DISCLAIMER

Publisher's and author's note

MEDICINE BEYOND

Biology and Healing In a World of Unseen Structures

" *A truth's initial commotion is directly proportional to how deeply the lie was believed. When a well-packaged web of lies has been sold gradually to the masses over generations, the truth will seem utterly preposterous and its speaker a lunatic.*

- Dresden James

Books by the same author
Allergies: What Everyone Should Know
The Allergy Handbook
The Poisoned Tree
The Complete Guide to Food Allergy and Environmental Illness
Diet Wise: Let Your Body Choose the Food That's Right for You
Cancer Research Secrets
Fire In The Belly
How To Survive In A World Without Antibiotics
The Parasites Handbook
The Waters Of Life
Love Your Liver

MEDICINE
BEYOND

New Dimensions Of Biology and Healing
Beyond The Everyday Laws Of Physics

by **Dr. Keith Scott-Mumby**
MD, MB ChB, HMD, PhD, FCRP (Medicina Alternativa)

Publishers

Supernoetics™ Inc.

10 9 8 7 6 5 4 3 2 1

© Dr. Keith Scott-Mumby 2015

Dr. Keith Scott-Mumby asserts the moral right to be identified as the author of this work.

ISBN 978-09884196-8-1

Printed in USA
by Bang Printing, 3323 Oak Street, Brainerd, MN 56401

To Emma and Katie, who are the future

Contents

INTRODUCTION

*Science should leave off making pronouncements:
the river of knowledge has too often turned back
on itself.*

— Sir James Jeans, *The Mysterious Universe*

THE HALF LIFE OF TRUTH

This ambitious book covers an immensity of time, from disputations over the origins of our universe at the very dawn of history, to the furthest future that science can foresee ahead of us and to which the human intellect can reach out… at least for the present. Of course the picture is changing all the time. We can never know when a shocking new insight into reality, such as Einstein's relativity or Max Planck's quantum mechanics, will burst upon the stage.

Nothing stays still. As Greek philosopher Heraclitus (c. 535 BC – 475 BC) told us, everything is change. His philosophy of this is summed up in a famous phrase: "No man ever steps in the same river twice". Incidentally, it was Heraclitus who gave us the term *Logos* (λόγος) in Western philosophy as meaning both the source and fundamental order of the Cosmos. Logos appears repeatedly as the suffix –ology, meaning science or study of.

In the first edition of *Virtual Medicine*, I wrote mockingly that science seems to undergo some major upheaval every quarter of a century or so.

Something that was proven to be true is later *proved* to be NOT true. Science is really a shifting quicksand of opinions and squelchy "facts". In the health field, readers will be aware there are rapid switches in what are supposed to be scientifically-proven truths. First you read that carbohydrates are good for us, then bad; saturated fat is bad and then it's good; we should eat meat, then we shouldn't; margarine is your best choice, now it is a dangerous option; we get all the iodine we need from bread, but the population of the Western world turns out to be dangerously deficient in this vital mineral... The discrepancies and contradictions go on and on.

The accepted idea that calling something scientific means it is a given or has been "proven" is thus a joke. The honest fact is that all truth changes. It would be hard to define anything as a lasting and permanent scientific "fact"; even gravity is now on the chopping block.

THE STATISTICS

Scholars in their halls have developed the concept of a "half-life of truth". Half-life, remember, is the measurement of how long it takes a radio-active substance to decay to half of its initial activity. This can be a matter of just minutes, as for Barium-122; 29 years, as in the case of strontium-90; or millennia, in the case of carbon-14, which has a half-life of 5730 years.

But here they are using the term somewhat flippantly to mean the point at which half the knowledge base is considered to be no longer valid. So, for a given body of facts, there will be a moment in history when half of it is no longer correct; the truth will have decayed. That means the body of data has become so corrupted, it cannot be taken seriously as fact.

It was always joked at med school when I was there that half of what we learned would be out of date in five years; trouble was nobody knew which half! That's the main problem actually: once data have become unreliable, certainty is to a large degree negated. *All of it* becomes worthless.

Surprisingly, it is now possible to put numbers to this. It started with a team of researchers at Pitié-Salpêtrière hospital in Paris, France. Thierry Poynard and his colleagues looked at the literature for their field: liver disease, especially cirrhosis and hepatitis. The team located nearly 500 articles in this field from over 50 years and gave them to a panel of experts to examine. Each expert was charged with saying whether the paper was factual, out-of-date or even disproved.

What they found was interesting. Yes, the validity of the papers had decayed significantly[1]. It emerged that the half-life for knowledge in this field was 45 years.

In another paper I found in *The Lancet*, a pair of surgeons went through a similar procedure with published papers in their field and came up with the same figure: 45 years[2].

CITATIONS

This isn't pure science, of course. The numbers and dates arrived at were themselves subject to mere opinion. Clearly, a panel of old goats who are clinging to the status quo will give more credibility to older trend-setting papers than a team of young bloods, anxious to move forward into their own bright future as experts.

But there is another way to estimate when data have become obsolete and that's by measuring *how often a particular paper is cited* by subsequent publications. Once no one refers to the material and conclusions any more, it is understood that it is probably no longer valid.

Of course this is not an absolute judgment, because a perfectly valid paper could be overtaken by torrents of later publications, which say much the same thing and therefore the original data are not disproven.

Nevertheless, there is a point to be made and these reviews somewhat prove what I said. What is "solid science" constantly changes and evolves.

What about other fields than health? What is the apparent half-life of knowledge in physics, say, or economics?

It has emerged that for physics, it's about 10 years for papers and 13 years for books about physics; whereas books on economics are 50% out of date after only 9 years.

CREEPING CHANGE

This is important because people often don't notice that change is creeping up on them. Things learned as a child or at med school could be completely overthrown before the end of a physician's working life, yet he or she may never notice. This is especially likely if that practitioner does not trouble to stay up to date with science—and most don't. Indeed, I have noticed, most physicians are not even up to date with changes in medicine, never mind progress in science at large!

Why am I dwelling on this at length? Because in the field of health and healing, my field, things are moving fast; so fast that my 1999 first edition of *Virtual Medicine* is w-a-y out of date and yet the medical establishment has barely registered any awareness of holistic and alternative health, never mind the validity of energy medicine!

But the medical orthodoxy is unaware of the changes in science and thinking that has crept up on them. We are talking about the "new physics", while they are still in Newtonian mode from high school days; centuries out of date science, in other words. It's no longer a good joke to scoff at energy medicine as a healing modality because, as I say often, advanced physics doesn't just tell us that these strange phenomena could it happen; it tells us they must happen!

The entrenched dogma has, quite simply, expired.

Add to that the degradation of the data set by lying and manipulation of drug trials by Big Pharma, the deprecation of studies demonstrating the worthlessness of many extravagantly expensive procedures (like stents and bypass) and the corruption of watchdog bodies like the FDA and it soon becomes evident that the so-called science of medicine is mightily unworthy of that label.

You can throw most of medicine in the trashcan and you wouldn't lose much of value; just a few common sense procedures. Ironically, these simple things work well and have never been tested "scientifically". It's only the stuff "proven" by science that is suspect or dangerous, like Thalidomide, which was *scientifically proven* to be safe for pregnant women. It caused women to give birth to children with abnormal or missing limbs. How safe it that? How good is the science, in other words?

WESTERN ENERGY MODEL

One of my pet hobbyhorses is the nature of Western energy medicine. Contrary to what many other people think, I do not believe it will be a watery make over of the Chinese, Ayurvedic, or similar models.

We have our own contribution to make and that is in the dazzling field of technology. In this book I have shared with the reader many devices which are so far beyond the limits of previous knowledge that they seem almost magical.

But then the late Arthur C. Clarke is famous for saying "Any technology which is sufficiently advanced is indistinguishable from magic".

This was the third of three laws by him. The first, "When a distinguished but elderly scientist states that something is possible, he is almost certainly right. When he states that something is impossible, he is very probably wrong" was proposed by Clarke in the essay "Hazards of Prophecy: The Failure of Imagination", in *Profiles of the Future* (1962).

The second law is offered as a simple observation in the same essay: "The only way of discovering the limits of the possible is to venture a little way past them into the impossible". Its status as Clarke's Second Law was conferred on it by others.

The third law appeared in a 1973 revision of *Profiles of the Future*. Clarke acknowledged the Second Law and proposed the Third in order to round out the number, adding "As three laws were good enough for Newton, I have modestly decided to stop there."

SO WHY DO THIS?

Given all that I have said about change and progress, it might seem rash for any author at the cutting edge to take on a catalogue of ideas, such as this.

I have had to introduce the reader to new and challenging principles in physics and new models of cosmology—simply because medicine has a context. All of science has a context. We cannot go on ignoring the nature of life and being, as the medical profession seeks to.

But soon it will be out of date. *Virtual Medicine* is history and *Medicine Beyond* will soon follow, if I do not rewrite it relentlessly. I have created a rod for my own back.

It may be appropriate to repeat for posterity my motivation for writing this book.

It's one of my sayings that the best reason to write a book is that it's the book you personally would like to read. *Virtual Medicine* did not exist in

1999, but there was a clear need, so I wrote it. The same is true of *Medicine Beyond*. I must say I don't consider it boastful to regard myself as the number one contender for the demands of this authorship. I have a very wide range of knowledge in all fields of healing.

Not quite a Renaissance man perhaps; but pretty well educated. I have also been used to getting outstanding results as a physician over the years. Not so much because I am amazingly competent but because I espouse and put to use good advanced and proven principles that help my patients. They get well more often. That's about the best measure of a physician's knowledge base!

The idea of "beyond" came from my time living in Spain. The Spanish have a term *mas alla*, meaning "more other", or beyond in the sense of something metaphysical or spooky even. Critics would readily describe my work as "very other", for sure! But I take pride in such a notion. My conscious intention has been to relay and openly discuss new possibilities.

I am respectful of the fact that many of my readers are willing and active physicians who have set aside their acceptance of current dogma and are looking for a gentler, validated and more worthy approach to their craft.

I hope in these pages they too find material that is deserving of their time in study. If there are omissions or weaknesses, I ask that they be blamed on me, not on my enquiries. Errors and inconsistencies are not to be taken as proof that the propositions I bring are faulty or nonsensical. Only that I am not perfect and therefore subject to the occasional mistake.

So, this is it then... the start of an incredible voyage, a journey back through time, into the far-flung future, sideways into very peculiar backwaters, downwards into profound concepts and upwards to the light, to joy and to the divine in us all...

A journey that I call *Medicine Beyond*!

Las Vegas, 4th March 2015.

CHAPTER 1

The Wild West of Science

<blockquote>

" *We have no right to assume that any physical laws exist, or if they have existed up to now, that they will continue to exist in a similar manner in the future.*

- Max Planck 1858-1947

</blockquote>

MAINSTREAM SCIENCE HAS BECOME JUNK SCIENCE

In 1999, I opened my book *Virtual Medicine* with these words...

Our view of the world is changing fast. A quarter of a century ago there were things that scientists were absolutely certain were true which, today, we are absolutely certain are not true. Nowhere is this more evident than in the physics of organisms. In just a few decades we have moved from the position where the human energetic aura was deemed not to exist, to the point where there is ample scientific proof of its existence and several good theories as to its nature and function. Studies have been carried out in many major universities of the world which, although they are largely ignored by those who have some other "truth" to peddle, have nevertheless done a great deal to unite realms that were once held to be only metaphysical (hence the name) with the accepted tenets of everyday science.

I pointed out that the reality of this "science", as its own proponents define it, is a shifting quicksand of fashions and opinions, which regularly contradicts itself—often embarrassingly so. And when there is clear evidence that the paradigm is heading in the wrong direction, it is always ignored. Nothing must disturb the status quo!

For example, two of the grandest and most revolutionary theories of the last century, Einstein's relativity and Planck's quantum mechanics, are in such disharmony that they appear mutually exclusive. All speculative talk of the grand unifying theory, which brings all the contradictions together, is just talk, nothing more. Yet we are promised that it is "just around the corner"; we are almost complete on physics!

Well, we've heard that before. In the 19th century, William Thomson, later Lord Kelvin, the most famous and influential scientist of the day (he gave us, among other things, the Kelvin scale of temperature: absolute zero is Kelvin zero), said that the future of physics lay *"in the last decimal place." "There is nothing new to be discovered in physics now. All that remains is more and more precise measurement."*

Yet within two decades of those complacent words, the discovery of radioactivity, the theory of relativity, and the development of quantum mechanics left his comfortable drawing-room science shattered in ruins. Almost overnight, waves were particles, then they were both, and now they are neither; matter is energy and vice versa; particles come and go in an infinite void. Everything Kelvin knew and believed in was turned upside down. One cannot help but believe that in modern times the only certain thing to have come out of science is Heisenberg's Uncertainty Principle.

In the 21st century, the zeal and self-delusion have only got worse. Scientific dogma is now running at the level of fanaticism and bigotry that characterizes the narrow-minded intolerance of the world's major religions. The term "scientism" has been coined to mean a level of pretense and rigidity that excludes all possible merits of true scientific undertaking. It is itself a kind of proto-religion, with people like Stephen Hawking as its prophets and Richard Dawkins as its ranting high priest.

I am not condemning real science at all. The scientific method is probably the greatest thinking tool that Mankind has. It means to observe accurately; to posit various explanations or hypotheses; to devise tests to see how close to the truth we have come; based on the tests and observations, to make refinements to our hypotheses and, in time, to choose the one that seems to fit the observed facts best...

There is no other path to truth, knowledge and understanding.

Instead, what do we have? - Dogma. Take the famous Big Bang theory. It's been dead for decades, disproven, it remains junk science today. Yet all mainstream scientists continue to subscribe to this silly model. The Wikipedia entry refers to it as the *"prevailing cosmological theory."* Never any explanation of what happened before the Big Bang! It started from a singularity, they say. Well, where did that come from?

Today the fashion is to say there was an earlier "multiverse," which gave rise to our universe. Within this multiverse, our own patch would be only one of an infinity of separate space-time mockups. In other words, universes indistinguishable from ours would be repeated infinitely, as would every conceivable configuration of mass-energy permitted by the laws of physics.

Don't ask the obvious question: where did that initial multiverse come from?

PROBLEMS WITH THE BIG WET FIREWORK

More than a quarter of a century ago (1988) the prestigious science journal *Nature* published an article with the startling title "The Big Bang Is Dead." In it were many reasons why this untenable model of the origins of the universe could not be true. Not that the evidence for it was weak, note, but that it *could not be true.*

For one thing, our universe is 40 orders of magnitude too flat for the Big Bang theory predictions. Worse still, something called the cosmological constant is 120 orders of magnitude too small ($1/10^{120}$) to fit with the predictions of the Big Bang model[1]. The cosmological constant, which governs the rate of expansion of the universe, cannot be changed because, if its value were even slightly different, the conditions suitable for life on Earth could not have arisen.

Unwilling to give up the theory, scientists have had to invent numerous patches for this ludicrous theory. It hinges entirely on the existence of something they call "dark matter." It's called dark because it isn't there, or at least no one can see it! It's never been found in the 50 years since the Big Bang model took the ascendency. How much dark matter is out there? Just enough to make all the silly equations work, no more, no less! Are you laughing at this? You should be.

Even allowing for so-called baryonic matter (optically invisible), there is still some 75% of matter missing.

By all that's proper, since there is no missing matter—or until it's found—the theory should be dropped completely. Instead they label the missing stuff as "dark" matter and say it MUST be out there. Why? - Because their theory won't hold up unless it is.

All this is based on an intellectually absurd proposition, which is that the so-called "laws" of physics are indeed laws and that they apply equally in all parts of the universe. Since no one has visited any other parts of the universe to test this assumption, it remains idle and unscientific guesswork.

Not that so-called scientists are strangers to fantasy and guesswork.

Take the mystical "black hole." It's just a fable. We'll never know if it's true because there is no way of testing or even identifying such an object. Subrahmanyan Chandrasekhar originated the idea. Sir Arthur Eddington, who created the gravitational star model, could not accept this "wild west" hypothesis, and complained, *"I think there should be a law of nature to prevent a star from behaving in this absurd way"* [2]. Such flippant pronouncements do not mean the black hole theory is wrong, of course, but invoking the old rule that "an extraordinary hypothesis requires extraordinary proof," one should regard this as no more than a fantasy, since it can never be verified.

Indeed, it has already been rejected by no less a luminary than Stephen Hawking (see below).

THE THEORY OF EVERYTHING DELUSION

Hawking's latest dreary nonsense is the M-theory he is promoting. That, in turn, is associated with string theory, where the assumption is that the ultimate constituents of matter are not particles but tiny vibrating strings. The trouble is that these supposed strings are so tiny that, for

10

purely practical reasons, we are not going to be able to verify that they're there. There can be no proof and so their "theory" is just an unsupported fable.

It's worse: these strings are supposed to be vibrating in 10 spatial dimensions. But there are only three proven physical dimensions. The rest are all mathematical abstractions. It is accepted that these missing dimensions are in some way real, because the math works so nicely. Well, if these extra dimensions should turn out NOT to be there, then the math isn't working after all, is it?

M-theory postulates the existence of many other universes; by definition, you're never going to be able to detect them, otherwise they'd be part of this universe. So we are not going to find a complete theory of everything any time soon, if ever.

Yet the press releases go on and on, as if it were all "in the bag." Trust me, when Stephen Hawking announces that M-theory is *the only candidate for a complete theory of the universe,*" he's talking nonsense.

The math hasn't even emerged yet! We can write down Schröding-er's equation of quantum mechanics; we can write down Newton's law of gravitation. But if you ask Hawking or one of his tribe to write down the equation that is M-theory, they can't: because they haven't got one.

Perhaps the perplexity is best summed up in a brilliant remark by Russell Stannard that appeared in The Times: *"A genuine theory of everything must explain not only how our universe came into being, but also why it is the only type of universe that there could have been - why there could only be one set of laws. This goal I believe to be illusory"* [3].

Please understand I am not trying to teach you physics here; I'm merely giving you enough data to grasp the massive fallacies and confusion that exist in science today. Since scientists cannot be honest about the almost total failure of science at being able to explain our world, someone has to say it for them!

THE WALL OF FIRE

In case you think I'm exaggerating, or maybe I'm just an ignorant fool who doesn't understand the majesty of true science, let me tell you this: in February 2014, Stephen Hawking shocked the scientific community by suddenly announcing that black holes don't exist, at least not as he's defined them for the last 40 years![4]

See, there's a problem. Black holes typify the clash between different orders of physics: quantum theory and relativity. The problem is what is called the event horizon, the border between reality and the sinkhole that prevents all light from escaping. As the theory was created, everything was supposed to vanish into the black hole and nothing could ever return—hence the term horizon—due to monstrous gravitational forces.

That means all information vanishes. But it's a core tenet of quantum theory that information cannot disappear in this way. So they invented the "firewall," meaning a ring of fire that could consume knowledge and information at the horizon, using the known laws of physics.

But that in turn violates the theory of relativity, which says that anyone passing through the event horizon would not be aware of doing so. It's a fundamental paradox. There is now a complete stand-off among scientists backing these two pillars of conventional physics. One or the other theory is wrong (or both)! It's a classic example of the way science digs itself deeper and deeper into the mud, using abstruse theories to "explain" the gaps in their models.

You will see in later pages that information is far more precious than material reality; indeed information is the progenitor of physical reality. The idea of it "vanishing" at the margins of a black hole makes no sense whatever.

They've come up with wildly fanciful patches, such as bouncing stars, stringy fuzz balls, and time machines to try to get round this problem. But, as Raphael Bousso at the University of California, Berkeley, so aptly puts it: *"No matter which way this goes, it's clear that things in conflict are very fundamental. You can't resolve this conflict without a revolution."*

Hopefully the revolution, when it eventually comes, will be to drop the gravitational universe model in favor of something more believable and, indeed, provable down here on Earth, in the laboratory - More of that later.

NEVER MENTION THESE IN POLITE SOCIETY

As I have said elsewhere, there are five things you must never even speak about, as a scientist. If you do, you'll be branded a fool and a crank. These are: free energy, antigravity, non-Darwinian evolution, cold fusion, and psychokinesis (telepathy, etc.). You could even lose your funding or your job if you step over the invisible line!

That's despite the fact that cold fusion, for example, has been proven over and over in more than 500 laboratories around the world[5]. All that scientists will ever quote is one hasty debunking of the original experiment by a bunch of self-interested scientists, who were involved with rival technologies. Why? Because it threatens all of physics if cold fusion were a fact!

This rigidity and narrow-mindedness is held in place by something called the peer review process. If you want to proclaim a discovery that is outside the existing scientific paradigm, you will not be able to get it published in reputable journals. Your peers and rivals will say it's nonsense and is "not scientific" or "junk science". No editor will take it on because it risks his or her very reputation in the scientific community. It's a kind of censorship, in effect.

The ordinary scientist plodder is led to believe that science is real and other subjects are "not scientific" because they have never been published in reputable journals. Unfortunately, it's a self-perpetuating exclusivity that serves nothing except the furtherance of the status quo and the reputations that depend on its continuation.

I found an interesting series of pronouncements from expert authorities, the kind of thing that would elicit peer review pressure to have any publication to the contrary banned. It makes hilarious reading! See what you think...

Heavier-than-air craft will never fly:

The demonstration that no possible combination of known substances, known forms of machinery and known forms of force can be united in a practicable machine, by which men shall fly long distances through the air, seems to the writer as complete as it is possible for the demonstration of any physical fact to be.

- Simon Newcomb, Rear Admiral, US Navy, Professor of Astronomy and Mathematics, US Naval Academy and Director, US Naval Observatory, The Outlook For The Flying Machine.

Galileo was ridiculed for his assertion that moons orbited the planet Jupiter (church elders refused to look down the telescope and see, because they "knew" Galileo was peddling heretical lies). Kepler was accused of mysticism for saying that the moon is the origin of Earth's tides. "Experts" laughed when Ben Franklin proposed that lightning was, in fact, electricity. When Alexander Graham Bell offered Western Union the telephone, they scoffed and said it was a trivial toy.

Sir Isaac Newton, no less, refused to accept that meteorites came from space, because he could conceive no way that could happen and considered the idea "unfeasible". (This is the guy who supposedly discovered gravity!)[6]

Lord Kelvin, already mentioned, supposedly the greatest physicist of his day, declared that x-rays were a hoax (presumably because seeing through solid objects was not part of his world view). About 10 years before the creation of the atomic bomb, (Lord) Ernest Rutherford—who was first to split the atom, incidentally—called atomic energy "moonshine."

So if contradicting or ignoring mainstream science worries you, don't let it get you down! They are an army of fools, masquerading as experts. They enjoy their exclusivity and the supercilious position that they alone know and you couldn't possibly understand all the issues; they are always right and to suggest other models that contradict their position is wrong, wrong, and damnably wrong.

Let me put it this way: properly conducted science can be a guide and may be useful. But it is NEVER right for certain and, for that matter, never right for long. I'm sure when Albert A. Michelson remarked in 1894 that, in physics, there were no more fundamental discoveries to be made, he was right at the time, within the boundaries of known physics. Probably quoting Lord Kelvin, Michelson continued, *"An eminent physicist remarked that the future truths of physical science are to be looked for in the sixth place of decimals."*

But this was far from the case and, with hindsight, one can say Kelvin's "science" was a laughable delusion. But have they learned to exhibit caution? No. Exactly the same dogmatic everything-we-have-is-final stance is the same pretense. In years to come, Stephen Hawking and his kind will be derided, as we now scoff at Lord Kelvin's foolish hubris.

WEIRDER AND WEIRDER

The multiplication of strangeness is one of the hallmarks of the utter confusion permeating modern-day physics.

There is a lot more hardcore weirdness in the makeup of our universe. It led British scientist John Haldane to famously remark, *"Our universe is not only stranger than we suppose, it's stranger than we can suppose"* [7].

For example, you have probably heard of the idea that the universe is continually expanding (the open universe). That was never proved. Another theory says it will expand for a time and then collapse back on itself (the closed universe). In fact, neither is correct.

In studies from a NASA space probe, published since the first edition of *Virtual Medicine*, the universe has been shown to be flat, meaning neither expanding or contracting but perfectly balanced and eternal[8]. The NASA website has updated us and says we now know (as of 2013) that the universe is flat with only a 0.4% margin of error. This suggests that the universe is infinite in extent[9].

Moreover, the quantity of matter in the universe needed to balance expansion vs. contraction is "correct" to the power 10^{50}. That's almost too staggering to believe. To me, that's akin to arranging a nuclear explosion in which the blast expands far enough outwards to knock over a target skittle 50 miles away but does not move the skittle standing next to it. Weird or what?

Entanglement is famous nowadays. It shows up as a given, even on popular TV. But to me it's no more than a crutch, a fable, to get round the presence of consciousness, which reductionist scientists won't admit to. The idea of a particle, somewhere in conscious reality, "knowing" what's happening to another separated particle and responding to it is not a mystery. It's no different to your left leg knowing what your right leg is doing!

It would be daft if the connection did not exist.

That says it all, really, in respect of non-locality. If all parts are connected and aware of all other parts, that's consciousness, not the zero field, not ether, not the quantum field or any other "magic" science. Just common sense!

Coherence is another term quietly slipped in and sounding scientific but is just another way of ducking the presence of consciousness. Of course, if our reality is one vast organism, as I believe and the evidence suggests, then it's going to be integrated and entire, or coherent and in phase, one part with another.

The famous double-slit experiment, in which photons appear to think and know what each other is doing, is actually a predictable result; prediction is a good test of the validity of a theory. It proves particles are not separate because they are united in one consciousness. But it blows the socks off mechanistic science.

THE REAL QUESTIONS ARE DEEPER AND HARDER

It is a disconcerting fact that electricity and magnetism, two of the absolutely fundamental building blocks of the universe, are so little understood that, at the deepest level, science cannot explain the nature of these energetic phenomena or how they exert their effect.

Newton's "law" of gravity has been with us so long, people have naturally assumed it was true. But it's never been proven and, according to some scientists, gravity itself is a hoax. The elusive "graviton" has never been found but, again, it must be there, so scientists blunder on hopefully, sincerely expecting it to be found some day. I'm coming to the alternative to gravity in the next few pages. Meantime...

In 1897 Sir Joseph John Thomson discovered the electron, which has basic particle properties, such as mass and charge, but a deeper explanation of how these properties arise is lacking. Moreover, his son, Sir George Paget Thomson, showed in 1925 that electrons sometimes behave as a wave. Both men received the Nobel Prize in physics, yet one contradicted the other!

Consider mass. This is not the same as weight, though many supposed scientists get this wrong. Mass is a property of matter and is representative of "amount," but we have no idea how this strange property of mass comes about. It persists in a space vacuum, whereas weight disappears. Some particles don't even have a rest mass. How is that even possible, you may ask?

16

Is this important? Yes, mass is crucial. Probably the most famous ruling equation in all of science is Einstein's e=mc². The "m" stands for mass, not weight, but we don't even know what mass is! It's supposed to be gifted to particles by the mystical Higgs boson, which has been called "The God Particle"; hmmm, might as well be called pixie dust, for all the science there is there.

I point out these enormous gaps in knowledge and the absurd contradictions that accompany them, in case the reader is under the illusion that science, in any meaningful sense, understands our world. It doesn't.

But my greatest complaint with so-called science is not that it is sometimes wrong; it's that it fails to acknowledge that whenever something cannot be demonstrated using the existing narrow approach, it is labeled a fake or delusion. There is never any suggestion that the problem may be the fault of science or its inadequate methodology or missing pieces of the puzzle in their erroneous model.

Yet if you searched for microbes with a hand lantern, you'd never find even one. The microscope is the only way to detect them. If someone describes the experience of being outside their own body, they say it cannot be true, because there is no non-material soul or spirit. But how would they know, since their instruments cannot—by definition—detect anything non-material, even if it's there?

One hundred and fifty years ago there was no way to detect radio waves. Did that mean they were an "unscientific" belief or a "delusion" if anyone had come up with the idea ahead of its time? Even more important, could it be said that because the science of the day failed to detect such a phenomenon that therefore radio waves did not exist?

That's the present stand: we didn't think of it, so it isn't there. Remember that when you read the science of strange manifestations in this book. Scientific dogma will argue, "It can't be true, therefore it isn't." I say: better to keep searching and hoping.

MISSING GRAVITY

Let me tell you how stupid and unfinished the gravity theory is: there are places on Earth with missing gravity. This shows most strongly around the Hudson Bay area, in northern Canada. Since the 1961 gravity geological survey, it's been known that the effect of gravity is less than it should be in that area ("missing gravity," screamed the headlines).

Various explanations have been brought forth to "explain" this anomaly. The two favorites seem to be that the tectonic plate is lower at that point; it was pushed down by the weight of the ice sheet in the last Ice Age and hasn't recovered. In other words, it dips down below Earth's mean surface level.

The other kooky idea is that magma circulating below the surface crust is less dense.

Both of these can be refuted by a schoolchild. Firstly, we know that gravity gets less as you go UPWARDS, not down. It disappears altogether when you are far enough above the Earth. A sinking surface plate would increase the Earth's gravity effect; you'd be lower and so weigh more! Objects in the bottom of Death Valley weigh significantly more than objects at the top of Mount Everest.

Secondly, gravity, by definition, is calculated from the center of the object in question, not its surface. There is just as much Earth underneath hot magma as there is under anything else on the planet. So unless the plate is HIGHER than everywhere else, there is no reason that gravity should be less.

The mumbling and bumbling is so ridiculous and so inconsistent with what they claim is the "science" of gravity, you think somebody would stop and say, "Hang on a minute, that can't be right…" But no, they continue with same-old, same-old junk science, because it must be so![10]

Of course there is no trouble with "variable gravity" if there isn't any gravity but it turns out to be electrical attraction and repulsion instead. In fact, you'd predict it could vary in different localities.

You might also predict that eclipses of the Sun would produce gravitational anomalies… and they do. Here's a graphic showing the nonsense that is gravity, in just one glance:

18

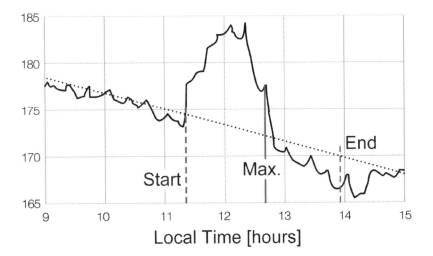

Local Time [hours]

What you are seeing is the effect of an eclipse of the Sun on a Foucault pendulum. Instead of the pendulum continuing on a supposed regular and predictable pathway (the diagonal dotted line), when the moon comes between Earth and the Sun, the pendulum swings speed up and veer off (shown by the peak at 12hrs, high above the predicted line).

This could not happen if gravity was real and was as everyone supposes. But it would happen like this if electrical attraction was the force involved. When the Sun is screened out, its effect on Earth objects is temporarily diminished. This is called the Allais Effect, after Maurice Allais, a French economist who made this observation in 1954 and it has never been explained. (Allais would eventually win the 1988 Nobel Prize for economics, not physics)

TOO MUCH LIGHT

The current model has another problem: too much light in the Cosmos. The universe is far brighter than it should be based on the number of light-emitting objects we can find, a cosmic accounting problem that has astronomers baffled.

The trouble stems from the most recent census of objects that produce high-energy ultraviolet light. Output from high-energy sources of UV light, such as quasars (galaxies supposed to contain "feeding" black holes) and young, hot galaxies filled with hot, bright stars, is far more than it should be from a tally of existing known sources.

"It's such a big discrepancy that whatever we find is going to be amazing, and it will overturn something we currently think is true," says Juna Kollmeier at the Observatories of the Carnegie Institution of Washington in Pasadena, California.

I'm certain she's right! I wonder if she's ready for the change or how many of her colleagues are.

Kollmeier started worrying in 2012, when Francesco Haardt at the University of Insubria in Como, Italy, and Piero Madau at the University of California, Santa Cruz, compiled the results of several sky surveys and found far fewer UV sources than previously suggested.

Then in February of 2014, Charles Danforth at the University of Colorado, Boulder, and his colleagues released the latest observations of intergalactic hydrogen by the Hubble Space Telescope. That work confirmed the large amount of gas being ionized. "It could have been that there was much more neutral hydrogen than we thought, and therefore there would be no light crisis," says Kollmeier. "But that loophole has been shut."

Now Kollmeier and her colleagues have run computer simulations of intergalactic gas and compared them with the Hubble data, just to be sure. They found that there is five times too much ionized gas for the number of known UV sources in the modern, nearby universe.

It's a simple enough message, easily predicted by models of the Electric Universe, which we will come to in the next chapter. But it's yet another death blow to the gravity model and all by itself should be enough to wake up astronomers and cosmologists that the Big Bang theory is wholly and totally unsupportable. *In over 50 years it has not made one single correct prediction of what is out there.*

It is now being claimed that "dark matter" may be the source of these radiations. Trouble is there's no dark matter! Even if there was, how is it dark if it's pouring out excess UV radiations?

The orthodox explanations just don't make any sense to a dispassionate onlooker[11].

AND WHAT ABOUT SHRINKING TIME?

What? Never heard that one? Well science has been baffled by the problem of the universe that's accelerating faster and faster (despite gravity's supposed hold). That's when they came up with the bizarre notion of dark energy: since it can't be seen, they can make up any story they like as an "explanation"! Maybe dark energy is working against gravity.

But Professor Jose Senovilla and his colleagues at the University of the Basque Country in Bilbao, Spain, have proposed an alternative mind-bending theory: they dismiss dark energy as nonsense and suggest instead that the universe isn't expanding at all. Time is shrinking. Seriously…this is real science, published in *Physical Review D*, a leading journal in elementary particle physics, field theory, gravitation, and cosmology.

Our current way of measuring expansion of the universe is via an effect called the red shift or Doppler effect (named after Austrian physicist Christian Doppler, who proposed it in 1842). The red shift depends utterly on time remaining constant. We don't need this effect in the Electric Universe model, by the way. But if time is dilating (slowing down), then the universe may not be accelerating at all.

According to this new theory, our solitary time dimension is slowly turning into a new space dimension. Therefore the far-distant, ancient stars seen by cosmologists would look as though they were accelerating from our perspective.

Eventually, if time stops altogether, we would be looking at a universe as unmoving as a photographic snapshot - weird stuff.

This curious idea is not without support however. Gary Gibbons, a cosmologist at Cambridge University, says the concept has merit: *"We believe that time emerged during the Big Bang, and if time can emerge, it can also disappear - that's just the reverse effect"*[12].

Is your head starting to hurt? Mine is.

END OF THE LINE?

Let's sum up a few of the holes and confusion in current scientific theory. You will rapidly see that it is the shakiest fictional contraption ever put together by the imagination of man! Even conventional science journalists are starting to say there may not have been a Big Bang.

It's based in gravity and gravity may not exist. Certainly, the existence of such a force has never been proven.

To make the gravity-based model work, they have had to invent dark matter (because there isn't any, so they made it up). How much? - Just enough to make their equations balance. Oh, pe-lease!

Other untenable discrepancies in the main theory have necessitated yet another patch: the concept of inflation. This says the universe is doing different things, at different speeds in different places. Where? Well, anywhere you want a patch, basically! Nobody knows, without touring the whole universe, which bits are playing the game and which bits are cheating!

It's a massive copout. Inflation can take almost any imaginable beginning and make it into the universe we see, says Stuart Clark in a recent edition of *New Scientist* open on my desk as I write[13].

Introducing the inflation idea has taken things from tricky to ridiculous. If such a phenomenon has taken place (ever) then there is no possibility of backtracking earlier than that point, because we don't know on what scale or over what time changes may have taken place. We simply can't work backwards to the supposed Big Bang. Anything earlier could have existed for 10^{36} seconds or a trillion years, said John Peacock, a cosmologist at the Royal Observatory in Edinburgh, UK (current theory says on 13 billion)[14].

So in a very real sense, cosmology has come to a dead end. The Big Bang, or whatever really took place at the start of the universe, is forever hidden from view, if inflation is correct.

And these guys are saying telepathy, prescience and homeopathy are fake and delusions? Isn't there a Biblical epithet about first getting the beam out of your own eye?

THERE IS NO OBJECTIVE UNIVERSE!

I'm sure you have heard of the "observer" effect, thrust on us by quantum physics. It's a doctrine that says you cannot observe or measure anything without participating in the aspect of reality you are trying to study and therefore (almost certainly) influencing it.

Neils Bohr gave it special emphasis and it became known as the "Copenhagen interpretation" (Bohr was Danish), but gradually most scientists have come to accept that it is a real and valid problem. Matters have been made even more extraordinary by the seminal experiments of my friend Bill Tiller, who has demonstrated conclusively that the experimenter's intention comes out strongly in the results. Apparatus can become imbued with the observer's thoughts and expectations and the results distorted accordingly. I said to him once, "You have destroyed science! It is no longer possible to measure anything with a real likelihood of an unbiased outcome."

It's not a problem in the conscious universe model Bill and I both espouse but it's a BIG problem to most scientists, who still like to believe in a mechanical, objective world, of which we are just passive observers.

When you move up to the metaverse idea, then the observer problem enlarges infinitely too! How can we, inhabitants on a planet in a solar system in a galaxy, meaningfully debate the existence of the so-called laws of physics as well as the origins of something, the very universe that we are part of? Can we evaluate the universe from within at all, or will it remain, forever, as Bertrand Russell suggested, "simply and inexplicably there"?

What about the parts of space-time we can never see? These regions could infinitely outnumber our visible patch. The laws of physics could differ there, for all we know. We may probably never know, in truth.

PARADOX SOLVED

Benoit Mandelbrot, virtually the "inventor" of fractals, who gave his name eponymously to the Mandelbrot Set, also put his fertile mind to work in cosmology. In 1974 he offered a new explanation of Olbers' paradox (the "dark night sky" riddle), demonstrating the consequences of fractal theory as a sufficient, but not necessary, resolution of the paradox.

In astrophysics and physical cosmology, Olbers' paradox, named after the German astronomer Heinrich Wilhelm Olbers (1758–1840) and also called the "dark night sky paradox", is the argument that the darkness of the night sky conflicts with the assumption of an infinite and eternal static universe.

The darkness of the night sky is one of the pieces of supposed evidence for a non-static universe such as the Big Bang model. If the universe is static, homogeneous at a large scale, and populated by an infinite number of stars, any sight line from Earth must end at the (very bright) surface of a star, so the night sky should be completely bright. This contradicts the observed darkness of the night.

Mandelbrot postulated that if the stars in the universe were fractally distributed (for example, like Cantor dust), it would not be necessary to rely on the Big Bang theory to explain the paradox. His model would not rule out a Big Bang, but would allow for a dark sky even if the Big Bang had not occurred.[15]

BIG BANG FUNDAMENTALISM

Let me finish this opening salvo with a great quote:

"Big-bang cosmology is a form of religious fundamentalism, as is the furor over black holes, and this is why these peculiar states of mind have flourished so strongly over the past quarter century. It is in the nature of fundamentalism that it should contain a powerful streak of irrationality and that it should not relate, in a verifiable, practical way, to the everyday world. It is also necessary for a fundamentalist belief that it should permit the emergence of gurus, whose pronouncements can be widely reported and pondered on endlessly—endlessly for the reason that they contain nothing of substance—so that it would take an eternity of time to distil even one drop of sense from them. Big-bang cosmology refers to an epoch that cannot be reached by any form of astronomy, and, in more than two decades, it has not produced a single successful prediction." [16]

Fred Hoyle, remember, was the person who invented the term Big Bang, as a sneer against this stupid, basically unbelievable, model.

CHAPTER 2

The Electric Universe

The cosmic web is spun from electricity.

- Dr. Michael Shallis, The Electric Shock Book

Let's now move away from the gravity-based model and try something better. If gravity exists, it has been calculated to be one thousand billion billion billion billion times (10^{39}) weaker than electrical force. Compared to other key forces that hold our universe together, it's almost ridiculously weak. The trouble is that, when Sir Isaac Newton formulated his theory of why objects fall to earth or why large planetary objects are attracted to each other, he had no knowledge of electrical forces; they were not discovered for another two centuries.

But modern scientists have no excuse. We know electrical forces attract and repel and can be extremely powerful. It's clear that we live in a violently electrically charged universe and yet mainstream scientists will only treat it as electrically neutral.

But that just isn't so. Space is flooded with wild electrical events: plasmas, solar coronal mass ejections, interplanetary and intergalactic electrical tides. Electricity is inescapably part of the fabric of our universe; it is not some glittering add-on, like chrome bumpers on an automobile.

The *"Electric Universe"* model, as it's called, is here to stay. It seems to me to have a few rough edges, yet it is inherently more plausible than the existing Big Bang model. It answers many riddles and fills in many blanks; therefore, it is definitely a more scientific view. For that reason alone, it should, by convention, be the ruling theory of the day.

It's based on the work of several Nobel Prize winners; it's accepted by the IEEE (Institute of Electrical and Electronic Engineers). But it contradicts the status quo in cosmology, which pays everyone's mortgages and mistresses, so it is artfully scorned and denigrated as folly.

BETTER MODEL

Why is the Electric Universe (EU) a better model? It doesn't need daft black holes, for example (whatever they are supposed to be) ... it has also made several successful predictions. The Big Bang theorists won't accept that their model has made no predictions whatever; they insist that the evidence they require will just "turn up" sometime.

The Electric Universe model has a lot to offer, not least in clearing up some fundamental confusions and mysteries, as we shall see. This important shift in postulated perception leads to a whole new way of looking at the creation of the universe and hence the origins and properties of life on Earth, including us. That in turn impacts any process of healing or transformation.

The Electrical Universe model redefines the meaning of the famous Einsteinian equation, $e = mc^2$. It's an electromagnetic equation anyway, since it rests upon the speed of light. Light is an EM wave; therefore mass and energy are functions of light. Indeed, David Bohm, the originator of the hologram model of our universe, said that *"matter is just frozen light."*[1]

Energy, mass, and the speed of light are actually all electromagnetic properties of the universe. Note that gravity does not even come into this all-defining physics equation! Since gravity is supposed to define mass—meaning mass is related to gravity, though not the same as weight—and gravity is not proven to exist, we have a tricky problem.

But in the Electric Universe it goes away. We get a new way of looking at the troubling property of mass, which is that the mass of a particle is now seen as a measure of how much energy is absorbed in the deformation of the particle, instead of its acceleration. This in turn means that energy requires the presence of matter; particles in space. There is no such thing as "pure energy" or "dark energy." Yet we honestly cannot say what matter is or how it could be formed, therefore we are not able to make any meaningful statement about how our universe came into being at this stage.

That may not sound like science but at least it is honest.

PLASMAS

It is strange that astronomers ignore the electric model, when 99% of the known universe is in a highly-charged electrical raw state called a plasma. We are used to thinking of astronomical bodies as "stuff"; something you could touch or kick, except that it might be very hot! But this "stuff" model is very out of date.

Almost all material content in the universe is neither solid nor liquid nor gas; it's in a fourth state of matter called plasma. In plasma, the atoms are torn to shreds. The energy is so intense that electrons are ripped from their corresponding protons. There are no atoms, as such. That means there are unmatched electrical particles on the loose: the electrons are negatively charged and the protons positively charged.

Our Sun releases plasmas all the time, which come screaming towards Earth. In our upper atmosphere there is plasma caused by the interaction of the solar wind and Earth's magnetosphere. This plasmasphere, so-called, is composed mostly of hydrogen ions. The base of the plasmasphere, which is the same as the top of the ionosphere, is about 1000 kilometers from the Earth's surface. The temperature in the plasmasphere is generally between 6000K and 35,000K or VERY hot, compared to temperatures we are used to![2]

The strange thing about plasmas is what we call "charge separation." It's supposed to be very difficult and require a great amount of energy. It's not possible in normal circumstances, say the physicists; only in fiercely hot states, like in plasmas and the interior of the Sun.

That happens to be yet another scientific hoax. Charge separation is easy for living forms and all our cell membranes do it at body temperature. Indeed, this charge separation is quite characteristic of life. With one charged particle inside the cell and the opposite charge held on the outside of the membrane, the difference between the two is what we call the cell membrane potential. The real identifier of life is this electric membrane phenomenon. Yet it's not supposed to be there!

It raises an interesting question I have heard before: is plasma a mark of life? Maybe ghosts, ball lightning, orbs, and other strange glowing electrical phenomena we hear about are actually life forms? You'll read in a subsequent chapter that consciousness does not need a physical matrix but it does need an electrically active milieu. The Sun might even be conscious!

I like the idea that there is life out there without bodies. In a later chapter (Chapter 26) you'll be reading about electronic voice phenomena (EVP), in which supposedly dead people communicate with us here via electronic machines, such as radios, telephones, and even televisions. It's stupid to argue these are all a hoax; it happens to far too many people, far too often, to merely be a delusion. We must ask instead a defining question: what exactly do we mean by life? Thinking? Communication? Consuming energy for effects and events?

A few paragraphs down, I'll bring in the concept of electrical nutrition. Maybe everything that transforms electricity is alive and our universe is, indeed, a vast living organism.

Anyway, this section is not intended to emulate a textbook on plasma physics or the electric universe. I just want to give you a heads up to some of what's out there and build enough context for my own model of *Medicine Beyond* to make scientific sense. I hope the reader will readily see how this alternative model of the universe is far richer, more active, more exciting and, well... more alive, than the cold, gravity-based machine world.

ELECTRIC GAIA

In the first edition of *Virtual Medicine*, I introduced readers to the blizzard of violent and dangerous energies that surround our planet and are held from frying us only by certain protective layers in the atmosphere above us.

Gaia is not the gentle goddess dreamed of but rather a harsh mistress, ravening with violent energies!

But is this hostility real or imagined? A better view is to regard the Earth as a step-down transformer, connected to the more powerful Sun's electrical energies and harvesting them safely for us. The Sun in turn transforms energy from other stars and the rest of the galaxies - more of that in a moment.

At the Earth's surface there is an electric field of about 100V per meter potential pointing straight up into space. What's that doing there? It's a complete mystery.

Around the world, lightning strikes the ground about 100 times each second, or 8 million times a day[3]. Each lightning bolt is millions of volts and tens of thousands of amps. That's big electricity.

Further out, between 50km and 100km, there are huge electrical events taking place over our heads, only recently discovered, that we call sprites, elves, and blue jets, reaching even further out into space. In fact most electrical storms seem to go upwards, rather as if Gaia was belching or breaking wind, shedding excess energy.

The next outer shell is where the famous Van Allen belts are found in the ionosphere. The inner belt, at about 1.6 earth radii, contains high-energy protons (positively charged atoms, sundered from their electrons). At 4 earth radii, we find the outer belt, with high-energy electrons to match. In other words, it's plasma, where atoms are split apart and behave very violently.

All this is happening as the Earth, with its giant iron core magnet, rotates on its axis at 1,000mph, and hurtles through the Sun's electric field at 60,000mph, making one orbit per year. Earth is actually a squillion-watt electrical generator.

Add in the fact that all the other planets have their own electrical plasma cloud, interacting with the Sun and with each other and we have some very complicated electronics indeed! The building of the EU model is only in its infancy. Still, it's more impressive and exciting than the cold, dark world of a gravity machine, where everything is separated by empty space.

The energy implications are staggering. Yet astronomers consider electricity unimportant. Yes, it's out there, they admit, but it doesn't DO anything. Huh?

But we are far from done: in the Electric Universe model, every star (sun) is transforming galactic electric currents; every galaxy is transforming the great currents and fluxes that flow through our universe as a whole. This is a process called induction. The strong electrical energies in the larger body "induce" a sympathetic current in the smaller scale body. It's like a series of step-down transformers, to get the "goldilocks" Earth environment, just right for Mankind!

It's no longer woo-woo to talk of our cosmic connectedness. The question is: How could worlds NOT influence each other? How could the planets NOT influence our lives down here on Earth? How can we not be connected to our Sun, whom the Egyptians regarded as the god, Ra?

My point is that we don't need "subtle" energies to model our universe and the mysteries in it. There are vast ravening clouds of raw electrical energy out there that can levitate a world never mind levitate or teleport a human!

As for magic, it's the mainstream theorists, like Stephen Hawking, who rely on magical, inexplicable events that "just happen." We free thinkers can do better!

ELECTRICAL NUTRITION

Given this simple and short explanation, the reader will appreciate that it is not at all far-fetched to reason that plants and animals are transforming the Sun's energy, here on Earth. Indeed, we have known about plant photosynthesis since school days. Plants use sunlight (electromagnetic energy) to manufacture sugars and amino acids. Animals eat plants. We eat both the plants and the animals. We eat sunlight!

Nutrition itself is electrical in nature. As you sit reading this and while you are breathing, there are in your body, in every cell and all your mitochondria, billions of individual electrons being guided down metabolic pathways and eventually reunited with protons. The mitochondria harvest the electrical energy this migration releases.

As Kenneth Nealson at UCLA explains, life, when you boil it right down, is a flow of electrons: *"You eat sugars that have excess electrons, and you breathe in oxygen that willingly takes them."*

Our cells break down the sugars, and the electrons flow through them in a complex set of chemical reactions until they are passed on to electron-hungry oxygen. In the process, cells make ATP, a molecule that acts as an energy storage unit for almost all living things. Moving electrons around is a key part of making ATP.

"Life's very clever," says Nealson. "It figures out how to suck electrons out of everything we eat and keep them under control." In most living things, the body packages the electrons up into molecules that can safely carry them through the cells until they are dumped on to oxygen. "That's the way we make all our energy and it's the same for every organism on this planet. Electrons must flow in order for energy to be gained. This is why when someone suffocates another person they are dead within minutes. You have stopped the supply of oxygen, so the electrons can no longer flow."

Now scientists have discovered a whole fascinating phenomenon, which is bacteria that "eat" electricity. It means some very basic forms of life can do away with sugary middlemen and handle the energy in its purest form—electrons, harvested from the surface of minerals[4].

Electrobiology is poised to swoop onto the scientific stage and take over completely from the biochemical model.

That's why we take antioxidants. We want to avoid our body chemistry being ripped apart electrically. Oxidation all comes down to electrical potential and events.

Our food is crucial. There is "live" food (electrically active) and "dead" food, where all the electrical energy is lost. In the latter case the food has become just a compilation of molecules, with no life energy. It does little or no good. We need to eat electricity for optimum health!

Now here's a whole startling extra take on electrical nutrition, that I consider very exciting and—knowing it will irritate the diehards who don't like new ideas—well, that just makes it an even more attractive theory!

HUMAN PHOTOSYNTHESIS

Maybe you have some trouble accepting that humans could get any nutrition directly from the Sun. Wasn't it drummed into you at school that animals can't do that? Only plants, using chlorophyll, are able to trap the energy of sunlight and convert it into forms usable by animals, such as us - right?

Wrong! By this stage in the book you should have realized that most "science" is just made up nonsense and this is just another instance of ignorance white-washed as knowledge!

The truth is one of the most ubiquitous substances in our body, a humble pigment melanin, is able to do what chlorophyll does... and very much more efficiently.[5]

Serious research has shown that melanin collects energy from lower-level radiation sources, shifting electrons into excited states, initiating a process that ends up producing electrical energy, similar to the way in which photosynthesis supplies energy to plants. Melanin works like a photoelectric cell. We are our own solar energy panel!

This is the "electric universe" gone crazy! Well, not crazy but so far beyond the bounds of simple science that it shakes the whole foundations of biology, never mind medical science.[6]

MARVELOUS MELANIN

Melanin is for the animal kingdom what chlorophyll is for the vegetable kingdom. Both molecules absorb photons and convert them into useful metabolic energy. But unlike chlorophyll, which is very unstable and lasts only a few seconds outside the leaf, melanin retains its bioelectrical properties outside the body for months, even years.[7]

Melanin (not to be confused with the pituitary hormone melatonin) is a red-brown pigment that gives rise to negroid and other skin color, brown and auburn hair, freckles and age spots, sun tans, and many other hues and tones in our skin and organs. Moreover, there is melanin scattered in parts of the body that are not visible from the surface, such as the retina and brain.

Most animals produce some version of the melanin family and those creatures adept at camouflage, such as the octopus and chameleon, have a large number of melanin-secreting cells on their surface that can rapidly show or hide melanin, so producing almost instant changes in colors and patterns.

In fact there is a whole range of melanins, such as skin melanin and brain melanin. Fungal melanin is being particularly well studied. Melanins, as a family, are unusual chemicals that are very species-distinctive and difficult to copy. One can always take a molecule from a frog, say a hormone, and manufacture it synthetically. But that is almost impossible to do with a melanin, according to experts.

Comparing melanin taken from the ink sack of a cuttlefish with commercially available synthetic melanins, for example, shows that the natural melanin, as an electrode material, has a specific capacity 50 percent larger than synthetic melanins.[8]

Melanin is remarkable in other ways too: it's a semiconductor, stable radical, conductor, free radical scavenger, and charge-transfer agent. It protects against many types of radiation and scientists now speculate that organisms that live close to radioactive sources can do so because of their melanin content, which is always enriched in such organisms. For example, fungi that seemed to flourish next to the Chernobyl disaster site all have extra melanin.[9]

Melanin is able to absorb low-energy radiation and throw it back out in enhanced form, releasing metabolically valuable energy. In fact, melanin can convert photo-excited electronic states with an efficiency approaching unity (1:1)[10]. It's so efficient at absorbing UV energies and converting it to usable energy that melanin-based solar technology is now a possibility.

Some scientists are predicting, based on strikingly high conversion efficiencies, which compete with those of conventional devices that organic photovoltaic cells, using melanin or derivatives of it, will soon come into prominence. Until now, the conversion of sunlight to electrical power has been dominated by solid-state junction devices, often made of silicon.

THE EYE IS KEY

If you follow the progress of a human embryo, large amounts of melanin are present in the eye from 35 days onwards, at a time when sight is of no value. You might begin to speculate whether this is an additional nutritional source for the fetus, over and above the obvious placental blood supply.

Birds have a remarkable small pleated structure in the eye called the pecten, which has eluded any credible explanation of its function. Numerous theories have been advanced, including enhanced vision and a magnetic direction sensor. Many tend to the explanation it somehow enhances eye nutrition by transporting nutrients from blood vessels to the iris, cornea and lens (there is no blood supply to the inner chambers of the eye).

The keynote is that the pecten is loaded with melanin and is soft, dark and velvety: perfect for absorbing light radiation. Given the properties of melanin now revealed, it seems entirely possible that the pecten does have a nutritional function—but as an amazing photo-electrical converter. This would indeed be a surprise.[11]

No-one can deny that what birds achieve with their tiny frame is almost unbelievable. Little humming birds, for example, migrate for thousands of miles and yet weigh less than a penny; the Arctic tern migrates 12,000 miles every year, from the Antarctic to the Arctic, and then back again, a round trip of 24,000 miles; the bigger wandering albatross truly deserves its name and stays aloft for 5-10 years at a time, circling the globe in the southern oceans, only coming to land to breed. We still have much to learn about how birds are able to accomplish such feats of endurance and strength. We do know that over the millions of years of bird evolution, they've been specially equipped to undertake the most arduous of travels.

The strange evolutionary organ called the pecten may just be a marginal but critical sunlight energy converter, to help birds cope with extra energy and nutrient needs under extreme conditions, fighting gravity, hypoxia, thirst and hunger during long-distance, frequently sub-zero flights, or in non-stop migration.

The human eye is a rich melanoid organ with higher-than-usual ability to photoconvert the Sun's energy. Maybe we all have something to gain by absorbing sunlight through the eyes, where it can be converted for us.

You may even have heard of people who claim to live on the Sun's light, without food and sometimes without water. Breatharianism or Ineda, it's called. I have had difficulty searching through the claims and accusations of fraud but having understood the properties of melanin and the fact that the human eye is richest in that pigment, you may now feel secure that at least there is a scientific model as to how such a strange effect could be plausible.

THE MELANIN BATTERY

A recent article in the journal *Bioelectrochemistry* relates how the researchers established that radiation interacts with melanin to produce an electric current.[12]

Over time, as melanin is bombarded with radiation and electrons are knocked away, it would be expected that the melanin became oxidized or bleached out. It would stop producing electricity. But that's not what happens. Instead, the melanin continuously restores itself. This led to the understanding that melanin can self-renew.

Dr. Arturo Solís Herrera of Aguascalientes, Mexico, has developed a "melanin battery" that is endless. Called the bat-gen and patented in many countries, Dr. Solis has examples of his battery that have been running for many years, without any charging or renewal. It seems like a biological free energy device!

In 2006 Solís and his team were producing 1½ liters of melanin every three months and had their first battery cells, generating 400 mV and 10 micro amps. Today that has risen to 200 liters of melanin daily and each cell now produces 600 mV and 200 milliamps; a thousand times more current and enough to power a small music player.

According to Solís, 1,000 liters of melanin can produce about 10,000 volts of charge.

This is not just one man's nonsensical obsession, by the way. Other orthodox sources are working on the same photosynthesis model. The first real confirmation of the electrical energy-producing power of melanin came from a study under Ekaterina Dadachova at the Albert Einstein College of Medicine, New York, looking at the way some fungi flourished in the intense electromagnetic radiation at the Chernobyl site.[13]

Melanin stands as one of the most remarkable biological substances known.

EDIBLE ELECTRONICS

On a slightly different note, it seems that melanin is likely to be medically useful in developing "edible batteries," that is, batteries that can be swallowed or used inside the human body at sites where traditional batteries would prove toxic. It's been christened "edible electronics"!

The batteries that power iPhones and laptops are optimized for performance but, for the circuitry that powers implantable or ingestible medical devices, the focus is biocompatibility. The challenge has been converting traditionally exotic and potentially toxic circuitry components into equivalent biomaterials that are safe enough to be swallowed but that can also provide a reasonable amount of power.

Conventional battery materials—used in pacemakers, for example—are not safe inside the body unless they're encased in bulky protective cases that must eventually be surgically removed. Electronics that can either be swallowed or implanted in the body without causing harm could be useful for things like monitoring wound healing and disease progression, releasing drugs at a critical moment, and enabling a more sensitive range of neural and cardiovascular sensors and stimulators.

One study paper that I found in the *Proceedings of the National Academy of Sciences* (PNAS) suggested that melanin would be a good vehicle. Professor Christopher Bettinger from Carnegie Mellon University, who led the research, developed a battery that uses the melanin from cuttlefish ink as an anode that exchanges electrons with a cathode made of manganese oxide. All the materials in the battery break down into nontoxic components in the body.

This first generation of edible batteries isn't powerful, especially when compared to highly toxic lithium batteries used in smart phones, but they're strong enough to fuel simple sensors, which makes them perfect for things such as arthritis drugs that typically can't be taken orally because the harsh environment of the stomach would destroy them. With this new battery approach, a patient could now swallow a pill that will detect when it passes beyond the danger zone and then self-destruct to release the drug into the gut.

Bettinger plans on boosting the power capacity by experimenting with different types of melanin[14].

This is intriguing and seems to me to be an ideal overlap between orthodox science and holistic models, giving impetus to my wide-ranging concept of *Medicine Beyond*.

ELECTRIC ORIGINS OF LIFE

Everyone has heard the proposition that lightning sizzling a primordial chemical soup could have given rise to life. Yes, it could, but it's hardly likely. For one thing, lightning is but a millisecond event. Moreover, it proverbially strikes each place only once (not strictly true but a statistical approximation). Continuous sparks in a laboratory culture have been known to result in a small yield of simple organic molecules, but that's if they are left running for long periods. The lightning flash-bang scenario is an unrealistic model, to say the least.

Let's get out of the laboratory and tiny sparks, or lightning flashes, and let's move upwards to a far, far greater "womb of life"…

What if particles falling to Earth, passing through the plasma clouds in the upper atmosphere, were transformed by the raw and very intense electrical energies up there? Almost any kind of molecules could be formed, as atom components combined and re-combined, though such adventitious compounds would only become stable as they fell below the hot plasma layer.

All elements, remember, are formed in the plasma of stars, so why not the outer space scenario? This hypothesis would certainly add a very plausible electrical origin to life. It's beginning to add up. Certainly, there is no other hypothesis that seems credible. The idea of life just somehow organizing itself from mud and molecules is virtually impossible, according to the laws of physics.

The famed Second Law of Thermodynamics says that things can't get more and more complex without some energetic input; in this universe everything is slowly decaying and disintegrating. It's a trend called entropy. It's supposed to be an unbeatable trend, though founder of quantum physics Erwin Schrödinger didn't think so (he wrote of life "eating negative entropy").

The point is that conventional physics forbids higher and higher levels of organization. As Lyall Watson pointed out in his groundbreaking book *Supernature*, "Any kind of order, even that as simple as the arrangement of atoms in a molecule, is unnatural and happens only by chance encounters that reverse the general trend. These events are statistically unlikely, and the further combination of molecules into anything as highly organized as a living organism is wildly improbable. Life is a rare and unreasonable thing."[15]

But the presence of ravening clouds of electricity throughout space changes all that. It can input vast amounts of energy, which may not even be reversing the trend; there are just such astronomical excesses (literally), nature can afford to waste energy on creating life. The model improves vastly too: lightning is a pitifully small source of creative energy, compared to the vast flows of electricity out there in space.

What say we scale this up and think in terms of life materials being formed in plasmas in space? There is good reason to look up above our heads for the origin of life. Organic life molecules are raining down on us from space all the time! It's not a wild theory; it's one that fits the known facts.

It's better yet: as you will learn in a subsequent chapter, experimental plasmas tend to give rise to organized groupings of atoms, which are helical in shape, just like the classical helix of DNA. You see how the Electric Universe model seems to suggest so many more answers than the machine universe of modern physics?

PANSPERMIA

The idea of life raining down on our planet from space is called *Panspermia* (literally: universal origins of life).

It will probably come as a complete surprise to many conservative thinkers that the idea of life tumbling to Earth from space is not totally derided in broader scientific circles. The prestigious journal *Scientific American* has published several serious articles on this topic and visiting the site of the even-more-famous journal *Nature*, I found 38 entries on the topic.

The idea was launched as a plausible scientific theory by none other than Sir Fred Hoyle, the man who coined the derisive term "the Big Bang"! In collaboration with his pupil, Sri Lankan mathematician and astronomer Chandra Wickramsinghe, Hoyle argued that life, at least in part, could have originated from extraterrestrial sources. The two even went so far as to propose that certain historical plagues were extraterrestrial in origin, caused by alien microbes raining down on Earth. Well, nobody can prove that isn't true! If it did happen, those organisms might have survived and be here with us now.

To my surprise, I learned that in a lecture delivered at Harvard University almost three decades ago, Nobel laureate Francis Crick, co-discoverer of DNA, declared that he had become disenchanted with the view that life arose on Earth. Instead, he too espoused Panspermia and proposed that the seed of life could have been an extraordinarily resistant spore of the kind produced by *Bacillus subtilis* and related bacteria, capable of enduring in deep space without air and water.

In response, Matthew Meselson pointed out that, if this were so, surely the extraterrestrial civilization would have sent a message or code in the spore. If only mankind was able to sequence DNA, he wistfully conjectured, then we could learn the secret of the Universe from the nucleotide sequence of the contemporary genome of the spore-forming bacterium. Maybe the SETI receivers, looking for radio signals, are going about it the wrong way and the DNA of life is the interplanetary equivalent of the Rosetta Stone, which allowed us to translate many early Earth languages![16]

This thought is echoed by Paul Davies, physics professor at the Arizona State University, in his 2010 book *The Eerie Silence* (because there is nothing coming through in space, no messages).

Physicist George Marx wrote in support of the concept by posing a question: "How does one send a letter to a faraway planet, a letter that is light enough for easy transportation, that multiplies itself on arrival, that can correct misprints automatically, and that will be read definitely by the intelligent race of the target planet after they have reached scientific maturity?"[17]

It's an idea called "directed Panspermia". And the best answer, you will have guessed, is DNA.

Of course this goes against the grain of orthodox science (Wikipedia remarks, almost coyly, that the idea of Panspermia is "essentially contra the scientific consensus"). Well, we all know what that means, don't we? Hitting a raw nerve with the diehards is not proof that a hypothesis is wrong or could not work. If you doubt that, re-read the words of Rear Admiral Simon Newcomb, already quoted on page 13!

The Panspermia hypothesis assumes that small organic grains, as Wickramsinghe called them, or spores, or chunks of organic matter, could remain viable after travelling immense distances through space and still be capable of replicating themselves. No problem with that.

The real test will be finding organic life forms, or at least proto-life substances, further out in space, say on an asteroid, in the tail of a comet, or on the surface of one of the many moons found in the Solar system. The more of it is out there, the more it is likely to be interplanetary or interstellar in origin.

Now scientists have found a significant organic molecule in the Sagittarius B2 system, which lies some 27,000 light-years from Earth. This carbon-based molecule is interesting because it has a branched structure, suggesting that it's probably isopropyl cyanide and that's important, because isopropyl cyanide is often found in molecules associated with life, such as amino acids. As a star forms, it produces isopropyl cyanide in an early part of its formation process.

Usually, organic molecules found in such regions of deep space are simpler: a single chain of carbon atoms. However, because of the way isopropyl cyanide branches off, it is easily identifiable and gives off a specific wavelength signature that telescopes recognize. That means that this is the first time we've detected this molecule in interstellar space, as opposed to nearby solar space.

This detection opens a new frontier in the complexity of molecules that can be formed in interstellar space and that might ultimately find their way to the surfaces of planets, says Rob Garrod, Cornell senior research associate at the Center for Radiophysics and Space Research. The branched carbon structure of isopropyl cyanide is a common feature in molecules that are needed for life—such as amino acids, which are the building blocks of proteins.

This new discovery lends weight to the idea that biologically crucial molecules, like amino acids that are commonly found in meteorites, are produced early in the process of star formation—even before planets such as Earth are formed. In other words, they can be formed in plasma! Remember you read the hot plasma origins of life here first![18]

CHAPTER 3

Strange Goings On

That the earth-as-a-whole is a gigantic electrical machine cannot be doubted. The constant turmoil of the atmosphere, its never-ceasing bombardment by the solar wind, the electrically charged wind-blown dust and snow, and the intense forces squeezing terrestrial rocks, all conspire to produce a wide spectrum of curious and poorly understood luminous effects

- William R Corliss, Lightning, Auroras, Nocturnal Lights and Related Luminous Phenomena, The Source Book Project, Glen Arm, Maryland, 1982

There are a lot of things taking place on our planet which, because they have no explanation within the existing scientific paradigms, are dismissed as nonsense or hoaxes. Never a suggestion that the existing paradigms are incomplete or defective!

Some of these phenomena have direct bearing on issues of health, medicine and biology. We need to absorb them into the *Medicine Beyond* model for it to be complete or even worthy. Strap yourself in for a wild ride;

there's some pretty amazing stuff to include, mostly from the Electric Universe.

If there is so much electrical energy around, how does that affect us humans? More than you could guess. If you remain skeptical about electricity's central role in life forces, you need to look at some genuine evidence (it's also evidence of the fact that science knows nothing, not even the limits of its own ignorance).

Consider the following intriguing and well-documented cases, which cannot be wished away by mere denial or refusal to acknowledge them. The fact is humans can act like lightning conductors, batteries, generators and highly charged capacitors.

HIGH VOLTAGE SYNDROME

One of the earliest investigated cases of an "electric person" was that of Angélique Cottin of La Perière, France. At the age of fourteen a strange condition befell her in which any object she went near would retreat from her, as if pushed, like magnets repelling each other. The mere touch of her hand was enough to send heavy furniture flying away from her. No one could hold down the furniture or stop it moving violently.

A study group was appointed by the French Academy of Sciences, and a well-known physicist of the day, François Arago, published a report in the *Journal des Débats* (February 1846). There is a lengthy translation of this report, entitled "The Electrical Girl", published in *Popular Science Monthly*, Vol 6, March 1875.

Here is an example of what they observed while studying the phenomenon. Angélique approached a table, which was repelled as soon as it came in contact with her apron. She seated herself upon a chair with her feet resting on the floor, and the chair was thrown violently against the wall, while she was sent in another direction. This experiment was repeated, over and over. Neither Arago, nor Gougin, nor Laugier, also present, could hold the chair immovable, and M. Gougin, seating himself in one-half of it, while the girl occupied the other, was thrown upon the floor as soon as she took possession of it.

They had no explanation, of course, nor even speculated much. But they did find that Angélique's unique powers seemed to emanate from her left side and were strongest in the evening. The episode lasted 10 weeks, before the strange manifestations finally ceased.

The Academy concluded that it was all a fraud by the slight little girl; apparently she had secret muscle reflexes that allowed her to throw a 100lb table or chair across the room, while disguising all movement from the observers! - Ridiculous but a predictable outcome.

Of course as soon as the word "fraud" is uttered, even be it by buffoons of the day, all scientific interest ceases and the eggheads no longer have to trouble their (tiny) minds with the issue. But for my readers, who are made of intellectually sturdier stuff than French Academicians, there's more!

George Gould and Walter Pyle, in their massive 1896 compilation of strange pathology called *Anomalies and Curiosities of Medicine* mention a six-year-old Zulu boy who gave off intense shocks and was exhibited at Edinburgh in 1882. From infancy he had been distinguished for this faculty, variable with the state of the atmosphere (which almost certainly connects it with electrical atmospheric phenomena).

Foder, in his *Encyclopedia of Psychic Science*, tells of a baby born at Saint-Urbain, France, in 1869 who badly shocked all who touched him. Luminous rays would shoot from his fingers, and when he died at just nine months old, radiance was observed around his body for several minutes. Later in the book we will be meeting biophotons, or light given off by living organisms. It's real and there is thus a plausible origin for these strange phenomena.

Let's call this "high voltage syndrome", since it is clearly pathological. Douglas Hunt, writing in *Prediction* (January 1953) gives two other cases of high-voltage infants: one was able to charge up a Leyden jar and the other could cause "vibrations" in objects held near him, and was seen to be surrounded by a soft, white radiance.

Colin Wilson, in his *Mammoth Encyclopedia of the Unsolved*[1] cites the case of Jennie Morgan of Sedalia, Missouri, who in 1895, generated charge sufficient to knock a grown man on his back and when she touched a water pump handle, sparks flew from her fingertips.

One of the most remarkable stories (to me) was a piece in *Electrical Experimenter* (June 1920) in which Dr. JB Ransom, chief physician at Clinton prison, New York, reported 34 convicts suffering from botulinus poisoning. One had tried to throw away a piece of paper and found it stuck to his hand. Soon all the afflicted inmates were in the same highly charged condition, varying in intensity with the severity of the poisoning. Compasses went wild in their vicinity and metal objects were deflected from their grasp. The effects faded as soon as they recovered from the poisoning.

A patient could make a torch bulb light up just by pointing at the torch, even though it was not switched on[2].

Why am I telling you this stuff? To make the point again that physics has no explanation for these phenomena. Scientists would simply say, "It's not normal." But there's a world of difference between not common and not "normal". Maybe these special individuals were normal and the rest of us are not? In any case, even if an event happens only once in the history of the universe, it cannot be shrugged off; it still needs explaining. If physics can't explain it then physics, (as normally described) is OUT!

They know that, of course, and so their only recourse is to pretend these events never did happen. But that's not science.

On the other hand I embrace this model because we are truly and irrevocably connected to the Electric Universe and we are surely part of it, not supernumeraries.

Let's continue with the fun…

BIOLUMINESCENCE

Consider the weird case of the "Luminous Woman of Pirano" (a tiny town in what is now Slovenia, on the Adriatic Sea). Anna Morano, aged 42, was an asthma patient. Over a period of several weeks, whenever she slept, a blue glow would be emitted from her breasts.

Dr. Protti from Padua University and a team of five other medical specialists kept a vigil at her bedside and witnessed the amazing phenomenon first hand, taking measurements and some cine film. Their work demonstrated that the subject doubled her heartbeat and respiratory rate during the brief minutes when the strange glow shone through her body. It was proposed that her sweating caused a luminous bacterium to glow but reports were very clear, her sweating and breathlessness came *after* the light.

None of the experts had any credible explanation for what was observed. Perhaps the best theory was that her weakened condition, due to religious zeal and fasting, increased the sulfides in her blood, which would be capable of glowing in ultraviolet light. But where did the ultraviolet light come from?

It remains a mystery. The effect disappeared after a few weeks and the woman was none the worse for her "affliction"[3].

Harry Wood Carrington tells of a child who died of acute indigestion. As neighbors prepared the shroud they noticed the body surrounded by a blue glow and radiating heat. The body appeared to be on fire; efforts to extinguish the luminescence failed, but eventually it faded away. Gould and Pyle also tell of a woman with cancer of the breast: the light from her body could illuminate the hands of a watch several feet away.

Then there was a letter to the *English Mechanic*, dated 24 September 1869, which described the experience of an American woman. On going to bed, she found that a light was issuing from the upper side of the fourth toe on her right foot. Rubbing made it worse and it spread up her foot. There was a bad odor and she tried washing her foot in soap and water, but it didn't decrease the glow (thereby rendering glowing bacteria out of the question). The whole phenomenon lasted for three quarters of an hour and was witnessed by her husband.

There have been many other cases of glowing humans. Indeed, they are rather common and may extend to include the halo effect seen around holy figures or those engaged in intense spiritual activity. Light capable of lighting up a darkened cell or chapel has been seen streaming from holy priests. There are simply so many of these accounts that they cannot all be dismissed as nonsense.

Rather, we need to explain how intense paranormal activity, immaterial thoughts, or transcendence can activate normal physical pathways, thereby leading to physical energy emissions. It's definitely a medical anomaly and demands proper and honest investigation by doctors and scientists who are not trying to disprove or disagree with what happened but who are motivated to find a proper explanation.

PATHOLOGICAL EFFECT

It's very clear these strange energetic phenomena are not normal, in any sense. In fact they tend to be pathological and mainly afflict sick people.

Even Angélique Cottin, the "Electrical Girl", was described as sickly and apathetic to an extraordinary degree both in body and mind. Colin Wilson, in his *Mammoth Encyclopedia of the Unsolved*, also describes the 1877 case of Caroline Clare of London, Ontario, who attracted metal objects and could deliver a powerful electric shock to as many as 20 people holding hands. She was suffering from adolescent depression at the time.

This may be the real clue we need.

I have been at pains throughout to point out that we live in a universe that is flooded with highly charged electrical flows. This current is transformed for us by our galaxy; this galactic electricity is transformed by our Sun; the Sun's violent energies are transformed by Earth herself. We live in a sea of electrical energies of unimaginable force.

It means that we must all be adapted to this high-powered environment. But what if we fall sick; go out of kilter; unadapt to our electrical environment? Could it not then be that, for some individuals, it means the electrical energy goes out of control and starts to work these strange manifestations?

I think so and this is certainly the most plausible explanation to date. That's why I have pushed and pushed the *Electric Universe* model: there is nothing in the "Universe as a cold machine" or a gravity-based physics that could possibly explain all that we have seen in this section.

It's a Universe that is vibrant and alive; it throbs with energy and electrical flows stream from end to end.

What's the number one sign of life that I keep telling you about? - Electricity. Not respiration, not reproduction or feeding: a cellular membrane electrical potential. In fact death is no longer determined by absence of breathing but by the cessation of electrical activity within the brain. Once that's gone; it's death. And in the reverse...

Mary Shelley may have had a strange prescience when she wrote her novel *Frankenstein*. We all know the story, even without reading the book: mad scientist stitches together a body of sorts, using dead pieces from the morgue and from graves. What is the one missing ingredient that is needed to make this monster come alive? - Electricity.

Frankenstein just has to wait for the fateful lightning strike to his laboratory roof and then...

ELECTRICAL BIOLOGY

Each cell in our body can generate a small charge. What does that really mean, in terms of quantification? Obviously, we all know that there are microvolt currents involved in nerve impulses and muscle discharges. But the real values are much more remarkable than that.

American doctor, Mayne R. Coe Jr. (*Fate*, July 1959), believed that a cubic inch of human muscle cells could in theory generate 400,000 volts but of very low amperage. Coe found he was able to move aluminum strips pivoted on the points needles by moving his hand over them.

He began various yoga exercises in an attempt to develop his bio-electricity; sitting one day in an easy chair, he felt a powerful current passing downward from his head throughout his body; he thought it was of high voltage but low amperage. He suspended a card-board box from the ceiling on a length of string, and found that he could cause it to move from a distance—when the room was dry, from as far away as 8 feet. Coe then charged his body with 35,000 volts DC, using an electric current, and found that he could move the box in exactly the same way. This seemed to prove that he was in fact generating a high-voltage current with his mental exercises.

Coe theorized that this could explain the phenomenon of levitation, when a yogi or saint's body floats off the ground; it could be the positively charged human body repelling the negatively charged Earth. It is significant that many of these strange experiences are accompanied by glowing light, as in the case of St Joseph of Cupertino (1603-1663) or St Teresa of Avila (1515-1582), and are therefore assumed to be holy in character.

Even if essentially electrical in nature, of course, that does not detract from the assumed holiness or the observable ecstasy of the experience. I speculate that the same electric mechanism may be connected with what are called "alien abductions" (see below).

Professor Ronald Pethig at the School of Electronic Engineering and Computer Systems, University of Wales, has estimated that the total number of chemical reactions involving electron transport along the metabolic pathways of our bodies generates a current on the order of 200 amps[4]. That's pretty big, compared to, say, 30 amps for an electric cooker going full blast on all heater rings and the oven.

Since the energy gap band of proteins is about 5 eV (electron volts), this represents a power output of about 1 kW: that's very significant. As my friend Dr. Cyril Smith, electronic boffin retired from Salford University, UK, pointed out, "If a man could synchronize all his chemical reactions to produce the energy of maximum metabolic output, he would be able to communicate with a hypersensitive individual anywhere on earth, just using electromagnetic radiations"[5].

Add the fact that a human holding his or her arms up above head height (a classic "guru" or preacher blessing gesture), would be the correct length for a quarter dipole aerial of 30 MHz or 10 meters wavelength. This frequency of 30 MHz is another curious "Goldilocks" coincidence, since it is the highest frequency that is reliably reflected round the planet by the ionosphere! In other words, such a guru could become a human radio and potentially influence the whole planet.

Smith later added a qualifier, especially for this text, as follows: "This example was intended to demonstrate the limits set by science. There would be 'Tower of Babel' problems if more than one person attempted this at any instant. Beyond this limit of science, one enters the realm of mind-to-mind communication outside space and time."[6]

BODY RADIATION EMISSIONS

I remarked in *The Allergy Handbook,* which I wrote in 1988, that allergy patients seem to have problems with electrical energies. Many of them give off unpleasant static shocks to the long-suffering nurses who inject them with test allergens. Nothing mysterious about this; there is a very high electric field across live biological membranes, in the order of 10^7 V/m (ten million volts per meter). This is far greater than anything likely to be experienced by an individual standing in the vicinity of high-tension overhead electricity cables[7].

We also give off EMF transmissions in the infrared or audio-frequency range of the electromagnetic spectrum. Cyril Smith points out that there are many resonances in the "ideal" cell, connected with the cell membranes and micro-tubular structures within the cell body. *"Living systems are making use of the entire non-ionizing frequency spectrum from Micro-Hertz to the optical"*, he points out[8]. These resonances radiate bio-information over at least several meters. We are a veritable radio station with lots of channels.

Years ago we used to record the biological emissions of an allergic patient undergoing a reaction by the simple expedient of having him or her hold a plastic-cased cassette tape recorder which was running without a microphone. The patient's body transmits a big enough signal to be detected by the machine and recorded on the tape. Usually a series of clicks and hisses can be heard on playback; it varies from patient to patient and even the same patient on different occasions. Obviously there must be a quiescent "control" recording in which the machine is left running in an empty room and the preceding remarks refer to sounds heard over and above the environmental background signals.

According to Cyril Smith, it should even be possible to compare the emitted frequencies with the endogenous frequencies associated with the acupuncture meridians to see which target organs are under stress. By the year 2000 he had done just that. It makes it possible to find allergens and environmental stressors and hence a *similimum,* the ultimate homeopathic treatment.

Smith showed that frequencies of acupuncture meridians can be entrained by homeopathic potencies which may stimulate or depress biological activity and hence can be "therapeutic"[9]. - More on this in the chapter on the science of homeopathy (Chapter 9).

Of course, today we have many sophisticated biosensors that are able to "read" body electromagnetic energy signals. Some can even hitch up to a smartphone and transmit data to any medical care service provider the patient chooses. Eric Topol MD, editor-in-chief of Medscape, has remarked that a sweeping transformation of medicine has begun that will rival in importance the introduction of anesthesia or the discovery of the germ basis of infectious disease. It will change how patients and physicians interact. It will change medical research and therapy. "Sick care", the current model of waiting for you to get sick and then trying to alleviate symptoms and make you well, will become true "health care," where prevention is the mantra and driving force.

ELECTRICAL HYPERSENSITIVITY

What began to emerge in the mid-1980s was that there are many individuals who are hypersensitive to electrical fields; "allergic to electricity" if you like. Cyril Smith and Dr. Jean Monro studied this in great depth and have created a whole new medical paradigm that is still so little known or studied that there have to be numerous avenues for a doctorate thesis in this field.

With Monro as the clinician and Smith as the gizmo-wizard, they began to experiment by subjecting patients to electrical fields of varying frequencies and strength. Two things became quickly obvious:

- only very low intensity fields were needed to produce an effect, using frequencies widely encountered in the environment and

- recognizable clinical syndromes could be triggered using this electrical approach.

Once a patient specific threshold of intensity had been exceeded, frequency was the relevant parameter. This is contrary to the present mantra that the only biological EM effects are thermal.

It was indeed a kind of allergy to electricity.

Monro, in her treatment facility, used a specialized form of allergy testing that provoked and then neutralized patient-specific symptoms. She and Smith found they could do the same with electrical sensitivity reactions: it was possible to set off symptoms with an electrical exposure and then use the neutralizing effect of a particular frequency or "dose". It was possible to afterwards imprint water with this healing frequency and administer it to the patient therapeutically (see page 170 for more on imprinting). I was able to confirm their pioneer work with a simple frequency generator in tests in my own clinic.

What was even more remarkable, Monro and Smith found they could trigger a food allergy symptom - by giving the patient an immunological dose of a known pathogen, and then "neutralizing" it with an electrical frequency. That's more exciting because it is a version of electrotherapy, the big bugaboo of orthodox science!

Their discovery much interlocked with work on bioresonance and other electronic devices, such as the SCENAR, which are discussed throughout the present work.

Now let's turn to something every bit as weird as some of the cases I have already cited, but very modern in its idiom!

CROP CIRCLES

Like most people, there was a time when I supposed that "crop circles" were either the work of extraterrestrials or just human pranksters; one or the other. Since I didn't believe that extraterrestrials with enough intelligence to reach our planet would waste their time fooling around in the corn—and since groups had been caught in the act of faking crop circles—I tended to the latter interpretation and didn't really give the matter much more thought for many years.

That is, not until I was in studio at the BBC to be interviewed about food allergies and met Colin Andrews and Pat Delgado, who were being interviewed on the same program, that same morning, to promote their new book *Circular Evidence*. The pair had been visiting crop circles, filming them, and told me that sometimes, when they stepped inside a formation, their electrical equipment drastically malfunctioned; the cameras wouldn't record. Yet, when they stepped outside the circle again, the gear resumed working normally. In other words, there was nothing wrong with the equipment; it just wouldn't work properly inside a crop circle[10].

That got me hooked.

But I'm not a "croppie" or cereologist, as they are sometimes called. There are too many hoaxers and timewasters who have made the topic an unrewarding one for me. Being the person I am I'd like to shift the debate from ETs vs. pranksters to the real issue: proper science versus prejudgment. The point is that, even if 99% of crop circles are faked, that still leaves 1% that needs a full and satisfying scientific explanation.

Could the phenomenon of crop circles be attributable to an Electric Universe? - Maybe.

The first scientific attempt to explain the appearance of crop circle formations was put forward by Terence Meaden, a physicist and meteorologist with masters and doctorate degrees from Oxford University and a Fellow of the Royal Meteorological Society. Meaden was originally part of the research team with Andrews and Delgado, but later began to distance himself from their remarks, which were that circles didn't just happen but were deliberately created by some form of consciousness, be it human or extraterrestrial.

Being very familiar with properties of atmospheric plasma, Meaden hypothesized that a whirlwind or tornado could potentially generate a plasma vortex that could account for the delicate and precise way that crop stalks appeared to be laid down in circles, as if from above. The plasma vortex theory could also explain the anomalous lights that were sometimes associated with crop circles[11].

However, as much more complex formations started to appear, the idea that these could really be created by a plasma whirlwind seemed less credible. There was simply no convincing way to argue that more complex crop circles were being created by a combination of merely wind and electrical charge.

This is where the pranksters got in the way of meaningful investigation, with their stupid tricks. Some of the designs you only had to look at to see quickly that they were manmade creations. One of the notorious howlers was a site which said in words, "We are not alone." Even if ETs knew the English language, they would still be expected to write, "You are not alone", surely?

Hard-line scientists continue to milk the notion of hoaxes, as if proof that circles can be faked means that they are all faked, which of course is intellectual nonsense. As I said, if there is but one authentic circle, it needs to be explained, not yapped away with pseudo-science, such as you read at the Committee for Skeptical Enquiry website[12].

PHYSICAL EFFECTS

For instance, there are certain physical changes at some of the circles that need explaining. I have already mentioned the malfunction of electrical equipment reported by observers; watches, mobile phones, batteries, and cameras are often affected during the examination of crop circles.

There are no explanations for these occurrences other than the influence of strong EM field distortions. Physical effects on people who enter crop circles have also been reported. While some feel elated, others feel nausea, headaches, dizziness, tingling sensations, pain, and giddiness.

Then there is the microwave energy and certain metallic residues found on the flattened crops. That's given rise to speculation about alien space-ships. I don't think we need quite such an elaborate and dramatic source of contamination, but how *did* such energies arise?

Also, there is the matter of the exploding nodes. Nodes are the thickened bumps marking joints along the stalks of a corn. Wheat stems taken from certain crop formations reveal a massive number of expulsion cavities at their stem nodes. This effect suggests they were subjected to an internal pressure so sudden and powerful that it blew holes through the node points of the stem walls, as the internal sap rapidly expanded.

LEVENGOOD'S MICROWAVE THEORY

Dr. William Levengood, in 14 years of scientific investigation on crop circles, has examined more than 250 crop formations in detail. Since 1992, he and his team have been involved in extensive on-the-ground surveillance and the collecting of samples and electromagnetic and other readings from crop formations. These samples are then sent for analysis in his private laboratory based in Michigan, where he compares the grain collected from in and around the circles with control samples taken from edges of the fields the formations were found in.

Levengood has concluded that the exploding nodes could be characteristic of electromagnetic radiation, probably microwave, emanating from the epicenter of the formation. He also noted other consistent characteristics of grain samples taken from the formations:

Stalks are very often bent up to 90 degrees without being broken, particularly at the nodes.

Stalks are unusually enlarged, stretched from the inside out by something that seems to heat the nodes from the inside. Sometimes this effect is powerful enough to literally explode the node, blowing holes in the node walls and causing sap to leak from the stalk.

Stalks are left with a surface electric charge, suggesting the force that flattened the crops was electrical.

The thin bract tissue surrounding the wheat seed shows an increase in electrical conductivity, consistent with exposure to an electrical charge.

The germination of some seeds found in crop formations has accelerated growth and vigor.

There are also significant reductions in the growth rates of subsequent seedlings, germinated from the wheat seeds taken from formations (up to 35% shorter than controls.

These results, Levengood concludes, strongly suggest rapid heating, such as would be caused by the exposure of the plants to microwave radiation or unusual electrical fields.

His results were published in the journal of the *Scandinavian Society for Plant Physiology*[13].

PRESENCE OF METEORITIC MATERIAL

Levengood's laboratory analysis of samples from crop formations also notes the presence of a gray dust of hematite or iron oxide, which is of a type found in meteoritic material. This suggests to Levengood that the formations were created by a close encounter between a meteoritic system and a plasma vortex. The vortexes described in Levengood's theory are created much higher in the atmosphere than those proposed by Meaden's theory. Beginning in the ionosphere, where there is an abundance of microscopic meteoritic material, the Levengood vortexes are drawn down to the surface of the earth, apparently to areas of significant electromagnetic charge.

This could be related to underground geomagnetic fields in the locations where the circles are found. Measurements taken by Levengood and his team in recently made formations have shown elevated magnetic levels that quickly dissipate, suggesting that a charge has somehow been released.

Unlike Meaden's theory, Levengood's model allows for the creation of complex shapes and geometries. His theory is also supported by the fact that the traces of hematite and microwave energy are not found in those circles that are known to have been a deliberate, manmade hoax. Levengood and his team have probably provided the most complete and comprehensive model of how crop formations could be made, but their research has neither been accepted by the scientific community nor widely covered in the news media.

Levengood's critics have focused on the fact that correlation is not causation. They also point to his self-expressed caution that *"node size data cannot be relied upon as a definite verification of a 'genuine' crop formation."* There has yet to be an independent replication of Levengood's work.

It remains a fact, however, that Levengood is a well-established scientist with an outstanding research record. His conclusions provide one of the most satisfyingly scientific explanations of the possible origin of these mysterious crop formations. Of course, Levengood does not attempt to explain why the formations seem to represent a symbolic language or interpret what kind of intelligence lies behind this phenomenon; instead, he focuses on the physics of how such a thing could possibly be accomplished at all.

THE HOEVEN CIRCLE (aka NOORD-BADANT CIRCLE)

Dutch engineer Eltjo H. Haselhoff wrote that a young Dutch man claimed he saw, at about half past one AM on June 7, 1999, a small pink light that moved in the air, then turned into an elliptic shape and slowly faded, leaving a crop circle of about nine meters of diameter, still hot (literally). The following morning the young man saw a second circle about 60 cm in diameter near the first circle. Five nights later, the (supposed) eyewitness saw a flash of pale blue light coming from a single point; this time the witness found another circle, nine meters in diameter, still hot.

Haselhoff arrived on the scene quickly and took samples. Later, using a mathematical model, he graded the lengthening of stalks between nodes and concluded that a radiation had been emitted by some unspecified kind of ball of light[14].

Self-affirmed skeptics attack Hasselhoff's mathematics and method with vigor. Yet they are strangely silent about the eyewitness account. Presumably they write off the youth as someone defective; he couldn't really have seen any such thing, could he? So they describe him as a "supposed eyewitness"!

ALIEN ABDUCTIONS?

Robbert van den Broeke seems to have the special ability to "feel" energies where circles are about to appear. He has been very close at the moment of causation and yet witnesses present insist he was not engaged in any fakery.

55

On one occasion when there were no immediate witnesses van den Broeke saw a "star-like" light-ball high in the sky, which seemed to be rotating, and he stopped to watch it. As it came toward him it became larger and larger and he could now clearly see that it was a light-ball and about the size of a soccer-ball, still rotating. When the light-ball was only about 15 meters above him he began to feel dizzy and as if he were losing consciousness and then felt as if his body was "flying" in the air, weightless (like a feather).

The next thing he remembers is finding himself sitting on the flattened grain in the larger (5.2m x 4.7m) of two small circles. He tried to stand but couldn't at first get his legs to work and says he could still see the light-ball, much smaller now, as it rose into the sky and then disappeared.

Van den Broeke's immediate impression regarding one formation was that it contained healing energy, which is one of the reasons I am writing about these "encounters".

But van den Broeke also got a second, very strange "message" that, if people would bring apples with them into this ring formation they might find, when they then took the apples home, that very clear dark markings or "symbols" would appear on them. And, further, that in those cases where this occurred, it would be good for the people to eat these apples, skin and all; that the apples would help promote healing.

Well, lots of people brought apples and lots of strange symbols appeared on them in subsequent days, all photographed and documented. Incidentally, strange markings have been appearing on apples in van den Broeke's parents' home, as well as his sister's, for many years since all this began and the family have noticed no ill effects from eating them.

OpenMindsTV is hosting a webpage with many photographs and a lot more data about van den Broeke and his uncanny connection with crop circles[15].

Real or fake? Mass hysteria? I really have no problem with electrical events in an Electrical Universe, so there is no reason to doubt people's integrity or powers of perception. I am on record (page 28) as speculating that ball lightning and plasmas could even contain intelligent life forms.

As to van den Broeke's account of being lifted by a ball of light and passing out; I couldn't help but note the similarity between this experience and so-called "alien abductions". I don't believe in alien abductions per se but I do believe in the authenticity of experiences like this, described by credible human observers like van den Broeke.

Maybe there are many such experiences that are not delusional, but based on a person becoming electrically charged up and then manifesting a strange glow and levitating. An electrical overwhelm could explain the supposed deliberate anesthesia induced by aliens, to cover up their nefarious presence! It's just electrical overload in the brain. No aliens are needed, not even the hand of God, but just plain physics.

CHAPTER 4

Information Rules

*All the phenomenon of non-local conscious-
ness—things like telepathy and psychokinesis,
and of course near death experiences—indicate
that consciousness is a far deeper, more profound
mystery than "kindergarten level" scientific materialism offers up.*

—Eben Alexander, author *Proof of Heaven*

I make the point that modern physics is very spiritual. It tells us that
our Universe is alive with interconnected energies and manifestations
that we would recognize as "consciousness." It is as if vital energy was
in-built into the fabric of reality. Nothing new here; it's been the teaching of enlightened seers and masters for millennia. But only in the last
century was science forced to come to terms with the fact that the way
to knowledge is personal involvement in creative experience. The vain
hope of the objectivists of conquering this reality by making it conform
to their preconceived "reasoning" seems doomed to failure, the more
facts are uncovered.

As Henry Stapp has remarked, *"It is the revised understanding of the nature of human beings, and of the causal role of human consciousness in the unfolding of reality, that is, I believe, the most exciting thing about the new physics, and probably, in the final analysis, also the most important contribution of science to the well-being of our species."*[1]

What defines thought? Logic or reason? No, not exactly. The structure of a crystal has logic and is very reasonable but such a formation is not thought as we mean it.

The defining quality of thought—awareness, consciousness, and mentation—relies on what we today call information. It has become a whole science in itself and now dominates the computer-driven age.

But one of the greatest information sources in our world, and crucial to life, is the structure of DNA. It's an encyclopedia, though it doesn't have functioning pages the way that most material scientists think of it; it's more like a biological PDA (personal digital organizer). We'll come to that shortly.

INFORMATION IMPLIES CONSCIOUSNESS

This is a long-standing contention of mine. What we call "information" is meaningless without some kind of conscious appraisal. Even the famous equation $e=mc^2$ means very little, except in abstract terms (what exactly is the speed of light squared? It's about as unreal as the square root of the river Thames).

The focus of this book is on a new model of reality: consciousness and information. They go together, like hand in glove. Using contemporary evidence (and a good deal of common sense) it overthrows the classic science model of matter or "stuff" ruling the universe. In the words of 1984 Nobel laureate for physics, Carlo Rubbia, whom I had delight in quoting for the first edition of *Virtual Medicine*: **matter is less than a billionth part of the manifest cosmos. The rest is pure energy and information.**

The twice-nominated Nobel Peace Prize systems theorist, Ervin Laszlo, said something similar: *"the fundamental furnishing of the universe is information and energy . . . Information is the 'software' that governs the mass/energy 'hardware.'"* And Albert Einstein himself, when referring to the seeming dichotomy between matter and energetic fields, stated that *"the field is the only reality."*

This is a staggering revelation, from some of science's top minds.

A healing discipline that looks only at such a tiny and inconsequential proportion of the whole (one billionth) is badly skewed, and is bound to get it wrong more often than right. Stuck in the incorrect "matter" paradigm, ignorant doctors are surely doomed to violate the first precept of Hippocrates' code, which is: "Do no harm."

Unfortunately, doctors are decades behind with this and are not even talking about the idea yet. Scientific attitudes here, I am sorry to say, are often no more than an affectation with which the medical establishment tries to browbeat its (many) opponents, rather than the humble reality of willing seekers of truth. It is a case where, as the founder of humanistic psychology, Abram Maslow, put it so well: *the pretense of science is being used to avoid the bigger truth.*

Later on (Chapters 8, 9 and 10) I shall adduce three different proofs that the "stuff" or matter is not really what makes it behave as it does, but the information/energetic signals it gives off. We can get biological changes from a substance that is not even present.

In other words, I will overthrow one of the core precepts of the "old" science: that only weighable substances with a rest mass and a sufficient biochemical gradient can affect biological organisms. Instead, I will show that unweighable (non-material) substances have profound measurable biological effects and that this may even be the paramount mechanism of their action.

Stick around for the proof.

INFORMATION FIELDS

Here's a clue.

The newest concept in biology is the information field. Information fields create reality; they put it there and hold it together the way it should be. Have you ever wondered why a teacup is a teacup? Why don't the atoms at the edge go wandering off and become, say, a spoon? The answer is an information field. When you drink a cup of tea you do so from something which, in material terms, is 99.999999 per cent not there (please don't count the decimal places, there are dozens that I didn't bother to type). Only the field is real. Matter, as quantum physics teaches us, is a mere illusion. It comes out of this "void" or vacuum, whenever we interact with it. Like the cavalry troops in the old B movies, it shows up just when it's needed!

It follows that a cancer, a parasite, and a virus are also just information fields. Everything in our life and being is energy and information. We come from fields in the egg; we go back to a field as a corpse. Indeed, there is the likelihood that we survive death at least as some kind of field (Chapter 26).

Biological information fields are unbelievably vast in the amount of data that they contain; many orders of magnitude greater than the combined total molecular complexity of our physical substances. In other words, there is no way that the biochemical matrix of our bodies could contain enough information to organize and control a living organism. We need the information field to put us there and hold us in place. Chemicals cannot 'think' and organize other chemicals without some initiating input! This one fact really does put paid once and for all to the idea of biochemically-based life, as espoused by the current drug-based medical culture. We exist as regulated and informed energy.

MORPHOGENETIC FIELDS

In the first edition, I didn't allow myself enough space to properly introduce Rupert Sheldrake's concept of the *morphogenetic field*. It's not an entirely new idea and contains echoes of an old idea from Plato: that of "forms" or secondary planes of reality which infer and perhaps create our world, rather like a reverse shadow, where it's the shadow that creates us, not the other way round.

More recently it was described by Hans Driesch (1867- 1941), who coined the word entelechy. He's out of fashion now because he espoused vitalism, instead of the dead, mechanical wilderness of modern science. But Driesch was able to clone the first animal in 1885[2].

Somewhat later, in Russia, the concept of biological fields, with the same manner of function as electromagnetic systems, was suggested by Russian Alexander Gurwitsch in 1922 and Paul Weiss in 1926. Gurwitsch (1874-1954) also launched the idea of biophotons, with

61

an interesting series of experiments involving onion shoots signaling to each other. We'll look at that later, in the section on light.

Paul Alfred Weiss (1898–1989) was an Austrian biologist who moved to the USA, ahead of the rise of Nazism. He also contributed early thinking on this topic.

But the excitement generated by Rupert Sheldrake is that he is a modern, highly respected academician (for instance a Frank Knox fellow at Harvard From 2005 to 2010; director of the Perrott-Warrick Project, funded from Trinity College, Cambridge University; a Fellow of the Institute of Noetic Sciences in California; a visiting professor at the Graduate Institute in Connecticut; fellow of Schumacher College in Devon, England).

That said, his first important book, *The New Science of Life*, was denounced by John Maddox, then editor of the journal *Nature*, with the infamous assertion it should be burned. Burning books is, of course, something we associate with the Inquisition and Nazis, not true investigative science and its deliberations. John Maddox, by the way, was the editor at the time of the Jacques Benveniste's "memory of water" debacle. The furor and criminal debunking of Benveniste that followed does no credit to anyone involved, but at least Maddox did have the balls to publish, urging readers to "suspend judgment" until the results could be replicated[3].

Meantime, a few words about entire fields, which the reader must supplement by study of Sheldrake's own very capable books.

It's a kind of consciousness effect, in which structure and form are held in a field that is superordinate to materiality, or at the level of information. It informs energy, which in turn creates and shapes the physical reality we see. That was the central proposition of *Virtual Medicine* at the time of the first edition and remains a key concept in *Medicine Beyond*.

This in itself is extremely revolutionary. If there are fields creating forms, they lie outside mathematics. Form is something quite special. Mathematically, we can show that energy is conserved, mass (perhaps), electric charge and momentum, but form is quite different. It cannot be conserved and if you take an object such as a vase and grind it to powder, the form is lost forever (you can use the dust to mix with stiffeners and make a new vase, but the old one is lost; or I should say the form of the old one is lost and gone forever).

In the polarization of today, Sheldrake has now been scoffed at by main-stream scientists, the Thought Police, who ignore his very meticulous and credible investigative methods and results. Using statistical methods, he has been able to show that there is some truth in old beliefs, such as the ability to know when we are being stared at or that dogs know when their owners are coming home.

He has also been able to show, to my satisfaction, that group knowledge is a field and that it can be added to by subsequent learning and accessed by other members of a tribe or species. He calls this phenomenon morphic resonance[4].

RADIO DNA

We cannot visit the topic of biological information without considering the mighty DNA molecule. It's supposed to hold the key information in its structure for how to create a living creature (it doesn't, by the way; more of that shortly). How does it do it?

Not by working as a "chemical photocopier," that's for sure. There is not enough room in the so-called genes to carry all the information that's needed.

It's better to think of DNA like Google: all the information is there (in Google search) but it's not contained in the computer chips that access it. DNA works "in the cloud", biologically speaking.

In *Virtual Medicine* (1999), I proposed that DNA works by being an in-formation transmitter, not a chemical processor. Advancing science has progressed to the point where this may be said to be a proven hypothesis. DNA has electromagnetic transmission properties; that makes it electri-cal in quality. "Radio DNA" is a core part of the Electric Universe model of life and reality.

As I pointed out, the DNA double helix is an ideal shape for a trans-mitter aerial, and in my view Nature doesn't waste her time on mean-ingless coincidences. In fact DNA very closely models the shape and performance of the highly efficient fractal aerials that are used in today's cell phones. Such an aerial is folded and refolded many times, so that a great deal of transmitting power can be transferred through a very small physical dimension.

Unfortunately, this ideal transmitter shape also makes DNA a very sus-ceptible receiver, sensitive to input from all external radiation sources, a matter which causes great concern. It has emerged clearly that cell phone dangers are due in part to DNA damage and this has been solidly proven, despite all the fake studies and posturing of T-Mobile and other providers.

THE REALITIES OF DNA

The first thing to grasp about DNA is that genes are basically a hoax; they do not chemically encode the characteristics of a human being or any creature. The delusion there is a gene for everything, such as blue eyes, is nonsense. Genes just don't work in the simplistic way that scientists have foisted on us over the years.

For one thing, human DNA has only 25,000 or so "genes." This is less than a tomato! Moreover we share a quarter of our genes with a daffodil, so only around 18,500 genes are uniquely human. It's just not enough.

All that genes really do is to encode proteins. The DNA sequence is copied to RNA strands and those migrate into the cytoplasm of the cell and cause the production of related molecular strands, mostly proteins. It's a sort of photocopy service for the cell; no more complicated than that.

But the biggest hoax is that genes are somehow fixed. Genes are very plastic and can easily be altered.

For example, the blue- or brown-eyes gene I mentioned: any good holistic therapist is able to change brown eyes to blue; as the patient detoxes, so the eyes clear. I have done this to some extent, even with Asians from the Indian subcontinent.

I have even reversed the "bad genes" of Duchene pattern muscular dystrophy, supposedly an autosomal dominant, which means you are doomed: you get it, end of story. They still think that, but once you have ever seen changes happen—that this or that gene can be switched on or off epigenetically—you realize the whole "photocopier" story is a hoax. Even just one example that breaks the "law" means it is not a law…

The streams of code orthodoxy had arrogantly labeled "junk DNA" on first inspection they are now saying are "switches" that turn genes on and off. There is talk of regulatory sections, as opposed to coding sections (of the genome). They still don't get it and are trying to make DNA autonomous and the origin of all transferred genetic information.

There is an important missing step.

If these groups of molecules really are switches, what activates them? Who or what is turning the power on and off? Lighting in your home does not come and go as it pleases; you have to make the decision you want light and then flip the switch. Something must trigger the trigger, unless they admit the trigger can think for itself! See, they don't even grasp this problem, never mind come up with a solution!

If all that happened is that DNA copied itself, it would soon discharge all its available material, like a ticker-tape machine gone mad, and then stop. But it doesn't do that. Some other outside force is regulating the process via these switches.

But this "stuff makes stuff" model will be around for decades to come and will persist, despite no clear way in which stuff can decide to make other stuff!

The ineptness of scientists at what discoveries are really telling them would be laughable, if it were not so frustrating. It's the classic case of scientists trying to project their theories onto Nature, instead of listening to her clear and capable messages!

DNA AN INFORMATION-TRANSMITTER

DNA contains vast amounts of data—but not as chemical strings. The whole human blueprint is there, as soon as the zygote forms. It's a radiated (broadcast) field image and the cells, as they grow and multiply, simply fit where they belong in the blueprint. It's what Rupert Sheldrake calls a *morphogenetic field* (shape-forming field): Hans Driesch's entelechy mechanism. That's how cells know how to grow and what position to take up. So a liver cell knows it's a liver cell, because it's sitting in that part of the field that says, "Liver goes here."

It cannot possibly be in the chemical helix because every single cell gets the same entire code. How do I know? It's easy to change the image and you get a new result!

In the 1970s, Dr. Vlail Kaznacheyev, director of the Institute for Clinical and Experimental Medicine in Novosibirsk reported some mind-boggling experiments. He took two samples of cell cultures, hermetically sealed off from each other. He then infected one sample with a disease process (a virus) and shone light through the infected cells onto the other culture with normal, healthy cells. The normal cells got the virus DNA/protein too!

That's simply not possible in conventional science. You would have to chemically transfer virus particles from one culture to the other. But Kaznacheyev did it by information transfer, using the electromagnetic spectrum—light.

This was backed up by the observation that, only when a quartz glass screen was inserted between the two cultures, did the DNA transfer effect take place. Normal glass blocked the process. We know that quartz allows UV light to pass; ergo: the energetic transfer agency was light at the UV end of the spectrum.

In other words, DNA is an information transfer vehicle.[5]

WHO ARE YOU CALLING QUACK?

Even more startling was the duck-chick experiment reported by Chinese researcher Tszyan Kangchen. He shone laser light through duck eggs, onto chicken embryos still in the shell and, when hatched, some of the "chicks" were found to have webbed feet, flat bills (like a duck), and eyes rearranged in the duck pattern.

Again, this is simply not possible in terms of modern science. However it's obvious enough: the laser beam carried some of the energetic field encoding of "duck" into the chick embryos and restructured their DNA so that a different creature was born. Again, no chemical "stuff" was required for the transfer.

This particular experiment put me in mind of another story about duck DNA and chickens: A bit of duck DNA might protect poultry from flu. In a study published online March 22, 2010, in *Proceedings of the National Academy of Sciences*, researchers said they've found that a key influenza-fighting gene in wild ducks is absent in chickens.

Genetically modifying chickens with a copy of that gene might render them resistant to influenza A, the most common form of flu infecting humans.

This raises the possibility of a whole new kind of medicine, which I will be expanding on throughout *Medicine Beyond*: one in which we could transmit the energetic equivalent of a therapeutic substance into tissues and bring about healing.

NOBEL LAUREATE DOES THE SAME

OK, some critics are going to say, Russian and Chinese researchers may be a bit weird; maybe they can't be trusted? (This is a common Western science attitude.)

Well, in a similar experiment, in a paper published in 2009, Nobel Laureate virologist Luc Montagnier (who shared the prize for discovering the HIV virus) described how he demonstrated the apparent ability of DNA fragments and entire bacteria both to produce weak electromagnetic fields and to "regenerate" themselves in previously uninfected cells.[6]

Montagnier strained a solution of the bacterium *Mycoplasma pirum* through a filter with pores small enough to prevent the bacteria from penetrating. The filtered water emitted the same frequency of electromagnetic signal as the bacteria themselves.

He says he has evidence that many species of bacteria and many viruses give out the electromagnetic signals, as do some diseased human cells. And that's what my book *Medicine Beyond* is about.

Georges Lakhovsky, whom we shall meet at some length later, pointed out that all cells capable of reproduction contain in their nuclei "filaments" of highly conductive material surrounded by insulating media. This filament, which may be the RNA-DNA complex, is always in the form of a spiral or helix—in other words, a coil. Therefore, each will react as a tuned circuit if its resonant frequency can be approximated by an external oscillating coil.

THE GRAMMAR OF DNA

Russian linguists have found that much of the DNA sequence follows a grammatical code, not unlike that of our language. They have speculated that language may be based on DNA, rather than the other way around.

This would go some way to explaining the possible phenomenon that words may influence DNA. Experiments suggest that imbuing laser beams with language concepts and information can influence the behavior of DNA. So it is not (scientifically) impossible that affirmations, prayers, and hypnosis could have an effect on the performance of DNA.

Note that the information has to be encoded in sound. Light or radio waves are only the carriers.

The the meantime—while Western scientists are cutting and pasting chunks of DNA (physical manipulation)—Russian scientists have created devices that influence DNA via radio and light frequencies and can transfer genetic information.

For example, frog embryos have been transformed into salamander embryos, using this process. By simply applying vibrations at sound frequencies, using laser light as a carrier, DNA is altered: no clunky cutting and splicing required[7].

Esoteric and spiritual teachers have known for ages that our body is programmable by language, words, and thought. This now has a scientific basis.

Of course the frequency has to be correct. And this is why not everybody is equally successful or can always do it with the same strength. The individual person must work on the inner processes and development in order to establish a conscious communication with the DNA.

It is assumed that higher conscious powers, which ride somewhat above physical factors anyway, can do this innately. It is already emerging that living organisms can whip up a gene out of nowhere, if they need it.

I like Russian scientists; they are open-minded free thinkers, not tied down to what they are "supposed to" find. They enjoy a candid resourcefulness that was long since lost in Western science. It's true that their science publications are not in line with Western methods, but the fact they won't sway scientists here doesn't bother me. Why? Because in turn most Western scientists are not moved by mere facts and data, only prejudice and theories. New discoveries are not going to budge them from their entrenched position.

For that reason, I include some speculative theories from Russian scientists here. Unfortunately, they are difficult to get sourced. The proposition concerning the language and syntax of DNA, attributed to Peter Garaiev, for example, seems to track back no further than the book *Ver-*

netzte Intelligenz (Networked Intelligence) by Grazyna Fosar and Franz Bludorf (ISBN 3930243237). There is no English translation.

GHOST DNA

Still not convinced by where I'm going with this? Consider the presence of a DNA "cloud" of imprinted energy but no "stuff" present...

Another Russian, Peter Garaiev PhD, the so-called "father of wave genetics," did this experiment in 1984. He discovered that DNA molecules absorb and hold photons; that is, small quantum packets of light.

That in itself is not surprising. Fritz Popp has been working in this area, too (p. 374). Maybe biophotons are the source of energy that DNA uses to work its effects. It could be storing photons, to use like a food supply?

There's more: the DNA held the light in a significant helical structure, which occupied the exact place of the DNA spiral. It was like a physical blueprint. Even more startling, when the DNA was removed and all physical traces of it had vanished, the light continued spiraling along in the same space, exactly as it had done when the DNA was present. The light knew where the DNA had been!

This remarkable effect didn't quickly vanish, either! It lasted up to 30 days after the dismantling of the DNA and equipment. Whatever was holding the photons in place did not need the actual physical molecule or "stuff" to be present. DNA, in other words, is seen to be an information field and not a chemical process.

REJUVENATING OUR BODIES

Peter Garaiev was in good form again in 2000. This time he took seeds killed by the Chernobyl nuclear blast; he shone non-burning laser light through healthy seeds onto the dead seeds, and they revived! They grew into fully healthy adult plants.

This is telling me that DNA as a molecule is dead; it's just "stuff." There needs to be that extra dimension of livingness-consciousness for it to do anything. The idea that molecules alone can "do life" is not consistent with observations such as this.

Here's the clincher. Garaiev tried similar experiments on rats. The animals were given a lethal dose of a toxin called alloxan; it destroys the pancreas and it is 100% fatal after a few days.

But if the rats were first irradiated with light shone through healthy pancreas and spleen, they did not die. That's amazing. There was no biochemical exchange, again, only an energetic/information transfer. Over 90% of the rats survived AND they actually regrew a healthy new pancreas. Within 12 days, they were as good as normal. So the DNA code was undisturbed and still carried all the necessary information.

So this is even beyond the discoveries I explained in *Virtual Medicine*. I was writing revolutionary theories about broadcasting the electromagnetic energy signals of remedies, such as penicillin or insulin (instead of the real stuff). But now it seems we could do better: to hell with the remedy, just send the message "healthy organs" at full volume (this is in fact the modality we call sarcodes, page 159)!

This discovery poses a whole new approach to aging: to transmit signals of youthful healthy tissues! Peter Garaiev stumbled on the possibility by chance. He was transmitting healthy messages from a youth to an elderly lady and this enabled the woman to start growing new teeth!

It is (almost) beyond belief, unless your theories are firmly rooted in the information and energy model of life and being. Yet they still want us to believe dead molecules are the "cause" of life!

BACK TO LUC MONTAGNIER

Everyone knows the sad story of Jacques Benveniste, the "memory of water" fiasco and James Randi's crooked posturings.

Benveniste, of course was right. There was no hoax. His work has been replicated many times since, in reputable labs. You never hear that, of course. Instead orthodox scientists (and twisted magicians) continue to broadcast that it was all discredited and Benveniste's work found to be "fraudulent".

Well, they now have something else to side-step. This time it's the memory of water imprinted with DNA particles. Moreover, the scientist this time was none other than Nobel Laureate for 2008, Luc Montagnier. It's going to be tougher to discredit him.

In what has been christened "the teleportation of DNA," Montagnier's team set up two adjacent but physically separate test tubes within a copper coil and subjected them to a very weak extremely low frequency electromagnetic field of 7 hertz. The apparatus was isolated from Earth's natural magnetic field to keep it from interfering with the experiment. One tube contained a fragment of DNA around 100 bases long; the second tube contained pure water.

There was no physical connection between the two tubes at all.

After 16 to 18 hours, both samples were independently subjected to the polymerase chain reaction (PCR). The gene fragments were found in both tubes, even though one should have contained only pure water. These additional fragments were replicants, generated by low-frequency electromagnetic waves transmitted from the original "real" DNA in the other tube.

Physicists in Montagnier's team suggest that the DNA structure is preserved and amplified through a quantum coherence effect and, because it mimics the shape of the original DNA, the enzymes in the PCR process mistake it for DNA itself, rather like the Garaiev experiment, where photons hung around in the shape of DNA, even when it wasn't there. In other words there was no actual DNA in the second tube, just information about its structure. To me this is just as significant; and still a real paradigm bender[8].

What was interesting to note that this effect didn't take place unless the DNA was diluted to homeopathic proportions around 10X to 12X (10D to 12D in Europe). Of course this defies the classical biochemical QSAR (quantitative structure activity relationship) models. But homeopathy isn't about "stuff," it's about information and energy.

All this will be everyday science in a hundred years or less but, for now, the dinosaurs are having a field day, scoffing and congratulating each other that they are the custodians of "real" science.

Gary Schuster, who studies DNA conductance effects at the Georgia Institute of Technology in Atlanta, called Montagnier's work "pathological science," according to a report in *New Scientist*. Jacqueline Barton, who does similar work at the California Institute of Technology in Pasadena, was equally skeptical. "There aren't a lot of data given, and I don't buy the explanation," she says.

"The structure would be destroyed instantly," says Felix Franks, a retired academic chemist in London who has studied water for many years. "Water has no memory," he says. "You can't make an imprint in it and recover it later."

(Didn't "experts" state categorically that heavier-than-air machines could never fly?)

DNA IS TELEPATHIC

The case against orthodox science gets stronger… Telepathy means sensing at a distance and strongly implies a non-material consciousness of the kind I have been describing. Yet DNA seems to have some kind of "telepathic" ability, according to a startling paper published in the journal of the American Chemical Society: *Journal of Physical Chemistry B*.

Apparently, intact double-stranded DNA has the ability to "recognize" similarities in other DNA strands from a distance. Somehow strands with certain characteristics are able to identify strands of similar base sequences and draw together. It's the spooky "effect at a distance" that Einstein found so disagreeable.

It's called *homology recognition*. There is no explanation from the material world or the known laws of physics at this time, but the research paper published in the *Journal of Physical Chemistry B* provided unequivocal scientific evidence that homology recognition was taking place.

In the study, British scientists observed the behavior of fluorescently tagged DNA strands of several hundred nucleotides placed in water that contained no proteins or other material that could interfere with the experiment or provide any kind of signaling mechanism. Yet, they found that strands with identical nucleotide sequences were about twice as likely to gather together as DNA strands with different sequences. Double? That's way, way beyond mere chance.

The "telepathic" effect is a source of wonder and amazement for scientists. It will seem less magical to my readers who have read this far. The DNA is a perfect electromagnetic signaling structure and it sends out signals loud and clear to help strands identify each other (like bird calls and animal cries). In this energy- and information-controlled universe, it is simple science. However, even this model doesn't explain how the molecules move towards each other; so this weird "behavior" of supposedly dead molecules is beyond current scientific explanations.

"Amazingly, the forces responsible for the sequence recognition can reach across more than one nanometer of water separating the surfaces of the nearest neighbor DNA," said the authors Geoff S. Baldwin, Sergey Leikin, John M. Seddon, and Alexei A. Kornyshev and colleagues.

Be sure of this: DNA is a consciousness-infused molecule and right at the heart of the manifestation we call life![9]

DID DNA COME TO EARTH FROM OUTER SPACE?

DNA, the ultimate life messenger, may have fallen to Earth from space complete. It's a bizarre new twist on the Panspermia idea (page 38). But consider this:

V.N. Tsytovich of the General Physics Institute, Russian Academy of Science, in Moscow, working with colleagues there and at the Max-Planck Institute for Extraterrestrial Physics in Garching, Germany, and the University of Sydney, Australia, studied the behavior of complex mixtures of substances in a plasma.

Until now, physicists assumed that there could be little organization in such a heated swirl of highly active particles. However, Tsytovich and his colleagues demonstrated, using a computer model of molecular dynamics that particles in a plasma can undergo self-organization as electronic charges become separated and the plasma becomes polarized. This effect results in microscopic strands of solid particles that twist into corkscrew shapes, or helical structures. These helical strands are themselves electronically charged and are attracted to each other.

That sounds just like DNA! Its most characteristic feature is the famous double helix. That would add an immense new argument to the possibility that we are, indeed, "stardust" or "billion year old carbon," as the Joni Mitchell song goes.

Quite bizarrely, not only do these helical strands interact in a counter-intuitive way in which like can attract like (doubling up!), but they also undergo changes that are normally associated with biological molecules, such as DNA and proteins, say the researchers. They can, for instance, divide, or bifurcate, to form two copies of the original structure.

These new structures can also interact to induce changes in their neighbors and they can even evolve into yet more structures, as less stable ones break down, leaving behind only the fittest structures in the plasma.

So, could helical clusters formed from interstellar dust be somehow alive? "These complex, self-organized plasma structures exhibit all the necessary properties to qualify them as candidates for inorganic living matter," says Tsytovich, "they are autonomous, they reproduce and they evolve." (Don't ask me what inorganic living matter means... maybe he just couldn't bring himself to say it's life!)

Tsytovich adds that the plasma conditions needed to form these helical structures are common in outer space. However, plasmas can also form under more down-to-earth conditions such as the point of a lightning strike. The researchers hint that perhaps an inorganic form of life emerged on the primordial earth, which then acted as the template for the more familiar organic molecules we know today[10].

There I rest my case.

DNA is the Cosmic messenger!

CHAPTER 5

Top-Down Creation

There is a philosophy that says that if something is unobservable—unobservable in principle—it is not part of science. If there is no way to falsify or confirm a hypothesis, it belongs to the realm of metaphysical speculation, together with astrology and spiritualism. By that standard, most of the universe has no scientific reality—it's just a figment of our imaginations.

- Leonard Susskind, *The Black Hole War: My Battle with Stephen Hawking to Make the World Safe for Quantum Mechanics*

WHERE DOES CONSCIOUSNESS FIT IN?

Information fields, although undoubtedly real, are not enough. Otherwise, it's like taking the painted picture but denying that the artist existed! Where do these fields originate? There must be something more, something that can grasp the concept of "information" and work with it. That can only be consciousness. But where does consciousness come from?

Can we know?

In 1957, Yorkshire astrophysicist Sir Fred Hoyle, Director of the Institute of Astronomy, Cambridge, and a Fellow of the Royal Society, wrote a brilliantly entertaining book called *The Black Cloud*. Richard Dawkins, no less, described it as "one of the greatest works of science fiction ever written" (probably because he believes it proves that consciousness can arise from pure matter).

A bunch of astrophysicists on Earth become aware of an immense cloud of gas that is heading for the solar system. The black cloud, if interposed between the Sun and the Earth, could wipe out most of the life on Earth by blocking solar radiation and ending photosynthesis. The UK's top scientists are gathered together to work on the problem and its implications.

The cloud unexpectedly decelerates as it approaches and comes to rest around the Sun, causing disastrous climatic changes on Earth and immense mortality and suffering for the human race (a bit like a nuclear winter scenario, popularized in the 1980s).

But then there is a stunning surprise: the cloud turns out to be a conscious life form. It's a Superbeing! - Almost a god, many times more intelligent than mere human beings. The cloud of electrically charged particles worked in concert, just like the human brain, to promulgate—or at least to relay—its thoughts to the human scientists.

It turns out to be a sentient and highly compassionate organism, distressed at the inadvertently caused suffering. But there is a problem… how to get the Solar system back to normal?

Well, I won't do a plot spoiler, in case you decide to read it. But there are some wonderful twists and turns in the tale. One, which foreshadows Hoyle and Wickramsinghe's hypothesis of Panspermia, is the cloud expressing surprise that intelligent life is capable of forming on solid planets. So far as the cloud was concerned, all life existed only in space and couldn't survive in tissues on a solid planet! Nice twist.

When the astronomers ask the cloud how such an electrical life form originated, it replies that they have always existed. Two of the scientists die in an attempt to learn some of the cloud's vast store of knowledge through visual signals, in order to gain further insights about the Universe. Their minds simply can't take the input.

In a tongue-in-cheek moment, one of the characters in the book suggests this idea is incompatible with the Big Bang theory. (Hoyle, I have already remarked, was responsible for inventing the derisory term "Big Bang," and his own theory of continuous creation cosmology lost out (at least for now).

It might all sound rather crazy and Hollywoodish, but in fact Hoyle's story is grounded in hard science. The detection of the cloud is described using physics equations, all of which are included in the book![1]

The fact that our universe is not alone is supported by information received via the Planck space telescope. Using the data, scientists have created the most accurate map of the microwave background, the so-called cosmic relic background radiation, which has remained since the inception of our universe. They found that the universe has a lot of dark recesses represented by some holes and extensive gaps.

Theoretical physicist Laura Mersini-Houghton from the North Carolina University and her colleagues argue that the anomalies of the microwave background exist due to the fact that our universe is influenced by other universes existing nearby, and holes and gaps are a direct result of attacks on us by neighboring universes!

See, the real science is fascinating and inspiring, whereas theories are not.

IS THE SUN CONSCIOUS?

Let's ask the question that Rupert Sheldrake asked over the summer solstice of 1997. He invited 13 people of diverse backgrounds and disciplines to meet in a secluded valley in the west of England to discuss the consciousness of the Sun.

As Kevin McCarthy, a contributing school teacher, pointed out, young children almost invariably draw the sun with a face and a smile. Its consciousness is not debated but simply accepted. And the face has eyes: the Sun not only emits light but it also sees. Similar imagery of the Sun as a living conscious being is found in all civilizations including Egypt, Babylonia, Greece, Rome, India, and in Christendom. - Just fancy? Read on.

There's a beautiful war poem *Futility* by Wilfred Owen: "Move him into the Sun..." move the dead soldier into the sunshine: "If anything might rouse him, rouse him now, the kind old Sun will know"... say the moving words. "Think how it wakes the seeds," Owen went on... "Woke, once, the clays of a cold star." That sounds like the beginnings of material life. I wonder if Owen had an intuition of what I am about to write[2].

THE SUN IS A MASSIVE "BRAIN"

Well, a conscious Sun is simply a folly, dismissed with the usual rhetoric: it can't be, therefore it isn't. For materialists, our consciousness is nothing other than the activity of our brains. Since the Sun, planets, and stars have no brain, they cannot be conscious.

But wait a minute: what does the brain do? It's a vast electrical matrix. Most materialists suppose that the complex electromagnetic rhythms in our brains provide the interface between brain activity and consciousness. Could rhythmic patterns of electromagnetic activity likely be associated with the consciousness of the Sun? Why not?

The Sun is extraordinarily dynamic. As well as its 11-year sun-spot cycles, the Sun has recently been found to reverberate, like a gong, to over a million pitches, each bouncing back and forth through the different layers of the interior of the Sun, with the resonance being determined by their pitch.

In addition to this extraordinarily complex spatio-temporal pattern of vibration, there are the oscillations, perturbations, and harmonics of the Sun's electromagnetic field. That's all we are picking up when we do an MRI scan of our brains at work!

As Sheldrake wrote afterwards: "Perhaps the Sun can think in a way barely imaginable to our more limited power of thinking, its thoughts interfacing with its ever changing patterns of vibratory activity. In this way, it is scientifically imaginable that the Sun could be conscious."[3]

Maybe Pharaoh Akhenaten was closer to the truth than any of us imagine when he had the Sun depicted as the God Ra, the rays tipped with tiny hands, reaching down to Earth, to cradle and cherish human life?

It's time to construct an intelligent, working model of what our universe is, how it was created and, most importantly, how we interact with it. We want a model that includes consciousness as a central ingredient. I'm talking now about the true nature of "reality," which must touch upon awareness and perception.

It would have to allow the presence of consciousness in everything.

MATTER IS ALIVE!

Everything points to the fact that ours is a sensory-aware, living Universe. Matter is "alive" in a very real sense. All the academic science that is supposed to disprove this is confused, absurd and contradictory... or the experiments are easily explicable in terms of the living Universe model anyway. There is no refutation, anywhere in science, of the conscious Universe; only the lame hypothesis that it *must be* wrong, therefore it is, but with no proof of this assertion.

I like the concept of "living matter" and often quote the work of Indian polymath genius Jagadish Chandra Bose. Working in a remote corner of the British Empire (Calcutta) around the turn of the last century, Bose carried out many pioneering feats, including the first research into microwaves and the very first radio transmission in 1895, fully two years before Marconi. He developed a device called the "crescograph," which would detect movement and response in plants. He was later knighted: Sir Jagadish!

The prestigious science journal *Nature* published about 27 papers written by him, which is remarkable when compared to even the greatest of scientists. He has been called the "Newton of the Orient." In 1894 alone, Bose published four major papers on the behavior of electric waves in the *Proceedings of the Royal Society* (London). A British editor once wrote: "In Sir Jagadish, the culture of 30 centuries has blossomed into a scientific brain of an order which we cannot duplicate in the West."

One of Bose's fascinating experiments was presented to the Royal Institution in London in May 1901. He "tormented" a metal plate with acid. The plate was then polished to remove all trace of the etching. Bose was later able to show a physical reaction, indicating a memory or "pain" at the site of injury to the metal. Strangely enough, this was not scoffed at; his methodology was not challenged. In fact one of the attendees, Sir Robert Austen, a leading authority of the day on metals, afterwards quietly confided in Bose: "I have all my life studied the properties of metals and am happy to think they have life."

Did Bose show conclusively that life energies exist, even within so-called inanimate forms? I think so. He died in 1934 and is still relatively unknown.

THE SCHISM

The schism between materialism and organism is even bigger than that. Egged on by fascinating devices like the microscope, spectrograph, chemical analyzers, and telescopes, science has come to believe we will understand our world better, by breaking it down into its component parts. We call this approach *reductionism*; reducing everything to the smallest common denominator.

So the belief has arisen that life can be understood by figuring out how cells work; that cells can be understood by studying complicated biochemistry; biochemistry can be studied by watching the performance of individual molecules and so on, down and down. It's only a belief, of course, but it is defended as pure science and every other view is voodoo science, they say.

It has reached the state where "life" is examined by electron microscopes but—by definition—nothing living can be seen under an electron microscope. All specimens are dead, killed in preparation. Yet they argue that phenomena seen on *live* microscopy don't even exist, because they cannot be seen in the dead sections. Unusual life forms are just dismissed as artefacts. This is about as daft as science gets.

The truth is, of course, that living organisms are a fully integrated whole. The idea of separating a "part" is ridiculous, because there are no parts, only the whole, with many aspects. It's the same with the biggest organism of all: the Cosmos. It too is a whole. Understanding stars doesn't tell us anything much about how the whole functions.

The fact that all parts are aspects of a wholeness is something that reductionist science just isn't seeing.

This blindness to integrated holism is akin to trying to figure out how a radio works by taking it to pieces. Examining a resistor, condenser, or rheostat will tell you nothing whatever about how a radio works. Even detailing and listing every single part of the radio will reveal nothing if you don't also know about radio waves and that a remote radio station is broadcasting them.

DOWNWARDS CAUSALITY

There is another way of looking at this conundrum: upwards and downwards causality. Reductionist science seems to believe that the universe was constructed from the bottom up (no mention of who or what is assembling everything). The research approach in this model is that by studying particles, we understand atoms and molecules; from atoms and molecules, we learn about biochemistry; from that we learn about how cells work and suddenly—bingo—we understand life.

A far more plausible model is top-down creation. That means we start with consciousness: consciousness has awareness and intentionality, by definition; the next level down is information. I have already remarked on my dictum that *information implies consciousness*. The concept of information has no starting point, unless there is something there to read it. Think about this: it applies whether we mean IT technology or living forms.

In the downwards model, it is consciousness that generates reality, via information which molds and directs energy, forms and systems. Of course that includes biological energy, forms and systems. It seems to me to make sense, in that you can take as many molecules as you like but nothing coherent will come from that unless you have a model, a higher plan, from above.

This may be counter to everything you are taught. It has always been supposed that information is something contained in matter and/or energy. A book, for instance, is black squiggles (ink) on a white sheet (the paper); or in the cyber world, information is stored as electronic bits in a silicon-based retrieval system we call a computer.

But the new scientific model says not so: the material lies within the information element. Our brain is in our mind, not our minds in our brains! That posits a different model for consciousness. Really, all I want to say about the nature of consciousness in this book, lest it become too long, is that consciousness is manifestly independent of any holding matrix.

They talk about the "hard problem" of consciousness: how could the phenomenon of self-awareness arise from a sticky blob of dead molecules? - A hard question indeed.

But consider these axioms (an axiom is a self-evident truth):

> It is a gross error of reasoning to hold that consciousness requires physical structures. There is no evidence or reason for such an assertion.

> It is a gross error of reasoning to hold that consciousness "must have" arisen from physical matter. There is no evidence or reason for such an assertion.

> It is a gross error of logic to hold that, because many mental and psychic phenomena can be triggered by brain stimulation, the brain is therefore the origin of these phenomena and the origin of consciousness.

> Denial of non-material states of existence is psychopathological science. Current reductionist science has no means of detecting or measuring such states, but that is not proof that they do not and cannot exist.

Just suppose, instead, that consciousness came first. That means consciousness would have no matter, energy, space, or time location. In other words it is immaterial. It follows that the entirety of the space-time continuum—our world, the Cosmos, the Universe (or multi-verses if you want to be sure of including everything)—is contained in consciousness, NOT the other way round.

There is then no hard problem of consciousness; *consciousness is a given of existence, the starting point.* Consciousness just IS. Moreover, it cannot see or investigate itself; like a knife that cannot cut itself.

The real "hard question" then switches to, "What is a Universe?" And "Why is it there?" "What is it for?" How does a Universe come into being and why should there be "rules" or "laws" for its functioning? These are difficult questions indeed.

CONSCIOUSNESS RULES

Starting from this new position—consciousness was there first—we can now posit an entirely different model of reality, in which consciousness is everywhere, immanent and pervading the entire space-time continuum: Ours is then a truly living, conscious universe. Consciousness is what pulls reality together. Consciousness is not just a spectator, or even just a participant; consciousness rules reality.

Space and time are properties of consciousness, not of the physical world. That fits very well with our experience, which is that both of these concepts are very abstract, rather than physical. Space is a consideration that things are united; that's the opposite of what we are taught, which is that space is supposed to separate things.

But that kind of space is found not to exist: non-locality, which is now beyond argument, no matter that Einstein found it "spooky", is effectively demonstrating that space joins things. It does not separate. In fact, it could be said that non-locality effects are proof that space, as we have always understood it, does not exist.

Time is an interpretation of change. In fact change is the *only* manifestation of the abstraction we call time. So in theory, if you reverse any change, you could go backwards in time. The Electric Universe advocates don't like the idea of time travel. And maybe time travel is too strong a proposition. But travelling backwards through time is implicit in Newtonian mechanics, which run just as accurately backwards as in the familiar direction. Check out my notes on retro-causality, as it's called (next chapter, page 94).

We can also postulate that spirit, which we hold to be non-material, would have no matter or energy and would not be located in space and time. The Being, the "I", or consciousness would only be located in space and time if it considered itself to be so located. In other words, it's a choice where we locate ourselves.

I can offer a suggestion for Ludwig Wittgenstein's aphorism: "the solution to the riddle of space and time lies *outside* space and time."[4] He's right. The solution, in one word, is consciousness and it lies outside space and time.

Hence, the supposition that we are inside our heads, peeping out through the eyes, is just an illusion: a postulated illusion. Zen writer Alan Watts used the expression "skin-encapsulated ego."

I could on like this for pages and eventually derive all of reality. Suffice it to say that my own science of being and knowledge that I call Supernoetics™ has torrents of answers to old puzzles and paradoxes, simply because it starts out in the right place (see Chapter 27).

What of God? That's just a word, remember. But the concept of a unifying and wise collective consciousness, that we may all be derived from, is a given in almost all religious mysticism. The idea that Christians, Moslems, Jews, or any other group in humanity could somehow possess this unifying consciousness as their special property is something I find so absurd as to be contemptible. It's as crazy as saying, "Our atmosphere is the right one and you others are breathing the wrong stuff!" I will say no more about it.

JUST A FEW MORE AXIOMS

If, then, consciousness subtends all and is outside the space-time continuum, we would expect that we as beings are omniscient; we would automatically have access to the full knowledge of everything. This fits with David Bohm's holographic universe. A hologram, remember, contains the whole in all the parts. The so-called "Akashik Records" would be a metaphor for this exalted state of knowing.

It means we would have to selectively UN-know things in order to function. If you knew everything, you would go crazy in a few seconds. But the selective unknowing process is the beginning of dysfunction and dismay among spiritual beings of all levels.

The good news is that we cannot die. If our awareness and being are not tied to anything physical, and especially not to a brain, then we cannot vanish. In fact, we couldn't "die" if we tried to, a thought which frightens some. In a later chapter you will be learning about authenticated messages from the dead, delivered by electronic equipment, such as telephones and recording apparatus. This is called electric voice phenomena or EVP (Chapter 26).

If consciousness is immanent in all things, isn't that the end of all science? Science as we know it, maybe. But don't despair; I think honest and open inquiry will eventually reveal the glorious truth, if we are humble and patient.

In the reverse, this explains why arrogant bombastic scientists, who already "know" the answers and the model they want to "prove" get exactly the results they expect. Then they whoop with delight and sneer at others who are exploring a different reality...such intellectual buffoons do not understand even the slightest nuance of the world they occupy.

The world is a conscious creation, not a machine with us hiding among the spars, cogs, and levers.

THE GOLDILOCKS UNIVERSE

It would be appropriate here to say a few remarks about what is called the "Goldilocks Principle", from the phrase in the famous fairy story that everything is "just right". It could be very direct proof of the importance of human consciousness.

Otherwise there is no explanation for the strange fact that our Universe is tuned perfectly for human life to exist. If any one of half a dozen parameters were different by even just a few percent, then life here would be untenable; indeed the Universe as we know it may not have come about at all!

Of course the God-squad jump on this and claim it is proof positive that God created the world and made it right for us. The trouble is, with such a hypothesis, there is no way to test it...ever. So it's not a very scientific theory.

But the mystery is undeniable. If the famous "moment of creation," when the Universe ripped into view, had been just one part in a million more powerful, the cosmos would have over-expanded and stars and worlds would not have been able to form.

If the fine structure constant were just 10% bigger than its present value, fusion would no longer occur in stars. The great physicist Richard Feynman once said, "All good theoretical physicists put this number up on their wall and worry about it. Immediately you would like to know where this number for a coupling comes from... Nobody knows. It's one of the greatest damn mysteries of physics: a magic number that comes to us with no understanding by man!"

THE ANTHROPOCENTRIC UNIVERSE

The technical term for this "Goldilocks" reality is *anthropocentric*, meaning centered around Humankind.

Perhaps I should explain that there are two models of this hypothesis, the "strong" and the "weak". The strong anthropocentric hypothesis says it must be that way by some sort of intention, in order that we could come into being. The weak hypothesis says we were just lucky and if it had come down any other way, we wouldn't be here talking about it.

The weak explanation to me seems rather foolish. It's rather like discussing why the moon is where it is and someone answers, "It just is, so get over it". A true scientific enquiry would want answers, like what, when, where and how? We don't just ignore why exercise is healthy; we want to know the mechanism and what kinds of exercise are best for us.

Personally, I am wedded to the strong anthropocentric view, accepting unequivocally that the conscious creation of the universe arose from an intention to have it be here and be occupied by aware beings. I'm not arrogant or foolish enough to suppose that humans are the only form of sentient life, so maybe the term "biocentric" universe would be better. I see that Robert Lanza MD has adopted the use of the term "biocentrism" for his book and defined it much as I am doing[5].

Either way, it means that biology—and therefore medicine—is a lot bigger in concept than just a bunch of molecules purring along in the space-time continuum, don't you think?

More pertinently, how can a model of life and healing pretend to be anywhere near complete if it doesn't include an accurate construct of our world?

EXTENDED REALITY

It doesn't stop there. If reality is generated by consciousness, we would expect aspects of conscious experience to lie outside the physical; other conscious entities would interact in ways that may appear to contradict the laws of physics. There would be "transpersonal" phenomena, to use an accepted word; non-ordinary realities.

It would need a whole book to do the search for such effects full justice. Suffice it to say we have many religious and philosophic dogmas to contend with. But there is enlightened science too. With a willingness to step outside the existing paradigm, an enquiring soul will quickly learn that there is a huge body of amazing research (and I mean research, not stories from dope-smoking truth hounds), from which to draw tentative conclusions.

We have to dump the extraordinary convoluted explanations of reductionist thinkers, who are still trying to stitch together a theory of "everything", but which excludes anything they don't want included! I mean: it's as laughable as that.

I think it's rather foolish, not to say conceited, of a materialist physicist to suppose he can make meaningful pronouncements about the nature of consciousness. It can badly misfire, as it has done in the case of Max Tegmark at MIT. He likens consciousness to another state of matter: solid, liquid, gas... and consciousness (don't laugh, he really means it). He likes to be quoted as saying "consciousness is the way information feels when processed in certain complex ways"[6]. I nearly fell off my seat laughing! Isn't that the same as saying an astronomer is what a star feels like when it's being looked at through a telescope?

A long way wide of the mark, Max. You need to take a deeper look at You-ness before you start trying to tie it into molecules and energy dynamics.

In fact we use the term "non-ordinary consciousness" for certain unusual states but maybe these experiences are much commoner than recognized and so much an everyday thing that it is hardly worth being considered abnormal. People who experience them tend to put them down to day-dreaming or hallucination.

Try your own experiment: every time you find yourself in the imaginary world, dreaming of another time and place, make a note of it. See how often it happens. Then ask yourself the killer question: could some of these moments represent real travel into other space-time dimensions?

It's been my assertion for most of my life that a child (or anyone else for that matter) who sits and daydreams that they are flying out of the window and off to do something more interesting than classroom work, *really are* flying in other dimensions, not just "imagining" it.

SHAMANIC WORLDS

Shamanism is one of the oldest healing modalities known. Essentially it means to travel or work in "other realities" to affect healing change in this reality. For example, much disease is modeled as missing soul parts; the shaman travels into other dimensions to find the missing soul part and restore it. The patient recovers.

It is customary to scoff at what is often called "witch doctoring." The typical Hollywood cliché is that of a grotesque fraud, splashing blood and chicken feathers, waving bones or a club, and chanting ugly incantations. Of course, in these stories the hero always has some penicillin to hand, the chief's daughter recovers and the witch doctor is exposed as a fake.

Well, that's the Hollywood version. Of course there are incompetent shamans, much as there are incompetent MDs. The focus is on the model. And it is my stated opinion that shamanic healing takes place far more often and far more successfully than in the drug-based modality. It's been around a long, long time and that alone ought to accord it some respect.

Maybe it's placebo effect. Who said there was anything wrong with placebo? It's a curse if you are trying to conduct a scientific experiment to prove your drug is superior to a null treatment. But otherwise there is nothing wrong with getting well because you believe in the practitioner. Ask any successfully treated patient!

But I believe shamanic healing is more real and defensible than just a placebo effect and will share with you knowledge that I have and refer you to others. Make of it what you will...

A SHAMANIC COSMOLOGY

In the shamanic paradigm, we commonly encounter three different "worlds", or realities. These are remarkably consistent everywhere on Earth. Each level contains within it a certain vibrational quality that holds specific wisdom and healing that is accessible to the shaman by entering a non-ordinary or altered state of consciousness.

Highest is "Upper World," an ethereal place which may have made some people think of a heaven. Often we find teachers here, with important messages for the seeker or sick individual. Maybe it's mythic, but I have been there, met a beautiful old man with flowing silver hair and saw my first wife running through the forest, her hair flowing free, and I was told, "All is well. She will be safe." At the time, it meant a great deal to me.

"Middle World" is much closer to our everyday reality. It's as if this dimension was just beyond a curtain, right here next to us. Just draw aside the curtain and there it is. In Middle World, we are closest to our own selves; a copy self; a mirror phantom, working or struggling with some issue. The reality we see is similar to our own life on Earth in present time, but there is always a subtle, detectable tone that's different. It feels like a dream.

"Lower World" is the big one! It is situated down beneath us and probably gives rise to notions of Hell. Whereas lower world is not a Hell, it's beautiful, it is certainly strange, shape-shifting, and at times scary. There we expect to meet unfamiliar and powerful creatures and must be on our guard not to be trapped or contaminated.

Nevertheless, lower world is where we meet our most profound mentors and have the most transformative insights. This is all put biographically, by the way, because I have explored this model and am satisfied with the truth or at least the workability of what I found. I consider it the duty of any decent self-respecting healer to look at other models and try them, even to integrate them into a modern clinical practice. I am not going to say anything here about the process of induction, except to say that I have never taken any mind altering substance and used only drumming rhythms.

I'm fairly open-minded, as you should have realized by this stage, but lest you think I'm crazy, let me introduce you to the work of US anthropologist Michael Harner. As a card-carrying academic scientist, he could be expected to hold to the view that the only reality is this one, the physical, and that any belief in other realities was merely a hallucination or a construct of primitive, superstitious minds.

But Harner's experiences led him to a different conclusion. While studying the Conibo people of the Peruvian Amazon, he agreed to try taking *ayahuasca*, the so-called "death juice" (anyone with the guts to swallow a substance so named has my admiration). In his book, *The Way of the Shaman,* Harner describes vividly what happened shortly after swallowing the deadly concoction.

Lying down outside a primitive hut, gradually his physical body began to go numb and seemed to turn solid, like concrete. Breathing became difficult and speech impossible. There came the most beautiful singing he ever heard and it was associated with a ship, floating above him, manned by strange creatures with bird-like heads and human bodies (reminiscent of the Egyptian god Horus).

The ship was drawing up his life force, out of his body. Harner was absolutely convinced he was going to die and a "voice" told him as much. He would be shown secrets, the voice said, which are only revealed to the dead and dying.

A vision of Earth appeared, as it was in the remote past, an ocean, barren land, and a bright blue sky. Suddenly a host of strange creatures appeared, black, wriggling, and dragon-like. They explained to Harner, in a kind of thought language, that they had come to Earth to escape from their enemies and they lived in hiding within the multitudinous forms of life on Earth, including humans. These creatures, if that's what they were, called themselves "Masters of Humanity and The Entire Planet."

This was 1961 and Harner had never heard of DNA but in later years he came to believe these squiggling strands might have been metaphorical DNA, though much larger, like dragons.

Eventually he mustered enough strength to cry out for the antidote and his Indian helpers administered the restorative medicine. He came round and slept well.

The real amazement of the story is what happened next day, when he explained his experience to an elder, blind Conibo shaman. When Harner's narrative came to the part about the black, sinister creatures that called themselves the "True Masters of the World," the old man grinned.

"Oh, they're always saying that. But they are only Masters of the Outer Darkness," he said, gesturing towards the sky. This gave Harner a chill. Because he hadn't mentioned seeing the creatures come down from outer space.

He was stunned. In a flash, Harner the scientist realized that he had been to a real dimension, a place that actually existed; the old man had been there before him, many times. The old man knew about these strange creatures! From that moment he decided to learn everything he could about shamanism. Today, he is a world leader among authentic "white shamans" and in 1979 he founded the Center for Shamanic Studies, now the Foundation for Shamanic Studies[7].

I have an interesting corollary to this account. In 1998 I explained this basic story to my former wife, Pauline. This was long after our divorce and we retired to bed separately. Next morning at breakfast she told me of vivid dreams she'd had of wriggling black creatures crawling into her body and lodging in the tissues. This was exciting to me, because I had not mentioned the squirmy "DNA creatures" to her.

So where does the mind and self end and these other realities begin? Who knows?

But such interactions virtually prove that consciousness is supreme and rules over the physical world. Heck, much so-called scientific evidence is far shakier than these observations and events! It's true that we are not very adept at using consciousness to alter the time-space continuum, but the era when we can do that, I believe, is just around the corner.

CHAPTER 6

A World of Structures Unseen

Science no longer holds any absolute truths. Even the discipline of physics, whose laws once went unchallenged, has had to submit to the indignity of an uncertainty principle. In this climate of disbelief, we have begun to doubt even fundamental propositions, and the old distinction between natural and supernatural has become meaningless.

- Lyall Watson, *Supernature*

To complete our model of the Universe as it really is, instead of just what physicists and mathematicians tell us it might be or could be or should be, we need to look at some levels of reality. I don't just mean physical dimensions here; I'm talking about other planes of existence.

Obviously, there is a physical plane. It's the only one most scientists will acknowledge but, in fact, is probably the most unreal of them all!

Nothing is quite so close to nothing as the something that's supposed to represent "reality." In a very real sense, there is no matter, energy, space, or time! Let's demolish so-called "reality" once and for all and replace it with the inner conscious Universe. What has been blessed with the term reality is probably the biggest illusion of all and it appears more and more confusing and counter-intuitive, the closer it is inspected.

In short, *it isn't real*!

TIME IS THE CRUX

We've got time that doesn't exist, according to some. In any case, time can go backwards in certain circumstances, so is that time? (More of that experiment in a moment.) There seem to be three camps.

There are those who think time is tensed or *sectioned*, that is, past tense, present tense, and future. The idea with this model is the familiar one: time past is gone and will never come back; time NOW is happening in a moment-by-moment stream; and then there is time future, which does not exist, because it hasn't happened yet.

Then there is the un-tensed or *block time* model, which says it's all out there, always was, and always will be. The future is just as real as the past, is just as real as the present; it's laid out for us, ready for examination, like a string of sausages. This one is harder to swallow. But this time value is closest to that in modern physics, in which there is no real NOW. This view is like a map without the "you are here" symbol[1].

The block time model allows for time running backwards and, strange to say, scientists do not object to this idea. Newton's laws of motion are "time symmetric", meaning they run just as well backwards as they do forwards. If the future and the past are not any different, there is no reason why you can't have causes from the future just as you have causes from the past. We call this *retro-causality* and I shall visit that in a moment.

Finally, there are those who boldly state, "Time doesn't exist." Not loonies or flakes but serious and well-qualified scientists. The idea goes back to Parmenides and surfaces convincingly in Zeno's paradox. According to Zeno's amazing and unanswerable paradox, if you shoot an arrow, you can split the time it takes to reach its target in half, then in half again, then again, then again, and so on, ad infinitum. No matter how small the increment of time remaining, you can always halve it. In other words the arrow will never arrive!

But we know the arrow does arrive. So that itself is almost a theorem to disprove the reality of time. Note that the original theorem was exposited by dividing distance in half but it works just as well dividing time; time and space, it seems, are fairly interchangeable. That fits with our experience, where we often label time as a property of place ("The time we were in Rome" or "Just before the first aircraft impacted the World Trade Center").

RETRO-CAUSALITY IN A NUTSHELL

But what if time can run backwards? Does that not finally dispel the illusion we call time? Richard Feynman lent credibility to the idea by proposing that perhaps particles such as positrons, the antimatter equivalent of electrons, are simply normal particles traveling backward in time.

John Wheeler of Princeton University proposed a method of testing retro-causality using a variation on the classic double-slit experiment. It required sending photons through a barrier with two slits in it, and choosing whether to detect the photons as waves or particles. All particles must go through one slit or the other, proving they are particles. But then an interference pattern is produced after passing through the slits, proving these are waves, not particles! (Yes, yes, I know: just another science contradiction—but this experiment has been done, it's not just theoretical).

What if, Wheeler asked, you wait until just after the photon has passed the slits to choose whether you will accept it as a particle or a wave? If that influenced the photons "choice" at the slit, then you have caused an effect backwards through time.

In 1986, Professor Carroll Alley at the University of Maryland, found a way to test this idea. Sure enough, the photon's path depended on the observer's choice made after the photon had committed to wave or particle![2]

Other groups have confirmed similar results but, predictably, most physicists don't accept this demonstration of retro-causality, on the time-honored principle that "It can't be true, therefore it isn't".

If these experiments do show evidence for retro-causation, it opens the door to some troubling paradoxes. If you could see the effects of your choice before you make it, could you then make the opposite choice and subvert the laws of nature? Some researchers have suggested retro-causality can occur only in limited circumstances in which not enough information is available for you to contradict the results of an experiment.

In the information-dominated world of *Medicine Beyond*, I can accept that caveat! For the moment, I have only wished to show that time isn't as real as you were told.

TIME CAN BE CREATED

Consider time in our healing context with the amazing story of Anita Moorjani. If you haven't come across this medical miracle, you should read more about it. In summary, here is what happened:

Anita was within hours of dying from terminal lymphoma; she had tumors the size of lemons all over her body. Her lungs were filled with fluid. She passed into a coma and her family was called to the hospital for the final goodbye. Her brother jumped on a plane from India, to be by her side at the end.

Although she was ostensibly unconscious, Anita heard and saw everything going on around her. She was later able to report a conversation going on down the corridor, way out of earshot of her bed. That alone tells us that consciousness is not located inside the head.

But the most moving part of the story is her experience of moving into "The Light" or near death experience (NDE). There she met her predeceased father and felt immense unconditional love from him and from other beings gathered around.

She was offered a choice: she could either go back and recover or leave her body permanently behind, dead. They even offered to fix her lab work, according to whichever she chose.

After much agonizing, she chose to live. And behold, she awakened in her hospital bed, to the astonishment and joy of her gathered family, not to mention the attendant physician!

Sure enough, her lab work had turned around and no longer showed any sign of the cancer. Within four days the tumors had vanished; within weeks there was not even any trace of cancer cells under the microscope. That's one heck of a recovery story. What makes it special is that Anita is so skilled and rational at communicating her experience while on the "other side" or the plane above this one.

My point is that so fast a recovery—lemon-sized tumors disappearing in just a few days—is hardly the phenomenon we recognize as healing: That process takes a while; weeks at a minimum. This reversal was so fast, it really does give the impression that time was running backwards at a rapid rate.

Maybe that's not so fanciful when you bear in mind that her helpers offered to rewrite reality backwards, depending on her wish, giving different lab results according to whether she wanted to return to this plane or give up and be absorbed into The Light.

If you are not willing to accept this story at face value, you are probably reading the wrong book. Please close it respectfully and give it to someone more open-minded.[3]

Be assured, Moorjani's is not a unique account. There are hundreds of such; she is simply more articulate than most. One current best-selling book of similar lucidity is *Proof of Heaven* by Eben Alexander MD. He recounts awakening experiences and conscious states, while his body lay in bed in a coma, his brain trashed from a particularly severe form of meningitis. Scans showed his brain was not active, yet Alexander vividly entered worlds that he knew, as a neurosurgeon, were not supposed to exist.

The only noticeable difference in his account I can observe is that he uses the idea of going *down* to deeper layers of consciousness, a hidden underbelly (Lower World of the shamans), whereas most individuals get the sense of rising, upwards (Upper World of the shamans). It's a particularly memorable account in that the author, as a doctor, knew for certain that consciousness was totally brain-based-being (B3 as I call it), until this illness, when he learned the exact opposite: conscious awareness does not depend on brain function.

SPACE, MATTER AND ENERGY

Then we have space that isn't really real. Entanglement suggests, amongst other mind-bending possibilities that space as we think of it doesn't exist. Particles are not "at a distance" when they respond to each other. We call this non-locality (literally: no place). In the living Universe model, they are together in consciousness.

The old-fashioned idea that space separates objects is gone. If anything, space unites objects! It's all very bizarre. Finally, we come down to the fact that we create space and time; they are properties of the mind, not something inhered in the fabric of reality. This is something propounded in the much-loved 1911 edition of *Encyclopedia Britannica*: we would not understand space and time until we fully understand the mind.

I would just tweak that and say: not until we allow consciousness to enter, as the true creator of reality.

So, with space and time dismissed, what about matter? That too is vanishing fast, under the onslaught of particle physics. We now have a veritable zoo of sub-atomic particles. They are all supposed to be made up of leptons, bosons, and quarks (up quarks and down quarks, charm quarks, top quarks, strange quarks, and bottom quarks to be exact).

But then what are leptons, bosons, and quarks made of? Nobody dare ask. But inevitably they will be split into yet smaller particles. While physicists believe only in "stuff," they will have to have their particles. But already these are vanishingly small.

We are used to the idea that solid matter is 99.99999% empty space: with a few protons and neutrons in the nucleus and electrons, weighing $1/1836^{th}$ of a proton whizzing around in orbit ($1/1836.15267245$ to be more exact). Nobody has any idea why an electron should be $1/1836^{th}$ of the mass of a proton. If there is a God, he has a weird mathematical sense of humor!

But when even subatomic particles are found to be composite, one has to ask where it will end. - Infinity?

WHAT IS ENERGY

Finally, there's energy. That's the most nothing of all nothings. Such a concept was unknown to Isaac Newton when he built his model of a mechanical universe. He knew about force but not energy. That came along in the 19th century, postulated by German physicist Hermann von Helmholtz (1821–1894). It works as a concept but is it real?

We can't touch it, hold it, feel it, or sense it in any way. All we can say about it is energy is the term we give to *that which creates change*. If a glass of water is taken from 10^0 to 20^0, we say that energy caused the heating effect. Beyond that, energy is wild speculation.

True, it is virtually interchangeable with matter. But I just disposed of matter as not very real anyway!

The big problem with energy is you can't create it or destroy it, or so says the famous Second Law of Thermodynamics. The gradual attrition of energy through time we call entropy and it's supposed to signal the eventual death of the universe.

But does it? - Only if true.

WHERE DO THE LAWS OF PHYSICS COME FROM?

I have trouble with so-called "laws" of physics. Who says they are laws? Our experience here on Earth may not translate fully to what goes on out there in the cosmos. Moreover our pitifully short experience of reality may not give any clues as to what is really happening in the long reaches of time. As Max Planck (1858-1947), the founder of quantum mechanics so capably put it, "We have no right to assume that any physical laws exist, or if they have existed up to now, that they will continue to exist in a similar manner in the future."

If the rules of the process can change, then it's not a law, is it? I'm not trying to hold science up to ridicule, merely pointing out that there are some very basic assumptions being made, which may not be valid at all. I urge an intelligent caution, not to abandon the scientific method.

Consider the suggestion of Paul Davies, theoretical physicist, cosmologist, astrobiologist, and bestselling author. He is Director of the Beyond Center for Fundamental Concepts in Science and co-Director of the Cosmology Initiative, both at Arizona State University. In Davis' view, *the universe might actually be able to fine-tune itself*. If you assume the laws of physics do not reside outside the physical universe, but rather are part of it, they can only be as precise as can be calculated from the total information content of the universe. One thing I'm fairly sure of is that the universe's total information is not infinite. Therefore laws derived from it are troublingly flimsy[4].

With that in mind, let's now look at some interesting and possibly useful alternative realities. These are every bit as real as the world of physics I have just painted. Maybe more so!

TELEKINESIS

Since the dawn of history, controversy has raged over whether there is anything other than simply what we see. The priest classes don't want us to look past that because their power derives from the pretense that there are levels of reality we can never know but which they fully understand and must needs interpret for us.

True, there are always stories that we can integrate with the Divine— that the Divine is within us and we are autonomous. But anyone who actually stood up and said that has ended up dead... very dead. Giordano Bruno, for instance, the Italian Dominican friar, philosopher, mathematician and poet, was burned to death in 1600 for saying, among other things, that God truly is within us and not something separate.

The Church has always had its say and clearly despises any suggestion we might not need priests to intervene for us.

Today, the emphasis has shifted to scientists. They are the ones who now tell us what we may believe and what we must not believe. Nothing seems to give scientists more trouble than the suggestion that there are things outside their ken and that they are unable to cut, measure, transform, photograph and pontificate about. In the face of clear evidence that there are other layers of reality, they retreat behind the dumb stance that there can't be. But the evidence? That's faked. Are you sure? Yes, of course, the phenomenon doesn't exist and therefore those who claim there is evidence are deluded or dishonest.

Take the case of telekinesis. I'm betting that the vast majority of the human race has no trouble with "feeling someone's presence", or telepathy, or just knowing when something is going to occur. We don't get this all the time (think how intolerable life would be!) but it does happen to most of us, at some time or another.

No it does not. It cannot, say scientists. But the experience I had? It's a delusion. - And the evidence? It's faked... and off we go again on the same old merry-go-round of accusation and denial. Oxford Professor of Chemistry Peter Atkins is on record as saying, "Work in this field is a complete waste of time... there is absolutely no reason to suppose that telepathy is anything more than a charlatan's fantasy."[5]

Note the word charlatan in his diatribe; it means to be deliberately misleading. I say you are wrong Atkins: silly, affected and wrong.

Nowadays we have a wealth of good studies to quote that really puts the matter beyond question; not that it requires "proof" in a conscious-based Universe: it's a given. Instead the skeptics should prove their point of view, since it's so aberrant. Unfortunately, badly designed and badly executed studies do not prove anything, either way. Failure to prove that something exists is not a proof that it doesn't exist. It's just a failure. It may just mean poor technique or a badly designed investigation, not factual findings.

Nevertheless, orthodoxy continues to howl "there is no proof" that any of these phenomena are real. Perhaps the real point, as David Wilcock wittily said in his treatise *The Source Field Investigations*, is not that there is no proof but "There is no publicity"![6]

It's usual to quote the foundational studies by Joseph B. Rhine in the 1930s as a starting point. In fact, that's not a good idea because, although Rhine did get a clear result at first, over time it faded. Skeptics insist this is proof the psi effect doesn't exist. In all probability, the reason was simply subject fatigue[7].

Let me quote instead from Dean Radin, author of *The Conscious Universe*. Dean is Senior Scientist at the Institute of Noetic Sciences (IONS), in Petaluma, California, and former President of the Parapsychological Association. He's a methodical and thorough enquirer and not inclined to fly off the handle, like Professor Atkins.

According to him, from the 1880s to the 1940s, 142 published articles described 3.6 million individual trials generated by some 4,600 percipients in 185 separate experiments. These figures exclude 3 studies involving mass ESP test broadcasts over the radio, which would add a million more additional trials and more than 70,000 participants to the 60-year database of ESP tests.

These are all Dean's carefully compiled figures. But what do they tell us? The overwhelming result was positive; there can be no doubt that the phenomenon of psi or ESP, whatever you want to call it, is real.

Of course the detractors were quick to jump on a landslide of figures such as this and try to discredit it. The results are skewed, they say, because everyone knows that successful trials are more likely to be published than unsuccessful ones. Dean has a comprehensive answer for that.

If we consider all the ESP card tests conducted from 1882 to 1939, reported in 106 publications by dozens of investigators around the world, the combined results of this huge database translate into odds of more than a billion trillion to one that the outcomes cannot be by chance alone.

So assuming there was selective reporting biased towards only successful outcomes, how many unsuccessful, unpublished studies would be required to nullify these astronomical odds? The answer is 626,000 reports. That's more than 3,300 unpublished, unsuccessful reports for each published successful report. In other words, chance results and selective reporting cannot possibly explain the positive findings obtained in these investigations[8].

My purpose for this book is not to argue the toss about ESP but to leave it with the reader as a scientific given. No matter what the critics say, the proofs are adequate. So, I can get on with my job here, which is to bring forth new models of biology, health and consciousness, acknowledging non-local consciousness as a force.

Let me just conclude this section with the words of Professor H J Eysenck, chairman of the Psychology Department at the University of London (1957):

> Unless there is gigantic conspiracy involving some thirty university departments all over the world, and several hundred highly respected scientists in various fields, many of them originally hostile to the claims of the psychical researchers, the only conclusion the unbiased observer can come to must be that there does exist a small number of people who obtain knowledge existing either in other peoples' minds, or in the outer world, by means as yet unknown to science[9].

The point is that if ESP is real then physics that says it is impossible must be wrong. We need some better ideas.

My only disappointment with ESP is that the effect is never very large (53- 55% at the 0.002 is typical). Plus not everyone seems able to do much with it.

I would prefer to see 90 – 95% success rates. I do believe that time will come, once the anchors of disbelief and propagandizing against it are off.

NON-SENSORY PERCEPTION

Let me now talk about what I call "non-sensory perception", which follows naturally from the matter of ESP. It sounds like an oxymoron, I know. But the senses, we have always been taught, come in via our eyes, skin, ears, nose, and so forth. This idea is so deeply ingrained, it is considered mad to challenge it.

If a person's eyes get too damaged, he or she is "blind" and cannot see; if the ears malfunction, the person is "deaf"; isn't this what we are supposed to believe? But it just isn't that simple.

What about people who can see things at a distance, far from their body and eyes (remote viewing)? What about people supposedly in a coma who can hear a conversation perfectly, going on well out of earshot down the corridor, and repeat it back verbatim when they wake? (Anita Moorjani's story)

How do those fit into the sense organ model? They don't.

What about out-of-body experiences? Those can't all be written off as delusional because the individual who experiences them may be able to accurately describe a scene in detail—who is observed, what was said—yet not be present with his or her physical body; sometimes even many miles away. No sense organs were on the scene!

Hypnotists tell of seeing a watch through a person's body—there is no line of sight, no reflection, no normal way in which the sense organs could have been involved.

There are many anecdotal stories of this sort; I have been out of my body many times and had vivid visual and auditory acuity, perceiving things that were supposedly not possible. I have no problem with the concept. There are just too many properly substantiated events of this kind (cross-checked) to dismiss them all as anecdotes.

In any case, if there is a report of a meteorite falling to earth in someone's garden, we don't say that's just an anecdote. We accept it as true. Science is very hypocritical like that and will accept observational (non-statistical) evidence it likes; but similar evidence, if it conflicts with the current model, is written off as just an anecdote!

The truth is that there is non-sensory perception. The late Cleve Backster famously showed that even plants have it. In his decisive experiments with a Dracaena plant (Cleve introduced me to the very plant and I was photographed with it!), it not only reacted to pain but could identify who ripped off its leaves and even reacted when brine shrimp were being killed elsewhere in the building. Yet plants have no nervous system at all, much less a brain, eyes, and ears!

Backster called this faculty "primary perception". I prefer my own term *non-sensory perception* and that's what I'll be using throughout.

Cleve was a very important figure in this field of science, because he was a meticulous observer and documenter and followed the scientific method closely. He irritated some of us by refusing to publish data he didn't feel met with robust criteria. But he was sober, scrupulous and trustworthy: qualities you could not attribute to "investigators" like conjurer James Randi, even in your most sanguine and generous moments!

Looking ahead, we shall encounter a new scientific discipline called "plant neurobiology" (Chapter 14, page 248). The point being that, if plants are conscious and aware, with no known nervous system, we must have got things completely wrong about the nature of consciousness, being and perception. Very wrong.

OK, now let's have some fun…

HEIM'S BRAVE NEW UNIVERSE

Forget Einstein, he's an also-ran. Burkhard Heim's our man. Einstein, and many others, attempted to derive equations that would describe all physical fields and their sources in a uniform manner, as dynamic characteristics of a purely geometric dimensional structure. They failed.

Now my math at school was dismal, so I do not snigger when telling you that Einstein and all the others, it turned out, worked with the wrong geometry (Riemann's). It fell to a pupil of Werner Heisenberg, himself one of the founding fathers of quantum theory, to solve the riddle. Burkhard Heim, a German theoretical physicist, using Weyl's four-dimensional space-time geometry and his own invention of metron calculus, helped out Einstein and fixed his problem; a small step for a mathematician but a giant leap for mankind, because he did indeed unify both theories beautifully.

Basically, what Heim showed is that we need more dimensions than we have hitherto relied on. We can start with 1- 4 (height, width, length, and time—the last of course introduced to us as a 'dimension' by Einstein). But, as soon as we take into account quantum-sized particles such as electrons, protons, neutrons, photons and the rest of the particle "zoo", the math comes to a standstill. That is, until we add two more postulated dimensions, 5 and 6. Heim gave them clumsy names, which we need not bother with, but tells us they are related to form (the morphogenetic field) and expression-in-time, respectively.

What is important to understand is that these are physical coordinates, meaning they are part of the real world. The true Cosmos thus has six dimensions (at least). This is what Einstein always believed, meaning there are 6 "manifolds" in Riemann's geometry. We can't understand or picture levels 5 and 6 except in the broadest terms of proof that "something higher" exists, as an information field, down from which come our vital form and organizing energies. The implications for trans-dimensional healing and *Medicine Beyond* are enormous.

Heim eventually deduced two further dimensions, 7 and 8, to complete the matrix derived from three intrinsic values in each of the four fundamental dimensions ($4^3 = 64$), and discovered that the math worked there too, perfectly. These last two coordinates prove to be physically empty—in other words, the associated equations do not yield any further information on the physical Cosmos—but they are incontrovertibly there, as *information space*.

Keeping solely to the physical dimensions, what Heim showed was that one can describe quanta, etc., perfectly in terms of dimensions 4,5, and 6; that is, with no location in space. But as soon as they interact with real matter, coordinates 1, 2, and 3 are needed. In other words, these quantum beasts only show up in physical reality when you need them to, which is what I was saying earlier about "virtual particles"!

The paradox of wave and particle dualism of quanta is resolved here. Everything about this new theory is neat, compelling and illuminating.

In case all this sounds too staggering to be believable, let me add that the most exciting part of this elegant model, which is about as mystical as mathematics gets, is that it is confirmed 100% by mass spectroscopic measurements and rigorous computer analysis. In other words, our Universe backs up Mr. Heim's theory and calculations to the last full stop.

ANTIGRAVITY LOBBY

It all went the way of novel science: *it was ignored to death*. Burkhard Heim was a maverick physicist, working entirely outside the mainstream of physics and publishing entirely outside peer-reviewed journals. The unappreciated researcher, isolated from the field, coming up with a revolutionary breakthrough theory that is unnoticed in his time, but found to be valid after he's dead...this is very much the plot of a romantic 19th century novel, not the way physics typically works[10].

Things changed in 2002, shortly after Heim's death, when Walter Dröscher and Jochem Häuser began to publish papers based on his work. Heim had developed a corrected gravitation law, which corresponds with Newton's gravitation law within the observable area of space. However for very large distances (as in interstellar travel) it provides completely different results.

Anti-gravity researchers took Heim's work very seriously. To this day we don't know if it's been dropped or has gone into a secret military "underground".

Be that as it may, Heim's matrix model is valid to me and is an almost exact fit to the kind of reality and super-reality I am describing here and upon which *Medicine Beyond* is grounded. Perhaps that is why Heim's brave new structure of reality is much loved by practitioners of electronic healing and bioresonance.

I found an entire webpage dedicated to links to Heim's theories, which the reader may enjoy: http://www.engon.de/protosimplex/index_e.htm

BOHM'S BOMBSHELL

While writing of the increasingly hazy demarcation between mind perception and so-called objective reality, it is essential to mention David Bohm's holographic universe concept. It is only a metaphor but it is an exciting one and it could well contain the essential truth needed to integrate our understanding of reality.

Firstly, let me explain an important point about holograms. Everyone knows that you can see them in three dimensions; it is a means of visualizing an object as a volume solid and is used in museums to preserve valuable specimens in storage while allowing the facsimile to be appreciated by visitors. What is less well known, but is actually a far more important property of holograms, is that each part contains the whole. If you take a pair of scissors and cut a photograph in two, you end up with two halves of the photograph - obviously. But if you cut a hologram in two, both halves contain the full picture, complete in every detail. If you cut it in half again, each new fragment still contains the whole picture. You now have four *complete* copies of the original image.

This can go on indefinitely; no matter how small the piece, it still contains the whole image, though obviously it becomes fainter and fainter as the representational elements become smaller and smaller.

Bohm's novel insight was to suppose that physical reality may be constructed in some similar fashion. In other words, the universe itself acts like a hologram. Bohm called the picture we see the *explicate order* (from explicit or obvious); and the hidden total inner picture, the *implicate order* (from implicit or hidden). What does this actually mean?

Well, if Bohm's conjecture is correct, it means that all parts of existence are contained in each tiny fragment of substance. The desk on which my word-processor stands has all the elements of creation and reality, from the dawn of time to the end of the universe; every atom, every galaxy. If I unscrew one of the drawer handles and inspect it, even that could contain the totality of everything!

In fact each of my fingernails contains a complete imprint of the *entire universe*! This is an appalling thought, hard to grapple with, but at the same time a thrilling one.

Certain threads from the *Medicine Beyond* paradigm now begin to converge. For example we saw that Sheldrake's morphogenic fields are something super-ordinary; something above and beyond the range of energy and matter, that acted as a kind of blueprint. Could these fields be part of the implicate order? If so, does it not mean that DNA, that wonder chemical substance that contains the codes for living organisms, could be the life bridge between the implicate and explicate orders? Remember from Chapter 4 that I proposed the DNA molecule works as a transmitter aerial. But what does it transmit; radio waves? Or some bolder cosmic message of order and creation? Maybe it transmits this deeper order of reality and creation.

The mind itself, of course, will form part of that bridge to reality. Information, as I have said before, implies consciousness and awareness. You can't really have one without the other. This is a potential paradox solved by reference to the eastern sages and the British Empiricist philosophers already referred to above: what we are is a product of what we perceive and vice versa. There is no difference between the perceiver and the perceived.

At this time, nobody knows if Bohm's hypothesis is the final answer to understanding our world but, in terms of consistency, it is a hard theory to beat, because almost all mysteries of the world we experience become understandable in simple terms of explicit vs. implicit order. Take telepathy or past lives as examples. If all of existence is wrapped up in every little fragment of reality, that would also include the matter inside our brains. Any piece of the brain has the whole of the rest of reality wrapped up in it somewhere. We can potentially know everything, all in an instant. Now that's what ancient sages have been saying, so the idea is not so alien. What is new is a means to understand how this could be true. Bohm's brave new universe is very satisfying in many respects.

The corollary is that, if we know everything, then we have to selectively UN-know things, otherwise our consciousness would just go into overdrive and burn out or... well, who knows what? We can speculate: because if knowledge is not merely brain, then perhaps all knowledge is potentially knowable.

We call that omniscience (knowing all) and it is held to be a recognition of the Divine. If we humans are potentially omniscient, would that not make us divine (small d)? Is it possible that Giordano Bruno (page 108) was right all along?

HIDDEN STRUCTURES

What has emerged, I think, from the investigations so far, is that we have a concept of the universe expressing itself from within; unseen inner structures exist which create and dictate what we see outwardly. Until science starts acknowledging these hidden layers or structures, it is never going to be science, in the full meaning of the term; just posturing and squabbling.

The truth is, ours is not a WYSIWYG reality (what you see is what you get); rather it is a case of *what you DON'T see is what you get!*

There is a layer or many layers beneath the outward reality, that have been variously called, the Source Field (David Wilcock), the Field (Lynne McTaggart), implicate order (David Bohm), the quantum probability field (Deepak Chopra), subspace (Bill Nelson), the morphic field (Rupert Sheldrake), possibly the Ganzfield ("whole field") of German psychologist Wolfgang Metzger (1899-1979), the Akashic field, and so forth.

As I hinted in Chapter 4, there may be a hidden structure field for every teacup, spoon and rock. Living forms, all plants and animals, would also need a hidden structure field. That field is what we would call life force or *"Elan Vitale"*, to use Henri Bergson's term. It follows that disease would be a disturbance of the pure, healthy field, whether that means a human cancer, a tree that grows bent, an animal with two heads or a supernova that went "Bang!" in the night!

See how big this becomes?

These hidden fields, or "structures" buried within, as I have called them, create, shape and energize our world. We have reached a point where it is simply absurd to believe that the only truth is one you can pick in your hand, photograph, measure or kick into a bucket. In fact, as I have said repeatedly, *that world* is the illusion.

THE ARROGANCE

Those who describe these hypothetical, even mystical, levels of experience I have been writing about are invariably written off as fools or cranks (because they cannot possibly be right). Everything is "stuff" the detractors say. At the same time, the scientists are extolling their own addled theories that are all equally unproven, can never be experienced, and are about as unreal and insubstantial as the word "theory" can imply.

String theory posits 10 dimensions, totally unprovable from this world, yet that is considered a scientific view. A few different experiential realities, difficult to put into everyday words but which people go to and *feel*, is considered too ridiculous for words. Such hypocrisy doesn't make sense.

They say 10 dimensions are needed to make the math "work." Is that proof that 10 dimensions actually exist? Of course not, at least not according to any logical system I have ever encountered. It's proof that the math is wrong, needing fancy tweaking to make it "correct." But that's just nonsense, as you can readily appreciate when I put it that way.

As I said before, scientific method is a very fine thing. But the idea of science as an established, real, and proven body of facts does not exist. It's the most confused, diffuse, contradictory and illogical set of propositions found anywhere! Science as the true custodian of knowledge is a cruel hoax. Everyone falls for it, because it is force-fed to kids as soon as they can read, write, and be imprinted by the system.

But I would like to think my readers are mature enough to step back, not react, but just look at the truth of what I'm saying and then start to question everything.

The whole idea of *Medicine Beyond* is that it's time to question what we think we know about biology, physiology, and healing. Our world is a deal different from the crude explanations of current science and, if the world is different, and reality operates in other ways than we have been taught, then medicine and healing too must learn to operate in new and better paradigms. I believe this passionately and want to see this more advanced medicine displace the current model.

I don't want "alternative medicine" to triumph; I want to see orthodox mechanistic medicine vanish and the model I espouse become the only *real* medicine!

CHAPTER 7

The Body Electric

The discarding of an old prejudice and the cultivation of a new outlook are not matters that can be completed in a moment. One first catches a glimpse of a new way of regarding things, and begins to see a few outstanding features of his surroundings in a new light. But he does not immediately realize that the whole scene has been transformed. Deep-seated beliefs remain, incompatible with the new outlook though they may be, and only gradually begin to take on a strange appearance and arouse misgivings.

—Herbert Dingle, Astronomer Royal

It will soon be revealed why the next logical step in our survey of "hidden structures" leads us inevitably to a new level of health awareness we may call "body consciousness".

First I want to start with a deeper look at the concept of holism. We use the word a lot, but what does it really mean?

Holism (and thence holistic) is a word that was originally coined by Jan Smuts, the South African soldier, statesman, and philosopher (1870-1950). He defined it in his 1926 book, *Holism and Evolution,* as "the tendency in nature to form wholes that are greater than the sum of the parts through creative evolution." Einstein himself studied Smuts' book soon upon its publication and wrote that two mental constructs will direct human thinking in the 21st millennium: his own description of relativity and Smuts' of holism[1].

The concept of wholeness and holism (sometimes incorrectly spelled *wholism*) has now become well integrated into our thinking in all spheres. Its simplicity and omnipresence belies the fact that it's basically a 20th-century concept. There are echoes of Leibniz's monads model here, but the German philosopher did not explain how small individual units would operate together; only that reality was made up of an infinite number of such units.

As originally conceived by Smuts, holism meant that small units and subdivisions would inevitably unite into larger wholes, which would in turn aggregate, and so on. Today we use the term mainly for wholes which are united and have been from the beginning. However, it does seem that, in a strange way, Smuts foresaw the emergence of chaos theory and strange attractors.

Let's see how far we have progressed down the road predicted by Einstein.

THE RADIO MODEL

If you took a large number of capacitors, wires, transistors, knobs, resistors, speakers, and a battery and threw them on the table, you could not realistically hope to tune into a radio station.

Yet that is the current approach in science, biology, and medicine: the belief that by the study of the fine details of the parts, we come to understand the whole. By studying molecules (biochemistry), we learn about life; by taking apart the components of a cell, we shall better understand its function.

But the only way the heap of parts in front of you would make sense is to create the whole: the working radio. So it is with living organisms and the "program" they broadcast, which we call life. How the parts are put together and the mutually interactive functions they perform are an entire complexity and without any one part, the entire radio will cease to work and is therefore useless.

So it is with living organisms.

I have already exposed the lie on DNA (Chapter 4) and how a mere listing of its small aspects, called genes, does not tell us how the entire molecule functions nor how different parts of an organism know where they are in the whole and what structural signals apply to them, as opposed to the other cells. The purely mechanistic deconstruction of life is unworkable. There is a living, creative entity that breathes life into the heap of electronic bits!

THE ELECTRIC CANCER MODEL

There is no more fundamental starting place for modeling health issues than cancer. I have said often, cancer is not a death knell, but it is a wake-up call, telling you your health is in ruins. It's about as bad as things can get.

Hans-Heinrich Reckeweg puts neoplasm (fancy word for cancer) as the final end game in a steady degenerative downhill process that he termed progressive vicariation. Controversial German MD Ryke Geerd Hamer, on the other hand, sees cancer as the inevitable result of severe life-changing psychic trauma. He calls it the "iron rule" of cancer, which is the whole foundation of his *German New Medicine*.

Using the electro-acupuncture approach (Chapter 15), an indicator read denoting a severe drop-off in energy along any meridian is highly suggestive of a cancer signal, even if it's many years before the physical tumor finally manifests. In this crossover model with Chinese traditional medicine, we learn that the electrical energy at the acupuncture point cannot maintain itself for more than a few seconds.

Cancer is the benchmark of bad!

With that in mind, let's see how the electrical model works with cancer.

I suppose we can start with Tesla (so many things start with Tesla!) It was claimed that his coil apparatus (page 223) was sometimes effective against cancers. But I always heed the warning words of Robert O. Becker, who quoted studies that showed conclusively that too much energy at the frequency of mains electricity (50-60 hertz) was likely to cause runaway growth in rogue cells and was most definitely contra-indicated in the treatment of cancer. This surprises many fans of Becker.

For example, he cites a 1971 study by Russian workers Mamontov and Ivanova, which showed that industrial-strength 50-hertz electric fields tripled the division rate of cells[2]. Several experimenters, notably Stephen Smith, showed that an electrotherapy bone-healing device increased the division rate of cells that were already dividing rapidly, which includes skin, gut, and liver cells and also, of course, cancer cells.

Wendell Winters, a researcher working at the University of Texas Health Services Center in San Antonio, provided some of the first laboratory evidence that power frequencies can accelerate malignant growth. He exposed human cancer cells to just 24 hours of the usual 60-hertz electromagnetic field and found that a week later the cells were multiplying *six times as fast* as a result.

As Becker warns, an electromagnetic field doesn't distinguish between desirable and undesirable growth. Processes susceptible to DNA stimulation include healing, embryonic growth, and cancer.

Quoting his own work and other studies, Becker concluded that only the magnetic element of an EMF had any healing potential. The electric component is hazardous[3].

L-FIELDS

After Tesla, the next significant figure on the stage is Harold Saxton Burr, professor of anatomy at Yale University School of Medicine and researcher into bio-electrics during the 1920s and 30s. His remarkable book, *Blueprint for Immortality*, after several decades of research, contended that the electrodynamic fields of all living things, which may be measured and mapped with standard voltmeters, are what control each organism's development, health, and mood. He named these fields "fields of life" or L-Fields[4].

Trees were particularly suitable for study and he wired up many specimens, some for many years. Burr was fascinated to note changes brought about by sunlight and darkness, cycles of the moon, sunspots and seasonal changes. The L-fields changed with the seasons and the Sun's activity, growing in magnitude when the Sun was most active and fading at night, when the Sun dropped from view. He took the very intelligent line that if it affected trees, the electrical fields would apply to all of life.

Naturally, conventional science wasn't in the least bit interested in this startling discovery.

Turning to the study of humans, Burr and his colleague Dr. Leonard Ravitz noticed that human emotions affected this field. Voltages would be high when a patient was feeling good and would drop when he or she was below par. Burr foresaw the fascinating possibility that "... psychiatrists of the future will be able to measure the intensity of grief, anger or love electrically—as easily as we now measure temperature or noise-levels today. 'Heartbreak,' hate or love, in other words, may one day be measurable in millivolts."[5]. If this thought interests you, then you will almost certainly be interested in my notes on psycho-galvanometry in Chapter 14.

Other fascinating discoveries about the electrical nature of life and disease included the observation that there was a voltage rise in a woman just before ovulation, which drops again as the egg is released. Healing wounds also changed this voltage.

Most remarkable of all, there were voltage changes due to malignant tissue and Burr was eventually able to predict, from reversal of the polarity across the abdominal wall, when a woman would in future develop cancer of the cervix. This anticipates the injury potential discovery of Robert O. Becker and later prognostic work with electro-dermal screening described in Chapter 19.

What Burr and his colleagues were measuring was simply voltage potential. But he himself points out that changes can be measured at a distance from the affected organ or even outside the body, holding the electrodes above the skin, showing it is therefore a true field effect; hence "Field of Life," or L- Field for short.

GEORGES LAKHOVSKY

The next investigative genius was actually born in 1869; his seminal book *The Secret of Life* was published in 1925. This puts him ahead (chronologically) of Saxton Burr, but the reader will soon readily appreciate that progressively he belongs here in the sequence, since his visionary ideas look far forward into the world of modern biophysics.

Georges Lakhovsky was a Russian engineer who became a naturalized French citizen and was ultimately awarded the Legion of Honor for his scientific technical services during the First World War. He had to flee his adopted country before the arrival of the Nazis, and died in New York in 1942.

Like those who went before him, Lakhovsky had to endure much calumny and ridicule. As one of his supporters remarked: 'The publication of The Secret of Life resulted in causing great annoyance to the custodians of infallible doctrines who made up with carping verbiage what they lacked in clarity of vision.'[6]

As Lakhovsky himself put it: 'I have been attacked by physicists ignorant of biology and by biologists ignorant of physics who consequently can neither understand my theories nor judge my experiments.'[7]

This extraordinary man of diverse talents showed that recorded sunspot activity paralleled magnetic disturbances and auroras on Earth. He also established a correlation between sunspot activity and good wine vintage years.

In my own 1992 book The Complete Guide to Food Allergy and Environmental Illness I called attention to Lakhovsky's observation that geological terrain seems to have a potentially dangerous connection with cancer causation[8].

Clay soils in particular, he found, were dangerous, probably because of the properties of water within the soil, whereas sandy and limestone soils had a very much lower incidence of carcinogenesis. Lakhovsky also foresaw that one day it might be possible to project images of cancer tumors as an energy disturbance onto a TV screen; today we have MRI and CAT scanners.

But it is Lakhovsky's ideas about biological radiation fields that concern us here. His fundamental scientific principle was that every living thing emits radiation. This has important health implications. According to Lakhovsky, the nucleus of a living cell may be compared to an electrical oscillating circuit. This nucleus consists of tubular filaments, chromosomes and mitochondria, made of insulating membranes but filled by an electrically-conductive intracellular fluid. These filaments have capacitance and inductance properties and are therefore capable of working like radio transmitters and receivers.

In Lakhovsky's model, life and disease are a matter of a 'war of radiations' between the body's cells and microbes. If the radiations of the microbe win, disease and death will result. If the cell's own energy transmission wins, then health is preserved. Thus he arrived at a very advanced and quite defensible energetic view of disease. Lakhovsky himself went on to conduct very many experiments in this vein. The results he got were little short of startling for his time, and so one may presume there is a lot to be derived from his theories.

Albert Nodon, President of the Société Astronomique of Bordeaux, studying ultra-short wavelengths in organisms, was able to prove Lakhovsky's hypothesis. He found radiation from all living plants and animals. Dead subjects did not, of course, transmit. Nodon produced remarkable figures showing that, weight for weight, radiation from certain beetles, flies and spiders was 3 to 15 times more intense than that from uranium.

He extended his studies to humans and was able to show that our bodies emit even more intense energies than plants and animals. Nodon also obtained what were termed 'spontaneous radiographs' by placing living things directly onto photographic plates. Clear pictures were duly developed, after several hours' exposure. This forgotten research anticipated Kirlian photography by many decades. Nodon's conclusion was 'It seems probable that matter, under the influence of radiation whose wavelength is less than the electron, may be subjected to certain modifications of an unknown nature which may confer new properties on matter, different from those conferred by radiations of a much greater wavelength, and not connected with electrons.'[9]

How right he was all those years ago.

A SIMPLE CANCER EXPERIMENT

If any reader would like to follow one of his simple experiments on plant cancer, it is not difficult to perform and will provide a fascinating home workshop on the properties of biological radiation. In this experiment Lakhovsky relied on the presence of ambient radiations. Remember that today we have over a million times the intensity of ambient radiation that was present in Lakhovsky's day. Yet he was able to demonstrate conclusively that extraneous radiations can cause disease; in this case a tumor of plants.

For this demonstration, Lakhovsky took a series of Geranium plants inoculated with the *Bacterium tumefaciens* (= tumor-making bacteria) which causes cancer-like growths on the plants:

A month later, when the tumors had developed, I took one of the plants at random which I surrounded with a spiral consisting of copper and measuring 30 cm in diameter, its two extremities, not joined together, being fixed into an ebonite support [a rigid plastic tube, such as a spent biro pen stem, would suffice perfectly well]. An oscillator of this kind has a fundamental wavelength of about 2 meters (150 million Hertz) and picks up the oscillating energy of innumerable radiations in the atmosphere.

I then let the experiment follow its natural course during several weeks. After a fortnight, I examined my plants. I was astonished to find that all my geraniums or the stalks bearing the tumors were dead and dried up with the exception of the geranium surrounded by the copper spiral, which has since grown to twice the height of the untreated healthy plants[10].

The oscillator was picking up and damping all kinds of atmospheric radiations. Lakhovsky bewailed the fact that so many radio transmitters were springing up (even in his day) that 'there is no detectable gap in the gamut of these waves'. Now, with millions of microwave cellphone users and uncountable powerful transmitting antennas, we are already waking up to the fact that cancer caused by these radiations is real.

Lakhovsky was yet-another genius before his time.

THE PRIORÉ AFFAIR

Antoine Prioré (1912–1983) was born in Trieste, Italy. He received training in electrical engineering and was a radar technician for the Italian Navy during the Second World War.

It is said by Internet sources that in 1944 Prioré noticed some oranges that had been left next to some electrical equipment. These oranges remained in a fresh state while others not near the electrical equipment became rotten and putrid. He naturally

wondered if the electromagnetic radiation had some kind of health-giving properties.

Over the years 1950 - 1975 Prioré built a series of electromagnetic devices producing a strong magnetic field (600 gauss or more), for the purpose of treating cancer and other diseases.

His last device was funded by the French government, with the help of one-time Prime Minister of France Jacques Chaban-Delmas. [11]

Prioré claimed to have cured a number of terminal cancer patients but there was much controversy. He was accused of manipulating his scientific data by the French Academy of Sciences and French journalists also accused Prioré of not understanding his own treatment technique.

In 1965, one event was said to indicate possible foul play in Prioré's experimental research. Mice with experimental cancers were sent to Prioré from the Chester Beatty Institute in England. He exposed the mice to radiation from his devices, they were sent back to the Institute. It was claimed that the mice returned to them were not genuine because they rejected new cancer grafts! That seems to me a particularly stupid criticism: that could just as easily be confirmation of his work—the mice were no longer vulnerable.

Unfortunately, Prioré never explained his exact method, believing others would only steal it for themselves. So we are left with the arguments and accusations unsettled, in what became known as "L'affaire Prioré "

ROBERT O. BECKER MD

After becoming noteworthy for calling the public's attention to the biological hazards of electromagnetic fields Becker, somewhat to his discomfiture, was quickly "adopted" by the New Age and holistic health field as the chief scientific credibility for some of their far-flung notions. He tried to play this adulation down but, in the end, many of these theories have proven correct!

Experimenting on salamanders, Becker discovered the "current of injury," or more exactly he stumbled across it in the Russian journal *Biofizika* (Biophysics) and began his own series of follow-up experiments. Becker, an orthopedic surgeon and twice a Nobel Prize nominee showed that living organisms propagate a DC electrical field and that this undergoes certain changes when the salamanders are diseased and injured (exactly what Burr showed). Subsequently, Becker developed elegant new theories regarding the electromagnetic regulation of life processes[12].

But Becker went further, with more advanced measuring systems, and has been able to show that body tissues act as semi-conductors, and that this is how the life-currents are transmitted. I find this exciting because it implies the possibility that living cells and tissues can function in the manner of a computer.

In the 1970s, Becker and his biophysicist colleague, Maria Reichmanis, were funded by the U.S. National Institutes of Health to study acupuncture scientifically. He chose to measure DC potential (electricity given off) at designated acupuncture points, and claims to have found that around 25 per cent of the points on the forearm were locatable using this method. He also showed that current is conducted by unknown channels that correspond to the stated acupuncture meridians.

According to Becker, the DC body field is not located in the nervous system itself, but in "perineural" tissues such as the glial cells in the brain and spinal cord and the Schwann cells encasing the peripheral nerves. This hypothesis would seem to conflict with the suggestion that the DC body field is correlated with the acupuncture system[13].

It is worth pointing out here that, later in the book, I will discuss research using changes in skin resistance at acupuncture points, which may be a more accurate method of detection. Proof of the probable nature of acupuncture meridians is found in Chapter 15.

Over the years Becker has expanded his authority and knowledge to be considered one of the best-informed scientists on the big issues of biophysics and environmental hazards, particularly those concerning the effects of electric and magnetic fields on living systems. His 1990 book *Cross Currents: The Perils of Electropollution; The Promise of Electromedicine* is an extremely powerfully argued and comprehensive overview of what has been going on in the last two decades in the field of electro-biology.

Some of his seminal work was on the subject of body consciousness. He showed that a fully awake, conscious organism has a definite electrical potential, head to tail; when a person is anesthetized, that electrical potential temporarily disappears. Moreover, if you switch that potential around (toe to head), you render the person unconscious[14].

In the late 1960s, Becker was probably the first person to predict that the magnetic field of the brain extends outside the head. He remembers how his idea was ridiculed by the audience at a scientific meeting of the time. Yet, he was eventually proved correct. This leads naturally to SQUIDs (without tentacles!)...

THANK YOU, MR JOSEPHSON

Finally today, we have gone on to develop instruments for the detection of biological energy fields. Notable among these is a device called the SQUID magnetometer. SQUID is an acronym for super-conducting quantum interference device. It has opened up a whole new world of bio-energetic science. The life field can be seen and mapped with an accuracy and sensitivity that would have been unthinkable 30 years ago.

The SQUID is based on a phenomenon known as the Josephson Effect after Brian Josephson, who predicted it in 1962 while working as a graduate student at the University of Cambridge. He received the 1973 Nobel Prize for his work. What his hypothesis means is that electrons, although we consider them particles (matter), can pass right through insulators as if they were waves.

Such a thing is impossible in the classical physics world, but natural enough in the quantum domain. We call this tunneling and we now know that Nature has many examples of this, including events inside the human body!

A SQUID consists of a Josephson detector, with an array of input coils to capture the bio-magnetic field, plus the necessary electronics to amplify and make sense out of the signal thus received. The whole setup is immersed in liquid helium, which makes the device exceedingly sensitive to magnetic fields, such as the delicate ones given off by living tissues and organs.

MEASURING LIFE

What can we do with such a sensitive device? One of the first biological experiments with a SQUID was carried out by John Zimmerman, who developed the SQUID, and his colleague David Cohen at MIT's National Magnet Laboratory in Cambridge, Massachusetts, in 1970. They showed the heart's magnetic field with vivid clarity. In fact, it was still detectable 15 feet from the body. Around the turn of the century, Dutch physician Willem Einthoven discovered electrical discharges from the heart. He received the Nobel Prize for Medicine in 1924 for this work.

Nowadays, routine electrocardiography is a standard part of the medical technological armory.

Each heartbeat is the result of an electrical discharge within the heart muscle; the current spreads to nearby tissues and can even be detected in the feet and hands. It travels in the blood which, being a salt solution, is an excellent conductor.

In 1821, Hans Christian Oersted showed that whenever an electric current flows in a conductor, a magnetic field is formed. If the current varies (flux), then the magnetism is even more intense. But the heart's magnetic field is very weak in ordinary terms, since the current is low. However, in 1963, Gerhard Baule and Richard McFee at the Electrical Engineering Department of Syracuse University, New York, used a pair of two million-turn coils (coils with one million loops of wire—that is, wrapped around the spindle one million times) on the chest of a subject and for the first time detected the heart's field.

It was in the same year that the tunneling or Josephson Effect was first published. Now SQUIDs can map the body's heart and other biological magnetic fields with amazing sensitivity. In 1971 Cohen went on to develop a brain magnetogram or MEG (magneto-encephalogram). The brain's field proved to be hundreds of times weaker than the heart field, necessitating that the patient be electromagnetically shielded in the room where readings take place. Clothing must be free of any magnetic material, such as zippers, snaps, and nails in shoes.

Since then there has been a real explosion in monitoring biological magnetic energy fields. It turns out that biomagnetic fields are often more indicative of events taking place within the body than are electrical measurements taken at the skin surface. For example, the eye acts as a remarkable battery and produces a substantial field which increases with the amount of light falling on the retina; we can obtain and study retinograms. Cohen himself, in 1980, reported detection of steady magnetic activity from growing hair follicles! Every muscle action creates a field effect outside the body. SQUIDs even show that there is more intense cortical activity in finger control areas of the brains of musicians than non-performers[15].

All this adds up to the fact that our living organisms are a field of teeming magnetic energy. There are other fields, too. These reflect what is going on within the body and, of course, it is entirely possible to influence the body in return. We live outside our skins! Life itself is an energy phenomenon. It no longer makes sense to practice medicine based on a biochemical or material paradigm; it's time to move over to the energy model.

So we can see that the magical, the mystical, the trendy, and what was once dismissed as hocus-pocus in fact have a very sound theoretical basis in physics and can now be measured objectively, using the necessary scientific instruments.

MICRO-SQUIDs

Researchers at the National Institute of Standards and Technology have developed a sensor that detects magnetic fields as weak as one pico-tesla (one-trillionth of a tesla). For comparison, the Earth's magnetic field is 50 million times stronger than a pico-tesla. The sensor, about the size of a sugar cube, contains about 100 billion rubidium atoms heated and vaporized into a gas. A low-powered infra-red

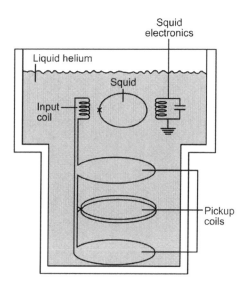

laser is fired into the atoms and a fiber-optic sensor detects how much of the laser makes it through the rubidium. Rubidium atoms absorb more light as the magnetic field around them increases, the quality that let the researchers actually measure magnetic fields.

The new device is slightly less sensitive to magnetic fields than a SQUID, which is considered the gold standard of magnetic sensors and is the preferred sensor in magneto-encephalography (MEG) machines.

MEG is a noninvasive procedure for imaging magnetic fields generated by electrical brain activity. It is used to explore the perceptual and cognitive process in healthy humans and to test the vision of newborns and map brain activity prior to brain surgery for removing tumors or treating epilepsy.

The downside of SQUIDs: they must be kept at −269°C to get good results, which requires they have cryogenic cooling. The new sensor, however, operates at room temperature and is small and lightweight. It can also be mass-produced, while squids are difficult to fabricate and assemble, therefore very expensive[16].

WE ARE LIQUID CRYSTALS

It's time to pull a whole bunch of threads together and explain why our bodies are such an integrated, dynamic whole, readily reactive and conscious. The model that emerges when sifting through the confusing wealth of science to choose from is both surprising and fascinating indeed.

We just need to go one step beyond Becker's insight that the body is made up of semiconductors. It's actually a *liquid crystal matrix*. It's the key to our holism. This model was proposed and amplified by Mae-Wan Ho from the Bioelectrodynamics Laboratory in Milton Keynes, UK, and her colleague James Knight, from King Alfred's College, Winchester.

In a well-referenced paper titled "The Acupuncture System and The Liquid Crystalline Collagen Fibers of the Connective Tissues," the pair reviewed supporting evidence from biochemistry, cell biology, biophysics and neurophysiology, and suggested experiments to test their hypothesis[17].

They proposed that the acupuncture system and the DC body field detected by Becker and others both inhere in the continuum of liquid crystalline collagen fibers that make up the bulk of the connective tissues. It constitutes a "body consciousness" working in tandem with the "brain consciousness" of the nervous system.

Harold Saxton Burr found that the electro-dynamical field of life can be detected in all early embryos and in plants and animals that do not have neural or perineural tissues and therefore it is independent of the nervous system[18].

It is likely that the DC field is functionally interconnected with the nervous system, and yet exists, to a large degree, outside the nervous system. One reason for supposing this is the fact that under a variety of conditions, the speed of communication in our body is much faster than can be accounted for by the known speed of nerve conduction[19], and nerves simply do not reach all parts of our body.

Mae-Wan Ho proposes that both the DC electro-dynamical field and the acupuncture system have a common anatomical basis. It is the aligned, collagen liquid crystalline continuum in the connective tissues of the body with its layers of structured water molecules supporting rapid semi-conduction of protons.

THE SPECIAL PROPERTIES OF COLLAGEN

The clue to the intercommunication function of connective tissues lies in the properties of collagen, which makes up 70% or more of all the protein in the connective tissues. These connective tissues, in turn, form the bulk of the body of most multicellular animals. Collagen is therefore the most abundant protein in the animal kingdom[20].

Recent studies reveal that collagen (actually a group of similar chemical substances) is not just a material with mechanical properties. Instead, it has dielectric and electrical conductive properties that make it very sensitive to mechanical pressures, pH, and ionic composition[21].

The electrical properties depend, to a large extent, on the bound water molecules in and around the collagen triple-helix. Three populations of water molecules associated with collagen have been identified:

1. the interstitial water, very tightly bound within the triple helix of the collagen molecule

2. bound water, corresponding to the more loosely structured water-cylinder bound on the surface of the triple helix

3. free water filling the spaces between the fibrils and between fibers[22]

Mechanical pressure on any part of the liquid crystal system results in an immediate global current of transformation. Also, the application of a current will affect the nature of the ground matrix, exactly as Becker found with his current of injury and anesthesia experiments.

The existence of the ordered network of water molecules, connected by hydrogen bonds and interspersed within the protein fibrillar matrix of the collagens, is especially significant, as it is expected to support rapid jump conduction of protons— positive electric charges—and this has been confirmed by dielectric measurements[23]. And note this: one outstanding characteristic of this form of semi-conduction in condensed matter is that it is much faster than electrical signals by the nerves. *Thus the "ground substance" of the entire body may provide a much better intercommunication system than the nervous system.* Ho and Knight actually speculate that the nervous system may indeed be a mechanism for slowing down signal transmissions to more appropriate speeds.

All very fascinating, once the full model is grasped.

CRYSTAL MEMORY

It's important to understand that the crystal structure of collagen will retain memory. According to Mae-Wan Ho, the collagens and bound water form a global network, in which there will be a certain degree of stability, or resistance to change. This retention constitutes a kind of memory, which may be further stabilized by cross-linking and other chemical modifications of the collagens. Of course it will also have the capacity to register new experiences, as all connective tissues, including bones, are not only constantly intercommunicating and responsive, but also undergo metabolic turnover like the rest of our body[24]. Memory is thus not inhered in structure, as the mainstream physiologists insist, but is dynamically distributed in the structured network and the associated, self-reinforcing circuits of proton currents, the sum total of which will be expected to make up the DC body field itself.

Rolfers and John Upledger fans will also recognize that tissues are able to hold onto a tissue memory or "engram," as first investigated by Lashley. It's not surprising that he (Lashley) removed almost all rat brain tissue and yet the living organism was still able to retain a memory of a maze, since memory is not confined to the brain.

WHO NEEDS A BRAIN?

This crystal memory effect may be at least a partial explanation of the remarkable phenomenon of humans functioning with virtually no brain!

In 1980 Roger Lewin wrote a famous paper, published in the journal *Science*, concerning the research of the late Dr. John Lorber, professor of neurology at the university of Sheffield, UK. It's startling title was "Is Your Brain Really Necessary?" It goes on to answer that question with very definite proof we do NOT need a brain.[25]

When Professor Lorber, as Sheffield's campus doctor, was treating one of the mathematics students for a minor ailment, he noticed that the student's head was a little larger than normal. The doctor referred the student to professor Lorber for further examination.

The student in question was academically bright, had a reported IQ of 126 and was expected to graduate. When he was examined by CAT-scan, however, Lorber discovered that he had virtually no brain at all. The student had less than 1 millimetre of cerebral tissue lining the skull, a condition called hydrocephalus, in which the cerebrospinal fluid pressurizes and destroys the brain.

Despite no brain, this Sheffield student had lived a perfectly normal life and went on to gain an honors degree in mathematics. His case is by no means as rare as you might think.

Professor Lorber eventually identified several hundred people who had very little actual brain tissue but who appeared to be normal intelligent individuals. Some of them he described as having 'no detectable brain', yet they had scored up to 120 on IQ tests.

The real truth, of course, is that we are not our brain. At best, the brain functions as a "tuner" to information fields out there in the surroundings. That's why, when you close your eyes and look at a mental picture, it seems to be outside your head. It is!

ANESTHESIA

That bound water plays a crucial role in conscious experience is supported by recent evidence that anesthetics act by replacing and releasing bound water from proteins and membrane interfaces, thus destroying the hydrogen-bonded network that can support proton jump-conduction.[26] I have already indicated that Becker found that general anesthesia also leads to the complete attenuation of the DC body field. It would be of interest to study the conductivities of collagen equilibrated with different solvents and anesthetics. We would predict that collagens equilibrated with anesthetics will show a decrease in conductivity compared to an equivalently hydrated sample.

Although brain and body consciousness are normally coupled to each other, they may decouple under certain circumstances. Indeed, Mae-Wan Ho asserts that brain consciousness associated with the nervous system is embedded in body consciousness and is coupled to it, rather than superordinate. This one sentence alone transforms all of the life sciences, if you think it through![27] Surgical patients under general anesthesia have been known to regain (brain) consciousness of pain, but not the ability to move or to express their distress. This might now be reinterpreted in terms of body consciousness having been insufficiently reduced, so pain is felt, but the brain remains "under", so movement cannot take place.

In contrast, acupuncture has been successfully used to anesthetize patients who are fully awake. The inference there is that body consciousness is reduced, but not brain function. Observations such as these have a great deal to teach us about the nature of consciousness and being, never mind brain function and anesthetics.

Further evidence that brain and body consciousness are to some extent independent is Becker's observation that during a perceptive event, local changes in the DC field can be measured half a second before sensory signals arrive in the brain[28].

Similarly, Libet et al. produced evidence suggesting that a *readiness potential* precedes the "decision" of a subject to move an arm or a leg[29]. It appears that the activities in the brain may be preconditioned by the local DC field. Materialists, desperate to prove we are just jelly after all (the brain) insist this means that a physical brain change precedes any decision being made. It does not. It simply moves the sequence further backwards.

Thought is not material.

CHAPTER 8

The Three Proofs: Cyclotron Resonance

Reality cannot be found except in One single source, because of the interconnection of all things with one another. ... I maintain also that substances, whether material or immaterial, cannot be conceived in their bare essence without any activity, motion being of the essence of substance in general.

—Gottfried Leibniz, 1670

Let's start bringing some of these wide-ranging ideas together and see where we have arrived. I have asked you to accept that our universe is built upon information, not matter. If I was to go further and tell you that we don't even need matter ("stuff") to have a biochemical effect, would you be startled?

I hope not - because the next three chapters are based on proofs of exactly that precept: that we can dispense with the material stuff and still get a full-on biological effect. We have already seen that we don't need DNA actually present, to have the same result as if it were present (Chapter 4). The information only of its presence is sufficient. Medicine has gone beyond the material world of conventional physics into the consciousness-driven reality of a new "information age".

It's breathtaking in concept and, for many, too scary for them to even contemplate. Yet scientists have known for many decades that it is the "real" world that is an illusion, built upon delusory perceptions of what we perceive is out there. Consider...

Some years ago, I used to travel the world with a talk entitled "The Non-Material Nature of Substances and Medicines." In it I take a major accepted hypothesis and show it to be false: *Only weighable substances with a rest mass and a suffcient biochemical gradient can affect biological organisms.* In other words, there have to be substances present in suffcient quantity, for there to be any measurable biological effect.

They call it "quantitative structure activity relationship" or QSAR for short. All of medical science is based on this idea, which is assumed to be a "given." It is not.

The truth - which I prove three times over in this and two subsequent chapters, using three different modalities - is that *unweighable (nonmaterial) substances have profound measurable biological effects and that this may even be the paramount mechanism.* If that is correct, then it must also apply to medicines and remedies. In other words, you may not need an antibiotic, after all; just the surrogate energy signal of the antibiotic!

This bombshell shakes so-called "scientifc medicine" to its very foundations! Let's take a look at the story...

DULL BELLY, NOT SO DULL RESEARCH

Let's take up the story at the start of the 20th century, as I did in *Virtual Medicine*, with the work of distinguished American neurologist Albert Abrams. He observed something remarkable, though for all his life he was totally unable to explain it. The man was no intellectual lightweight and had studied conventional medicine with the best doctors of the time in Europe—Virchow, Wasserman, Helmholz, and others—winning top honors and a gold medal from Heidelberg University. You can be sure he knew what he was seeing, even if he couldn't understand it.

Abrams returned to the U.S. and taught pathology at Stanford University's medical school in California. One day, when he was percussing (tapping on) the abdomen of a patient with his fingers, the resonant note went suddenly dull. It coincided with the moment when a nearby x-ray machine was switched on. But what was remarkable was that when Abrams rotated the patient, he found the dull note was only present when the patient was oriented east-west. It was a spectacular example of science from a serendipitous moment, where the prepared mind, in the right place at the right time, observes something that everyone else would surely miss.

Subsequently, during a routine examination of a patient suffering from cancer (of the lip), Abrams noticed the same strange dull percussion note when tapping certain areas of the abdomen. It turned up on other cancer patients and tuberculosis cases, but again only if the body was aligned with feet towards the west. Abrams subsequently found this dullness in healthy cases when they were merely in close proximity to cancer or tuberculosis specimens and, most astonishing of all, in cases where the patient was remote from the pathological disease specimen but connected to it by means of a wire[1].

Abrams' conclusion, quite logically, was that unknown energy waves were being emitted by diseased tissue and that these could produce physical alteration within the body. He went on to fnd that he could pass a metal disc over the patient's body, connected to the wire, and when he came to the site of pathology the note would again go dull. When a skeptical colleague challenged him to fnd the exact location of a tuberculous infection of the lung, Abrams did so accurately. He was able to repeat this numerous times in different cases and with uncanny accuracy.

Abrams went on to develop an instrument he called the "Reflexophone" as a means of detecting and quantifying the strange radiation. A variable resistance altered the current and the machine emitted a sound which varied in pitch, thus eliminating the need to percuss the abdomen. He spoke in terms of differing "rates" for each disease process and he compiled a disease register: 55 for syphilis, 58 for sarcomatous tissue, and so on. Even when testing blind, he could infallibly detect or "diagnose" diseased tissue using his device. Even more incredibly, Abrams found that by adding new resistors to the Reflexophone, he could calibrate the device in such a way it would say how far advanced the disease process was!

Finally, as if to annoy his conventional colleagues to the extreme, Abrams announced that he could dispense with the patient's physical presence altogether and use only a spot of the subject's blood, hair or urine for testing. Not only that, but he could obtain his "electronic reactions" by having a healthy subject point to the part of their own body that was diseased in the patient, while connected to the Reflexophone. It was all too fantastic to believe. Trouble was just around the corner…

Then one day, while Abrams was demonstrating to a class the reaction produced by the blood of a malaria patient, he went one stage further. The known treatment of malaria was quinine, an alkaloid from the bark of the Cinchona tree. Abrams put a few grains of quinine sulfate into the test tray, together with the malarial blood and, to everyone's amazement, the dull percussion note vanished. The reaction was cancelled out.

Other known antidotes behaved similarly; for example, mercurial salts for syphilis. With the insight of genius, Abrams suggested there were unknown radiations emitted by the quinine molecule that exactly cancelled out the emanations from the malaria specimen.

THE OSCILLOMETER BROADCASTS HEALING FREQUENCIES

From this he reasoned, logically, that it should be possible to build a machine that could broadcast electrical oscillations at just the right counter-frequency, thereby altering the characteristics of diseased tissue and effecting a cure.

Medicine Beyond was on the way!

In co-operation with Samuel O. Hoffman, a radio research engineer who had distinguished himself in World War I by devising an early form of radar to detect approaching German Zeppelins at a great distance, Abrams came up with his "Oscilloclast." It did indeed offer some remarkable cures. His ideas began to spread and shake the foundations of the medical establishment. In his prophetic words, "As physicians we dare not stand aloof from the progress made in physical science and segregate the human entity from other entities of the physical universe."

However, conventional science was not ready for this new wisdom.

Predictably, Abrams was attacked by orthodoxy. When he perhaps unwisely announced in 1922 that he had used his instruments to successfully diagnose a patient over telephone wires, he was quickly denounced as a quack in the *Journal of the American Medical Association*, mouthpiece of the American Medical Association, which then, as now, seeks to bring down ideas contrary to the status quo or which threaten the rich pickings of the medical profession in the USA.

When the *British Medical Journal* repeated the scurrilous and defamatory attack, Sir James Barr, past president of the British Medical Association, wrote furiously in defense of Abrams:

> You [BMJ] very seldom quote from the *Journal of the American Medical Association* and one might have expected that when you did you would have chosen a more serious subject than an ignorant tirade against an eminent medical man, against, in my opinion, the greatest genius in the medical profession.

Abrams died in 1924. The vituperation continued for some time, including 18 consecutive issues of *Scientific American*. One of the worst insinuations was that Abrams had no scientific motive but was merely trying to make money by gulling an unsuspecting community. In truth, Abrams, son of a rich San Francisco merchant, had inherited a vast fortune and was a millionaire in his own right. He had written to Upton Sinclair, the American writer and journalist, offering to donate his devices to posterity and work unpaid for any institute that would develop the "Abrams Box" for the beneft of humanity.

Such is the integrity of medical journalism.

THE EMANOMETER

There was another twist to the enthralling story, in which the truth fared a little better. In 1922 a British homeopathic physician, Dr. William Boyd, built a modifed version of the Oscilloclast, which he called an "Emanometer," and was able to confrm all Abrams' findings.

Boyd was a keen researcher, particularly in the field of electro-physics, and he published extensive scientific physiological and biochemical research. He presented a very detailed paper on the workings of the Emanometer at the International Homeopathic Conference in London in 1927. As well as diagnosing, Boyd used it to test homeopathic remedies and let the instrument choose a suitable *similimum* (for a full account of homeopathy and its terminology, see Chapter 18). It was quite successful by all accounts but it was all so startling that controversy was, of course, inevitable.

Accordingly, in 1924 a committee was set up by the Royal Society of Medicine to investigate Boyd's claims, under the chairmanship of Sir Thomas Horder (later Lord Horder). The results were reported to the Royal Society of Medicine in January 1925. It is little short of astonishing that Horder found the Emanometer and percussion method quite valid; over the space of years I pay respect to his integrity. One would have expected official fudging.

The fact is, all the committee members were able to detect the change in percussion note first described by Abrams, and the detector apparatus was considered to offer important new diagnostic possibilities. In a series of 25 trials, Boyd's method was shown to be almost 100 per cent accurate according to the investigative committee, identifying chemicals and tissues presented in a manner that was "indistinguishable by visual or other normal" means[2].

THE BLACK BOX AND RADIONICS

Unfortunately, the committee made no cogent recommendations for further research, and since neither they nor Boyd had the faintest idea how the equipment might work, the black box was subsequently ignored and passed into medical history. It now stands as a watchword for humbug and pseudo-science among the skeptics. However, this story is far from ended, as later chapters on electro-acupuncture and electro-dermal screening with a modern computer will reveal.

Meanwhile, George de la Warr in Britain and Ruth Drown in the U.S. had devised their own versions of Abrams' instrument and, for a time, considerable interest began to develop in radiesthesia or radionics, as their new technique became known. However, the enthusiasts were to remain entirely outside the medical profession and detector instruments were soon being sold to all and sundry, most of whom had no legal medical qualifications. Inevitably bizarre, exaggerated, or just stupid interpretations were being made which soon brought the whole system into grave disrepute.

The catastrophic and manifestly unjust imprisonment of Ruth Drown for supposed fraud shattered any remaining credibility and heralded the end of any chance for the new medicine to slip into mainstream practice (she had been tricked by use of a spot of chicken blood on which she had passed a "diagnosis").

Radionics limps on, staunchly defended by a few nobly indignant devotees but hardly taken seriously, even by most fringe practitioners. It has been unable to shake off the stigma of its shaky beginnings and the criminal indictment of its principal founder.

However, there are many well-documented and fascinating phenomena in the field of radionics which must have some explanation (other than fraud) and seem to go very far beyond current medical models.

GEORGE DE LA WARR'S MYSTERIES

Radionics pioneer George de la Warr in England (1904-1969) developed a radionics camera. It was an advance on a device developed by Ruth Drown. De la Warr soon thought of putting a bottle of homeopathic *Aconitum napellus* remedy (monks' bane) into the camera and tuning the instrument to the rate of the aconite flower.

When the plate was developed, he was amazed and delighted to find a clear picture of a fully developed monk's bane flower on its stem.

To follow up, he then took a lily seed and "tuned" the camera to *potentiality to germination* and the plate yielded a clear picture of a lily bulb. When he tuned the camera to *potentiality to flower*, the plate showed a faint but perfectly formed image of a lily in flower.

These remarkable experiments which are, in every sense, of historic significance, yielded the first photographic evidence of the energy and information that resides in homeopathic dilutions, though, as we have seen, William Boyd and other radionics pioneers had found that these dilutions could produce reflexes in a subject.

The results were very reminiscent of the work of Dr. Harold Burr and his electrodynamic "fields of life." However, de la Warr knew nothing of Burr's work and called his images—a kind of electronic matrix holding the information of a living entity—"energy-patterns," "counterpart bodies," or "force-field bodies," for want of any other name.

Perhaps the most remarkable claim for de la Warr's camera was that it could travel through time and photograph the past or the future (hang on to your hat!) Apparently, in front of a group of journalists, he tuned his camera-connected machine to thoughts of his own wedding, 30 years earlier, and also introducing blood samples from both him and his wife (called witnesses).

The resulting photograph showed the couple, at the younger age, complete with outdated clothes.

There were over 10,000 photographic plates from this device, many of which have survived and are now in the possession of my friend Irene Mosvold, wife of the late Peter Moscow. Stand by for developments as I secure access to the device in the UK.

The whole field of investigation has given us new words: psionics and, later, psychotronics.

Interestingly—and perhaps not surprisingly—such devices as the camera can't be readily subjected to an objective evaluation. If anyone hostile to psionics is present, the device just won't work. The camera can only respond to the presence of the operator thoughts and is easily rendered inoperative by hostile mind energies.

I don't have a problem with that but of course skeptics hoot with laughter from their high tower of infinite learning!

BIOLOGICAL RESONANCE

The key question for this work is: "What scientific effect had Abrams found?" It might be argued that one or two paid practitioners were fraudsters; but members of a UK Government committee were hardly likely all to be stooges. They had seen something credible, after all. Can we put a name to it after all this time? I believe the answer is an unqualified "Yes," and it is not magic moonbeams or alien rays! I published the credible scientific explanation that follows in the original *Virtual Medicine*. So far as I am aware, I was the first person to go into print with the scientific connection.

Abrams himself discovered a major clue. While he was in Naples, he watched the famous tenor Enrico Caruso flick a wine glass to produce its note or tone and then, by singing the same note, shatter the glass. We call this phenomenon resonance. You can try it for yourself in the bathtub; simply sing or hum a higher and higher note and at some point you will hear a loud booming effect where the loudness of the sound is markedly enhanced. At this exact pitch your voice is resonating with the basic wavelength of the room, according to its size (the smaller the room, the higher the resonance note).

In my view, the so-called Abrams reflex was a spectacular example of the principle of cyclotron resonance, though demonstrated over half a century before this important magnetic phenomenon was recognized and explained. With the discovery of the cyclotron resonance effect, advanced physics is almost ready to shake hands with energy healing and telepathy. It is critical to the understanding of the functioning of most of the remarkable new diagnostic and therapy systems in the chapters that follow.

Nobel Prize double-nominee Robert O. Becker tells us, "The electromagnetic resonance concept may provide an intriguing link to a number of little understood and disputed phenomena, such as extrasensory perception and the ability of 'healers' to diagnose and treat patients. In both these activities, the participants may be unconsciously using an innate biological mechanism similar to that of magnetic resonance imaging (MRI)."[3]

Everyone today is familiar with MRI, though usually without necessarily comprehending the technicalities involved. In principle it isn't difficult, though of course the reality may be far more involved than we know. A charged particle or chemical "ion," when in a fixed magnetic field such as the earth's own field, is made to spin; the stronger the magnetic effect, the faster the spin. Each atomic substance has different spin characteristics.

If a second oscillating (ON–OFF) field is applied, at an angle of (exactly) 90 degrees to the original field, then the spin motion is enhanced according to the principle that we call resonance; it is the same effect as piano or violin strings beginning to hum in sympathy with musical notes of the right frequency sounded nearby. The particles gain energy. If the field is suddenly interrupted, the particles give up this extra energy, which is radiated outwards (Figure 1). An image can be formed by placing the body in a fixed field and then bombarding it with an oscillating field, flowing at right angles. When the oscillating field is ON, the ions pick up energy; when the oscillating field is OFF, the ions re-radiate the energy in a form which can be picked up and displayed on a computer as a three-dimensional image. That's really all there is to MRI.

136

The enhanced energy effect we call *cyclotron resonance*. What is important is that the weaker the static field, the smaller the oscillating cross-field needed to create the resonance effect.

Cyclotron Resonance

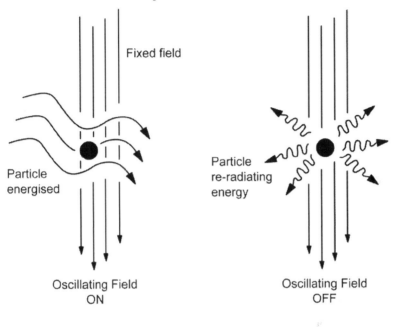

Fixed field

Particle energised

Particle re-radiating energy

Oscillating Field
ON

Oscillating Field
OFF

To be exact, the non-local effect that would best explain Abrams' findings is nuclear magnetic resonance (NMR). Whereas cyclotron resonance is a phenomenon of classical physics, nuclear magnetic resonance belongs to the strange world of quantum physics, where non-locality rules.

That is why practitioners are able to "act at a distance", to use the conventional physics term. Remote healing is credible, when resonating information fields are invoked.

RATS ON PARADE

It is impossible to overestimate the biological importance of this magnetic resonance effect. Living forms exist within the Earth's field, which is very weak. Thus only the slightest disturbance, if at the right frequency and in the critical direction, could have profound effects on important ions such as calcium, sodium and potassium (note how Abrams' reflex only operated if the body was oriented feet to the West). It is only a matter of time before scientists begin to wonder if certain diseases are not becoming more common because the typical fields we experience are the ones that interfere with the ordered metabolism of critical ions (the rise in osteoporosis, which depends on functioning levels of calcium ions, is an example I have in mind).

To show how easily this could come about, consider an experiment carried out at the U.S. Naval Research Center, Bethesda, Maryland, and published in the journal *Biomagnetics* in 1986. In this study, the effects of cyclotron magnetic resonance on lithium in rat brains was monitored, using a fixed feld of 0.2 gauss (low end of the Earth's field strength) and an oscillating field of 60 Hz, which is the frequency of U.S. domestic electricity. The reasoning was that, if the lithium was truly enhanced by the magnetic resonance effect, then the rats should display more subdued behavior, since lithium is known as a central nervous system depressant. In fact the rats were exposed to:

1.   a sham (null) field

2.   the 60 Hz field alone

3.   lithium frequency alone

4.   a combined oscillating and lithium information field

Unexposed controls were used, as part of standard scientific protocol[4].

In due course, it was obvious that the rats exposed to cyclotron resonance (combined oscillating field plus the lithium information code (4) were indeed significantly subdued, compared to control rats receiving an incomplete information package (1-3). This result was the equivalent of giving the rats a substantial dose of lithium; in fact they had been given none.

It's a very fine example of information field therapy, using biological effects created without any material substance present; just the information of a substance.

The study is important because it shows major biological effects with low-strength fields acting on chemical substances common within the body. It also shows that fields in a typical home are significant biologically. In fact we worry a great deal these days about the particular frequencies between 10 and 100 Hz. These are considered extremely-low-frequency, or ELF, fields. They are the most active biologically.

What's more, you will later learn, very low-intensity fields have the most effect; turn up the juice and the effect often disappears, probably due to overwhelming the biological tissues, rather than inducing a gentle resonance.

BIOLOGICAL DANGERS

The most obvious question, of course, is: how does this affect our health? Clearly we are all meeting cyclotron resonance conditions and NMR effects every single day. It can tune up our nutritional building blocks or, more dangerously, tune them out.

NMR can produce perturbations of normal cell cycle time by inducing resonance changes in the atoms of DNA molecules. We all know that DNA damage can, potentially, cause cancer.

But this isn't confined to the DNA molecule. For every chemical element, an oscillating field at a specific frequency will induce resonance within a steady-state field at a certain strength. In 1983, a research team under A. H. Jafari-Asl showed that, while the Earth's magnetic background could serve as the steady field, the harmonics of power-line frequencies could produce a time-varying field that would induce nuclear magnetic resonance in at least two crucial atoms of living tissue – potassium and chlorine.

Other elements might also be susceptible to the effect. Bacteria and yeast cells exposed to these NMR conditions doubled their rate of DNA synthesis and proliferation, but daughter cells were half size. Liboff, analyzing contradictory studies, found that the contradictions disappeared when he calculated resonance conditions for the Earth's field where each test was done. Previous work must now be reinterpreted as one vast experiment in adding new frequencies to the varying background.

Almost all experimenters to date have tested the response of organisms to a single specific frequency and intensity. This approach was needed in the beginning to provide a basic level of knowledge, but it's far removed from everyday life, in which we are all exposed to many frequencies simultaneously. A synergism between electromagnetic energy and radioactivity has already been suggested by the fact that cancer rates among nuclear power plant workers are higher than was predicted solely by the higher levels of ionizing radiation in their environment.

Nuclear power plants abound in multi-frequency radio waves and other electromagnetic radiation. In addition to inducing NMR in the building blocks of living cells, multiple frequencies may likewise interact synergistically to yield biohazards greater than the sum of their individual dangers[5].

CONVENTIONAL MEDICINE CATCHES UP

I knew it was coming and in 1999 predicted that conventional medicine would eventually start using cyclotron resonance for diagnosis and, ultimately, treatment. Science demanded it and such a step forward seemed only justice for Albert Abrams, after he was so reviled for first discovering its benefit.

Even so, I was startled when, only a few years after the publication of *Virtual Medicine*, I heard that the famous Mayo Clinic was installing a monster cyclotron resonance machine. Then, shortly afterwards, I learned of a diagnostic device, used to detect testicular cancer, developed in an Italian university. Things were moving fast.

Today we have MRI scans, nuclear magnetic resonance imaging (NMRI), and magnetic resonance tomography (MRT). All use the same basic technology, which is to subject the body to a static magnetic field and simultaneous radio frequencies (oscillating field) and then study the displacement of hydrogen ions. Using a complex imaging procedure and a computer analysis, the data can be assembled into an image of the body.

All other ions are realigned too, which is one of the reasons this is a potentially dangerous process, using a very strong magnet. It's much overused in diagnosis but is certainly safer than using ionizing radiation, as in x-ray imaging.

The technique provides high-quality cross-sectional images of internal organs and structures. Paul Lauterbur, an American physicist, and Peter Mansfield, a British physicist, shared the 2003 Nobel Prize in Physiology or Medicine for pioneering contributions that later led to the application of magnetic resonance in medical imaging. I have often thought that Albert Abrams deserved at least an honorable mention!

The emerging possibilities are almost endless and science is moving fast. For example, I found a 2008 paper by researchers at the Institute of Neurobiology and Molecular Medicine in Rome, Italy, proposing the use of the cyclotron resonance of calcium ions to assist the formation of new heart tissue from cardiac stem cells. The idea was to regenerate damaged hearts with newly-formed tissues; something that supposedly does not happen in nature.

Feasibility was demonstrated and tissue markers improved. As the authors speculated, this may pave the way for novel approaches in tissue engineering and cell therapy[6].

In another study, cyclotron resonance treatment to the blood significantly reduced malondialdehyde levels. MDA is a known marker for oxidative stress, so this is a clear indicator of improved tissue sustainability.

Researchers studied 32 healthy volunteers. Each received 15 cyclotron resonance treatments, 27 minutes in length, distributed over 5 weeks. The highly significant reductions in MDA concentrations (53.8%) were noted just after the 15 treatments. There was no effect on cholesterol levels. The implication of this work is that this type of therapy may be a profound contribution to antiaging science[7].

Resonance magnetic applications in mice brains have been used to visualize and even dissolve amyloid plaques, the characteristic lesion of Alzheimer's disease. Think what that means, though I do not accept that these plaques are necessarily the cause of Alzheimer's. Moreover these same resonating magnetic fields can significantly reduce cancer growth, also in mice[8].

A paper presented at the SENS 2013 conference in Cambridge, UK (SENS is dedicated to anti-aging research), introduced a device known as the QUEC PHISIS, which uses cyclotron resonance to generate coherent domains in water. Coherence is the hallmark of life and not shared in nature. Randomness and chaos are the norm. Artificial man-made coherence is a very new phenomenon (as, for example, the laser).

I can go further and state that lack of coherence is the basis of all disease states. Not surprisingly, therefore, a device able to create biological coherence had numerous benefits that were presented at the conference: optimizing redox balance (rH2) and the acidity (pH) of body fluids, correction of membrane potential, activation of enzymatic processes, promotion of intra/extracellular ionic balance, enhancement of the bioavailability and the absorption of the fundamental elements in the cellular metabolism[9].

What were really fascinating to me were the comments on this paper: "Extremely suspicious technology", "This trips my 'bogus science' detector" and "certainly sounds like quack physics to me", for just a few examples! This underpins my whole problem with pretend scientists, which is that *they know next to nothing.*

How can anyone pretend to science and yet not be aware of—indeed, even predict, as I did—that a phenomenon as powerful as cyclotron resonance would be a strong influence in all of biology?

QUANTUM JAZZ

The fact is that we vibrate. It is our nature. We are a kind of musical instrument, resonating at uncountable multiple frequencies. It's what Dr. Mae-Wan Ho, author of *The Rainbow and The Worm*, called Quantum Jazz. Dr. Ho is one of our most gifted holistic scientists, but with a flair for poetry and phrase, as her suggestion reveals.

By Quantum Jazz she means the holistic and fully orchestrated way that organisms resonate in harmony; she means the way creatures like us are swarming with spontaneous activities at every level, right down to the molecules inside their cells.

It's a dance with rhythms and harmony over more than 70 octaves (each octave is double the previous frequency of the same tone). There are colors too. That's not as trivial as you might think. Coherence in fact is a very big deal. It isn't supposed to happen in living organisms. But that's just another scientific myth, like the Big Bang, and other weird and wonderful "explanations" of our world. Coherent biological organisms are the norm; indeed the ones that are not coherent are dead! Color is about coherence.

We are an orchestra, all playing at once. We are not a bunch of soloists with a copy of the tune in the same key. In fact it wouldn't be wrong to say we are the actual melody, we embody the song!

SHIVA'S QUANTUM DANCE

Quantum coherent action is effortless action, effortless creation, the Taoist ideal of art and poetry, of life itself.

142

The parallel between Shiva's dance and the dance of subatomic particles was first discussed by Fritjof Capra in a 1972 article titled *"The Dance of Shiva: The Hindu View of Matter in the light of Modern Physics,"* published in Main Currents in Modern Thought (Sept-Oct 1972).

> Every subatomic particle not only performs an energy dance, but also is an energy dance; a pulsating process of creation and destruction...without end... For the modern physicists, then Shiva's dance is the dance of subatomic matter. As in Vedic mythology, it is a continual dance of creation and destruction involving the whole cosmos; the basis of all existence and of all natural phenomena.[10]

Shiva's cosmic dance then became a central metaphor in Capra's subsequent international bestseller *The Tao of Physics*, first published in 1975 and still in print with over 40 editions and going strong.

It may surprise my readers to know that in 2004, a tall statue of the dancing Shiva was unveiled at CERN, the European Center for Research in Particle Physics in Geneva, Switzerland. CERN has oversight of the Large Hadron Collider (LHC) and is also the place where core technologies of the internet were first conceived.

Ananda K. Coomaraswamy, late curator of Indian art at the Boston Museum of Fine Arts, is quoted on a plaque accompanying the statue:

> Shiva's dance is the clearest image of the activity of God which any art or religion can boast of.[11]

By contrast, the dead biology and lifeless physics of conventional science is like pulling apart a saxophone and saying, "There's no music in here!"

MUSICAL RESONANCE

OK, with that cue, I cannot finish this chapter without bringing in the power of music as a resonance phenomenon. Indeed, the whole thread of reasoning began with music (Caruso shattering glasses). Resonance is a core principle in music and is the reason why instruments speak so clearly and sweetly: the resonance of bow on string, a wooden cavity or the voices of a choir in a large auditorium. Music has power beyond its ability to sooth and charm!

If you are not familiar with the work of Fabien Maman, it's time you were. He was able to destroy cancer cells by singing at them. No, really!

Maman is a French composer and bio-energeticist, who explored and documented the influence of sound waves on the cells of the body. He was fascinated with energetic healing techniques, and wondered if we are really affected biologically, or even changed by music? If so, how deeply does sound travel into our bodies?

He began a year-and-a-half study joined by Helene Grimal, an ex-nun who had left the convent to become a drummer. She supported herself by her profession as a biologist at the French National Center for Scientific Research in Paris. Together they studied the effect of low volume sound (30-40 decibels) on human cells.

The pair mounted a camera on a microscope where they had placed slides of human uterine cancer cells. They proceeded to play various acoustical instruments (guitar, gong, xylophone as well as voice) for periods of twenty-minute duration, while they observed the effect on the cells.

Sounding the notes of the Ionian Scale (nine musical notes C-D-E-F-G-A-B and C and D from the next octave above), the cellular structures quickly disorganized. Fourteen minutes was enough time to explode the cell when he used these nine different frequencies, reported Maman.

The most dramatic influence on the cells came from the human voice: when he *sang* the same scale, the cancer cells literally "exploded" in less than 10 minutes.

The vibration of sound literally transforms the cell structure. As the voice intensifies and time passes with no break in sound, the vibratory rate becomes too powerful, and the cells cannot adapt or stabilize themselves. Therefore, the cell dies because it is not able to accommodate its structure and synchronize with the collection of sound. Cells cannot live in an atmosphere of dissonance and they cannot become resonant with the body. Therefore, the tumor cells destabilize, disorganize, disintegrate, explode and are ultimately destroyed in the presence of pure sound.

What was especially exciting to me was that one particular note—A at 440 Hertz—seemed to carry the most healing power. Maman has produced numerous photographic images, showing that A (the note an orchestra tunes to) turned cell energy fields Indian pink. Pink is a healing color and associated with love, as we all know. This Indian pink effect on cells appears, no matter what instrument the note A is sounded on.

As Maman said excitedly: What if, for 20 minutes, radio stations and hospital intercoms played pieces in the key of A? What if children sang songs, mothers hummed to their babies and public PA systems all broadcast this note? Perhaps for 20 minutes, at least, our world could be harmonized.

What if, indeed?

A full treatment of healing by musical resonance is not appropriate here but if you are indeed interested, then you can follow up with Maman's book *The Role of Music in the Twenty-First Century* (Redondo Beach, CA, 1997). You will also enjoy *The Healing Forces of Music* by Randall McClellan (Element, Rockport MA, 1991).

CHAPTER 9

The Three Proofs 2: Homeopathy

 Relativity theory has had a profound influence on our picture of matter by forcing us to modify our concept of a particle in an essential way. In classical physics, the mass of an object had always been associated with in indestructible substance, with some "stuff" of which all things were thought to be made. Relativity theory showed that mass has nothing to do with any substance, but is a form of energy.

—Fritjof Capra, *The Tao Of Physics*

The second proof of the non-material nature of substances I use is homeopathy, which I introduce more fully in Chapter 18.

These days it's fashionable to decry homeopathy and say, "It's proven not to work." That's the claim of dishonest scientists like Edzard Ernst, one-time professor of complementary medicine at the University of Exeter (a political joke, clearly). These phony opinions, which seem to me to be libeling good, honest practicing homeopathic physicians, are repeated frequently in journals, newspapers and all over the Internet, with no one quoting any source. Of course there can be no "proof" something doesn't work; only the failure to demonstrate it does.

These vicious attacks are simply insupportable and there are many scientific studies showing that homeopathy works and works well, all ignored by Ernst and his like. Moreover, it is very safe. Switzerland recently accepted its workability officially and in India homeopathy has been widely practiced since 1839, when Romanian doctor John Martin Honigberger successfully treated the Maharaja of Punjab for paralysis of the vocal cords. After treating the Maharaja, Honigberger moved to Calcutta, where he was known as the "cholera doctor" because of his successful treatment of the disease using homeopathic remedies.

In 1960, the Maharashtra Act—also known as the "Bombay Act"—set up a court of examiners concerned with the teaching of homeopathy and the creation of new colleges to do so, and a board of homeopathy to regulate and license practitioners.

Despite the hue and cry, homeopathy is available quietly at select U.S. clinics, such as the M.D. Anderson Cancer Center in Houston. Moreover, the U.S. National Cancer Institute wants to fund more studies - More of these breakthroughs for *Medicine Beyond* in a later section.

For now, let me quote a typical strong, well-designed study showing homeopathy works: a study which the fraudulent critics say doesn't exist!

HOMEOPATHY IN A NUTSHELL

One of the big problems that conventional scientists and doctors have with homeopathy is that most of the active therapeutic solutions are so dilute there is clearly none of the original substances left. Once past the so-called "Avogadro number" or "Loschmidt number," which is a 10^{23} dilution or 23 zeros, we know from simple chemistry that no molecules remain, since there are 10^{23} molecules in a standardized (molar) solution.

That sounds a lot but when homeopaths dilute 100 x100 x 100 x 100... they only have to do this 12 times (12C which is 12 followed by 24 zeros) and they have gone beyond the Avogadro number. 12C is actually not very dilute in homeopathic terms: solutions of 200C are used routinely or even 1000C (1M as it's called).

But that does not mean these ultra-dilute remedies can have no effect! It's an obsession of the reductionist scientists, stuck on "stuff," that only material substances can have any biological effect. These are the same people who insist that the Sun and moon can have no biological effects on us, when in fact it would be absurd for there to be no influence.

We homeopaths think of the substance's unique property as an energetic signal or, in the very high dilutions, pure information. This energy or information is "printed" on the water and so can be used therapeutically, long after the actual substance is gone.

However, here's a finding that surprised even me! Maybe the actual "stuff" doesn't entirely disappear? Properly conducted studies on market samples of homeopathic remedies, using Transmission Electron Microscopy (TEM), electron diffraction and chemical analysis by Inductively Coupled Plasma-Atomic Emission Spectroscopy (ICP-AES), have shown the presence of the starting metals and their aggregates, in the form of nanoparticles, even at these extreme dilutions.

The study is was carried out at the Department of Chemical Engineering, Indian Institute of Technology, Bombay and published in the journal *Homeopathy* and was reported on PubMed.[1] That puts an end to that particular debate, I think.

The Avogadro number "theory" doesn't seem to apply.

DILUTE A POISON AND WHAT DO YOU GET?

Notice that in the process of ultra-dilution, a toxic substance is transformed to being one of beneficial healing. Consider the homeopathic master remedy Lachesis, derived from the South American bushmaster snake, which is very venomous indeed. The symptoms of being bitten include a weak heart; a rapid, weak, irregular pulse; palpitations; angina; and difficulty in breathing—leading eventually to circulatory collapse and death. Yet these symptoms are the very ones eased by taking the much diluted form of the venom (Lachesis). This is rather wondrous to behold.

Turned around, this means that even poisonous substances can be beneficial, if used in small enough quantities. Strychnine, a deadly poison, was once used in bottled "tonics," which older readers will remember in the medicine cupboard. Instead of killing you, it revitalized (i.e., put life back in) you. - More on this principle in the section on hormesis below.

Now there is substantial proof from a different direction that, like it or not, homeopathically potentizing (diluting) a substance, even beyond the point where there is any physical molecules present, still creates a biochemical effect.

THE MEMORY OF WATER

In 1988, Jacques Benveniste published a now-famous paper in the journal *Nature*, reporting experiments showing that extreme dilutions of water solutions of an antibody could still evoke a biological response long after the active substance was diluted away, provided the solution was agitated after each dilution[2].

Non-agitated solutions produced little or no effect. This pointed clearly to transmission of information via some kind of water-organizing process. Benveniste was bitterly attacked by his peers and even denounced by Sir John Maddox, the then-editor of *Nature*, who had first commissioned the article.

For such an affront on the narrow-minded tenets of science, Benveniste lost his government funding and his laboratory was closed down. There were even some attempts to prove he had perpetrated a fraud, but in the end this was toned down to hints that his work was not reproducible by others. In fact there have been several published papers since this "memory of water fiasco", replicating Benveniste's work.

First, there were the South Korean chemists who discovered that molecules dissolved in water clump together as they get more diluted[3]. Furthermore, the size of the clumps depends on the history of dilution, making a mockery of the "laws of chemistry."

Then in 2003, Swiss physicist Louis Rey published the results of a startling experiment in *Physica A*, a reputable journal specializing in statistical mechanics. Rey was investigating the effect of sodium and lithium chloride on the dissociation of water molecules, using a well-established conventional technique called thermoluminescence.

In fact, Rey used "heavy water" or deuterium hydroxide, since it performs better. When heated steadily from deep frozen, irradiated deuterium gives off two distinct luminescence peaks: one around 1220 K and the other at 1660 K. Adding sodium chloride or lithium chloride enhances this process and results in a larger dissociation.

That's all very mainstream; but in a fit of curiosity (which could have cost him his job!) Rey decided to see what happened if he used only homeopathically diluted sodium or lithium chloride. He followed the proper procedure, including succussion (shaking) between dilutions, and went to a dilution way beyond the Avogadro number, which the reader will now be aware means that no physical substance remains.

The results? Exactly the same! The two charts are identical and one could be laid over the other, they are such an exact match. Homeopathically prepared substances, diluted beyond the presence of any weighable rest mass, still created a potent physico-chemical effect[4].

Predictably, Rey has been attacked and criticized, just as Benveniste was. Martin Chaplin from London's South Bank University, an expert on water and hydrogen bonding, for instance, claims "Rey's rationale for water memory seems most unlikely." Chaplin suggests that tiny amounts of impurities in the samples, perhaps due to inefficient mixing, could be getting concentrated at the boundaries between different phases in the ice and causing the changes in thermoluminescence. This is mere speculative comment, of course, disguised as science.

Contrast Chaplin's shaky intellectual position with that of thermoluminescence expert Raphael Visocekas from the Denis Diderot University of Paris. Visocekas took the trouble to visit Rey and watched him carry out some of his experiments.

"The experiments showed a very nice reproducibility," Visocekas told *New Scientist*. "It is trustworthy physics."[5]

Just be patient. In time, as with Benveniste's memory of water, the results will be repeated and confrmed quietly in many independent universities.

But the critics of homeopathy, like Professor Edzard Ernst, will ignore these later fndings and go on spouting their dogma that "there is no proof" that homeopathy works.

WHAT COULD BE MORE ABSURD?

A good article published in the prestigious journal *The Lancet* (1994), showed that homeopathy is unarguably effective. It will also give the reader great insight into the specious convolutions imposed in the name of science to try and twist or evade an unpopular truth, to make it fit with accepted facts, in spite of all the evidence.

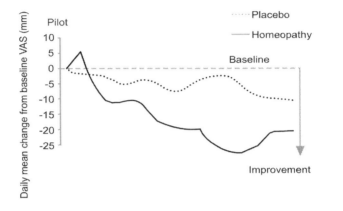

A series of asthma patients were given either a placebo or a homeopathic remedy, chosen by a suitably knowledgeable doctor, assigned on an entirely random basis in a double-blind test. "Double-blind" means that neither the investigators nor the patients have any idea who is getting the "blank" and who is getting the real remedy. But when the code was broken, it was abundantly clear that patients receiving the homeopathic regimen became steadily better and better over several weeks, many even giving up their conventional drugs. No such benefit was noted in the placebo group.

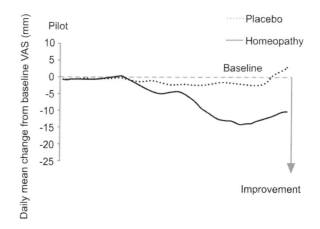

We'll call that the "pilot" study, they said. So they did the whole thing again, just to be sure. The second series of cases came out with exactly the same decisive result. This was the principal study.

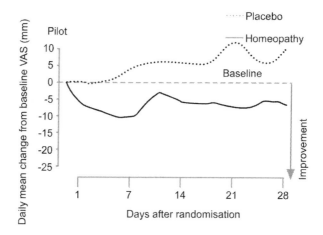

You would think that was the end of it. But no, the investigators decided that, since the findings were "controversial", they would do it again, a third time. This was the confirmatory study!

Anyone would be forgiven for supposing that the aim was to go on and on until a negative result was obtained, which would then would be published as "proof" that homeopathy was worthless. I remind the reader that many killer drugs find their way into the market after only one poorly conceived trial to back them up, and do great harm before being recalled.

At least, in this instance, *The Lancet* editorial had the frankness to admit this was a trial conducted with "exceptional vigor."

In this neatly designed and simple trial, there was no escaping or fudging the facts. Did the researchers conclude that homeopathy is valid? Well, not quite—they had the unbelievable effrontery to suggest that maybe the real explanation was that the scientific method was somehow faulty: "... we must ask if the technique of randomized controlled trials is fundamentally flawed, and capable of producing evidence for effects that do not exist, by, for example, the effects of clinicians' expectations of outcome transmitting by subtle effects that circumvent double blinding?"[6]

In other words, "We know homeopathy doesn't work so maybe this is telling us that double-blind crossover trials are faulty"!

This really is going too far and borders on deception; the authors quote an explanation that maligns good homeopathic practitioners, for which there is no scientific justification. The whole point of double-blinding is that it means the clinicians' expectations are removed from the equation.

I find it appalling that the scientific community can criticize others for failing to measure up to the scientific canon they impose, yet when proof is amply forthcoming showing those who are being attacked are undeniably correct, then, suddenly, the scientific method becomes debatable!

However I do have some sympathy with the researchers and understand the difficulty they must have faced in getting this study into any decent journal. Personally, I am grateful to them for managing to report in such a prestigious publication. The editor, too, must be complimented for what would have been professional suicide as little as a decade ago.

Nevertheless, he could not resist sniping in his accompanying editorial, presumably to cheer along the regular troops, who must have been sickened by such clear evidence in favor of something they hate!

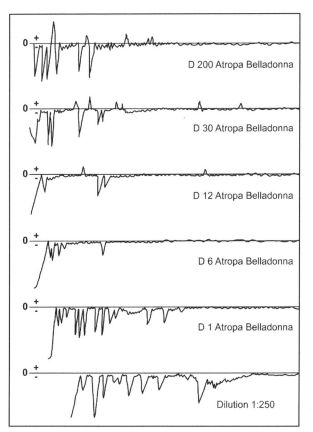

Proof that homeopathic *Belladonna* broadcasts energy

What could be more absurd than the notion that a substance is therapeutically active in dilutions so great that the patient is unlikely to receive a single molecule of it?[7]

RADIO BELLADONNA

OK, to settle all argument, consider this spectrographic analysis of several homeopathic Belladonna dilutions. It shows *unequivocally* the capability of water for retaining information. The spectrograph is probably
the most exquisitely sensitive scientific detector we have. It is a device
that can show us traces of an element on remote stars, billions of light
years away (indeed, helium was first discovered in our Sun, using a spectrograph, before it was ever found here on Earth).

154

It should be noted that, according to physical science, dilutions of D23 (one-in-ten dilution repeated 23 times) or higher cannot possibly contain any chemical residue. What is being measured is an energetic information signal. It can be seen that even at high dilutions (D30 and D200) frequencies above the positive line are recorded, meaning that *the solution is actually transmitting information.*

This cannot be explained by merely substance-based thinking. There is no "stuff" or mass present, though in fact it should be explained that school-level physics leads us to consider mass too simplistically. Scientists now recognize "weighable" matter, which has a rest mass; but also non-weighable matter, which has only energetic properties and no detectable rest mass.

Whatever is in the Belladonna "solution" or residual water after the chemical has left, it carries recognizable energetic properties. It can interact with the tissues and with the disease process to effect a cure. It does this by resonance, that is, striking a frequency chord (as in music) where the two oscillators (or notes) together match up and create a much-intensified response.

Your radio set does much the same thing. The incoming signal is very attenuated but when you tune the dial, you are altering a resonator (the amplifier) until it matches; at that point, the signal becomes much stronger and can be used in a modulating electrical circuit, without it being drowned out. In other words, the information (broadcast) is singled out from the surrounding "noise."

Thus there may be no belladonna carried by the water, but its "radio transmission" is still present and will resonate with scarlet fever, or any similar combination of symptoms.

The point is that, even without knowing anything about resonance frequencies and "vibrational" medicine, the pioneers of homeopathy somehow understood that a certain message or signal, mimicking the disease, had the power to dislodge it.

It's not quite as dramatic as singing in resonance with a glass tumbler and shattering it, as Caruso did (page 135). But the principle is worth bearing in mind. No "substance" actually passed between Caruso's vocal cords and the glass tumbler but the effect was... well, no glass tumbler!

DRAMATIC BENEFITS FOR CANCER PATIENTS

It's quite an historic day when a study showing homeopathy works as well as a major (very expensive) drug gets published in a prestigious peer-reviewed journal (*International Journal of Oncology*).

So: what did this landmark paper show? Four homeopathic remedies, Carcinosin 30C, Conium maculatum 3C, Phytolacca decandra 200C, and Thuja occidentalis 30C, had a pronounced cytotoxic effect against two human breast cancer cell lines. Phytolacca is better known as poke-weed root, which grows as a towering weed in the US and elsewhere. Conium maculatum is poison hemlock, while Thuja occidentalis comes from the eastern arborvitae tree. Carcinosin is the only non-botanical in the group. It is made from a highly diluted extract of breast cancer tissue.

All four remedies were capable of inducing apoptosis, the "cell suicide" effect that causes cancer cells to self-destruct. This was so startling that the experiment was repeated three times. Two of the remedies—*Carcinosin* and *Phytolacca*—achieved as much as an 80-percent response, compared to only a 30-percent reduction by placebo. In other words, the homeopathic effect was more than twice that of a placebo.

Also, the effect was strongest with the greater dilution—which is why we call it "potentizing."

The study was originated by Dr. Moshe Frenkel, who was at the time working at the MD Anderson Cancer Center (MDACC) in Houston. Frenkel had been to India and was astounded by what he witnessed. "I saw things there that I couldn't explain. Tumors shrank with nothing else other than homeopathic remedies. X-rays had shown there had been a lesion on the lung and a year after taking the remedy it had shrunk or disappeared"[8]. In India, homeopathy is big. The pharmaceutical industry does not have a stranglehold on medicine there, unlike here in the USA. Doctors are free to tell the truth; they won't lose their jobs. What's more, the whole ethos of medicine is looking for simple, safe, effective cures, not profits over patient health.

What was especially interesting to me was that the cell-killing effects of Carcinosin and Phytolacca appeared similar to the activity of paclitaxel (Taxol), the most commonly used chemotherapeutic drug for breast cancer, when it was tested in the same two adenocarcinoma cell lines investigated in this study.

The use of poisonous plants to treat cancer is commonplace in orthodox medicine. The periwinkle plant (Vinca) has given us vincristine and vinblastine, two very powerful chemo drugs. The aforementioned drug paclitaxel (Taxol) is derived from the bark of the Pacific yew tree.

So, next time you hear somebody claim there is no proof that homeopathy works, just remember this study, published in a major peer-reviewed journal!

Meantime, the British medical establishment has just pronounced there is "no proof" that homeopathy works and has removed financial support for it as a therapy. Taxol costs $20,000 US for six rounds of therapy. The homeopathic remedies, $20 for all four! Do you think this makes sense? It makes perfect sense if the British establishment is controlled by Big Pharma money and bribes!

BEATING THE DREADED BRAIN TUMOR

Incredible as it seems, homeopathy can bring good outcomes for brain tumors, such as gliomas, generally considered to be incurable and swiftly fatal.

Researchers treated human brain cancer, leukemia cells, normal B-lymphoid cells, and mouse melanoma cells with different concentrations of Ruta 6 in combination with tricalcium phosphate. In addition, 15 patients diagnosed with intracranial tumors were treated with the mixture, including 7 with gliomas. Of these 15 patients, 6 of the 7 glioma patients showed complete regression of tumors.

Six out of seven glioma patients with complete regression of tumors is remarkable, to say the least. Compare that with orthodox figures, as follows: 10,000 Americans diagnosed each year with malignant gliomas, about half are alive one year after diagnosis, and 25% after two years.

Although the number of patients in the group was small, the outcome of homeopathic treatment was highly encouraging and novel. The researchers went out on a limb when they proposed that Ruta 6 in combination with tricalcium phosphate could be used for effective treatment of brain cancers, particularly glioma.

That's a pretty good score for what critics insist is just water! (In fact dilution 6X is not beyond the Avogadro number and therefore, technically, contains a small residue of Ruta)[9].

I will conclude these comments by saying this: you must not be persuaded to rely on just homeopathy to treat your cancer. It's good in good hands. But there are very few really good practitioners of homeopathy today. It's been opened up too much to medically untrained individuals.

MORE MINIMUM DOSE MAGIC

Other homeopathic substances may be helpful, however, such as clearing old diseases (nosodes) and hereditary weaknesses (miasms). You will learn more about these specialist approaches from a practitioner and also in the section about electro-dermal screening.

In brief, a nosode is a homeopathic formulation of the actual disease substance or pathogen (cancer cells, or bacteria). This aligns with the key precept of homeopathy: like cures like.

Another type of remedy we call a sarcode, which is made from good healthy tissue of the diseased organ. Remember we are talking information transfer, not biochemistry here. There are no substances present, just the "message," as it were. So it makes logical sense to supplement the treatment with healthy signals from healthy tissue (I already referred to this principle in the section on DNA, where healthy pancreas signal was used to protect rats from deadly alloxan poisoning; see page 69).

Nevertheless, the controversy rages. To understand the raw stupidity of the establishment, consider this quote, also from the aforementioned journal *The Lancet*:

> The conflict between observation and theory has raged ever since Bacon advocated the experimental method. Homoeopathic research epitomizes this conflict; on the one hand, Klaus Linde and colleagues' meta-analysis shows that the effects of homeopathy are unlikely to be due to placebo, but on the other, Vandenbroucke refuses to accept this evidence "because it runs counter to current scientific theory."

To be skeptical is to be rational, but Vandenbroucke betrays this by suggesting that if Bayesian analysis should support homoeopathy, then Bayes' theory should be abandoned. In other words, if a phenomenon exists, but cannot be explained, it does not exist.

This is wholly unscientific and portrays a rabid dogma, rather than any methodical thinking.

A commentator on that same *Lancet* piece spikily remarked, "Like many facing the seemingly absurd, he (Vandenbroucke) seems to be frog-hopping from pad to pad trying to find one which supports him. But none will. Such an attitude, blinded by dogma, almost robbed us of the discoveries of Galileo, Semmelweis, Pasteur, Einstein, and Bohr." Ouch![10]

THE TRUE BASIS FOR DISEASE

Awarded the Nobel Prize for Chemistry in 1947 for his work on non-equilibrium thermodynamics, Belgian boffin Ilya Prigogine has become a key figure in redefining physics as something inherently cheerful and nurturing, instead of decaying and dismal. His work is largely theoretical and on those grounds we must be cautious. But what Prigogine showed is little short of a scientific bombshell; he demonstrated scientifically that order can come from disorder.

That's not supposed to happen. The hallowed Second Law of Thermodynamics says it cannot.

It takes a perturbation or overthrow of the existing order by an exterior source. This leads to the acquisition of new levels of order. These dissipative (nonlinear) structures, as he called them, can go through periods of instability and then self-organization, resulting in more complex systems whose characteristics cannot be predicted except as statistical probabilities.

Basically, a dissipative system is a local manifestation which defies the surrounding order which is bound towards entropy. Instead of less organization and decay, a dissipative structure becomes more complex and more orderly as a result of perturbation. It's a superb line of discovery. But basically *life* is the principal known dissipative structure! And does it not appear that life is somehow able to evolve to a higher order? Evolution creates more and more complex systems from the old order. Materialism creates more and more decay from the previous order.

There is proof that life is non-material. In the words of Prigogine: "We know we can interact with nature. That is the heart of the message I give... Matter is not inert. It is alive and active. Life is always changing one way or another through its adaptation to non-equilibrium conditions. With the idea of a doomed determinist world view now gone, we can feel free to make our choice for good or ill. Classical science made us feel that we were helpless witnesses to Newton's clockwork world. Now, science allows us to feel at home in nature"[11].

THE LESSONS OF DISEASE

What Prigogine's theory says is that perturbation stimulates more complexity. But the reverse of this is that life cannot create increased order without being subjected to stresses (perturbations).

Attack and stress is what drives evolution. Now do you see the importance of this new line of science for our attitude to disease? What Hippocrates, Thomas Sydenham, and all those who followed this line said all along was that disease creates health! They were correct. The illness we recognize is the response to perturbation; it creates newer order. We can learn from our sickness; it is sent to teach us.

This model tells us that modern reductionist medicine, which insists on treating disease by head-on confrontation and attack, is fundamentally flawed. Toxic therapies, by their very nature, drive the organism, the patient, further towards disintegration and entropy.

This new theory also makes it clear that the study of life in the form of increasing analysis by breaking it into parts is fundamentally flawed. Since life comes with increasing complexity or order, by taking its structures apart we get less life, less complexity, less energy. So the main thrust of science—reduction and analysis—leads away from the very phenomenon it purports to study. The result is the fundamental mistake orthodox medical science makes: that disease is caused only by microbes, stress, nutrient deficiency etc.

Suddenly disease becomes essential to the life process. Disturbance and conquering it becomes the basis of renewal and advancement for life. Only by coming to wholeness, in the fullest meta-religious sense, can we hope to understand the complex dynamic nature of health and illness, and therefore *Medicine Beyond*. So really, the holistic movement, for all the criticisms laid against it for being unscientific, is in many ways being the more scientific of the two approaches.

SO, WHAT IS HORMESIS?

Hormesis (from Greek *hórmēsis*, "rapid motion, eagerness," from ancient Greek *hormáein* "to set in motion, impel, urge on") is the term for generally favorable biological responses to very low-level exposures to toxins and other stressors. It's a biological version of the old saw: *That which does not kill me makes me stronger*. Increasing doses stimulate at first and then steadily suppress (inhibit). See graph.

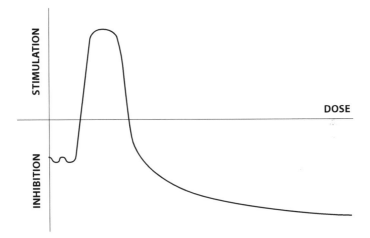

Paracelsus was there first, working with micro-doses of noxious agents and obtaining significant therapeutic results.

An example from contemporary study is the fact that, in 2012, researchers at UCLA found that tiny amounts (1 mM, or 0.005%) of ethyl alcohol doubled the lifespan of *Caenorhabditis elegans*, a round worm frequently used in biological studies. Higher doses of 0.4% provided no longevity benefit[12].

One of the valuable areas where the concept of hormesis has been explored extensively with respect to its applicability is aging. Since the basic survival capacity of any biological system depends on its homeodynamic (homeostatic) ability, biogerontologists proposed that exposing cells and organisms to mild stress should result in the adaptive or hormetic response with various biological benefits. This idea has now gathered a large body of supportive evidence showing that repetitive mild stress exposure has anti-aging effects[13].

In 1998, Edward J. Calabrese and Linda A. Baldwin at the Department of Environmental Health Sciences, School of Public Health, University of Massachusetts, published a survey of publications, judging their worth and validity, and found over 4,000 relevant research papers. Their analysis suggests that hormesis is a reproducible and relatively common biological phenomenon, pertinent to many living species and a wide variety of tissue insults, including radiation, temperature extremes, and chemical toxins[14].

This is probably why resistant organisms evolve when we use antibiotics; some at least receive only small doses and are stimulated rather than suppressed.

I have considered the possibility of another mechanism that may be involved in hormesis: that unhealthy cells and tissues may be far more susceptible to toxins than normal tissues. They may be damaged or destroyed at a level which might only be stimulating or inhibitory in healthy circumstances (compare this phenomenon with an inflamed eye, which is sensitive to the least light, while a healthy eye is traumatized only by the brightest sunlight). The result of such a differential destruction of poor or weakened cells and tissues would be a sort of "culling," without doing harm to the main body. This could, in turn, result in regeneration and renewal of existing healthy tissues that were no longer negatively influenced by adjacent sick signals.

All this goes to show that the diseased parts are sensitive to the smallest stimuli. This fits with the overload theory I have expounded here. On the plus side, the same observation might give a clue as to how the homeopathic medicine works. It is seen that the sick organism responds to extremely small doses of the similar drug, whereas the healthy organism is unaffected by such a small dose. Professor August Bier has shown that it requires 250,000 times as much formic acid to produce symptoms in the healthy person as it does in the case of a patient with gout (formic acid, prepared from ants, is one of the homeopathic remedies for rheumatism and gout).

As Johnson and Bruunsgaard at the Institute for Behavioral Genetics, University of Colorado, Boulder 80309, USA, wrote: "Rather than being an exception, non-linearity between dose and response is the rule in biological systems. It might even be anticipated that at some doses a response opposite to that seen at high doses could be elicited (hormesis). Such non-linearity with dose has multiple implications for numerous aspects of biomedical research on aging and in designing experiments. Moreover, the implications of such non-linearity are such that governmental regulatory activities and other areas of public health administration will be affected to a large extent, once hormesis is widely recognized[15].

The authors are referring to the fact that the authorities would like to accept radiation hormesis as a surprise benefit, meaning that sub-lethal doses may not be as harmful as logic says they must. If low levels seem to benefit the organism, rather than harm it, that lets them off the hook morally and legally!

We don't know enough to allow us to go along with that. Furthermore, it does not address the issue that what may be a hormetic level for some is a dangerous dose for others. The only totally safe dose of a toxin is zero!

MITHRIDATING

A strange variant of this low-dose-protects phenomenon is mithridatism, named for King Mithridates VI, who was a ruler of Pontus in Asia Minor in the second century BC, and who was said to take daily increasing doses of known toxins to render himself immune from assassination by poisoning. Gradually the body becomes accustomed to the harmful substance and "normal" (i.e., an assassin's) dose has no effect.

Rasputin survived several murder attempts, including one attack in which he was administered enough cyanide to kill several people. Yet he did not die (his assailants had to shoot him and then drown him to finally assassinate him). It has been theorized that frequent attempts to kill him with poison had resulted in mithridating him, so that subsequent attempts not only failed, but strengthened his resistance.

In my allergy work I have long utilized a similar principle: low-dose desensitization. For decades it was scoffed at by orthodox colleagues but today you can Google it and find 100,000s of returns about it.

In a nutshell (no pun intended) the patient takes sublingual doses of carefully titrated end-points that work as a "neutralizing" dose. After an allergen is found, we go more and more dilute, to find the correct end-point that can be used therapeutically. A personal formula, containing numbers of such neutralizing doses will, over time, see the patient able to tolerate food or inhalant antigens far better.

The regularly repeating doses of the pathogen—in this case an allergen—bring about resistance to its ill effects.

ADEY'S WINDOW AND THE ARNDT-SCHULZ LAW

Alchemists all knew that a poison taken in small dosage was not necessarily dangerous and might even be helpful. A few generations ago, physicians carried strychnine in their bags as a tonic; only in high dose was it considered a harmful poison. Today we refer to this effect as Arndt-Schulz's Law, after the chemists who described it so well (1888). It is one of the very earliest laws of pharmacology. It states that for every biologically interactive substance: small doses stimulate, moderate doses inhibit, and large doses kill.

In other words: *more is not better*. Elementary-school science drums into us the linear or quadratic relationship and we are taught that if a quantity of some substance has a particular effect, then larger amounts will perforce induce a greater effect. But this is often not so.

There are very good biological reasons for the magic of the minimum. If the body is subjected to too strong an input signal, this often has a negative rather than a positive effect. This can be likened to turning up a radio set so loud that it begins to distort. The extra volume is counter-productive and the program broadcast will be heard better by turning down the volume to a more comfortable level. Overdosing is the way in which many drugs work. I am convinced that much allopathic medicine is simply poisoning out some part of our physiology; for example, painkillers poison the full working of the nervous system.

Medicine Beyond practitioners have come to understand that the biological information field is paramount, and that the field only needs to be modulated slightly for there to be a major change in output. This is summed up in an important holistic principle known as the Arndt-Schulz's Law, which applies to homeopathic prescribing, but again also to many other interacting living systems:

- A small stimulus will provoke positively.
- A larger signal has no further beneficial effect.
- A very large signal actually has a suppression effect.

W. Ross Adey of Loma Linda University showed this effect experimentally while studying calcium influx in irradiated animal brain cells. He showed that the brain cells not only responded to quite specific frequencies (approx. 10 Hz), but did so only at extremely low intensities[16].

There was, in effect, only a very tiny spread of values in which the optimum effect could be detected. Outside that range, either nothing happened or function was suppressed. This gives us a new term, the Adey Window, meaning a narrow effective low-level band or response-slot. Adey received the Hans Selye Award for this holistic insight in March 1999, at Montreux in Switzerland.

CONSIDER VACCINES

I often wonder why orthodox doctors have such a difficult time with the concept of the "minimum dose" when, really, that's what vaccination is all about.

The idea is to give the body a small dose of something, to educate it and for it to adapt to and for the body to work out it's own natural resolution to the encounter and to learn defensive responses.

The idea of using a medicine, prescribed homeopathically, for the *prevention* of disease, rather than just a cure, was present from the very beginning of homeopathy. I believe the first presentation of this idea was by Samuel Hahnemann himself in an article, entitled *Cause and Prevention of the Asiatic Cholera*, which was published in 1831. In this article, Hahnemann suggested a list of possible remedies (*Camphora, Veratrum, Bryonia, Rhus toxicodendron, Cuprum*) that would be of most use in the cholera outbreak that was raging at that time.[17]

This was without being involved in the outbreak; just speaking from first principles. Hahnemann's followers quickly put these suggestions to the test with remarkable results. Prediction, you may know, is the keystone of any scientific hypothesis. If you have a theory and it can predict something which turns out to be true, your science is 100%, until something better turns up!

OK, that takes care of the dilution principle. Now let's move on to another dimension, in which non-material effects may come from substances which are not physically present, via an information package, like a computer download!

CHAPTER 10

The Three Proofs -3: Digital Substances

Quantum theory has... demolished the classical concepts of solid objects and strictly deterministic laws of nature. At the subatomic level, the solid material objects of classical physics dissolve into wave-like patterns of probabilities, and these patterns, ultimately, do not represent probabilities of things but probabilities of interconnections.

—Fritjof Capra, *The Tao of Physics*

The third proof of my *Medicine Beyond* hypothesis that physical substances are not needed for a biological or healing effect lies also in the work of the late Jacques Benveniste, who went on to study far more than just the memory of water.

It rests with the fact that when atoms come together they form a molecule held together by energy bonds which both emit and absorb certain specific electromagnetic frequencies. No two species of molecule have the same electromagnetic oscillations or energetic signature. Each vibration is unique.

SIGNATURE OSCILLATIONS

Seventy years later, Benveniste was able to use the unique radiations of molecules and substances to create an "electronic signature". He went further, however, and showed that the characteristics of a biochemical substance did not depend on its physical presence but could be replicated digitally and used to "inform" water. He meant imprinting the energetic signal into water. This informed water would then generate the characteristic response attributable to the substance in question: but there was no trace of the physical substance present in the test medium.

The technicalities are challenging but need not concern the average reader. Basically, the substance under review was turned into a digital (binary) signal, using a transducer via an ordinary computer sound card (I think he told me, or I read, he used an ordinary Sound-Blaster card).

Once in the form of an electronic file, the "substance signature" or EMS as he called it (electromagnetic signal) could be handled like any other computer file. It could be burned to a floppy disc, attached to an e-mail or sent via the Internet as a download.

A typical experiment of this type would proceed as follows:

A quantity of the substrate would be obtained, say phorbol myristate acetate (PMA), a useful test agent capable of generating reactive oxygen metabolites or "free radicals". This was then turned into an electromagnetic signature file.

Using a transducer, water would be treated or "informed" with the PMA file, played to it through a transducer. This could be compared to the effect (if any) of plain water as a control. The effect of real PMA was known and, as a further investigation, the team tested whether SOD (superoxidase dismutase), a substance known to block reactive oxygen species, had any detectable effect.

Results were tested by measuring production of reactive oxygen metabolites (ROM). The reader will be pleased to hear these studies were very reproducible and measurements of ROM consistently showed identical effects, whether the chemical substances used were "real" or digitized water[1].

It is very satisfying that the SOD blocked ROM release, even by the "informed" or digitized water. This suggests to me at least the probability that the real mechanism of most biochemical reactions is that of electromagnetic signaling and not "stuff" interacting with other "stuff" at all!

This relates to a thread going elsewhere, when I mentioned that my friend Cyril Smith was able to use electromagnetic frequency signals to switch off the effect of a real challenge pathogen, such as an allergen. (page 50)

Later as well as replicating these results elsewhere Benveniste and colleagues at the Northwestern University in Chicago were able to send digitized biological information via telephone, on a floppy disc, via the Internet, even as an e-mail attachment and still replicate the effects at the other end[2].

THE BIRTH OF DIGITAL BIOLOGY

Benveniste has successfully given birth to a whole new paradigm he christened "digital biology". It's going to be a rough ride getting it accepted in the die-hard community of people who believe utterly in the untenable model of biochemical collisions as the basis for life (that's how molecules are supposed to signal to each other).

Follow along with Benveniste in his own words:

> Life depends on signals exchanged among molecules. For example, when you get angry, adrenalin "tells" its receptor, and it alone (as a faithful molecule, it talks to no other) to make your heart beat faster, to contract superficial blood vessels, etc.
>
> In biology, the words "molecular signal" are used very often. Yet, if you ask even the most eminent biologists what the physical nature of this signal is, they seem not even to understand the question, and stare at you wide-eyed. In fact, they've cooked up a rigorously Cartesian physics all their own, as far removed as possible from the realities of contemporary physics, according to which simple contact (Descartes' laws of impact, quickly disproved by Huygens) between two coalescent structures creates energy, thus constituting an exchange of information.

For many years, I believed and recited this catechism without realizing its absurdity, just as mankind did not realize the absurdity of the belief that the sun circles the earth.

The truth, based on facts, is very simple. It does not require any "collapse of the physical or chemical worlds." That molecules vibrate, we have known for decades. Every atom of every molecule and every intermolecular bond—the bridge that links the atoms—emits a group of specific frequencies. Specific frequencies of simple or complex molecules are detected at distances of billions of light years, thanks to radio telescopes. Biophysicists describe these frequencies as an essential physical characteristic of matter, but biologists do not consider that electromagnetic waves can play a role in molecular functions themselves. We cannot find the words "frequency" or "signal" (in the physical sense of the term) in any treatise on molecular interactions in biology[3].

Like most readers, I too was raised on the old-fashioned view of "lock and key" molecular activity and believed in it utterly at the time. So I know how deeply entrenched this model has become. That's the problem. It's like wearing glasses: you don't see the lenses, just the view beyond (altered by the different focus).

But, thanks to Benveniste, I'm as sure today it's wrong as I was sure then it was correct.

Let's compare the two models and see which is more plausible. First, the background to the digital biology model:

• All cells communicate via molecular resonance

• Mutual resonance extends outwards, like chain reactions, spreading to other molecules nearby (just like piano strings vibrate when something nearby excites them!)

• All fields extend to the ends of the universe, even though they get fainter and fainter (basic physics)

• Almost instant (speed of light)

• Every substance is known to have characteristic frequencies which, theoretically, can be detected right across the universe

The traditional model, on the other hand, relies on molecules actually bumping into each other. I blush when I think I once believed this! It's almost impossible!

TENNIS BALLS SERVE FOR THE MATCH

The more of a substance is present, the more likely a collision, that much I can agree with. This model has a technical name QSAR (quantitative structure activity relationship). In simpler terms we would say that it relies on a concentration gradient.

The QSAR model therefore has the following characteristics:

- Needs direct contact

- Relies on random collision

- Uncontrolled, trial-and-error basis

- Statistically virtually impossible

- The simplest biological event would require a very long time

The way I illustrate this in my public lectures is as follows: Let's suppose we take 10,000 super-elastic white tennis balls, which bounce almost indefinitely, and set them all in motion in the Carnegie Hall auditorium. Then we follow up by launching 100 yellow super-elastic tennis balls, which are also in motion nearly indefinitely. How long do you think it would take before 2 of the yellow balls actually collided?

Well, the answer is that it could happen in the first fraction of a second. But it could also take a week. All we can say is, with precise probability math, we can predict the likely length of time it would take. I don't need to do that here; it's a very long time. Just follow the reasoning.

This reliance on chance encounter is virtually impossible for biological functioning. On a reasonable timescale, even for molecular-size systems, it's going to take too long. Or it would require a huge presence of the active substrate (a lot of the yellow balls). Yet we find in typical biological systems that concentrations of very active substrates (like hormones) are almost infinitesimally small, the equivalent of say 6 - 8 yellow balls among the 10,000 white ones.

Nevertheless there is an effect.

The digital model explains this easily: substances do not need to make contact, ever. The resonating field extends outwards to infinity (OK, classical physics resonance is going to fade slowly with distance. But nuclear magentic resonance is a quantum effect and therefore non-local and does not attenuate).

Digital biology:

- Requires no direct contact

- Therefore distance not a problem

- Resonance enabled by geomagnetic field

- Instantaneous (before there is time for one cycle of blood circulation), which is often seen in medical biology.

- Extremely low frequencies work at very attenuated levels

- Even high-frequency molecules can "beat" at an ELF, which we have seen is more powerful biologically.

Let me explain the last two points, which to me are the clinchers.

The cyclotron resonance effect we began with in Chapter 8 relies on a simple mathematical equation as follows: $v = (1/2\pi)(\rho/\varphi)\beta$. It probably looks scary but it isn't really. All the funny Greek letters in brackets are just math symbols, which can be substituted, giving the cyclotron resonance characteristics of any known substance. Just ignore them.

We only need to consider the $v = \beta$ elements of the equation. Those are saying that v (frequency) is directly proportional to β (the intensity). Turn that around and it means the lower the frequency, the lower the corresponding intensity needed to create an effect.

This is why extreme low frequencies are so powerful, biologically speaking. ELFs need only a very low strength field to work!

So you see even if the field was weak (not many yellow balls, or too far apart), it doesn't matter on this model. The molecules can still talk to each other, without ever making contact. Neat, isn't it?

Now the only bit we have left to clarify, in order for you to know 1,000 times more physics than your medical practitioner, is what I mean by "beats" and how that phenomenon fits into the picture.

Many molecules have quite high frequencies. They don't qualify as ELF. But simultaneous high frequencies which are close, but not identical, resonate with a very slow secondary rhythm which is the difference between the two frequencies. Stay with me for a moment: if you sounded a tuning fork at 440 cycles per second (middle "A") and then started off a second tuning fork doing only 443 cycles per second, you would hear a wu-wu-wu-wu-wu-wu "beat" of 3 cycles per second (perhaps you wouldn't hear it at first but with practice…).

In fact that's how orchestral musicians all tune their instruments together. They listen for beats and tune until the beats get slower and slower (less difference) and then finally the beats disappear altogether, meaning the two instruments are perfectly in tune.

In fact this is where the sound element comes in. Benveniste, you'll remember me saying, was recording electromagnetic signatures via a computer sound card; well, now you know why. Many specific frequencies he was working with fall within the range of "sound" or the infrared spectrum.

DIAGNOSIS

But wait a minute! Could this signature idea be used to detect the presence of pathogenic substances and organisms? Maybe we could do away with the need for blood samples, biopsies and other physical sampling in order to make an accurate diagnosis?

You bet.

And in the course of time that may become Benveniste's greatest legacy.

In his Portakabin laboratory in Paris (all that was left to him after the "memory of water" debacle), he and his DigiBio team went on breaking the frontiers of science and medicine.

One of the headline studies involved a detection method for the bacteria E Coli, an occasional human pathogen. The K1 strain, particularly, is a major cause of enteric/diarrheal diseases, urinary tract infections, and sepsis.

In line with their previous work, the team electronically captured, digitized, and transmitted the specific electromagnetic signal (EMS) of the K1 bacteria to a biological system sensitive to that exact pathogen (or its EMS).

First they digitally recorded the EMS from E. Coli K1 and two other substances as controls: staphylococcus (3.5 million/ml) or saline.

Next, they set up latex particles, sensitized by a K1 antibody, from Pasteur Diagnostics. These particles will clump or aggregate in the presence of real E. Coli K1.

When the Staph EMS was played, little happened; when the control (saline) EMS was applied, little happened.

But the E. Coli K1 EMS induced the formation of significant aggregates (larger than that of Staphylococcus or saline).

What was curious—and here's the integrity of the man—is that Benveniste reported that the magnitude of aggregation varied from day to day. It was not consistent. Yet, always in comparison for the controls of that day, the team seldom made a mistake in separating E. coli. This was repeated over hundreds of experiments[6].

This is remarkable in that a diagnostic test was performed with none of the pathogenic substance present, only it's electromagnetic "signature". Incidentally, these were common or garden ".wav" files, familiar to any computer literate individual.

As Benveniste remarks, since these signal files can travel a long distance, it should become possible to detect any immunogenic substance from a remote location. Don't send blood or urine: send an .mp3 file!

So finally we are tying together all the strands from Albert Abram's Reflexophone and Oscilloclast, via the dermatron and Voll's EAV machines, to modern day computer analysis and digitized "specimens".

174

DIGITAL TREATMENT!

Remember, part of Abram's original discovery was that pathogens could be eliminated by playing them hostile frequencies, through his "Oscillo-clast" (page 131). What is the current state of play on this?

In Chapter 17 I refer to so-called bioresonance therapy, where specific chosen frequencies can be played to the tissues, producing a therapeutic response. MORA machines, the BICOM and similar devices have now reached a state of sophistication where they are practically, in themselves, a new healing paradigm. Even the mighty little SCENAR (Chapter 20) can be considered to belong to this family of healing devices.

But this would be a good place to introduce another electronic healing model, which is scandalously controversial (I love it), and at the same time fascinating and instructive in its scientific, biological and medical impact.

I'm referring to the work of Royal Raymond Rife.

It's an involved, bitterly disputed story, generally distorted with fanciful embroideries and has reached near mythic proportions in some accounts of his life and work. Moreover much of the supposed teaching and documentary material in circulation about Rife comes from people who are trying to promote their own me-too versions of the Rife machine and their documentary evidence is often suspect, to say the least.

Let's stick with the main therapeutic facts.

ROYAL RAYMOND RIFE

Rife was unarguably a brilliant technician. He was hired by Henry Timken, an industrial magnate, and under Timken's sponsorship produced the most technologically advanced speedboat marine engine of the day (1915), generating 2700 HP.

Rife went on with Timken's support to develop microscopes and almost perfected the art, producing compounded quartz prisms in a glycerin bath, which gave resolutions of up to 50,000 diameters; this was at a time when the best commercial laboratory microscopes could give only up to 2,000 diameters. Rife's Universal Microscope was without doubt the greatest optical instrument ever designed; no one can seriously question this aspect of Rife's work.

It's what he *saw* that started the acrimony and disputation.

Rife illuminated the microorganism (usually a virus or bacteria) with two different wavelengths of the same ultraviolet light frequency which resonated with the spectral signature of the microbe. These two wavelengths produced interference where they merged. This interference was, in effect, a third, longer wave which fell into the visible portion of the electromagnetic spectrum. This is exactly the same process by which Benveniste got his frequencies down to the human auditory range.

Rife painstakingly identified the individual spectroscopic signature of each microbe, using a slit spectroscope attachment. Then, he slowly rotated the block of quartz prisms to focus light of a single wavelength upon the microorganism he was examining (you will remember from high school physics that a prism splits white light into its component frequencies). The selected wavelength was chosen because it resonated with the spectroscopic signature frequency of the microbe based on the now-established fact that every molecule oscillates at its own distinct frequency (this was 50 - 60 years before Benveniste came across the same realization).

The result of using a resonant wavelength is that microorganisms which are invisible in white light suddenly become visible in a brilliant flash of light when they are exposed to the color frequency that resonates with their own distinct spectroscopic signature, coordinating with the chemical composition of the organism. Rife likened this effect to using light as the equivalent of a chemical stain in conventional microbiology. In fact the particles Rife was able to visualize were smaller than the molecules of typical acid and aniline dye conventional stains!

This new technique gave Rife a unique advantage and enabled him to see things nobody had ever seen before with ordinary microscopes.

Rife became the first human being to actually see a live virus, and until quite recently, his microscope was the only one which was able to view live viruses. Even more amazingly, he saw that when a Tubercle bacillus was destroyed, it split into many smaller living particles that he called TB viruses (a virus at that time was just considered to be a filterable bacterium).

These altered forms we call pleomorphism and it is bitterly disputed, even today, that such a thing can take place. Of course none of the experts who deny its existence has ever looked through a Rife microscope!

But Rife also saw something else, something startling, and something that shouldn't be there!

BACILLUS X

Rife saw curious tiny little living virus-size organisms in the blood of cancer patients. They were too small to be bacteria but were not viruses. He found they gave off a distinctive purple-red emanation when viewed in the microscope. He named this entity bacillus X, or "BX" and claimed to have verified its existence in every instance of carcinoma he examined.

At that time virus causation of cancer was unheard of. Moreover it was not known that viruses were simply protein capsules containing either RNA or DNA. On our present model, BX was cancer trouble just waiting to happen. In fact Rife was able to convert from cancer to the organelle and back 104 times. He injected rats with the organelles and created cancers. These were then used to obtain more organelles and pass the disease on to the next rat and so on. He did this 411 times in total, with the same result. Cancer was transferred by a small filterable moety he called "BX". That's pretty convincing.

He also found another organism associated with sarcoma he called "BY".

But few were prepared to believe Rife. Despite widespread media of the day claiming that "The cure for cancer has been found", the idea of a cancer virus or cancer bacterium was too far beyond the boundaries of knowledge at the time (1932).

LETHAL RAYS

Rife discovered that if you play a resonant frequency to an organism it will oscillate or vibrate with it, until it bursts, like the singer's trick of singing the specific note of a drinking glass and make it shatter. The same thing happened with cancer cells and other pathogens. This killing disruption is called electroporation, and led to the cell's immediate malfunction and death. The fatal frequency Rife termed the MOR or mortal oscillatory rate.

Now, here is another loop closed by this present text: Rife's early investigations were contemporaneous with that of the still-living Albert Abrams. Rife, it is known, actually had one of Abrams' Oscilloclasts (page 131). From this prototype, Rife also designed and had constructed his own oscillator which was capable of generating a wider spectrum of individual frequencies than the Abrams' machine. By a painstaking process of examining the BX in culture while stepping through a wide array of frequencies, Rife found the one which "devitalized" it.

Rife isolated the organisms and found the MORs for tuberculosis, E. Coli, tetanus, chickenpox, herpes type virus, pin worms, streptothrix (fungi), rabies and altogether, over a forty year period, the MOR for about 600 different forms of bacterial and viral forms. The primary frequencies used ranged from the low audio up as high as the limit of short-wave, with several frequencies being combined, and acting both as a carrier as well as a treatment frequency.

Now, this is critical: Rife stated quite clearly that you need the MOR killer frequency of the rod form of the bacillus and the viral form simultaneously to get any effect. Otherwise (his words) you either kill the patient or nothing happens.

This feature is missing from most me-too "Rife machines".

Fortunately, perhaps surprisingly, normal healthy human cells were completely unharmed by these lethal waves.

The MORs for the BX (cancer) and BY (sarcoma) forms of malignancy were listed by Rife as follows:

- 1,604,000 Hz

- 11,780,000 Hz

- 17,033,663 Hz

These are radio frequencies (RF).

By 1935 Rife was ready to begin experiments using his "ray" machine on humans with cancer and TB. Out of 16 terminally ill patients, 14 were pronounced clinically cured after 70 days; the other 2 subsequently recovered after the end of the trial: in other words a 100% success rate on patients in the worst possible condition. This result is outstanding and passes into medical history as a truly great achievement. More shame on those who still refute it, over 70 years later.

THE END

In his career Rife won 14 government awards in recognition of scientific achievements and was honored with a medical degree at the University of Heidelberg in Germany. Yet today his name is often viewed as synonymous with quackery and "Rife machines" are illegal in his home country (though not, of course, elsewhere in the world). That's how far Rife's star has fallen and has yet to be resurrected.

Much has been written about the final destruction of the Rife microscope and "Rife Ray" machines. We have accounts claiming the FDA burst into his office at gun point and smashed all his equipment. The stories of raids are more likely distortions of actions taken against Life Lab Inc, a later company making copy-cat frequency machines, with Rife as a titular research head but without much involvement (he was scared of further litigation).

It's true that Morris Fishbein, editor of the Journal of the AMA tried to buy into Rife's company Beam Ray Corporation and became very maliciously vindictive when he was not allowed to. As a result of his actions doctors using the device were "visited" by the AMA and told to send it back, or face loss of their license (incidentally, Fishbein and the AMA used the same tactics against Harry Hoxsey, who developed a successful herbal cancer cure).

But Rife's own colleagues probably did him nearly as much damage by producing machines which did not stick to the proper specifications and failed to work consistently. Philip Hoyland, the electronics engineer, was paranoid about others stealing the design, which was unpatentable. He tried to disguise the frequencies. Scruples reached a low ebb when a group of British doctors were sold two machines which had been deliberately mis-wired, in order that they could not guess how it worked. They figured it out anyway and, not surprisingly, were very upset at the fraud.

Bertrand Comparet, Rife's lawyer of the time even speculated that Hoyland was sabotaging the program because he desired to grab the action for himself. Hoyland, we know, accepted $10,000 from Fishbein's associates and subsequently was a stooge in their attempt to grab Rife's Beam Ray Corporation. The ensuing litigation was disastrous and although Rife "won" the case, the little company was virtually bankrupt and ceased trading.

Regardless of all this, I think the final demise of the machine was much simpler to explain and far less dramatic.

Rife came to the market with his machine in the 1930s. It cost $7,000 which in those days was a very considerable investment, even for an MD. No matter, he sold a number.

But also in the 1930s, by a twist of fate, sulfonamide antibiotics swept over the horizon, followed rapidly by penicillin, and this new class of drugs soon overran the therapeutic picture at a fast gallop. When it was possible to knock out virtually any pathogen with a drug costing just a few dollars, quickly, safely and simply (according to perceptions of the day), who would want to invest in a costly machine that was inconveniently large, expensive to run and difficult to operate?

It was the same bad luck with his advanced microscopes. They were the very best of the day, precise and advanced, but very costly. Unfortunately for Rife, the electron microscope was just around the corner (1931) and optical microscopes, no matter how powerful, were doomed to be eclipsed. Of course electron microscopes can only ever look at dead tissue; but that's the fashion in so-called science. Nobody, it seems, wants to do anything as corny as to look at real living organisms!

There is another factor little talked about, which is that the authentic Rife machines were super-regenerative RF transmitters. Without going into the technical details, that meant they ultimately fell afoul of Federal Communications Commission regulations. Remember, by this time radio stations were springing up all over the US and the FCC developed strict guidelines as to who was allowed to broadcast, where and at what frequencies. Rife machines were really doomed by this one factor alone.

Rife was simply a man out of his time. He died in 1971, frustrated and sad, a broken man, an alcoholic. Most of his knowledge has passed into history and most claims for authentic "Rife machines" are bogus.

In the 1960s a man called John Crane, who had worked with Rife, started selling off the shelf frequency generators as authentic Rife machines; he merely changed the labels on the casing. Crane created the myth that the lower audio frequencies, developed later by Rife and supposed to be used in conjunction with the RF carrier frequencies, were in fact the real MORs.

Clearly this is not true. Recorded MORs are in the far higher RF range. Unfortunately, most modern machines are really derived from Crane, not Rife. Most are even from the same manufacturer, sold under different brand labels. You can tell any of these knock off fakes because they use disease "codes", instead of displaying a frequency.

Don't be fooled by the present Beam Ray Corporation, which is NOT the original Rife company and doesn't have true Rife machines but are simply cashing in on the present interest.

WHAT HAVE WE GOT LEFT?

The real challenge is that, because of the controversy, most modern manufacturers don't want to be known for selling "Rife machines". They use the term frequency generator.

If you want to explore or be part of this technology, choose carefully among the offerings. Let's take one model as an example, the GB-4000. It is made in the USA. Moreover it was designed by a man who has studied and re-created a Rife Ray machine, so at least he knows what he's trying to parallel.

The first good point is that it uses a frequency band-pass or "sweeping", like the BICOM (page 294). That means that it will carry out a sweep, passing through a wide range of frequencies.

It has "gating", a surprise new discovery from recent investigations into Rife's old machines, some of which are still around for boffins to pore over. (See below)

It also uses the RF carrier wave method, as well as the lower audio frequencies. It delivers the energy through direct contact (pads and electrodes), so the need for Rife's old-fashioned glass tubes, which generate huge power, are not needed.

IRREVERSIBLE ELECTROPORATION

I have startled my subscribers in the past by pointing out that Rife technology has gone main-stream recently—only they don't mention Rife and most investigators have never heard of him.

Blowing apart microbes and cancer cells using electronic means is now called "irreversible electroporation" and it's being researched a lot.

Studies were initially carried out using RF frequencies to push chemotherapy agents into the cancer cells; the idea being that this could be done with far smaller, and therefore non-toxic, doses.

But investigators have now moved on to the point where they have realized they can dispense with the chemical agents and just use electromagnetic frequencies. According to one study published in the *Journal Of Cancer Related Research*, cytotoxic frequencies appear to be tumor-specific and treatment with tumor-specific frequencies is feasible, well tolerated and may have biological efficacy in patients with advanced cancer[7].

The FDA's stand that Rife's technology was a fraud now looks wholly untenable, scientifically.

GEMM THERAPY

While we are on the topic of EMF devices and electroporation as a cancer treatment, do not forget the work of the late Suleyman Seckiner Gorgun in Turkey. In fact his reputation spread throughout and he enjoyed considerable credibility. He is a largely unknown modern equivalent of Rife and, it has to be said, he carried out far more scientific proofs of his method than Rife ever did!

Gorgun was born in Istanbul on 12th of May, 1950 and graduated in medicine in Pakistan.

In 1972 he began working on cell cultures at the Marine Biology Laboratory in Izmir, Turkey, to observe the effects of external electromagnetic fields on cells. He developed what was first called the "Method of Gorgun" but later became known as GEMM therapy (Italian: Generatore Elettro Magnetico Modulato), a therapeutic device generating specially modulated, low power (0.25 watt) radio waves (don't mix this up with gem therapy, which I write about in chapter 22).

In 1974 Gorgun had fine tuned his method and went to Germany to present the outcomes to Prof. E. Shaumlöffel at Marburg University. There was significant regression of the tumors on mice inoculated with cancer.

In 1982 Dr. Gorgun went to France to work with the renowned French Immunologist Prof. Raymond Pautrizel at the University of Bordeaux to demonstrate the effects of his treatment on Trypanosoma and Plasmodium, which also proved susceptible to RF terminal electroporation.

PROCEDURE

Therapy sessions are carried out daily, generally lasting around 30 minutes through antennas directed towards the patients lying in therapy beds.

Depending on the type and stage of the disease & the condition of the patient, the therapy may last anywhere from a few weeks to several months.

GEMM Therapy is very safe. It is CE certified. It uses a power of only 0.25 watts). Compared to X or Gamma Rays used in conventional radiotherapy, radio waves have at least a billion times less energy and have no direct destructive effect on normal, healthy issues.

Gorgun went further with our understanding of what happens (remember, Rife was not medically trained and knew very little medical science).

Gorgun focused on molecular communication. In this sense he is closely aligned with the writings of Georges Lakhovsky and his theory of molecular and cellular frequencies (page 116).[8]

CHAPTER 11

Biology Beyond the Skin.
Traditional Models

And a new philosophy emerged called quantum physics, which suggest that the individual's function is to inform and be informed. You really exist only when you're in a field sharing and exchanging information. You create the realities you inhabit.

— Timothy Leary, *Chaos & Cyber Culture*

When I came up with this chapter title I used in *Virtual Medicine* nearly twenty years ago, it seemed very daring, clever and revolutionary. Now, you could almost say, "It's obvious!" Knowing as we do about the life force, the electromagnetic field surrounding us and the non-locational effects demonstrable in living systems, it seems absurd to doubt that the nature of our creature being extends outwards, well beyond the confines of the skin.

In fact amazing experiments conducted by my friend the late Cleve Backster show that, if cells from an individual are retained in the laboratory and he is sent hundreds of miles away, those cells will react when he is emotionally disturbed, even though there is no physical connection whatever[1].

I'm also fond of telling the story—it is amusing, as well as instructive—of experiments done by Pierre Paul Sauvin, an electronics expert from New Jersey. He showed that plants wired to electronic detectors reacted briskly whenever he experimentally hurt himself. Also, at the precise moment he and his girlfriend were having orgasmic sex, in a forest eighty miles away, the plant reactions sent the needles off the dial! This says remarkable things about plants.

But don't forget, it says something amazing about us: we are a sphere of energetic influence at the very least 160 miles across[2]. Of course if this is a true non-locational effect, instead of a field force effect, distance is of no matter. Sauvin and his plant pals could be a million miles apart.

The thing is scientific scrutiny of non-locational quantum events and biological energy is enabling us to re-evaluate older Oriental and other models of health, such as vitalism and entelechy.

Often we find surprising concordance with these older, colorful models, and the realization is gradually dawning in the West that other models are not arcane or naïve constructs born out of ignorance but simply strange words attached to a very precise and more or less demonstrable and accurate body of knowledge.

This chapter proposes to visit some of these other energy-based models. Each has aspects which we will certainly need on our journey into the exciting world of *Medicine Beyond*.

Let me start with the acupuncture model.

THE CHINESE MODEL

Chinese philosophy, upon which Traditional Chinese Medicine (TCM) is naturally based, recognized an underlying ultimate reality which unifies everything. It was known as *Tao*, but this should not be confused with the later use of the same term by Confucius and his followers, meaning 'a path in life' or a code of conduct. In its original sense Tao means something very like our quantum field or zero-point energy; it is seen as something uniquely dynamic in character, flowing, ever-changing, creative and continuous. Thus the whole basis of TCM is energy and information; it is definitely not a substance-based medical model.

Tao also has the quality of being somewhat reflexive and circular—that is, coming back on itself, repeating endlessly rather than being linear. 'Returning is the motion of the Tao,' says the great classic *Tao Te Ching* by Lao Tzu, which also says 'Going far means returning'. This too reminds us of the new physics, which is teaching us a new reality that is flexible, flowing, reflexive and certainly non-linear. Effects become their own causes.

The well-known symbol the *Tai-Ch'i T'u* shows these several elements: change, movement, dark and light, circular, returning and complementary balance.

The two dots symbolize the fact that when one reaches the outer limit of a certain trend it must then reverse and come back on itself; each form or event contains the seeds of its own opposite.

That's an awful lot of philosophy in one small motif!

Ancient Chinese medical theory is really a whole gestalt (composite) and it is somewhat artificial to separate out the parts. Life energy is called *Ch'i* and it flows in and around the body, constantly changing, interacting and influencing the physical domain. Blockages and disruption of the free flow of Ch'i is seen as the basis of disease. Other aspects of TCM include balance of energies (*yin* and *yang*), the five key elements (earth, air, water, wood and metal), the body clock (different organs dominant at different hours of the day) and the concept of Earth energies, or Feng Shui, interacting with all in a harmonious totality.

But what we are most concerned with here is acupuncture, the medical art of unblocking and balancing the flow of *Ch'i* energy through the meridians, or invisible energy channels, which run through and around the body. The practice of acupuncture goes back over 4,000 years.

In fact I have revealed amazing look-up research I did in Sri Lanka that suggests that acupuncture may have arisen there, perhaps as long ago as 20,000 years BC[3].

But its great flowering was the publication of a book called Huang *Ti Nei Ching* around 400 BC (The Yellow Emperor's Classic of Internal Medicine) available in translation by Ilza Veith[4]. The use of fine metal needles, inserted at key points in the body in order to stimulate Ch'i, was evidently first introduced about this time also.

WHAT IS CH'I?

Ch'i is the word used to denote the vital breath or energy which pervades and animates all the cosmos. This sounds similar to the quantum information field or vacuum in which virtual particles come and go. Understanding the manifestation of Ch'i is central to TCM. It is also a key concept in which our Medicine Beyond models come into direct contact with ancient wisdom.

There are easy parallels to draw between earlier descriptions of quantum probability fields and texts about Ch'i:

> When the Ch'i condenses, its visibility becomes apparent so that these are then seen as shapes (of individual things). When it disperses, its visibility is no longer apparent and there are no shapes. At the time of its condensation, can one say otherwise than this is temporary? But at its time of dispersing, can one hastily say that it is then non-existent?[5]

This is a brilliant insight into the way that particles form and vanish alternately in the quantum probability field. How could the author of this ancient text know that, in centuries to come, physics would show that indeed the cosmos—far from being a vacuum containing fixed matter—would be seen instead as pervaded with information fields which cause 'matter' (virtual particles) to come and go as they need when interacting with something else?

Again, our understanding of the true nature of disease turns on this point: if information energy of a disease is present but the disease not apparent, is it truly manifest? Or do we have to wait until structure alters and decays before we allow ourselves to be interested in healing? It is a crucial question, since now with *Medicine Beyond* we are able to see the forward projection of disease, *before it becomes apparent*.

WHAT ARE MERIDIANS?

In the human body Ch'i flows through discrete pathways called meridians and these affect the vitality and function of the organs. There have been many attempts to explain the nature of acupuncture meridians. At the last count there were some twenty different theories, which tells us that the problem has not been solved yet.

It is accepted, however, that a "blockage" of flow in a meridian will result in a malfunction of any organ through which it passes. It is worth pointing out here that a meridian passes through more than one organ and a disturbance in the meridian need not be confined to that organ alone. Thus for example the gallbladder meridian transects the canine tooth (eye tooth), upper and lower, as it passes across the face. An abscess in these teeth can cause gall-bladder dysfunction and vice versa.

Not only that, but we can bring in the 'organ clock' notion described in the *Nei Ching*. The gall-bladder meridian is dominant between 11 p.m. and 1 a.m. Thus the toothache due to a canine is likely to be at its worst around midnight. Observations of this sort often astonish patients but are simple when you have the right biological model.

THE WINDS OF CHANGE

The meridians have been a source of great fascination to doctors and laymen alike in the West. Because of the craving for anatomical certainty, there has been a continued search to find some kind of structural explanation for the existence of meridians. They are clearly not nerve channels, blood vessels or any kind of duct system. Since no obvious anatomical structures mimic the described pathways of meridians, the tendency for Western science has been to dismiss the concept as something fanciful; this has not been helped by the choice of unusual metaphorical names given certain points such as *The Sea of Energy* (Conception Vessel 6), *The Marshes of the Wind* (Bladder 12) and *The Door of the Mental* (Heart 7).

Gradually the climate has changed however. During the 1960s and 1970s the world's attention was increasingly drawn to Chinese traditions, partly accelerated by President Nixon's widely broadcast visit to mainland China. At around that time we first saw dramatic TV footage of major operations being carried out with no more anesthetic than needles placed at exactly the right places in the skin.

188

It was obvious to all and sundry that acupuncture worked, and worked at least as well as Western scientific medicine in some surprising ways, no matter how alien the rhetoric and however unfamiliar the mechanics and model.

Since then, science has begun probing to see if it can establish at least some objective evidence for the Chinese model (evidence, that is, within its own paradigm and criteria of judgment).

We seem to have made a certain amount of progress.

THE ESTABLISHING OF MERIDIANS

There are at least four possibilities I should point out to the reader:

1. Some as-yet-unknown mechanism.

2. The concept that the energy somehow follows existing anatomical structures, diving into the interstices between cells, through connective tissue, along fascia lines and so on, but not necessarily nerves, blood vessels etc.

3. Standing waves in a fractal-based anatomy, which need not necessarily correspond to anatomical structures.

4. The "liquid crystal" model I described on page 123. Collagen is a remarkable substance which has piezo-electric potential and is more than capable of distributing energy and information swiftly through the body.

Let's take each in turn:

As I reported in *Virtual Medicine*, in February 1937 the prestigious *British Medical Journal* carried an article by Sir Thomas Lewis describing a hitherto unknown network of cutaneous nerves[6].

He called it the 'nocifensor system' and deduced, from his experiments, that it was an independent cutaneous nerve system, unrelated to known pathways and unconnected to the autonomic nervous system. It was composed, not of nerve fibers, but a network of thin channels, similar to meridians.

This may have been the very first Western science peep at the TCM model!

The second model continues in a more modern style, from an article published by researchers at the US Science Research Institute. Their proposal is that the meridian system mostly operates via interstices in or between other physiological systems; in other words the pathways, however indistinct, can be found flowing through connective tissues, electrolytes, cells and proteins; the electrolytes provide rich fluids and ions for processing, transportation or propagation of information, matter and energy in the meridians[7].

This echoes an earlier paper (1985) from Pierre de Vernejoul at the University of Paris. He carried out a definitive and much-quoted experiment. He used a radioactive marker, technetium 99m, which he injected into subjects at classic acupuncture points. He then used gamma-camera imaging to track the subsequent movement of the isotope. He was able to show that the tracer migrated along the classic meridian lines, travelling quite quickly: a distance of 30 cm in 4–6 minutes[8].

As a control he made a number of random injections into the skin (not at acupuncture points) and also injected the tracer directly into veins and lymphatic channels. There was no significant migration of the tracer at other sites than an acupuncture point.

What this simple but helpful study proved is that meridians are definitely real 'vessels' but they conform to no macroscopic anatomical structures whatever. Somehow the flow takes place but is not a function of any known channel.

I rebut and deplore the squabbling and pseudo-critique of Vernejoul's paper that has appeared on Wikipedia (remember a wiki, by definition, can be edited by anyone, ignorant or knowledgeable). The basis of the attack seems be that it couldn't have worked, so obviously it didn't. They berate Vernejoul for failing to provide adequate data and then quote someone's opinion that he photographed lymph vessels, without citing any data whatever to justify such a wild claim. Numerous "failed" attempts at replication have been cited; supporting papers which replicated Vernejoul's work are virtually ignored or given only in very small print.

So if meridians are not nerve-conducting channels or other anatomically visible vessels, what are they? How is the energy conducted?

There are two up-to-date theories and they are not mutually exclusive, by any means.

FRACTAL MODEL

The fractal-field model of biological systems and structures would tell us that meridians are wave cycles in the coherent field of the organism, with projections on the body surface at the acupuncture points.

We can actually view the points as sites where an informational exchange is taking place between the organism and the environment. The goal of this exchange is the adaptation of an organism to the environment's changeable conditions[9].

Fractals, it must be understood, enable the exchange of information, without an expenditure of energy.

Please do not suppose this is a fancy dressed-up model using pseudo-science language to disguise New Age whimsy. The matter is discussed at some length on PubMed and serious science papers are discussing the topic.

One paper I found described as "plausible" a pain relief mechanism based on the wave theory of a fractal continuum and how it interacts with the neuro-vascular network (brain and blood). The authors theorized two possible explanations why acupuncture needling could be effective against pain.

If the impedance of the meridian *hugely mismatches* with that of the brain after acupuncture, then the traveling wave of the pain signal will be largely reflected back and only partially transmitted to the brain, hence pain relief can be achieved.

If the impedance of the meridian *entirely matches* that of the pain source after acupuncture, then the pain wave would appear to be in phase or "nonexistent" to the brain, hence analgesia can be achieved.

The former mechanism can be used to explain the relief for chronic pain and the latter one for acute pain[10].

Note that, according to the principles of fractalization, an organism creates a lot of quantum copies of itself with projections on the skin, mucous membranes etc. This accords well with recent discoveries and intervention systems, which claim there are body images on different areas of the skin.

In fact one may posit that it's all a significant hologram effect, where any small part contains the information of the whole. Certainly, the "projection" concept is explicable only in terms of information science, not biological science, neurology or hormones, etc. information.

These innovative mini "projection" models are called *micro-acupuncture systems*: the best-known by far is Auriculo-therapy (Nogier). Others (there are many) include Su Jock-therapy (Park Jae Woo), ECIWO-therapy (Zhang Ying Qing), oral acupuncture (J. Gleditch), iridodiagnostics, nasal therapy, different modifications of scalp therapy (including Yamamoto New Scalp Acupuncture-YNSA), vaginal acupuncture (H. Buchheit), clavicle needle injection and numerous others.

LIQUID CRYSTAL MODEL

The second big contender for energy and information transmission via channels and meridians is conduction of energy signals via the collagen fibers of the connective tissues, as already mentioned in Chapter 7.

As the name suggests, connective tissue fills in between the main organs and layers. There is thus a continuum of liquid crystalline water-bound collagen fibers running throughout the whole body. Recent studies have shown that these are not just mechanical fibers but that they have dielectric and conductive properties that make them sensitive to pressure, pH, local ionic composition and surrounding electromagnetic fields. In fact these collagen fibers, like a network mesh of fine electrical fibrils, form the ideal conductor medium in which many of the electromagnetic phenomena described in this book may take place.

Remarkably, and very conveniently for us, this network of semi-conductor material can enforce a one-direction flow on the electrical current, acting rather like one-way gates called diodes. This is interesting because energy is said to flow in only one direction through each channel; the Ch'i passes up one meridian, down the next, up a third, and so on. Once again, scientific testing has validated ancient wisdom, as described in the original *Nei Ching* text.

It is important to note that the acupuncture system is traditionally looked on as an active *flowing* system for mobilizing energy and for intercommunication throughout the body. Thus it is unlikely to be completely understood in terms of the *passive responses* of skin conductance to electrodermal stimulation. So the most important correlate of activity is going to be the body's DC field, as investigated by Robert Becker[12]. As Becker showed us, this DC body field is involved in morphogenesis during development, in wound-healing and regeneration subsequent to injury.

The direct currents making up the body field are not due to charged ions but instead depend on a mode of semi-conduction characteristic of solid state systems (Becker, 1961). The acupuncture points, it is speculated, may act as "booster amplifiers" of the very weak currents that typically flow along the meridians.

The collagen network is everywhere in contact with the intracellular chemical fluid medium; this matrix in total provides an excitable continuum for rapid, coherent intercommunication throughout the whole living system of a human body. It also reaches all parts of the body, even where there is no nerve supply.

ACUPUNCTURE POINTS

In tandem with the concept of energy meridians comes that of acupuncture "points". These are spots on the skin where the energy wells upwards from within and the energy escapes. Blocked points are where needles are placed, to stimulate the flow of energy so that healing can take place...

But what are these points exactly?

The first extensive investigation was by my friend William A. Tiller of the Department of Material Sciences and Engineering at Stanford University in California. During the 1970s Tiller and other material scientists were investigating the properties of skin to determine the requirements for prosthetic replacement skin, which could be used to treat burns and other skin graft procedures. Tiller studied elasticity, resistance, permeability, chemistry and many other biological properties of skin.

Acupuncture points typically represent local maxima in conductance, elevated by a factor of 10 to 100, compared with the surrounding skin[13].

Tiller has presented several models to account for the electrical properties of acupuncture points based on charge movements and selective permeability of ions through different layers of the skin.

Research showed that certain points on the skin had much lower resistance than elsewhere. They soon surmised that what they had located were acupuncture points. Tiller studied the dynamics of acupuncture points. The data obtained during these investigations revealed a complex, changing system of information. His model grew to include several electrical properties, such as resistance, conductance and capacitance:

- Conductance is the reverse of resistance and measures how well electrons flow.

- Capacitance is caused when charge builds up across an electrically resistant barrier; there are several such layers in the skin.

Tiller pointed to at least two layers of the skin: the epidermal and dermal layers as two domains in series, each with its capacitance and resistance with very different response (relaxation) times. There is a fast component associated with the dermis, and a low frequency component, the epidermis. This model identifies the differing electrical properties of the dermis and epidermis, which could account for some, though not all, of the responses of the acupuncture system to electrical stimulation[14].

Tiller has further suggested that the fast conductance might be due to hydrogen ions, as the DC voltage supplied in testing was sufficient to ionize water.

All of this means that skin conductivity is far more subtle than just the properties of a wire cable. Many factors play a part, the cells of the different skin layers influencing the diffusion and permeability of electrically-charged ions such as sodium, potassium and chloride ions. Tiller began to refer to acupuncture points as 'windows of information'. According to his model, the health status of the organ in question affects the concentration and diffusion of ions at the points along the meridian, and thus the rate of electron flow, which is what EAV measures.

We need far more studies in this area. Unfortunately, research in the alternative medical field is grossly underfunded. We are lucky, therefore, when a leading figure from an academic institution chances to become interested in this way (Bill tells me they would have loved to get rid of him once he started his holistic investigations but he had tenure and could not be removed just for political reasons!)

THE ACUVISION

Let me contribute here, with a report on an amazing machine in my possession. It's called the Acuvision and was developed by Romen Avagyan from Moscow. Avagyan got his PhD in radio and quantum physics in 1977 from Moscow State University.

The Acuvision uses high frequencies and high-voltage electronics, which in the presence of a dielectric, causes the acupuncture points to become illuminated and visible on the skin. This clearly hearkens back to the cellular emissions of biophotons, as described by Fritz Popp. The points are about the size of a pin-head and can only be seen in a darkened room.

It is thrilling and eerie to see the living body behaving like a lamp and throwing out blue light through real skin "pores". Apparently there are many more points than appear in classic texts or even Voll's extended system. It is of note that the Nogier ear acupuncture points stand out particularly well (see next section).

To date this device is no more than an interesting medical curiosity. Avagyan is of the opinion that this phenomenon can be further exploited for diagnostic potential by measuring the intensity of light emitted by the points. It appears that they glow more intensely where there is excess Ch'i energy and are dimmer when the energy is lower than it should be. This is logical and fits in with everything else I have written in these pages.

NOGIER'S

As an example of a comprehensive micro-acupuncture system, let me take up Paul Nogier's auriculo-acupuncture. Strange though it may seem to some, Nogier's method has been in use successfully for many decades, for pain relief, stopping smoking and changing of eating habits in obesity. It has become widely adopted, even in China, where it has sparked a wave of research into the apparent embryonic connections.

French neurosurgeon Dr. Paul Nogier based his system upon the idea of an image of a fetus projected onto the external ear (see diagram). It includes some 200 points.

Historically the Chinese, Arabs, Romanies, Hindus and some Europeans advocated needling a point on the ear lobe to remedy "eye deficiencies". Even today some European doctors recommend the insertion of a gold or silver earring to stimulate this spot continuously in cases of eye "deficiency" (whatever that is). Currently auriculo-acupuncture is much used for anesthesia, obesity and addictions such as smoking. An ancient Indian text, the Suchi Veda (which translated means 'Science of Needle Piercing') gives detailed techniques and points for needling the ears. It is interesting that the Arabs should use the ear mainly for the treatment of low back pain and kidney trouble, when it is known that the ear is seen by the Chinese as the outward 'flowering' of the kidneys[15].

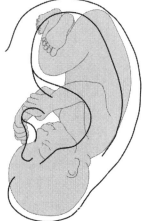

The purpose is not to discuss the method in detail here but to offset it somewhat against what was discussed earlier about the proving of meridians. If Nogier's theory is correct and there are connections from the ear points to each individual organ, we find ourselves very unsettled on the idea that meridians are anatomically proven. Indeed, it rather opens the debate up again. What had Nogier discovered? There is no arguing his powers of observation; many other people have confirmed the efficacy and accuracy of his correlations. Rather, I think, Nogier's idea is one of neurological energy conduits projecting into the body field and so influencing it.

But it does not seem to rely on the concept of independent energy channels running through the body. That's probably true of all micro-acupuncture systems; unless there are an infinite number of multiple channels, each represented repeatedly on body parts. So perhaps these micro-systems are pointing us more towards the fractal model?

Auriculo-acupuncture is another example of a "structure unseen" and a very welcome contribution to the body of knowledge I call *Medicine Beyond*!

THE CHAKRA MODEL

Now let's go to the ancient Ayurvedic healing tradition, which is considerably older than TCM, indeed is probably the oldest surviving model of health and disease. It has certainly stood the test of time and therefore deserves to be accorded respect. It would also prompt the wise scientist to begin asking what is workable about a system which has endured so long.

For the longest time, the Indian tradition of health has been that of *prana* energy concentrated in energy vortexes attached to the body, called chakras.

The universal energy, which the Chinese call Ch'i, is here known as *prana*. Instead of the meridians, the Indian system introduces the concept of chakras. These are the gates or channels by which the life-giving universal *prana* energy enters (and leaves) our bodies, thus influencing our bodily functions and vitality.

I have to give my opinion, which is that the chakra system seems to be more of a belief system than an established scientific structure in the way that acupuncture meridians have become a measurable reality. That's not to say chakras don't exist. But I don't think it's a mandatory model of health and reality; more a sort of "option".

But why seven? I'm always suspicious when a system has the "perfect" number. Seven has always been seen as the heavenly number, like the original seven planets, the seven deadly sins, seven days of the week, seven colors of the rainbow, seven notes on a musical scale, seven seas and seven continents.

Snow White ran off to live with seven dwarves, there were seven brides for seven brothers, Shakespeare described the seven ages of man, and Sinbad the Sailor had seven voyages. And when Ian Fleming was looking for a code number for James Bond, he didn't go for 006 or 008. Only 007 had the right ring[16].

Do you get my point? It's a suspiciously "correct" number.

I am not saying that those who can "see" chakras are deluded. In fact all through the book I have made it clear that anyone will see what they want to see. This is in fact the true nature of reality, rather than some objective sounding board. I will be introducing a completely different and extremely plausible Western model in the next chapter which, in a sense, trumps other Eastern interpretations.

There are said to be seven main chakras. Each one of these has a correspondence with anatomical structures, notably a nerve plexus and an endocrine gland. The names and correspondence of these main chakras are as follows:

CHAKRA	NERVE PLEXUS	ENDOCRINE GLAND
Base	Sacro-coccygeal	gonads
Sacral	Sacral	Leydic cells in gonads
Solar plexus	Solar plexus	adrenals
Heart	Heart plexus	thymus
Throat	Cervical ganglia	thyroid
Head	Hypothalamus/pituitary	pituitary
Crown	Cerebral cortex	pineal

NADIS

What is less widely known is that Ayurvedic texts refer also to other energy centers associated with major joint structures of the body, like the knees, ankles, elbows, etc. These are called *nadis*. Taken altogether there are over 360 chakras of the body. These in turn are said to be joined together by a network of etheric channels called nadis, which are interwoven with the nervous system. Thus, unlike the TCM meridian system, chakras and nadis display considerable correspondence with anatomical structures.

The best work to date seems to be that of Japanese psychic and clinical psychologist Hiroshi Motoyama. He is also a Shinto priest and a yogi adept of some ability. At his research faculty, the Institute for Religious Psychology, he developed the AMI scanner, an acronym for Apparatus for Measuring the Functional Conditions of Meridians and their Corresponding Internal Organs.

Motoyama also claimed he had developed a 'Chakra Instrument' able to detect minute electrical, magnetic and optical variables in the immediate environment shell of the study subject[17].

The detectors have to be used in a light-proof room, shielded by lead sheeting on the walls and lined with foil which is grounded, to keep the electrical potential at zero. A 10 cm copper disc plus a photovoltaic cell (which generates electricity when light is detected) is positioned in front of the chakra being 'sensed', off the body. The magnetic detector is simply placed on the floor beside the subject—in other words within his or her magnetic field.

Changes in readings are processed and stored by a multichannel recorder, along with a number of conventional variables such as respiration rate, ECG and galvanic skin response (similar to a lie detector). Using questionnaires and evaluating disease susceptibility and organ function, and intercalating that with his 'detector' readings, Motoyama claims to have had some degree of success in objectifying the chakras. However the obvious criticism seems to be that he is depending heavily on the correlation between chakras and nerve plexuses. He could arguably be measuring nothing more than autonomic nerve activity, not energy vortexes in the ether!

SPIN

On the subject of vortices, this is probably a good opportunity to describe the phenomenon that practitioners using the systems described later in the book call 'spin'. In physics there is a phenomenon known as 'optical rotation', which comes from the helical structure of crystalline solids, or helical molecules in liquids and solutions. Spin is designated either right or left (*dextro-* or *laevo-*).

What practitioners come up with is that healthy blood and saliva have a right-spin; urine and feces have left-spin. When a person is under considerable duress or experiencing geopathic stress, this reverses.

Is it relevant? Certainly. Many patients with 'reverse spin' will not recover therapeutically until the spin is back to normal. The truth may be that spin-reversal makes one susceptible to outside events, such as geopathic stress, rather than vice versa.

But spin could have far wider implications. In 1995 I attended a conference in St Petersburg, Russia, in common with many other colleagues from the Scientific and Medical Network (a group of doctors and scientists dedicated to finding out more about the metaphysical and transcendent aspects of creation). There we heard lecture after lecture from leading Russian scientists about the properties of what are known as torsion fields.

Matter, we now know, has three basic physical properties: charge, mass and spin. Each of these gives rise to a characteristic field. Charge creates an electromagnetic field, mass gives rise to a gravitational field, and spin generates what we call a torsion field. It was high-level stuff, but what we learned is that torsion fields are different in having instantaneous effects at all points. Gravity fields (if they exist at all) have a distance effect, and electromagnetic propagation has a time (frequency) effect, even though the ruling speed of light is pretty fast! Torsion fields, almost by definition, have neither a distance nor a time effect. In other words, we were hearing about yet another information model which could explain telepathy and other supposedly etheric phenomena.

I was particularly pleased at the St Petersburg conference to hear through our discussions that thought could almost certainly be imprinted in space outside our skulls and left there for others to 'walk into'. There was a perfectly scientific explanation for certain strange and creepy feelings many of us experience from time to time. It could be the basis of déjà vu, though my *Tunnels of Time* project means I am heavily committed to the validity of past lives.

The potential for health effects from torsion fields, especially some of the strange outer-limit manifestations that you will read about in this text, is of course considerable. Readers will be able to work out many ways in which this obscure but enriching model could apply to the body-mind-spirit composite we call our Being.

CHAPTER 12

Western Energy Systems

It took less than an hour to make the atoms, a few hundred million years to make the stars and planets, but five billion years to make man!

— George Gamow, *The Creation of the Universe*

Now we are going to take a look at Western energy systems. It has long been a contention of mine that energy medicine in the West will not simply be a watery makeover of acupuncture or Ayurvedic medicine. We have our own brand of brilliance: technology!

How far back do you want to go in history? As I wrote in *Virtual Medicine*, you could pick up the threads at least as far back as the Ancient Egyptians. The Ebers papyrus gives clear instructions for what we would now call "hands on energy healing". It is entirely possible that the Bible stories of Jesus healing people recount a form of beneficial energy transfer.

Schiegl also describes the technique of *shunomatism*, named after a woman known as Abishag from Shuna who slept with King David to bring him back to health[1].

The concept of lying down with someone ill in order to take on their evil humors is told of in other tales as well. According to one story, Lady Bath of England slept with two young women; she recovered and they were left drained and ill. One might imagine other explanations for this type of recovery, but it is entirely consistent with Tantric teachings of energy transference.

The great Middle Age physician who called himself Paracelsus (Theophrastus Philippus Bombastus von Hohenheim, 1493 – 1541), had theories of health and disease based on an astral fluid, which he called *archea* and which sounds to me remarkably like the quantum field.

Paracelsus virtually founded the modern discipline of toxicology, presumably in the wake of Lucrezia Borgia's murderous antics. He is also known as a revolutionary for insisting upon using observations of nature, rather than looking to ancient texts, in open and radical defiance of medical practice of his day. He is also credited for giving zinc its name, calling it Zincum. Modern psychology often also credits him for being the first to note that some diseases may be rooted in psychological illness[2].

In every way (except tactfulness) Paracelsus was a visionary and brilliant man, centuries ahead of his time and someone who is still revered, and rightly so, by all practitioners of holistic and spiritually-oriented therapies. His major tract *De Origine Morborum Invisibilum* (The Invisible Causes of Diseases) nicely presaged the title for my own *Medicine Beyond*! I like to think he would be pleased to see the revelations that science offers the true-healing medicine I have described in this book.

ANTON MESMER

The other early guru who must be introduced in any review of electromagnetic medicine and biology is Anton Mesmer. Born in 1734, he properly belongs to the modern scientific (post-Newton) age. Few gurus have ever made such an impression on their era or paid so dearly for assaulting the vagaries of medical orthodoxy. Even today his name is synonymous with smoke-and-mirrors mystification - to "mesmerize" someone often means to somehow overthrow their common sense and harness their credulity. Yet this is to woefully misinterpret Mesmer's work.

Mesmer took some of his inspiration from earlier thinkers, including Paracelsus. He worked on energetic healing using systematic movements of the hands. Judging by the enormous numbers of people who came to him, he must have been very successful. He recognized a healing force of some kind coming through his hands; he even found he could transfer it indirectly through other individuals. He invented the term "animal magnetism." Unfortunately there was no way in his day to measure such a force field and he was ultimately discredited. Yet he was right, as we shall see. Today, just before the close of the 20th century, we are able to visualize the energies that he could sense and describe.

In Mesmer's book, *Report on the Discovery of Animal Magnetism*, he describes 27 axiomatic principles, which many enlightened doctors today would consider to remain valid. Only the terminology has changed. Here are a few of these key principles:

1. There is a mutual influence of celestial bodies, the Earth and human bodies.

2. The medium for this influence is a universally present and continuous fluid, which permeates everywhere. It is fine beyond comparison and, by its nature, is capable of receiving, spreading, and communicating all influences of movement (the quantum field).

3. The mutual influence is subject to laws of mechanics that are as yet unknown (quantum mechanics).

4. The living body feels the alternative effects of this fluid: by penetrating the nerves, these are directly affected (neuro-peptide release; current model for much successful therapy).

Again, Mesmer was a man far ahead of his time and we have to move to the 20th century for further significant advances.

THE HUMAN AURA

People claim to be able to see many layers of aura, which they attribute to the mental, emotional, astral and other aspects of the individual's composite being. I can only say that not everyone can do this and therefore it is not truly objective. Further confusion is added by the fact that even I can see 'auras' around buildings, rocks and other formations, if the lighting and climatic conditions are right. It's not that big a skill.

With this in mind, what objective evidence is there for such a thing as an aura? In 1911 Dr. Walter Kilner, working at a London hospital, published a book entitled *The Human Atmosphere or the Aura Made Visible with the Aid of Chemical Screens*. He invented the Kilner screen, which was effectively a pair of glasses in which double screens held a liquid containing dicyanogen blue dissolved in alcohol.

Kilner described three zones around the body:

1. a thin dark layer close to the skin

2. a more vaporous layer, with rays pointing away from the skin

3. a tenuous outer layer about 6 inches across, with varying density and colors.

He found that this 'aura' would change with age, sex, mental energy and health factors. He was able to see shadows in the aura and could tentatively diagnose diseases such as hepatitis, cancer, appendicitis, epilepsy and psychological states.

Nowadays we can buy Kilner 'aura glasses' on the Internet. These are glasses with specially coated lenses which allow through only certain colors and screen out incident light. Some practice and concentration is required, but by all accounts most people can master it.

PHOTOGRAPHS CANNOT LIE: OR CAN THEY?

In 1939 Semyon D. Kirlian, a Russian technician, was repairing hospital equipment when he noticed something strange. It was another case of the right mind prepared to benefit from a chance event; Kirlian thought it through properly and went on, with his wife, to develop what we now call Kirlian photography.

What he had discovered was that by the interaction of a very high-frequency electric discharge and a photographic plate, energy imprints of living organisms can be revealed on the film. The subject, enclosed in a light-tight bag, is in contact with a charged metal plate backed onto a photographic emulsion. At the moment of discharge, high-energy electrons jump from the plate to the subject, resulting in ionization of a thin layer of air between the two. The photographic emulsion is excited in the normal way and can be developed to reveal what may best be described as a visualization of the subject's energy field (which may or may not be the same as the aura).

Further research by scientists at the Kirov State University of Kazakhstan extended the discovery. They found that the light emanated was polarized (blue or red-yellow). This seems to accord with the traditional Chinese view of yin and yang energies[3]. These scientists began to refer to the visible energy shell beyond the body surface that was being recorded as the bioplasmic body.

Testing showed it was affected by atmospheric conditions and cosmic events, such as sunspots. The Kirlians had already noticed rapid and pronounced changes in the energy photographed, caused by emotional disturbance. Increased light seemed to pour out with anger and (perhaps surprisingly) exhaustion. So here we seem to be looking at an actual visual confirmation of Burr's L-Fields (page 113).

Experiments with plants and animals showed that each had a unique, defining energy field. What is most impressive is that even if half a leaf is cut away, the Kirlian photograph still shows the full field, the whole leaf energy appearing to be present even when the cut-away particles or mass is absent. Could it also be that the leaf 'ghost' photograph is defining one of Sheldrake's morphogenic fields? If not, what holds the energy vibration in place? It must surely be an information field of some kind.

The Kazakhstan workers also tried to record objectively the bio-physical changes that may take place in the hands of healers when treating a patient. What was visualized on the print when the hands of the healer were held close to a patient under the Kirlian camera was a narrow stream of energy, concentrating into an intense band which streamed into the area of the illness. What appeared to be happening was the transfer of energy from the bioplasmic body of the healer to that of the patient[4]. Life force energy is finite otherwise we would not die. Healers who use their personal energy can become prematurely exhausted when older as they have given a lot of their life energy away to others.

Other applications of the photography, to demonstrate energetic transference of vital energy to water or seeds which had been held in the hands of a talented healer, were also successful. Photographs of manufactured or junk food show that it lacks the vital energy field which is present in and around fresh or whole food. The conclusion seems too obvious to comment upon.

CROSSOVER

In 1953 Dr. M. K. Gaikin, a Leningrad surgeon, made an interesting discovery. He realized that the position of the main flares on the skin, which are characteristic of Kirlian photographs of humans, did not correspond to anything anatomical—but that they did appear at classical acupuncture points! This effect mimics the *Acuvision*, developed by Romen Avagyan (page 195).

For a long time Kirlian photography had mainly the status of a party trick or an engaging exhibit at psychic fairs and carnivals, where practitioners charge a small fee for a 'picture of your aura'. Ironically, most of these aura-simulation cameras are not true Kirlians. There has to be direct contact with the plate, impossible at even a tiny distance or through a lens.

But there was always hope that Kirlian photography would be able to offer the means to diagnose disease and initial studies suggested that Kirlian imaging could reveal information about the state of a person's health. For example, it was possible to evaluate the general level and character of the organism's physiological activity judging by the size and shape of the fingertip and toe captures, as well as to assess the state of various systems of the organism.

Today I can report two major systems of diagnostics based on Kirlian effect: Peter Mandel's system of Energy Emission Analysis (EEA) using a high-voltage analog camera and dark-room technology and more recently, Dr. Konstantin Korotkov's Gas Discharge Visualization (GDV), using a camera of his own design and sophisticated software to interpret and display the camera image as data sets.

EVALUATING REMEDIES

The Journal of Alternative and Complementary Medicine carried an article in 2003, showing—under blinded, controlled conditions—that it may be possible to evaluate homeopathic remedies, using GDV techniques or similar[5].

The experiment used 30c potencies of three homeopathically-prepared remedies from different kingdoms, for example, *Natrum muriaticum* (mineral), *Pulsatilla* (plant), and *Lachesis* (animal), dissolved in a 20% alcohol-water solvent versus two different control solutions (that is, solvent with untreated lactose/sucrose pellets and unsuccussed solvent alone).

GDV measurements, involving application of a brief electrical impulse at four different voltage levels, were performed over 10 successive images on each of 10 drops from each bottle (total 400 images per test solution per voltage).

The procedure generated measurable images at the two highest voltage levels (17kV and 24kV), which differed from controls.

Moreover the journal *Homeopathy* reported in 2008 on the use of high voltage plasma images of high dilutions of sodium chloride (30C). Thus dilutions, even beyond the Avogadro number, clearly differed from 'pure' water and the action of sodium chloride on the electrical properties of water is inverted at high dilution[6].

So the Kirlian effect is gradually moving over into the science arena.

THE CATALYST OF POWER - THE ASSEMBLAGE POINT OF MAN

I now come to an energy model which is "Western" in the sense that it is not from Asia but rather from the North American Native Tradition. I feel sure it will greatly appeal to many readers who have not encountered it. And for the detailed description which follows, I am indebted to my friend Jon Whale, director of Electronic Gem Therapy Ltd. who could fairly be described as the world's number one scientific expert on this topic.

I'm talking about the human "Assemblage Point".

Like many practitioners, I had never heard of this model, until it was published in the journal *Positive Health*, in the October 1996 issue entitled: *Core Energy Surgery for the Electromagnetic Body*. They have since reported that this article was the most outstandingly popular and ever-in-demand article their journal has ever published[7].

I was intrigued and spotted that the author, Jon Whale lived in Arnside, Cumbria (England), only a few miles from my own home at that time, near Lake Windermere. I could not resist visiting him and spent a very fascinating half day learning a whole raft of new ideas, not confined to explanations of the Assemblage Point, but including the scientific principle of electronic gem therapy.

I learned to move the assemblage point to a healthier position, as Jon taught me, and it remains a fascinating model of health, much more realistic and rewarding for me than the chakra system.

I must here caution the reader that the description of this process given by Carlos Castaneda in his book *The Fire from Within* is not only unhelpful but definitely misleading. I have reason to believe that what he describes is a special variant of the technique used by shaman Tom 'Two Bears' Wilson (on whom he may have modeled Don Juan, the sorcerer). This was an atypical version because Castaneda himself was in bad shape!

In any case there continues real doubt about what Castaneda's sources were; he was certainly good at hiding them. Indeed there are many who consider his whole evocation of shamanism a fraud. The years before his death hardly add to his image; in the words of Mick Brown, 'Rather than dying the immaculate death of the sorcerer, it's suggested that the sorcerer's apprentice died a frail, paranoid and angry old man lashing out at the world with lawsuits'[8].

Over the years 1996 and 1997 Jon Whale published two more comprehensive articles in *Positive Health*, detailing the medical symptomatology and dangers of unhealthy Assemblage Point locations 3-part series and the methods for correction. The following year Jon received a litigious restraining fax from Carlos Castaneda's offices. It stated that only Castaneda had the rights to the medical applications of the Assemblage Point. The irony is that Carlos Castaneda failed to provide his readers with any methods or details on how to correct an unhealthy or detrimentally located Assemblage Point and besides the work denied had already been done.

In fact Castaneda had no such rights. He was far from the discoverer.

MEETING SWIFTDEER

A decade previously (September 1988) Jon Whale had met with a well-known North American Indian Shaman called Harley "SwiftDeer" Reagan. SwiftDeer employed large specimens of machined and polished quartz crystals within his Shamanic work and teachings. At that meeting Jon Whale showed SwiftDeer one of his early prototype electronic gem therapy instruments. SwiftDeer said that he was all in favor of combining electronics with crystals and gem stones for the purpose of increasing their healing power. See Chapter 22 for the fulfillment of this.

SwiftDeer also explained the human Assemblage Point and demonstrated how he used a large rose quartz crystal to shift it to the center of the chest. This was a ritualistic practice used at important events, such as before entering a native Indian 'Sweat Lodge' ceremony.

All those present at the meeting had their Assemblage Points moved, followed by a 'Sweat Lodge' ceremony. This event was for Jon and other people present a profound experience, each person experiencing the living proof that their Assemblage Point was a life giving reality.

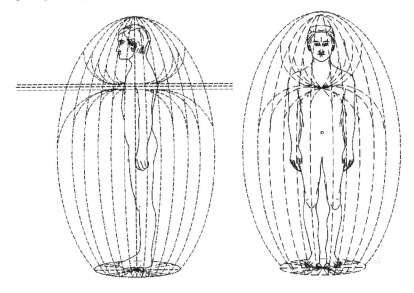

Incidentally, SwiftDeer—a real life shaman, not a fictional character—was not complimentary about Castaneda's books, intimating to Jon Whale that it was important to research, record and publish the different Assemblage Point locations relating to medical health problems; he as good as charged Jon with this important task.

SwiftDeer used 'The Sliding Shift' method to relocate the Assemblage Point described by Jon Whale below, as opposed to the back slapping method described by Castaneda. Jon Whale taught this technique directly personally to me, along with the other methods he had developed. It is neither a version of chakras nor meridians but the similarities are startling. Again we are talking of a universal life energy flowing in and around the body. But in this shamanic model there is a definite vortex coming in at the chest, an actual assemblage of energy flows (assemblage: gathering together).

Let me give here the "seven rules" which govern this model:

THE SEVEN RULES

1. At the physical, emotional, atomic and quantum level, a human being is an independent oscillating energy field. All oscillating energy fields, by virtue of the fact that they are oscillating, must have an epicenter or vortex of the rotation. The epicenter of the human energy field is called the Assemblage Point.

2. The location and entry angle of the Assemblage Point with respect to the physical body dictates the shape and distribution of the human energy field.

3. The shape and distribution of the human energy field are directly proportional to the biological energy and activity of the organs and glands in the physical body, also to the quality of the emotional energy.

4. The biological activity of the organs and glands determines the position of the Assemblage Point, and thus the shape and distribution of biological energy throughout the physical body.

5. The location and entry angle of the Assemblage Point has a direct influence over the biological activity of all of the organs and glands including the brain and these have a direct influence on the location of the Assemblage Point.

6. The location and entry angle of the Assemblage Point regulates how we feel and behave. Disease also dictates the Assemblage Point location and entry angle.

7. The way we feel and the manner in which we behave; our state of health or disease and our ability to recover is reflected in the location and entry angle of our Assemblage Point.

HOW IT WORKS OUT

Our Assemblage Point location fixes in a healthy, stationary, near-central position at around the age of seven if we are brought up in a stable home environment and positively identify with good parents. The Assemblage Point has a critical relationship with our embryonic life force.

A stable location near the center of the chest is essential for good mental and physical health.

But an unstable and displaced Assemblage Point is likely if we had a consistently negative relationship with our parents, a troubled background or having a displaced upbringing. Genetic reasons or disease can similarly produce abnormal and unstable Assemblage Points.

Sufferers of an involuntary Assemblage Point shift downwards experience that 'something' deep inside them has changed. Although they can remember how they behaved and felt before the incident, returning to their former energetic and happy self is impossible for them. That indescribable 'something' deep inside all of us that can suddenly shift following an adversity, changing our whole perception of reality and our physical health, is the location and entry angle of our Assemblage Point.

Gross misalignment of the Assemblage Point location is present in many diseases such as: depression, bipolar syndrome, paranoia, schizophrenia, drug and alcohol addiction, epilepsy, senile dementia, coma, Parkinsonism, toxicity, leukemia, cancer, AIDS, myalgic encephalomyelitis (ME or fibromyalgia), multiple sclerosis, and many others. Many of these conditions are accompanied by compromised pathology of the patient's hematology and biochemistry.

The diagram below should make the basics clear. Above center is over-stimulation, below center is depression; to the (patient's) right means anxiety/tension states (extrovert psychosis), to the left means hallucination and delusions (introvert psychosis). With this in mind, it is possible to tell, from the position of the assemblage point, a great deal about a person's energy state.

Note: The location for an average healthy woman is 2–3 inches higher than that of an average healthy man.

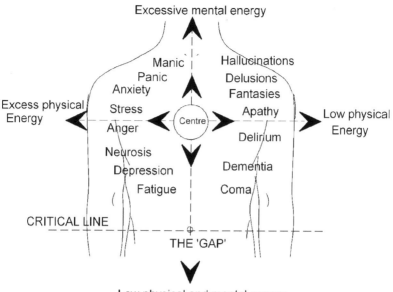

Excessive mental energy

Manic
Panic
Anxiety
Stress
Anger
Neurosis
Depression
Fatigue

Hallucinations
Delusions
Fantasies
Apathy
Delirium
Dementia
Coma

Excess physical Energy

Centre

Low physical Energy

CRITICAL LINE

THE 'GAP'

Low physical and mental energy

Locations higher than the optimum are accompanied by symptoms of too much energy: hyperactivity, anxiety, panic, insomnia and so on, along with hyper liver/adrenal activity. Attention deficit hyper activity disorder (ADHD) in children is now very common and is an example of this.

Lowered locations are accompanied with hypoactivity: the depressive illness spectrum and hypo liver/adrenal/thyroid activity.

The bipolar disorder spectrum or manic depression is accompanied by an oscillating Assemblage Point location, which switches between a high manic location and a low depressive position on the right side of the chest.

With the schizophrenic spectrum there may be several Assemblage Point locations, as often happens with the epilepsy spectrum.

DANGEROUS DROP

If the Assemblage Point drops beyond a certain distance for example, with chronic fatigue, down to or below the liver area, despite what medications or therapies are employed, it is very difficult for the individual to recover their former health and state of being. Their Assemblage Point is

212

most unlikely to return unaided to its previous healthy location. Literally the biological energy levels are too low, so preventing recovery.

Raising the Assemblage Point location and angle upwards, closer to the center of the chest, is an essential intervention in such cases. Unfortunately, accepted orthodox diagnostic and management procedures do not take the patient's Assemblage Point location into consideration.

States that can drop the assemblage point below "the gap" and into the danger zone include the following:

1. Serious accident, bereavement, disease, fever, tragedy, chronic stress or depression.

2. Distressed or oppressed childhood, rape or sexual assault, violent intimidation, kidnapping, abduction, enslavement.

3. Self laceration, mutilation or poisoning, attempted suicide, substance and drug abuse, an overdose, mental institutionalization.

4. Mugging, robbery, burglary, fraud, identity theft.

5. Genocide, war, terrorism, homicide, torture, post military combat trauma, imprisonment.

6. Physical or psychological intimidation, interrogation, brainwashing.

7. Betrayal, financial or legal intimidation, blackmail, malicious divorce, bankruptcy, redundancy, home repossession, arrest, prosecution[9].

Under any of these circumstances many people can undergo a significant and seemingly permanent lowering of mood or even a personality change. They may also develop physical symptoms and illness. This may eventually lead to more serious disease. Any of these incident types can and do cause an involuntary shift of the Assemblage Point to a dangerous dropped location.

LOCATING THE ASSEMBLAGE POINT

Finding the precise location and entry angle of the average, healthy, balanced person is a very quick and simple affair. The following is a description of one the numerous methods used to locate the Assemblage

Point. You can find detailed and clear graphics of how to do this on Jon Whale's website: www.whalemedical.com

1. The person should stand upright, looking ahead at the horizon. The investigator should stand facing the person's right-hand body side.

2. Form your left hand into a shallow cup shape. Use it to 'feel' for the person's Assemblage Point at the back around the area between the shoulder blades.

3. Form the fingers and thumb of your right hand into a tight, concentrated point, like a 'bird's beak'. Use the fingertips of the right hand to 'feel' for the cluster of energy lines entering the person's chest.

4. Hold both of your arms wide apart. Hold your left hand behind the person and your right hand in front. Standing relaxed, be keenly aware of your physical feelings and your weight on the floor. It helps to close your eyes or look away. Moving both hands in a slow circular motion, slowly bring your hands towards the back and towards the chest, feeling for the maximum energy disturbance or potential in the fingertips of your right hand and in the palm of your left hand. Allow the person's energy lines to control your arm muscles.

5. The difference in energy potential along the collection of energy lines of the Assemblage Point is easy to distinguish, being concentrated and stronger closer to the chest. When your cupped left hand and right hand pointed fingers are lined up with the person's cluster of energy lines, you will experience an 'energy surge'. This will pass along your arms and through your chest between your shoulders.

6. Bring your hands together, feeling for the maximum power and connection with the person. Allow your hands to touch the person's back and chest at the points of maximum energy connection.

7. Move your right-hand fingers back and forth across the energy lines of the Assemblage Point. Most subjects will feel a 'pulling' sensation deep inside their chest. Use small, adhesive labels to mark the front and rear position.

The location of a woman's Assemblage Point is generally, but not always, several centimetres higher than that of a man. Broadly speaking, a woman's vibrational rate, her behavior, the way she feels and her view of the world are quite different to a man's vibration. Therefore, female and male locations tend to be different.

At the location of the Assemblage Point, the skin is less resilient and more painful to the touch. The skin may occasionally be blemished or marked in some way, sometimes by a small diameter reddish spot. Touching or pushing the spot with a fingertip will cause the skin to redden more than skin elsewhere on the chest. The spot is tender, sore or uncomfortable.

Pushing it causes the person a feeling of slight unease. The feeling passes deep into the chest, often right through to the shoulder blade or the place of exit at the rear. Any sensitive person touching the precise location of a person's Assemblage point will feel an exchange of energy. It will feel like a faint or weak electric shock and often has a vibrating quality to it[10].

SHIFTING THE ASSEMBLAGE POINT

Obviously all this new knowledge would be of little value, unless some means were known that could shift the Assemblage Point back to the central healthy position. But in fact it's surprisingly easy! I learned to do it in less than an hour. The procedure takes mere minutes.

Those with the requisite skill, such as Tom 'Two Bears' Wilson, can probably correct it with a well-placed whack on the person's back! The way Jon taught me to do it was to use a crystal rod (as an attractor) and just "bump" or drag it to the desired location. It's easier to describe than do, but it is certainly not difficult. Anyone with enough life energy in them should be able to do it for another individual.

Doing it for yourself would be near impossible, I think.

There are a number of methods of doing it. The following is the one I learned from Jon and is good for beginners. You will need a heavy chunk of quartz crystal, about 200 grams (7–8 ounces), a length of at least 18 centimetres (6 inches) and a thickness of 3 cm or more (1½ inches). Most large towns and cities will have shops that support the sale of crystals.

The crystal must have a ground and polished dome at one end and must have a well-defined point at the opposite end. It should be as clear as possible. The point should have at least three perfect triangles among its six facets and it must be energetic and dynamically "alive" (the crystal should be washed in running water after each use, to keep it energetically clean).

Check its power: hold the crystal with your right hand and direct the point at the palm of your left hand. You should feel a breeze of cool, tingling energy penetrating the skin of your left hand, where the crystal is pointing. If it's "dead", switch for another one which isn't. The crystal is a crucial tool.

Just don't drop it on a hard floor!

Here's the procedure:

Having found the Assemblage Point, front and back (previous section), you now know the start position. Your intention is to literally drag or shove it to the center ideal location. Done right, you can get this shift in one go. If not, repeat the procedure. You'll see an immediate change in the patient's body and energies. When Jon first showed this to me, an MS patient of his, who could barely walk, was instantly able to walk normally!

1. Mark the Assemblage Point position, front and back, with a felt tip marker or small self-adhesive labels.

2. Instruct the subject to stand upright and look straight ahead, not at you.

3. Position yourself to the left-hand side of the patient's body. Holding the crystal in your left hand, place the smooth, domed end on the precise location of the subject's Assemblage Point, where it enters the chest.

4. Place your right hand over the exit point on the rear of the chest, ready to slide it to the desired location.

5. Have the subject take three deep breaths, exhaling slowly over several seconds. Make sure they really are deep and if not ask for three more, to really expand the lungs and chest cavity.

6. On the third inspiration, instruct the patient to hold their breath and squeeze their perineal sphincters (anus and genital area).

216

At the same time instruct him or her to half swallow, which closes the throat, and then hold that moment.

7. With the retained breath and closed body exits, pressure will build up and this "loosens" (for want of a better word) the person's energy field. It becomes detached from the body. Act swiftly and firmly, executing the next step...

8. Using the quartz crystal as a kind of handle, slide your subject's Assemblage Point to the center of the chest. At the same moment, drag the rear location to its correct position, between the shoulder blades, using your right hand. The direction of movement is critical: you must sweep up, across and DOWN onto the desired position.

9. Twist the crystal a half turn and remove it from the chest. At the same time tap the person's head with the palm of your right hand and instruct him or her to resume normal breathing.

10. If you fluffed it or the patient is nervous and fails at keeping still or holding their breath, start again with locating where the Assemblage Point has now moved to and its new angle and repeat the procedure, beginning from this new position.

Obviously, you should instruct your subject beforehand what to do and what to expect. Then these verbal instructions while doing the procedure are merely reminders.

Confirming the shift: - Once done, you will need to orient the subject to the new location. Have them feel it and notice that the spot may be tender. He or she may have reduced or vanished symptoms, as a direct result of the shift of Assemblage Point[11].

For comprehensive information and instructions on locating and correcting the location and entry angle of the Assemblage Point, please refer to Jon Whale's EBooks and paperbacks entitled: *The Naked Spirit* or *The Catalyst Of Power,* available on Amazon or via Jon's website: http://www.whalemedical.com/

These are both extremely insightful and innovative books, in my view. If you like brilliant and novel ideas, you will also enjoy learning about Jon's electronic biologic energy devices. (www.whalemedical.com). I feature one called the Stellar Delux (former Caduceus Lux) in Chapter 22.

CHAPTER 13

The Emergence of Electroceuticals

 There is something fascinating about science. One gets such wholesale returns of conjecture out of such a trifling investment of fact.

—Mark Twain

Bio-electronic medicine (BEM) is the most recent medical revolution. It has become clear that it should be possible to treat human illnesses using electrical signals to replace some drugs. Orthodox medicine is grasping this at last and, in a sense, it's the birth of "orthodox energy medicine", though that sounds something of a contradiction.

How things have changed. True to its ridiculous history of attacking anything they didn't think of first, medical orthodoxy has always viciously impugned any suggestion that electrical healing has validity and it's been labeled charlatanism for the best part of a century. Now they are having to eat humble pie and admit that claims, all along, had some validity albeit in a rather hit and miss fashion until the advent of modern scientific trials.

In an electric universe, with a clear electrical basis for life, the use of electricity in healing seems obvious. Let me introduce the term "electroceuticals", in line with pharmaceuticals and nutriceuticals. When you look back, the concept has been around for a very long time.

We're now learning to speak the electrical language of the body—and using it to develop treatments for diseases from arthritis to diabetes and possibly even cancer. And I'm talking orthodox treatments; nothing outlandish.

Internally generated electric fields are an inevitable product of biological systems. Cell membranes and epithelia—flat sheets of cells such as the outer layer of your skin and the lining of your gut—routinely pump ions from one side to the other, creating gradients of electrical potential. This makes them resemble charged batteries, with an excess of negative ions on one side and positive ions on the other. All it takes for current to flow is for a channel to open up linking the two sides, either through damage or deliberately. And where there is a current flowing, an electrical field inevitably follows.

Researchers have measured naturally occurring electric fields in organisms ranging from microbes to humans, and in biological systems ranging from cultured cells to embryos—in which an ion-separating epithelium is the first functional tissue to form. The strength of the field is typically between 10 and 100 millivolts per millimeter, but can sometimes reach 1600 millivolts per millimeter.

Until recently, no one had shown that such fields had any function.

But as I have remarked several times in this text, an electrical potential in living organisms is THE characteristic of life that is universal: no membrane potential, no life. So it seems only logical that electrical control factors are senior considerations in examining life force and healing.

Cell migration and multiplication plays a key role in development and healing. Yet most research in this area, true to form, has been on chemical factors, totally ignoring the electrical element (bio-electro-magnetism). Now several studies have shown that applying electric fields can affect cell migration and division as well.

Take, for example, a study, at the University of Aberdeen in Scotland, looking into repair of the cornea (in the eye).

In a healthy eye, cells pump positively charged ions into the cornea and push negatively charged ions out, creating an electrical potential of 40 millivolts. But in damaged areas this voltage disappears, setting up an electric field between the damaged area and the surrounding still-charged corneal tissue. By enhancing or diminishing this electric field, scientists found they could speed up or slow down the rate of healing[1].

The conclusion: the electric field is the primary driver of the healing process. As one of the researchers stated, it's a big step forward to realize that fields play an important part in healing. They are just so far behind the pioneers in this[2]!

It's no surprise to me, of course, nor should it be to anyone who knows of Robert O. Becker's classic book *The Body Electric*. Becker first wrote vividly about experiments with salamanders, in which correctly applied electrical currents could stimulate the regrowth of amputated limbs[3].

Becker's seminal work can only be regarded as the start of a rebirth of electrotherapy. The concept has been around for centuries, yet until recently has attracted nothing but vilification and ire from orthodox doctors and scientists, who roundly pronounce the very idea as nonsensical and fraudulent. All evidence to the contrary is dismissed as the rantings of fakers and crooks. Once more we are treated to the ubiquitous scientific principle: it can't possibly work, therefore it doesn't.

And yet again, they are proven the fools and retards!

One is reminded more than ever of the old adage, that discovery goes through four stages:

1. It's quackery and nonsense

2. There might be something in it

3. There might be something in it but where's the proof?

4. We knew that all along!

Stage 2 (anecdotal evidence, so-called), is where we are supposed to be at. But how long does anecdotal remain a valid accusation? If orthodoxy simply ignores the pioneering work of Robert Becker, Andrew Marino and Joe Spadaro and the many other published authors in this field, does that mean evidence is still anecdotal? How is a large body of peer-reviewed and published research on micro-currents and voltages in healing in bone and other tissues considered "anecdotal"?

It's farcical.

A LITTLE HISTORY

Electrotherapy has a long history. William Gilbert, the Cambridge mathematician who later read medicine and became Queen Elizabeth's court physician in 1600, experimented with static electricity.

In 1757 John Wesley (1704-1791), the founder of Methodism, wrote in his diary of prescribing treatment with a specially made electrostatic machine for people "ill of various disorders: some of whom found an immediate, some a gradual cure".

In 1760 Wesley published *The Desideratum* or *Electricity made Plain and Useful by a Lover of Mankind and of Common Sense,* based on his use of electricity in free medical clinics which he had established for the poor in Bristol and London. Although not widely appreciated by either science or medicine, or even by religious historians, Wesley appears to have been one of the most notable electrotherapists of his day. In the tradition of English parish priests, he combined remedies for illness with rescue of the soul. Moreover, his work stimulated nineteenth century developments in psychiatry and general medicine.

By the end of the 19th century, the work of Faraday and many others had produced a host of convenient ways of generating electricity of various kinds: electrostatic, direct current and low-frequency and high-frequency alternating currents. Each had its advocates and to each were ascribed marvelous healing powers for every conceivable medical situation.

Catalogues of the General Electric Company in the late 19th century had a number of such devices. Its 1893 catalogue illustrates nine magnetos, ranging from one 20 centimeters long, boxed in pine, to the Phoenix, boxed in mahogany with a dial "to measure strength". Assorted electrodes "for foot, tooth, and ear, with plated handles" were available for the device.

Crank the handle and it generates a low-voltage alternating current. Instructions inside the lid claim that, when wound at the speed "most

221

agreeable to the patient", this magneto will treat no fewer than 50 ailments, from weak eyes to spinal and nervous diseases, debility, fits, paralysis and gout.

Another type of device was the induction coil, originally developed to detonate explosive charges. By 1888, GEC was offering induction coil apparatus for medical use, complete with bichromate battery, in a wooden case. By 1890 their range had grown to 10 models, with many variants, and electrodes engineered to treat particular parts of the body, from eye muscles to the spine. Early in the 20th century so-called "hydroelectric baths" became fashionable. A wooden or porcelain bath was fitted with plate electrodes. Sometimes medicines were added to the bathwater in the belief that the patient would thereby receive whole-body treatment through the skin, *cataphoresis* as it was called. Knowing what I know now, all these devices make sense and although they were not subject to modern-style scientific trials, there is little question they had benefit to some, at least equivalent to the majority of today's pharmaceutical drugs.

I was pleasantly surprise in my research to find that the famous Mayfair chemists John Bell and Croydon, just around the corner from my former Harley Street clinic, at one time carried a range of such electrotherapy devices. They even had their own workshop, making induction coil machines tailored to what the doctor wanted for his patients in terms of output, portability and price, and the electrodes necessary to deliver the current where it was needed.

Historically, as far back as 1890, the American Electro-Therapeutic Association conducted annual conferences on the therapeutic use of electricity and electrical devices by physicians on ailing patients.

The effect of an electrical current on the body depends on its intensity. At 25 milliamps, the current, if it lasts for about 20 seconds, can stop the heart beating, so they are not inherently safe (the electric chair operates on this principle). But below 10 milliamps, whether direct current from a battery or an alternating current at ordinary mains frequencies (50 to 60 hertz), the current can create a rather pleasing tingle.

David Fishlock, an avid collector of these early devices, tells us that in the 1920s, a version of the Tesla apparatus (see below), known as Roger's *Vitalator*, began to make its appearance in barbers' shops as a way of treating minor ailments, including bald patches and dandruff. The barber would fit one of a number of glass tubes into an ebonite holder and switch on, whereupon sparks sizzled from the tube to scratch and tickle the pate. The maker recommended it for 127 conditions, including sexual debility, impotence and breast development. That's barbers for you[4]!

Fishlock asks the question: do black boxes emitting electricity or rays have a serious place in medicine? There is no doubt that the early inventions attracted the "snake-oil merchants" but that does not justify dismissing the entire topic. As early as 1882, Silvanus Thompson, a fellow of the Royal Society and president of the Institution of Electrical Engineers, warned of the "gross impositions of the quacks and rogues who deal in the so-called magnetic appliances and disgrace alike the science of electricity and medicine while knowing nothing of either".

We shouldn't worry. Don't forget Lord Kelvin, the greatest scientist of his day, declared that x-rays were a hoax!

My own reservations simply arise from the fact that it is a rather hit and miss approach, to drench the entire body in electricity in the hope of hitting something. It's not unlike chemotherapy, in which the whole body is soaked in deadly chemical, when the target is really only a relatively small tumor (yes, of course there will be cells in the bloodstream). It makes more sense to accurately target the pathology, using devices that can focus energy or tap into existing narrow pathways, such as meridians and acupuncture points.

As this 1917 quote says, it's important to be accurate and focused for meaningful results: "Success in electrotherapeutics depends on an adequate knowledge of physiology and pathology as related to the human body; on a mastery of the laws that govern electricity [physics]; on the possession of efficient apparatus, the achievement of good technique by practice and the good judgment to apply all these requirements ... Electrotherapeutics is not a system to be used to the exclusion of other therapeutic measures, but is a worthy addition to any physician's armamentarium ..."[5]

It's strange the orthodoxy should have such a problem with a fully validated physiological modality. Our bodies run on electricity!

THAT MAN TESLA

In 1908 another black box appeared in the GEC catalogue. It offered two models of high-frequency transformer, one based on designs by Arsène d'Arsonval, a French professor of experimental medicine, and one by Nikola Tesla, the Croatian-born American engineer. This Tesla coil, was already being used "in several leading London hospitals for the treatment of lupus and other skin diseases", GEC claimed. "Strong violet rays are produced on the skin of the patient by means of a special electrode."

Nikola Tesla (1856-1943) discovered the rotating magnetic field, the basis of most alternating-current machinery and today's mains electricity. He was born in Smiljan Lika, Croatia and worked as a telephone engineer in Prague and Paris, where he conceived a new type of electric motor which had no commutator, as direct current (DC) motors have, but instead worked on the principle of a rotating magnetic field produced by alternating currents (AC). He produced a prototype, and finding no interest in Europe, emigrated to the United States in 1884.

Tesla worked briefly with Thomas Edison, who cheated him over payment for designs, then left to establish his own lab and continued his prodigious output of inventions. Tesla obtained patents on motors, dynamos, and transformers for a complete AC power system.

Tesla is now credited with inventing modern radio as well, since the Supreme Court overturned Marconi's patent in 1943 in favor of Nikola Tesla's earlier patents. When an engineer (Otis Pond) once said to Tesla, "Looks as if Marconi got the jump on you" regarding Marconi's radio system, Tesla replied, "Marconi is a good fellow. Let him continue. He is using seventeen of my patents."[6] But see my remarks about Chandra Bose, page 79.

Largely as a result of this carelessness with worldly success, Tesla died destitute having lost both his fortune and scientific reputation. Interestingly, almost immediately upon his death, the US Office of Alien Property moved into Tesla's home and labs to take possession of all his notes and property—a highly unorthodox move, since Tesla was by then a US citizen.

Today the man is revered by an army of followers, who consider him probably the greatest technical genius of all time, a visionary who pulled world-transforming devices seemingly from thin air, often without any theoretical precedent. It is highly probable that he invented the first laser, with his button lamp, using precious crystals. Certainly it was known Tesla worked with rubies and he describes the production of a "pencil thin beam of light" produced by this device[7].

TESLA COILS

One of his major inventions is the Tesla coil, invented in 1891, and still used in radio and television sets and other electronic equipment. A Tesla coil is an electrical resonant transformer circuit used to produce high-voltage, low-current, and high frequency alternating-current electricity. It can develop far higher voltages than electrostatic machines such as the Wimshurst machine.

For example Tesla coils are used as a high-voltage source for Kirlian photography, which we visited in the previous chapter[8].

A large Tesla coil is capable of sending electric currents through the atmosphere (which was the origin of the "death ray" myth). I'd like to point out that such a device is exactly in line with the electric universe where current flows through spaces; just reducing it down to a human scale.

In 1898, Tesla published a paper that he read at the eighth annual meeting of the American Electro-Therapeutic Association in Buffalo, NY. In it he stated that "One of the early observed and remarkable features of the high frequency currents, and one which was chiefly of interest to the physician, was their apparent harmlessness which made it possible to pass relatively great amounts of electrical energy through the body of a person without causing pain or serious discomfort."[9]

THERAPEUTIC USES

On September 6, 1932, at a seminar presented by the American Congress of Physical Therapy, held in New York, Dr. Gustave Kolischer announced: "Tesla's high-frequency electrical currents are bringing about highly beneficial results in dealing with cancer, surpassing anything that could be accomplished with ordinary surgery."

This has certainly not been followed up with any published studies I am aware of. Nevertheless, "Tesla coils" are being widely promoted for their health benefits.

Safety may be a debatable feature. Tesla himself warned that the after-effect from his coil treatment "was certainly beneficial" but that an hour exposure was too strong to be used frequently. The danger has not gone away, though enthusiasts tend to play it down.

A coil-generated high-frequency current is said to travel across rather than through the skin: long sparks leap from the machine to the patient's nose and ears, but the patient feels no more than a tickle. This is based on erroneous science.

Although Tesla currents penetrate only the outer fraction of an inch in metal conductors, the 'skin depth' of human flesh at typical Tesla coil frequencies is still of the order of 60 inches (150 cm) or more. This means high-frequency currents will still preferentially flow through deeper, better conducting, portions of an experimenter's body such as the circulatory and nervous systems[10].

The reason for the lack of pain is that a human being's nervous system does not sense the flow of potentially dangerous electrical currents above 15–20 kHz. For nerves to be activated, a significant number of ions must cross their membranes before the current (and hence voltage) reverses. Since the body no longer provides a warning 'shock', the unsuspecting subject may touch the output streamers of a small Tesla coil without feeling painful shocks.

But, I repeat, it may not be harmless. Anecdotal accounts from Tesla coil experimenters indicate tissue damage may still occur and be observed later as muscle pain, joint pain, or tingling for hours or even days afterwards. Nevertheless, healing claims abound.

Before entertaining the idea of submitting to a Tesla coil machine, the reader would be well advised to study all the later material in this book covering exposure to electric and electromagnetic fields, including the appendix.

THE MULTIWAVE OSCILLATOR (MWA)

It would be wrong to mention Tesla coils and not introduce George Lakhovsky's multiwave oscillator (MWO), which is also a whole-body device. It uses a dampened Tesla coil, with far less biological impact.

For many years Lakhovsky (1869-1942) had a great interest in the mechanism of cancer formation. This in itself was unusual in his time. There were no 'Fight Cancer' media campaigns running then, and a leading London surgeon of the day pointed out that funding of cancer research did not even amount to one penny per person in the British Isles!

There are many aspects of cancer-causation from genetics, to environmental toxins and emotional traumas. I have already referenced Lakhovsky's work on soil types throughout Paris, identifying which soil types were most carcinogenic (page 115 and again on page 444).

But Lakhovsky was convinced that oscillatory disequilibrium—that is, cellular radiation energy disturbance—was the predominant factor in the onset of malignancy.

The problem was how to reverse it.

According to Lakhovsky, our bodies consist of some 200×10^{18} cells (most modern estimates would lower this to 100×10^{12} or 100 trillion) and hardly any two oscillate exactly alike. This is partly due to differing tissues but also variation through time in the status of each individual cell. The impact of extraneous radiation would also produce additional modulations, such as the resonance effect.

The basis of Lakhovsky's reasoning was that healthy cells carry a healthy frequency which keeps them energized. Unhealthy cells, on the other hand, have weakened radiations and are prone to be overwhelmed by oscillations from pathogens or nearby cancer cells. In other words, pathology was not really a tissue event but an electrical one; therefore the therapy should be electrical.

But finding a standardized harmonizing frequency would seem to be a Sisyphean task.

With brilliance and ingenuity, Lakhovsky invented his celebrated Multiple Wave Oscillator. As its name suggests, the MWO put out a large range of frequencies, generating a variable field in which every cell could find its own frequency and vibrate in resonance: the practical successes he began having in hospitals soon confirmed the validity of his theory. Numerous cases recovered and were documented by excited doctors.

Lakhovsky was careful to avoid talking in terms of a cancer 'cure'. No treatment is 100%, but Lakhovsky's MWO was certainly remarkably effective.

In 1925, he published a paper with the explicit title of "Curing Cancer with Ultra Radio Frequencies" in *Radio News*[11].

The MWO device was used in the USA until 1942 and in Europe for about another 15 years. It was ordered removed from the US hospitals that were using it shortly after Lakhovsky died mysteriously in 1942. He was hit by a car: Coincidence? You be the judge.

ORTHODOX RESISTANCE TAKES A HIT!

It had to come. The volume of bluster, derision, self-righteous indignation, huffing and puffing about electricity and healing that has come from orthodox medical colleagues over the last century only serves to make them the more laughable, now they are forced to admit that it's not only possible: it's of crucial importance!

The structures of life have been known over that same period to have a largely electrical function, yet they wanted to believe it was all somehow unimportant. "Life" was down to molecules and biochemical substances, not energy and, supposedly, not electromagnetic energy. Electrical phenomena, they claimed were confined to the nervous system.

That's just not true. Science is awash with pretenses like that.

The reason nerve cells can transmit electrical signals is because the inside of the cell is negatively charged relative to the outside, known as its resting potential. When a nerve cell fires, there is a sudden influx of positive ions into the cell through channels in its membrane. These ion channels open and close much more quickly in nerve cells, but other cells speak this electrical language too. "All cells maintain a resting potential. They use it to signal to their neighbors," says Michael Levin of Tufts University in Medford, Massachusetts.

Scientists have started waking up to the fact that an electrical language might be spoken more widely in the body than anyone thought, playing a pivotal role in coordinating the actions of our organs, glands and cells. It may even be possible to use the nervous system to coax the body into healing itself in ways we never dreamed of.

Now we know that autoimmune diseases, asthma, diabetes and gastric conditions are just a few of the disorders that appear amenable to electrical intervention. There are even hints it could reappear as a radical way of treating cancer. Within a decade or two, electrical implants could replace many common drugs.

In the late 1990s, Kevin Tracey of the Feinstein Institute for Medical Research in New York made a remarkable discovery. He and his colleagues were testing a new anti-inflammatory drug and when they injected it into rats' brains they noticed it also dampened inflammation in their limbs and peripheral organs. This shouldn't be possible, according to the accepted model.

It was, in effect, an electrical analgesic.

Moreover, the quantities injected were vanishingly small, so researchers knew the signal wasn't going through the bloodstream. It had to be a neurological response, mediated electrically. To test this idea, the team started electrically stimulating different nerves to see if they could reproduce the effect. Sure enough, electrically stimulating the nerve fibers that linked to the spleen—home to immune cells known as T-cells—dampened their activity. It was one of the first hints that the brain might be talking to the immune system after all.

What followed was a new clinical application, with physicians grafting an "electrical implant" into patients likely to benefit from this kind of stimulation. Here is another hidden structure that was hitherto unknown to medicine. This is *Medicine Beyond* (beyond the existing) at its finest!

Best of all, this intervention had no serious side effects. You will see more and more of these "electroceuticals" in the future.

For example, in the first edition of *Virtual Medicine* (1999) I introduced the world to a remarkable new device from Russia that was capable of stimulating an electrical response from anywhere on the body surface and even some orifices. It's called the SCENAR and we will revisit it again, for an update, in Chapter 20.

Through its use the body could be trained to release its own on-board pharmaceuticals, in the form of signaling compounds, such as neuropeptides. There was no question of the effectiveness of this family of devices. It was simply a matter of time before Western science began to wake up to the new world of bio-electromagnetism and energy healing.

ELECTRICAL STIMULATION OF IMMUNE FUNCTIONS

Tapping into the vagus nerve has shown other possibilities. It supplies tissues in the thorax and abdomen, all the way down to the end of the gut, including the spleen. So here is an important pathway, through which the brain can "talk" (electrically) to the spleen. Why is that important?

The spleen is no longer thought to be just a reservoir for blood. In recent years scientists have discovered that the spleen is a manufacturing plant for immune cells, and a site where immune cells and nerves interact. The fact that the brain can rapidly influence immune function via this organ is probably of critical importance.

In fact research performed at the Feinstein Institute showed that stimulation of the vagus nerve increased survival in laboratory models of sepsis. A sharp fever resulted which, you may know, is an important part of a healthy immune response. No fever; no attack on the pathogens. If the vagus nerve is cut, fever doesn't occur. That means the vagus nerve is telling the brain to start a fever: But how?

It's a whole new language. But it is telling us that the grammar is electrical.

The findings were published July 22, 2014, in the Proceedings of the National Academy of Sciences.

OPENING DOORS

Why confine this to the vagus and spleen? Gradually, we are learning more and opening up more avenues of enquiry. I have already remarked on the 1937 article in the BMJ by Sir Thomas Lewis describing a hitherto unknown network of cutaneous nerves[12]. I speculated that this cutaneous nerve mechanism could well overlap with acupuncture meridians (page 189). They even could be one and the same thing.

Naturally, my interest was piqued when I read that Clifford Woolf of Harvard Medical School and his colleagues had found a second nerve network in the skin, which was able to suppress infection when stimulated.

Similar circuits are cropping up elsewhere too. A team at the New University of Lisbon found that the carotid body—a cluster of cells that sense glucose levels in the main artery carrying blood to the head—has a connection to the central nervous system that can affect rats' insulin sensitivity and blood pressure[13]. They speculate that implanted electrodes might manipulate these nerve signals to tweak insulin sensitivity. At any rate, it is becoming clear that these circuits are all plugged into a body-wide electrical grid.

Note that I foresaw all this burgeoning science almost 20 years ago, when I wrote *Virtual Medicine*. Also note that British medicine was once very adventurous and men like Sir Thomas Lewis anticipated today's claims by many decades!

THE ELECTRICAL BRONCHO-DILATORS!

Electrocore, a New Jersey electroceutical device manufacturer, has come up with a device which is able to stimulate a region of the brain involved in the physiological response to stress and panic. Zapping them triggers the release of noradrenaline, which dampens the activity of neurons that control the airways—prompting them to open—averting the asthma attack.

It appears to work. In 81 people admitted to emergency departments during an asthma attack who didn't respond to standard drugs within an hour, electrical stimulation with Electrocore's implanted electrode led to a significant improvement in their lung function. Electrocore is now testing a device that activates nerve fibers through the skin.

The problem to date is that it is not yet possible to accurately target select fibers in a major nerve. Brendan Canning of the Johns Hopkins Asthma and Allergy Center in Baltimore, Maryland has come up with a work around, which is to tune the amount of electricity from a "smart electrode", so that it only stimulates a small subset of the fibers.

It should even be possible to create a device which can detect changes in nerve activity, provide therapy as needed and then shut off. Pharmaceutical giant GSK (GlaxoSmithKline) has people working on just that.

This is a huge paradigm shift in conventional medicine. Just a few years ago the idea would have been derided as absurd, that electrical signals could take the place of "real" medicines (drugs). Well, today the chemical approach has completely discredited itself. To practice medicine using only these tools is actually a serious degree of fraud by physicians.

The thing is electroceuticals can be far more precise than pharmaceuticals. In autoimmune diseases, for instance, it may make sense to place an electroceutical device on a well-chosen nerve rather than to blast the entire body with a drug. Disorders that involve specific organs and their innervation via electrical impulses seem ripe for electrical interventions.

With that in mind, last December GlaxoSmithKline announced a $1-million prize for the first team to develop a miniaturized, implantable device that can read specific electrical signals and stimulate an organ to perform a specific function reliably for 60 days[14]. The company has spent $50 million on in-house electroceutical research, and it is also funding a consortium of scientists at 25 universities to develop devices that can be made available to the broader research community.

On 1 May 2014, the US Food and Drug Administration (FDA) approved a device by Inspire Medical Systems of Minneapolis, Minnesota, that stimulates airway muscles to treat sleep apnea by regulating breathing while a person sleeps.

And on 17 June, an FDA advisory committee recommended that the agency approve a weight-control device from EnteroMedics in St Paul, Minnesota. Implanted between the esophagus and stomach, it stimulates the vagus nerve to make a person feel full.

The NIH is in on it too. Their electroceuticals project, tentatively called Stimulating Peripheral Activity to Relieve Conditions (SPARC), plans to bridge the knowledge gap by focusing on the mechanisms that underlie electrical control of organ systems. Its first grants will be awarded in early 2015. Over the next six years, the agency hopes to map the nerves and electrical activity of five yet-to-be-decided organ systems and then develop electrode devices that can attach to the nerves and maintain high-resolution recording and stimulation interfaces with them for decades without causing damage.

Conventional science seems to be getting the idea. It is most definitely not quackery. It's energy medicine become respectable. Yet again, I give you *Medicine Beyond!*

They are almost catching us up, with the SCENAR and like devices! Look out for rapid progress during the lifetime of this book[15]!

MICROCURRENT THERAPIES

Today the big thing is micro-current therapy (MCT), sometimes referred to as MENS (Micro-current Electrical Neuromuscular Stimulation). It uses extremely small pulsating currents of electricity to generate healing.

Because these are very low-level currents, this approach is more biologically compatible than any stronger electrical stimulation device. The effects can therefore penetrate the cell—as opposed to passing over the cell as other stimulation devices do. It works on the Arndt-Schultz principle (page 164), which states that weak signals will create a positive stimulus but stronger signals will reduce it; a very strong stimulus will inhibit or abolish activity altogether.

The idea is to normalize the electrical activity taking place within the cell if it has been injured or otherwise compromised. The external addition of micro-current is known to increase the production of ATP, protein synthesis, oxygenation, ion exchange, absorption of nutrients, elimination of toxic waste, and at the same time neutralizes the oscillating polarity of deficient cells.

MCT uses include treatments for diabetic neuropathy, age-related macular degeneration, wound healing, tendon repair, plantar fasciitis and ruptured ligament recovery. However pain is the commonest use for micro-current treatments, to speed healing and recovery. MCT is commonly used by professional and performance athletes with acute pain and/or muscle tenderness as it is drug-free and non-invasive, thus avoiding testing and recovery issues[16].

It can also be used as a cosmetic treatment; causing tightening of skin and reduction in wrinkles.

The Russian SCENAR device (Chapter 20) and similar devices such as the Avazzia, are typical micro-current therapy devices.

CHAPTER 14

GPS FOR THE MIND

The diversity of the phenomena of nature is so great, and the treasures hidden in the heavens so rich, precisely in order that the human mind shall never be lacking in fresh nourishment.

—Johannes Kepler

For some years now I've been using novel ways of exploring the mind; especially locating and eliminating distressing emotional "charges". Some people are gifted at doing this in a traditional consultation format. But unfortunately the vast majority of practitioners are ignorant, highly opinionated and unable to resist the temptation to make themselves seem clever and important by "explaining" to the patient what's wrong.

It never works. The patient has to work it out for himself or herself for there to be any valuable transformation. Other approaches, like emotional freedom technique (EFT) and NLP are really ways of papering over the cracks and getting the patient to take their mind away from hidden issues. That doesn't work either, because the issue remains present but out of sight. Sooner or later, it will blow up in a person's face.

I can't tell you how many patients I have worked with who said to me, "I've dealt with this issue," and yet he or she ends up bawling in grief, within minutes of finding the real emotional charge and releasing it.

What's needed is some reliable, proto-scientific way of tracking down trouble at source and, furthermore, we need a dependable way to know when the charge really has gone and not just been buried once again.

Can electronic devices help? After all, I've been explaining the electrical nature of Being and how the mind interacts biologically with electronics and electromagnetic phenomena.

The answer is a resounding YES.

A SHORT HISTORY

Active work on medical applications of electricity began almost as soon as Michael Faraday had invented a means to create electrical currents and it was generally accepted by 1840 that the body's electrical characteristics provided not only a basis for a new theory of disease, but for diagnosis and therapy.

The first observations of psychological factors in relation to electrodermal resistance phenomena are generally attributed to Romain Vigouroux at the Pitié-Salpêtrière Hospital in Paris (1879).

But the story really gets started in earnest with French physician Charles Samson Féré (1852-1907), who in 1888 published the earliest-known scientific paper on this. Féré was a gifted student of Jean Marie Charcot and set about defending Charcot's electrical and magnetic theory of hypnosis and hysteria[1].

However the usual starting place, and certainly a major milestone, is the work of Ivan Tarchanoff (1846 – 1908). He was professor of Physiology at the Academy of Military Medicine in St Petersburg, Russia, from 1877 to 1895 and authored a slew of articles on physiology for the Brockhaus and Efron Encyclopedic Dictionary. Tarchanoff was the first to study extensively what I call a psycho-galvanometer, a machine which measures electrical changes stemming from mental energy, emotion and effort.

His seminal paper, two years after Féré, was published in Pflüger's Arch. Für Physiologie, 1890, and entitled "Galvanic Phenomena in the Human Skin in Connection with Irritation of the Sensory Organs and with various Forms of Psychic Activity."

Tarchanoff employed saline-soaked skin pads, attached to a galvanometer device which detected change by deviations of light reflected from a mirror. The instrument was so sensitive that nerve impulses from a frog's sciatic nerve deflected the mirror off the scale.

In the course of experiments, electrodes were applied at various times to different portions of the body, such as the hands and fingers, feet and toes, the face, the nose, the ears and the back. It was found that tickling of the face, ears, or soles of the feet, with a camel-hair brush or a feather, induced a significant deflection in the galvanometer. The same results were obtained by stimulating the skin with a faradic brush, with hot and cold water, and by pricking with a needle. Irritation in analogous ways of other sensory organs, the ear, the nose, the tongue and the eye, affected the galvanometer in a corresponding manner.

What interested Tarchanoff was that it didn't need a physical stimulus but merely the fact of the test subject thinking about being touched was sufficient to cause a response. It was observed furthermore that the recollection of some strong emotion, such as fear or joy, produced the same result. The emotion of "expectant attention" or anticipation had a marked effect upon the galvanometer.

Tarchanoff attributed the phenomena he observed to a secretory current of electricity associated with the sweat-glands. That cannot be correct, as we will see later, though it is an idea which has stuck ever since, probably because individuals wired up to a lie detector are likely to sweat if they are in fear of being found out.

Like many discoveries of importance, Tarchanoff's remarkable work lay buried in medical literature for years, and it was not until 1897 that any further contribution on this subject appeared. In that year Georg Sticker published a repetition of the work of Tarchanoff. He thought the sweat secretion theory was wrong, because the response was still present when the skin areas were anesthetized (no neural activity)[2].

Then, in August 1906, Dr. O. Veraguth, a Zürich neurologist, published his own findings in Arch. De Psychologie (Geneva). Again he corroborated Tarchanoff's findings. He called this the "psycho-physical galvanic reflex". You may also hear it referred to as the Tarchanoff phenomenon, an electrodermal response, the Féré phenomenon, galvanic skin response (GSR) or psychogalvanic response.

Veraguth went further than mere physical stimulus as a trigger, however. He found if the individual under observation is read to, there was deviation of the galvanometer when passages associated with emotional tone are reached. He also tried calling out a list of emotionally-charged words, as suggested by Carl Jung, which produced a response, while indifferent words did not.

He concluded from his studies that only sufficiently intense and actual emotional tone would induce a response measurable on the galvanometer. That conclusion remains true today.

Veraguth admitted he was not able to explain the phenomenon, but he did not think it due to alterations in the quantity of blood in the parts beneath the electrodes, for the phenomenon takes place whether the hands be emptied of blood by an Esmarch bandage or supercharged with blood by artificial venous stasis. Moreover, he too excludes the sweating hypothesis, because the results were the same with hands made dry by the application of formalin[3].

CARL JUNG

The best-known figure in early psycho-galvanometry was Carl Jung. We still today sometimes refer to the "Jungian" GSR meter.

With colleagues, notably Frederick Peterson MD, Jung began further investigations and together they made certain consistent observations. For example, as soon as the circuit through the test person is closed, there is a rather rapid response apparently induced by expectant attention. Tarchanoff himself was much struck by this. Attention is nothing more than a special form of affectivity. Attention, interest, and expectation, are all emotional expressions.

Expectation is not only manifested at the beginning of an experiment in the degree of galvanometer response, but may be observed throughout the experiment in connection with every stimulus, sensory or verbal. It is particularly strong when there is a threat of pricking with the needle, or threat of letting fall a heavy weight.

They also found, like Tarchanoff, that not only emotions created a response but the thought of an emotion did so too. They measured delayed response to emotionally-charged words and topics and took repeatable measurements.

For example: by questioning one patient, they learned that recently, when greatly depressed, he had determined to commit suicide by drowning. Water, lake, ship, swim, were words that excited this complex in him. The complex brought about lengthening of the reaction time. We know this today as "word association" and, contrary to popular belief, it is not the first word the patient thinks of that reveals the truth; it's the delayed reaction time, which gives a measure of emotional confusion.

To the end, Jung remained enamored of the "sweating" theory, even though it was disproved on all counts! However, he did admit in his 1907 paper with Peterson there was insufficient knowledge to put forward a fully cogent theory of how these emotional electrical responses happened.

To add to the uncertainty, a deep inspiration alone, or a deep expiration, without alteration in the contact of the hands, increases the deflection of the galvanometer, while ordinary respiratory movements did not affect it. Coughing also causes a considerable galvanometric wave. Because of this, Jung was inclined to think that this response to changes in breathing rate and depth, and with coughing, may in fact be emotional, rather than being just an artefact.

These physiological reactions, or body movements as we may call them, are readily differentiated from those depending wholly upon psychic influences.

Warm hands naturally permit a larger current than cold hands. The level of the response increases when the skin in contact grows warmer or moister, and descends with increase of coldness in the skin.

In the end Jung was thwarted in creating a new science, since his devices were limited in scope. It would have to wait for amplification technology (valves, transistors and eventually silicon chips) before fuller investigation could be mounted.

ENTER VOLNEY MATHISON

Volney "Dex" Mathison (1897- 1965) was a US chiropractor, psychologist and inventor. In 1935, Mathison was employed building short wave radios. He invented a device called an electroencephaloneuromentimograph or E-meter for short.

By this stage he was able to use a needle-on-dial arrangement for detecting responses or "reads". The device was initially known as the "Mathison Electropsychometer" and he used it with his patients in order to investigate their inner problems.

Soon Mathison was writing and talking of "clearing" mental image patterns and he called at least some aspects of this work "Creative Image Therapy".

Mathison went on to develop a word-list to be used in conjunction with the GSR meter, just like Jung. He would ask the subject under analysis, to take hold of the meter-electrodes; then he would read this list of words to him or her. Without fail, some of these words would trigger a response on the meter and in some cases violently. Whenever this was the case, Matheson knew that these words were associated with strong and negative fear or resentment that had its origin in unconscious (reactive) complexes in the subject's mind. Most of the time, the subject was completely unaware that he was reacting on the meter in this way.

The Mathison Electropsychometer became popular and was used among other chiropractors. John Freeman writes in Suppressed and Incredible Inventions, "Recalling my visits at the height of his career, I remember that, while his results were outstanding, he was typically fought by the Medical Profession."

However, Mathison's problem turned out not to be the medical profession but L. Ron Hubbard, founder of Scientology. Hubbard coveted Mathison's meter and demanded the patent rights which Mathison refused to surrender, even though he was a follower of Hubbard's new theories.

What followed was a long and acrimonious dispute, which was never resolved. For a time Hubbard pretended such a meter was of no value anyway: "Yesterday, we used an instrument called an E-Meter to register whether or not the process was still getting results so that the auditor [practitioner] would know how long to continue it. While the E-Meter is an interesting investigation instrument and has played its part in research, it is not today used by the auditor.... As we long ago suspected, the intervention of a mechanical gadget between the auditor and the preclear [client] had a tendency to depersonalize the session...."[4]

But within a short time Hubbard was busy having his own knock-off of the Mathison meter manufactured and sold to his followers, such that, as pointed out by holistic method basher Edzard Ernst, to this day most Scientologists believe that the E-Meter was invented by their founder L. Ron Hubbard."[5]

Mathison never litigated the appropriation of his invention, but he felt bitter and disillusioned about Hubbard. Mathison remarked in 1964, "I decry the doings of trivial fakers who glibly denounce hypnosis and then try covertly to use it in their phony systems"[6].

Apparently the battle continues and I heard recently that Scientology missionaries had struck a deal with Mathison's estate (one would suspect under some coercion) in which all Mathison's research papers were sold to The Church of Scientology, presumably to destroy them and further the myth that Hubbard invented this device[7].

Of course its connection with what is widely regarded as a cult has meant the idea of psychometric reactions has come under intense scrutiny. Critics even pretend that Jung had concluded his experiments were worthless. The ramblings of such fools, with their pseudo-science would be amusing, if it were not for their false claims and absurd manipulations of what were once facts, leading away from a useful truth.

The bottom line is that such detection devices can tell you nothing about a person's life and history. The client does that. The meter simply tells us what is significant and what is of no account for the time being.

THE SPREAD OF ELECTRO-PSYCHOMETRY

Scientology propaganda and crude attacks by the uneducated critics notwithstanding, Mathison's breakthrough device is here to stay and is in widespread use today among many practitioners and in many disciplines. I have several models, including Hank Levin's Clarity Meter, the Ability Meter, Levin's InnerTrac for which Hank coined the phrase "GPS for The Mind™". I also have a computer mounted version.

The latter is particularly significant, in that I can conduct a guided session with someone anywhere on the globe. By using the remote screen share function I can talk to the individual, see their countenance and observe the meter responses, from thousands of miles away!

There is now a gathering consensus on how to adapt Mathison's discovery to modern transformational discovery processes. I belong to a worldwide network of healers and researchers who are pushing this technology forward. It is important to say that these meters have no power to heal or produce change in their own right but they can tell us where to look. The term GPS is helpful, in that it implies a geographical location. It may be a revolutionary view, to see the mind in structural terms but in fact it works well.

Users are very clear about the following: meter "reads" (GSR responses) are operative only in the pre-conscious area. If a trauma is buried too deeply, there will be no read. If it's trivial, fully cognized in consciousness, it will not read: no "charge" as we say. A read is telling the practitioner that something is lurking just below the surface, within reach but momentarily out of view—something significant.

So we want to process memories and cognitions that are reading well, for the best results, exactly as Tarchanoff, Jung and Mathison found. No charge, no gain.

THE MISUNDERSTANDINGS OF MODERN SPECIALISTS

Instead of advancing, psycho-galvanometry has stagnated, left in the wilderness by untested opinions current among investigators. Here's what current thinking believes: That a GSR reaction merely indicates general arousal and can never be used to detect meaningful states within a person. It's true that a response means arousal. But look: if the person is talking about mother (say) and the GSR reactions are pronounced, it means mother is a "hot" item.

If a person talks about rough times in life and one reads strongly (a serious illness, for example), then you know that it is a significant episode. In 1936, in his famous book *Science and Sanity*, Alfred Korzybski pointed out that you can use a GSR meter to detect charged or misunderstood words and process the negative emotions associated with them which he called semantic reactions. That's extremely useful for an educator and allows us to clear up a person's schooling mishaps.

So to say you cannot know what is significant for a person using a GSR meter is really rather stupid; it's how you use the device that makes it so valuable. The skills I teach in my own specialty of Supernoetics™ and the "GPS" guidance techniques I call Transformational Mind Dynamics™, enable the practitioner to rapidly locate and discharge negative emotions.

But what is taught today as orthodox psychogalvanometry is that arousal is bad. What they consider ideal is a person in a relaxed, unaroused state. A high unresponsive reading shows the person is not in a state of stress (arousal).

But in terms of useful change and transformation, that's merely a state of avoidance and the patient is not looking at their issues, is "switched off", and so is totally unable to access or eradicate problem areas. I see that as pointless and although arousal may be low, that is not the way forward.

REVERSAL THEORY

Let me take a few paragraphs to explain arousal-calm theory, based on the work of British psychologist Dr. Michael J. Apter and psychiatrist Dr. Ken Smith. You'll see that arousal is not always bad!

Basically there are thousands of adjectives that may be used to characterize a person's current operative mental state, such as 'angry', 'fearful', 'bored', 'serious', 'excited', 'sensation-seeking' and many others. This is clearly impractical as a basis for the understanding of psychological processes; a better solution is to look for clusters of inter-related states and their behaviors that are amenable either to direct observation or psychometric measurement. Such a model would need to explain why individuals do not remain in one constant state of arousal, but change from introvert or extrovert, withdraw or become involved, be thoughtful or spontaneous. This backwards and forwards inversion is what is meant by reversal of states; hence reversal theory, as it's known today.

Take the example of a person riding a bicycle: the behavior is cycling; the goal is arriving at a certain place. If the cyclist needs to get to work on time, his behavior is chosen to meet the goal that is in the foreground (arrival); the means of doing this is secondary. This is a telic state - the person is serious-minded, planning oriented and seeks to avoid unnecessary arousal (distractions).

The alternative experience is for the behavior to be in the foreground and the goal in the background; the person may simply like the feeling of the wind in his hair as he cycles down a hill; the destination is unimportant to the experience. This is the paratelic state; it's exciting, the person is playful, prefers to be spontaneous, is 'here and now' oriented (pursues goals only insofar as they add to the immediate pleasure of the situation) and prefers arousal to be high, since it is pleasurable.

This can be shown on a simple graphic:

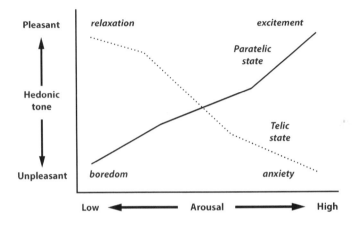

The telic line (dotted) shows high arousal as anxiety (unpleasant); the paratelic line shows high arousal as excitement; a pleasure stimulus.

Now looking at your life issues and hurtful moments may not seem like a pleasant activity. It isn't. But if the person is in agreement with the procedure and wants to recover from hurt and expand their mental powers, then such explorations may not only be acceptable but actually high on the hedonistic tone (hedonism: seeking pleasure).

The patient knows the journey is towards release and a shift of state into something better. Therefore becoming engaged would mean a positive experience to that person, even if there are tears during the transition. "The best way out is the way through", as poet Robert Frost worded it ("A Servant to Servants", 1914).

In this arena, the way out is signposted by GSR responses, which is our GPS system for the mind!

SO HOW DOES IT WORK?

Let's look at the proper procedure, as I use it. First the psychometer:

There are three useful GSR meter measurements: the overall state of arousal (base reading); individual responses or needle "reads", which indicate charged areas; and the accumulated change over time during a therapy session (differential).

The overall (basal) reading of skin resistance, itself provides the analyst with useful information about the subject. Values lower than 5K ohms indicate a high level of brain arousal, with high anxiety (towards overwhelm) and concentrated introspection. At the other extreme, values higher than 25K ohms indicate low arousal and withdrawal from the mind (dissociated states of poor concentration, limited self-awareness, non-confront, over-reactivation, boredom, fantasy, switch-off, apathy).

Generally down-trending readings between these extremes indicate progress of the client during a session of therapy. Most modern devices have an automatic accumulator, which collects the total down-trending or "differential" for a period.

Of course the base has to go UP in order to come down. So the base or regulator is continuously rocking backwards and forwards (up and down values). When formerly repressed material is coming to the surface (for example, memories associated with guilt), the skin resistance rises and the client experiences feelings of tension, that is, if he is involved with his inner feelings, and in a paratelic mode of experiencing rather than a telic avoidance.

Then, when the repressed material finally reaches the surface and the negative emotion discharges (often with some anxiety in the process), there is usually a large drop in skin resistance and the client experiences relief.

Any experienced observer will tell you that the total accumulated differential from a session is a direct monitor of how the patient will feel afterwards. Large amounts of differential equate to a light, pleasurable, relaxed state of mind; a sense of being freed from turmoil, with a new clarity and wisdom, coming from insights gained during the release process.

Temporarily, the meter will stop responding and the needle simply drifts idly to and fro, in a null or undriven pattern.

244

GIVING BIRTH TO THE TRUTH

Next the method:

What we do in Transformational Mind Dynamics™ is an advanced version of the maieutic or questioning method, attributed to Socrates. In actuality, the term originated with the Greek philosopher Plato, writing about Socrates.

In *Symposium*, we are told that Socrates said that a seeker is not an empty vessel to be filled with wisdom from a teacher ("If only wisdom were like water which always flows from a full cup into an empty one..."). But it's not like that. You can't "transmit learning"; you can only draw it out—which is what the word, educate means: *e(x)-ducare*, Latin).

So it is with Transformational Mind Dynamics™: nothing can be achieved by telling the client stuff or explaining how it is. He or she has to discover the truth, following a series of clever questions, delivered in a clever and impactful way.

The Supernoetics™ approach is virtually unique in taking a question and really "milking" it with continuous repetition, until the client has nothing more to give in answer. We have squeezed all the juice out of the orange. We then go on to the next question and do the same.

But guess what? After lots of different answers, the problem or perspective starts to shift and the person sees things in a new light. The early answers are the more obvious ones. With continuous inspection of the issue, it starts to take on new shape and significance. Things really do change. Clients educate themselves and we are glad to be witness at the birth of the new self!

Giving birth to truths from within was Socrates' actual concept: literally midwifery! *Maieutikos*, from which we get maieutics, meant midwifery. In the *Theatetus* Socrates explains: "My art of midwifery is in general like theirs; the only difference is that my patients are men, not women, and my concern is not with the body but with the soul that is in travail of birth." (Remember women were not given much importance in Ancient Greece).

THE BILATERAL METER

If it were left to some of today's armchair critics and writers, no progress would be made in any direction. They Google each other's opinions and pretty soon start to accept mere musings as data. Nothing, apparently, has any worth to this crowd, unless someone of authority makes a pronouncement, at which point they are suddenly experts in this new aspect of knowledge.

Unfortunately, as we have seen repeatedly in this volume, expert opinion is almost a watchword for folly. Give me the maverick and pioneer every time; at least their ideas are filled with life, not dogma, derision and accumulated dust!

So it is with newer discoveries in psychogalvanometry. I am now one of the world's leading pioneers in this direction and as such I am free to choose what I describe as fact, experience and veracity; and also of course to reject what I know to be nonsense.

What am I effusing about now? The bilateral GSR meter (patent pending). It can identify and measure right and left brain arousal.

We all know the right-left brain activity model. It's definitely an oversimplification, since functional MRI studies make it plain that both sides of the brain actively participate in what are supposed to be unilateral (one side only) functions.

Leaving aside the extensive current beliefs around this model, I can share this: the right brain is where the emotions, turmoil and trauma reside; the left brain is where logic and language reside. What I find in clinical practice is that the left brain tries to be rational and will come up with an explanation for emotional and behavioral follies, even to the point of inventing a story or telling "lies".

The right brain, on the other hand, can't tell lies. It can only "know" what is, with no way of expressing what's going on, without adequate words (which is a left-brain function). In short, it's impossible to process and eliminate emotional and other traumas, without invoking the agency of the left-brain, which acts as an "interpreter" and verbalizes the patient's understanding.

So we can string the two psychogalvanometers together and learn more about what is happening in the person's psychic space. If there is a "read" on the conventional GSR meter, that means stress. If, at the same time, the bilateral part moves to the right, it means "true". If it shifts to the left, there is some untruth, whether intentional or not. Maybe, in the latter case, the patient really believes the fabricated story they are telling. But deep inside, the mind knows that something is wrong.

It goes without saying that only the truth releases unpleasant emotional stresses and their accompanying dysfunctional behaviors.

WORK ON YOUR SENSE OF CURIOSITY!

One thing I know for sure, having used these devices for decades, is that they can detect deep psychic responses. Whereas I fight shy of the idea you can play the lottery using one, I do sincerely believe that it can be used as a kind of "dowsing" tool, meaning that it will react on non-brain thoughts, in other realities.

One friend of mine sincerely proposed we use a psychometer to dowse for gold and other precious metals. It would be easy to agree with him, since I have already explained that in electronic dowsing, the operator works as the instrument or "sensor" (page 282). The electro-psychometer reads on what we, as fully-aware conscious beings, know, or think we know.

A more appealing idea was to use it in the direction of, say, detecting food allergies or hidden pathogens. What I can report is a simple and quite thrilling application, which is using the sensor to take readings on plants. It's the science of phyto-galvanometry... a word I just created!

I think everyone knows the seminal experiments of my late friend Cleve Backster, who wired plants to a galvanometer and found that they were sensorily aware (see also page 103). They seemed to react to being "hurt", as when leaves were torn off. Not only that but it emerged the plants could later identify the person who did it and reacted violently on the meter when he or she came into the room[8].

It is now clear that, despite supposedly having no brain or nervous system, plants are clearly aware of their surroundings. Cleve Backster was convinced that plants could "see" better than humans. In 1900, Indian biophysicist Jagadish Chandra Bose began a series of experiments that laid the groundwork for what some today call "plant neurobiology". He argued that plants actively explore their environments, and are capable of learning and modifying their behavior to suit their purposes. The key to all this, Bose said, was an electrically-based plant nervous system.

However Bose did not use a galvanometer but a spring-loaded sensor device of his own design that he called a crescograph.

PLANT NEUROBIOLOGY

Bose was remarkably far ahead of his time. It wasn't until 1992 that his idea of widespread electrical signaling in plants received strong support when researchers discovered that wounding a tomato plant results in a plant-wide production of certain proteins and the speed of the response could only be due to electrical signals, not chemical signals travelling via the phloem, as had been assumed.

Anthony Trewavas at the University of Edinburgh, UK, became the first person to seriously broach the topic of plant intelligence. The trouble is, plants grow and change so slowly. There are a few exceptions, such as the closing of the Venus flytrap around an insect. But the most visible plant behavior is simply growth, and growth is a very slow business. However, this problem has been reduced with the advent of time-lapse video and photography.

The speeded-up behavior is remarkably snakelike, says Trewavas. Take the parasitic vine Cuscuta, also known as dodder. In time-lapse, a dodder seedling seems to sniff the air looking for a host, and when it finds one, it lunges and wraps itself around its victim. It even shows a preference, choosing tomato over wheat, for example.

Once witnessed, it is hard not to believe that plants are behaving in ways that you expect animals to behave. They manifest intelligent behaviors. In 2005, the *Society for Plant Neurobiology* was formed to foster debate and change the way we think about plants.

Unfortunately, there were very many biologists hostile to the notion that plants were sentient and would not accept the term neurobiology for organisms without a brain or nervous system. After much controversy therefore, the name of the society was changed to *The Society of Plant Signalling and Behavior*.

In fact plants may have a real "brain". It's called the transition zone, in the growing root. Researchers have found that the transition zone is electrically active. What's more, within it is a hormone called auxin, which regulates plant growth. Auxin is ferried around in protein containers called vesicles. This is exactly what happens in the human brain, where vesicle recycling is thought to be important for the efficient and precise information exchange across synapses. The transition zone is also a major consumer of oxygen, which is just like the human brain.

This echoes the "root brain" hypothesis of Charles Darwin. In the last paragraph of The Power of Movement in Plants (1880), Darwin challenged readers to think of the root as the intelligent end of a plant. Referring to a plant's primary root, or radicle, he wrote: "It is hardly an exaggeration to say that the tip of the radicle... acts like the brain of one of the lower animals."

Remarkably, Susan Murch of the University of British Columbia in Kelowna, Canada, has shown that drugs like Prozac, Ritalin and methamphetamines, which disrupt neurotransmitters in human brains, can do the same in plants. "If you really mess with a plant's ability to either transport or make melatonin or serotonin, root development is very strange – they are malformed and disjointed," she says[9].

THE SINGING TREES OF DAMANHUR

Recently, my wife and I visited the Eco-Community of Damanhur in northern Italy. One of their on-going experiments has been dubbed "the singing plants" and was reported in Digital Journal.[10]

Since 1975 researchers at Damanhur have been experimenting with plants, particularly trees, measuring their reactivity to the environment and their capacity to learn and communicate. The conscious reactivity of vegetative life has been monitored by special electronic devices, allowing researchers to listen openly to the "thoughts" of trees, by translating responses into sweet-sounding music.

It's quite remarkable and very engaging to listen to!

Electrical differences between the leaves and the roots of the plant are measured. Using a simple principle, the researchers utilized a variation of the Wheatstone bridge, exactly like the psycho-feedback meter I use with humans, but instead of feeding into a meter, the changes in electrical status are used to power a variety of effects, including music, turning on lights, movement and many others.

It is clear that every living creature whether animal or plant, produces variations of electrical potential but plants seem exceptionally sensitive and, depending on the "emotions" being experienced at the time, they signal the arrival of the person who cares for them, when being watered, when spoken to, during the creation of music, etc.

Non-sensory perception (page 102) within the plant induces a physiological reaction, which then expresses itself in electrical, conductive and resistance variations. These variations can be "translated" in different ways, including into musical scales.

The experiments have shown that plants definitely appear to enjoy learning to use musical scales and also making their own music with the use of a synthesizer.

Damanhur workers have given demonstrations in public parks and schools and have also held concerts in the woods.

PHYTOGALVANOMETRY

Back to the subject of struggling plants. Personally, as an accomplished gardener, I have no trouble seeing plants as sentient aware beings, who understand us very well when we communicate with them.

So why can't they be "unhappy" or sick? Some emotions, it might be argued, are uniquely human (a doubtful claim anyway). But a plant, overwhelmed by challenge from its environment, can be seen to visibly wilt, not unlike depressed human beings. Those people we might call "sensitives" can be with plants and "feel" their messages and emotions. It's not my place to argue this is all nonsense.

What I do say is that when ordinary humans are fully in the presence of healthy, vigorous plants, there is an easily-detected energy or humor about them. It actually feels good to us. Plants make admirable company!

And don't forget the homeopathic remedies of Edward Bach, the so-called "flower remedies" (page 322). Bach was very clear in his mind that plants had emotions and attitudes and these "humors" could be dissolved in solution and used to modulate human feelings. Anyone who has ever taken Bach's Rescue Remedy in an upset or emergency will know these remedies really work.

Moreover, Rescue Remedy can work on plants, animals, insects and other life forms, as many experiences attest.

So it is not surprising that plants can be evaluated and transformed, using a GSR meter, involving simple questioning.

Well, Eric Swanson, from Leytonville on the Eel River in California, together with Hank Levin, carried out a simple "proof of concept" experiment with plants. Eric was a gifted gardener and had no trouble raising vigorous, healthy plants and flowers. But he met a challenge: a particular azalea was not doing well—in fact it was on the point of death.

Wiring up the plant and calling off a series of questions (akin to Jung and Mathison's pre-prepared list of words) they got a read on "root rot, due to too much water"! This was surprising in a way: azaleas are famous for being very thirsty plants. But apparently the issue was drainage. Azaleas like water but not soggy roots. Eric corrected the problem and the plant recovered in no time[11].

CHAPTER 15

The Birth of
Electro-Acupuncture

*Are we biology or God or something higher? I
know my heart beats and I listen to it. The beat is
biology, but what is the song?*

— James Frey

Electro-acupuncture, the application of a pulsating electrical current to acupuncture needles as a means of stimulating the acupoints, was developed in China as an extension of hand manipulation of acupuncture needles around 1934. It is described, though
only briefly, in most comprehensive texts of acupuncture[1]. The procedure for electro-acupuncture is to insert the acupuncture needle
as would normally be done, attain the Ch'i reaction by hand manipulation, and then attach an electrode to the needle to provide
continued stimulation.

Then, in 1951 Yoshio Nakatani presented his research and theory of
RYODORAKU Acupuncture. Nakatani had found that there were a series of low electrical resistance points (or high electrical conductivity)

running longitudinally up and down the body. When linked together these points closely matched, but were not identical with, the acupuncture meridians.

Nakatani called these lines (or meridians) "Ryodoraku" (*ryo* = good, *do* = (electro) conductive, *raku* = line). The points along the Ryodoraku he named *Ryodoten*.

Thus Nakatani was probably the first person to measure the electrical activity of acupuncture points and the first to formulate diagnostic and treatment criteria from these measurements.

He also introduced the concept of using electrical stimulation of acupuncture points; something that is now widely accepted. Notwithstanding, Ryodoraku detection, analysis and point selection for electrical stimulation is much less popular than EAV, which is what the present chapter concerns.

This is unfortunate as Nakatani's concepts provide an accurate pulse-organ diagnosis, accurate location of required treatment points and a much quicker treatment regimen. It has been said that a classic electro-acupuncture treatment, lasting an average of 30 minutes, would only take 2 - 3 minutes using Ryodoraku.

A Ryodoraku device is called a "Neurometer". To provide consistency and avoid problems because of dryness/wetness of skin, a moist electrode is used to locate the points of lowered electrical resistance or Ryodoten points.

The moist electrode is run lightly over the skin until a high reading points to an area of low resistance, high conductivity. As in other forms of electro acupuncture practice is required to achieve consistent results. Too much pressure or repeated checking of a point can change the electrical properties of the skin in that area and lead to error.

Computerized Ryodoraku sensor units are available in Japan. These give a steady 3g electrode pressure to the skin. Reproducible pressure is one of the problems that dog the usual electro-acupuncture system (Voll's).

VARIABLE POINTS

Nakatani discovered that the number of electro permeable points not only varied with any disease process but also with the voltage of the detector probe. Most of the traditional acupoints could be located if a 21 volt circuit was used. However if a 12 volt circuit was used, there were other electrically conductive points over the body, not associated with any specific acupuncture points. He called these Responsive Ryo-do-points or reactive electro permeable points (REPPs).

These Ryodo-points often correspond with myofascial painful "trigger points". The term "trigger point" was coined in 1942 by Dr. Janet Travell to describe a clinical finding with the following characteristics:

- Pain related to a discrete, irritable point in skeletal muscle or fascia, not caused by acute local trauma, inflammation, degeneration, neoplasm or infection.

- The painful point can be felt as a nodule or band in the muscle and a twitch response can be elicited on stimulation of the trigger point.

- Palpation of the trigger point reproduces the patient's complaint of pain, and the pain radiates in a distribution typical of the specific muscle harboring the trigger point.

- The pain cannot be explained by findings on neurological examination.

Nakatani showed that stimulating these trigger points or REPPs for 7-10 sec with a 200μA charge would render them electrically inert and produce symptom relief.

ELECTRO-ACUPUNCTURE ACCORDING TO VOLL

Enter Dr. Reinhold Voll, physician extraordinary. He is the very stuff of which legends are made: dark, irascible and arrogantly conscious of his abilities. Originally trained in architecture, he qualified and became interested in technology as well as preventative medicine, an ideal combination to set the stage for his future. Voll contracted cancer of the bladder but refused to accept the Western dogma of terminal decline. Instead he sought relief through the intervention of traditional acupuncture methods. Remarkably, although he needed life-long catheterization, Voll conquered the disease sufficiently to continue working for over two decades – a testimony to the effectiveness of his teachings. Many people over the years have had cause to be grateful for this minor miracle.

Voll set about the business of trying to marry up Chinese medical wisdom with Western technology, a transition which had to come sooner or later, but with Voll it came soon and comprehensively to boot. He began to survey acupuncture points and their related meridians, using a modification of a standard valve ohmmeter which he called the diatherapuncteur, and with it he founded the science of 'electro-acupuncture' in the 1950s. You may also at times hear of the dermatron, a later transistorized version of the same instrument.

The patient holds one electrode while the investigating physician uses a probe to complete the circuit by touching the skin at the point being tested. The small tip of the probe allows remarkable accuracy of placement, yet yields a great deal of information other than just skin resistance, as we shall see. The current is in the region of 10 – 12 micro amps at a potential of 1.0 – 1.25 volts; in other words, quite safe.

Any more and the current itself would become stimulating and produce changes, instead of monitoring the status quo. Indeed, just the very act of pressing firmly on the acupuncture point is sufficient to stimulate it, and very sensitive patients may even feel unwell due to this effect after such a test session.

Voll's first interesting discovery was that almost all Chinese acupuncture points are detectable by a change in skin resistance at that spot and are remarkably accurately located; most are within a millimeter or two of where the classic texts say. At these sites the skin resistance is a fairly constant 95,000 ohms (elsewhere the skin is highly insulating, at around 2 million ohms, except when wet). However, Voll also found many more such points than the Nei Ching and other classic texts tell us. So far this is simply a matter of scientific detection and there can be no argument; anyone who wants to measure these points for themselves can do so easily.

ADDITIONAL VESSELS

There are 12 main acupuncture meridians recognized in TCM and two principle governor vessels running in the midline, front and back (Conception Vessel and Governor Meridian, respectively).

It very quickly became obvious to Voll that there were other conducting channels, many extra points, and at least eight new 'vessels' were

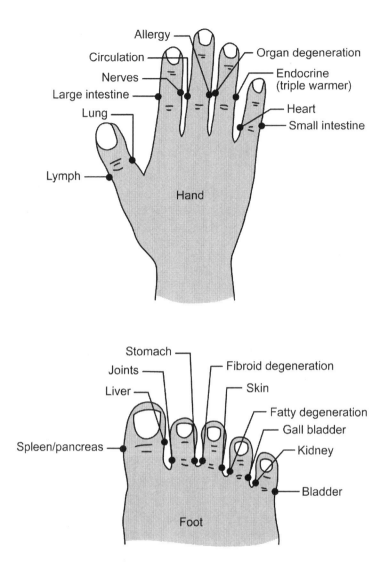

Hand

Foot

mapped, then labelled according to what he felt they represented in terms of biological function, namely: lymphatic drainage, nervous system (including the autonomic nervous system), fatty degeneration (including fat-soluble toxic chemical deposits), organ decay (including malignancy), non-malignant cystic fibrosis and other benign degenerations, skin, joints and allergies. His system brought the total up to 20 bilateral channels, two to each digit, fingers and toes, making a total of 40 channels in all.

There has also been the opportunity to rename some of the classic meridians with names more in line with modern Western science; thus the Chinese 'triple-warmer' has become linked with the endocrine system; the circulation-sex meridian (heart master) is now linked with vascular degeneration.

The illustration below shows the hands and feet and each vessel named on the Voll system. The only asymmetry is that the channel on the medial side of each big toe differs; on the left foot it is taken as indicative of *spleen* function, whereas on the right foot the same vessel is named for the *pancreas*.

TOO MUCH OR TOO LITTLE ENERGY FLOWING?

From here on it starts to become increasingly contentious. What Voll did is to arrange that a normal 'balanced' reading on a true acupuncture point is set at 50.

At the upper end, 100, this would represent no resistance to current flow. A reading of 0 would mean total resistance (no current flowing whatever). Readings significantly higher than 50 on this scale mean too much energy (this may not at first sound an obvious problem, but remember all such excess energy must be stolen from somewhere else).

Generally we take readings of 65 or more to mean an excitation (or irritation). Over 80 is an active inflammatory process and over 90 an active inflammatory process that is pronounced in grade.

Conversely, readings below 50 mean degeneration and decay, which is more serious because destructive changes are less readily reversed. Below 40 is considered a sign of danger and below 30 an indication of an already established cancer or dead tissue (for example, I have observed readings as low as 27 at the point representing the defunct adrenal gland in a case of Addison's disease but without malignancy being present). I know of no EAV practitioner who has recorded less than 20 on this scale of values, but it would represent the final stages of tissue degeneration and death. The scale of pathological readings is shown here schematically:

Value	Significance
90–100	Total '-itis'. Whole organ inflamed

80–89	Partial '-itis'
70–79	Cumulative irritations, premorbid
60–69	Physiological irritant values only
48–59	Normal range of variability
40–47	Incipient degeneration
30–39	Serious degeneration, pre-malignant
20–29	Advanced degeneration, almost certain malignancy
Under 20	Degeneration in the final stages

This may be summed up as: increasingly serious inflammatory and active organ disease above 80; serious degeneration and risk of malignancy below 40.

INDICATOR DROP

In addition to the general level of readings, Voll recognized another phenomenon, which is where the reading is fine at first but after a few seconds it begins to die away to a lower level. What was observed is that the meridian somehow could not hold on to its energy. The interpretation of this is that there is diseased tissue present somewhere in the indicated tissue of that meridian, influencing the energy levels.

Voll called this phenomenon the Indicator Drop (ID), and he considered this to be the most important reading of all. It points clearly to some significant pathological process taking place, regardless of what level the initial reading was found to measure.

Put another way, a meridian which is high but where there is no Indicator Drop is not nearly so much a problem as one which reads nearer 50 but has a major drop. For example, a high liver reading (90+) means a major detoxification is going on, with high liver energy and possible inflammation of liver tissue.

Voll called this reading the 'speeded Indicator Drop' and declared it indicative of chemical intoxication. But providing there is no die-off effect, the problem lies elsewhere. The liver overburdening is a secondary manifestation. The source of the toxins is the matter which needs rectifying, which when solved will ease the liver problem.

Basically, the bigger the Indicator Drop, the more serious the pathology giving rise to it. The electro-acupuncture practitioner will seek out the biggest drop in the measurement system and choose to treat that first, as a priority. This leads almost inevitably to the concept of 'most stressed organ' and implies a necessary treatment regimen.

ORGAN CORRELATIONS

Where Voll became decidedly controversial is the systematic way he went about trying to find correlations between each electro-acupuncture point and specific organs and diseases. In my view he may have been stretching his cloth to fit!

Most scholars of the Chinese system are content to view the 'gall bladder' or 'large intestine' meridians as concepts or qualities of energetic potential, rather than being related necessarily to disease of those organs. Voll thought otherwise and, over many years of painstaking and detailed research on many thousands of clinical cases, he gradually catalogued enough data to be able to associate certain points with certain organs or relevant tissues.

Gone was the old system of colorful metaphors such as *The Sea of Energy* (Conception Vessel 6) and *The Door of the Mental* (Heart 7). Instead, in Voll's system, the first point on the endocrine meridian is associated with gonadal and adrenal function; the fifth point on the heart meridian connects with the mitral valve (left) or tricuspid valve (right); the ninth point on the lung meridian is larynx, and so on (all examples counted from the tip of the relevant digit, whether the start or finish of the meridian).

Existing meridians were found to have several additional points, so a new naming system had to be devised. The first point between 1 and 2 became 1a: then came a 1b. But then further divisions led to 1-1 and 1-2 and so on. The result is confusing but there is a certain amount of consistency based on function. For example, Voll considered the second Voll-point on each finger (just distal to the last knuckle joint) to be concerned with lymphatic drainage, so these are always designated 1-1; the point immediately proximal to the last knuckle joint he associated with the sympathetic plexus of the system concerned, and these are always designated 1a.

Conveniently, Voll's method concentrates mainly on taking readings on the hands and feet and nearby skin, so the patient is spared much disrobing.

Eventually Voll published a complete knowledge system of all the above which we now call 'electro-acupuncture according to Voll', or EAV for short. It is the first real model outside Abrams' original work of what I have chosen to call *Medicine Beyond*.

CRITICISM

As a user of the EAV method with some years' study it is possible to say that there are indeed some remarkable correlations between EAV points and meridians, but overall, I feel that Voll has invited criticism by trying to fit the clinical findings into his mental hypothesis. After doing so he has come up with a useful but partly inaccurate 'map'.

That said, there is nothing that even comes close in scientific terms to such an advanced energy diagnostic system and it does indeed go a long way to combining the intuitive genius of the Chinese system with the preciseness of Western electronic technology.

Perhaps, as the idolization accorded to Voll fades into a brilliant historical perspective, it will be open to others to question some of the master's dogma and make changes which reflect more accuracy in what is being tested and more humility concerning the fallibility of the method.

CENTRAL MEASUREMENT POINTS (CMPs)

There are many points to measure, over a thousand in all. We don't try to measure every one on each patient. An obvious question would be: is there any way to establish quickly the general state of each meridian? One suggestion is to measure the ends of the meridians. These points are called 'Ting points' in Chinese nomenclature.

Without going into the arguments for and against, it has been settled that it is better to measure a little further up the meridian, at what we call the central measurement point or CMP. With one or two exceptions, like the thumbs, big toes and heart meridian (inside of the little finger), this point is just distal to the second knuckle joint. This gives an overall idea of the energy of that meridian. If there is suspicion of a problem then it is very simple to delve deeper and check other points related to that meridian.

By using the CMPs as quick reference points it is usually possible to home in on the problem area. However, nothing in EAV overrides the common sense of history taking. If the patient says she has lung problems and the CMP has no Indicator Drop (ID), it is mandatory to check other points on the lung meridian.

As with conventional medicine, electro-acupuncture is about establishing a hypothesis as to the causation of illness and then dealing with it. The fact that different criteria and an unfamiliar frame of reference are called into play does not alter this basic logic or mean that we ignore what clues there may be in the patient's description of his or her problem.

PRACTICAL CONSIDERATIONS OF EAV

EAV is not easy, though simple enough in concept. It is rumored that it takes five years to make a good EAV specialist. That may be true, but being able to get useful readings and helpful therapy pointers can be learned in a matter of days. After all, one does not need to be a brain surgeon to learn to dress wounds and set up an intravenous line. Consistency of probe pressure is the hard part to master. Once the practitioner can do that, everything else follows.

The real difficulty is to learn the remedies. It's a whole different repertory (see Chapter 18) and certainly does take years to get to grips with. But there are always textbooks to help.

It is also important to respect certain general rules. We know, for instance, that testing after a heavy meal obscures the results. We call this a parasympathetic dominant state, when the patient is lethargic and the energetic system somewhat closed down (yin state). But TCM tells us more: that, as in all things, the body cycles through contrasting phases; midnight to noon is a time of sympathetic dominance (yang); noon to midnight is parasympathetic dominance (yin). Moral: don't test after about 6 p.m. and never after the patient has eaten a big meal!

These are things one learns gradually.

Other factors which can reduce a patient's energy are lack of sleep, severe stress, cold or medications.

QUADRANT MEASUREMENT

A quick and easy test to see if the patient's energies are adequate for EAV testing is what we call quadrant measurement. It can be shortened to a hand-to-hand reading. Provided the energies fall in the 80–90 range, there is sufficient energy for testing. If not, some means of stimulating the patient is required. This could be having the patient run on the spot, clap his or her hands together forcefully a few times, or tap repeatedly on both temples.

Quadrant testing is a useful preliminary procedure. Readings are taken from hand-to-hand, right hand to right foot, left hand to left foot, and foot-to-foot (foot measurements are made with the patient's soles on electrode plates). If there is a significantly higher or lower reading in one of the quadrants compared to the other three, it suggests that the key pathology is in that quarter.

HYPOTHALAMIC DISORDER

Dr Sam Williams, an advanced EAV specialist physician, taught me the importance of checking hypothalamic status. It happens sometimes that when recording meridian energies at the CMPs that everything seems 'irritable'—that is, a great many small Indicator Drops register, but nothing really stands out. This makes it difficult to know where to enter the case. Systemic steroid therapy can produce a similar picture, where IDs are being clearly suppressed. However, in this case there is usually some reading which enables us to break into the problem.

Screening for hypothalamic disorder is done by measuring at the traditional Chinese point of Triple Warmer (TW) 20, which lies just above the ear pinna. Measurement is made while the patient is in contact with the ground with one hand, touching TW 20 with the probe.

Alternatively, the patient uses the index finger of the hand holding the bar electrode to touch TW 20, while the therapist uses the probe on the allergy vessel CMP of the opposite side. An imbalance of readings on the two sides indicates either hypothalamus disorder, or possibly a dislocation of cervical vertebrae at the level of C3 or C4.

If one or the other condition exists, it will skew the results and it would be best to remedy this problem first. Subluxation will need a realignment manipulation by a skilled chiropractor or osteopath. If it is indeed a hypothalamus problem, matters can be improved by choosing a suitable restorative remedy or light therapy (see Chapter 22).

Unless a hypothalamus offset is corrected first, the therapy regime will not be totally accurate and consequently less effective.

FOCI (singular FOCUS)

Using electro-acupuncture, one is given several new insights into the disease process that are not obvious to the traditionally-orientated clinician. For example we have the concept of a 'focus' (plural: foci). No matter what the presentation of the patient's complaint, it often emerges that there is some area of the body which is distressed and 'transmitting' a trouble signal which influences the energy body adversely.

Common examples would be old tonsillitis, appendicitis, what I call pelvic 'anger' in a woman, prostatitis in a man or teeth and gum problems (see Chapter 24 for startling new revelations about the dangers of teeth foci). These foci can appear 'silent' clinically but they are certainly not so electromagnetically.

When a focus is active within an organ tissue it will disturb the body's homeostatic regulatory mechanism. The body needs to divert a great deal of its energies to cover up and compensate for the focal disturbance. This causes imbalances in other organs, with fatigue and global low energy states. Therapy may be blocked until the focus is corrected.

It soon becomes evident to the budding EAV specialist that these hidden and smoldering foci are quite dangerous and can create a great deal of chronic ill-health, rather like the 'smoldering virus' that we began to talk about in the 1960s.

Spread of infection and toxins by blood transportation is obvious. But another largely unsuspected route is retrograde seepage along nerve channels. We know that viruses and bacteria can travel in nerves: rabies, herpes and poliomyelitis are just three diseases where this is known to happen. In 1923 two groups in Paris and the US chanced upon identical experiments. Each inoculated rabbits in the eye with Herpes simplex virus ('cold sore' virus) and showed clearly that the virus tracked along the trigeminal nerve to the brain stem. This is the critical area of the brain pathways, where all the key functions converge.

What wasn't said, though quite obvious and pointed out by Patrick Stortebecker of Sweden is that teeth are also supplied by the trigeminal nerve and dental foci could also track into the cranium and attack central brain tissue in this way (page 423).

Payling Wright, pathologist at Guy's Hospital in the 1950s, showed the poliomyelitis virus and even inert substances such as ink particles and dyes could travel at a remarkable 2-3 millimeters an hour (5-7 centimeters a day) in this way[2].

Unfortunately, this kind of observation is not given any currency and the vast majority of doctors and medical students do not know of this phenomenon and the appalling health risk it poses.

REMEDY EVALUATION

If the testing system described so far were not enough for a lifetime of work by one man, Voll gave us another gift of technological insight. We call it 'remedy evaluation'. How this came about is ascribed to one of those lucky accidents, a case of the prepared mind being ready at the right place at the right time to be able to benefit from what, to others, would merely be a baffling observation.

Let Voll tell his own story:

> I diagnosed one colleague as having chronic prostatitis and advised him to take a homeopathic preparation called Echinacea 4X. He replied that he had this medication in his office and went to get it. When he returned with the bottle of Echinacea in his hand, I tested the prostate point again and made the discovery that the point reading which was previously up to 90 had decreased to 64, which was an enormous improvement in the prostate value.

> I had the colleague put the bottle aside and the previous measurement returned. After holding the medication in his hand the measurement value went down to 64 again, and this pattern repeated itself as often as desired.

Voll went on to verify this startling discovery with many other patients and found it to be consistent and very helpful in choosing appropriate treatments.

Thus was remedy evaluation born, though Abrams and Boyd had reported it earlier (page 131) and it was subsequently forgotten.

HOW IT WORKS

Part of the EAV circuit includes a test plate or a 'honeycomb'—that is, a metal block with slots to take small phials of test substances for comparison. The plate has to be on the passive electrode side of the circuit, so that the remedy 'signal' has passed through the plate and then the patient, before being picked up by the probe and completing the loop back to the instrument (See illustration).

If we accept the presence of the Indicator Drop as indicative of a pathological process somewhere along the meridian system, then logically any remedy which removes that drop and restores the reading level will have a beneficial impact. We can put a remedy into the circuit and test the response. If it improves matters somewhat but does not eliminate the adverse read completely, it is open to the practitioner to add other likely therapeutic agents until a satisfactory formula is obtained.

Thus we can build a therapeutic regimen with the assurance that it is at least likely to work.

Dr. Kuo-Gen Chen of the Department of Physics at Soochow University in Taipei has researched medicine testing extensively and explains that *'When a medicine sample is put on the metal plate of the EDS (electro-dermal screening) circuit, the electron waves passing through the plate will be phase modulated. When these waves later pass through the patient's body, a given signal is transported to the proper organ or tissue by resonant absorption.'*

In his view, testing is an application of quantum mechanical quasi phase matching.

Rapid large-scale testing of remedies can be done by arranging racks of trays containing large numbers of phials. The Dermatron or other sensing device is then connected to each rack in turn; when a rack reads positive, individual trays are tested until the right one is identified; finally each individual phial in this tray can be switched into the circuit until the necessary remedy is located.

In this day and age you would expect computers could help and you would be right. We come to this in Chapter 19.

ALLERGY TESTING

The alert reader will probably quickly deduce the reverse side of this remedy-testing coin: that it is possible to identify substances which bring about an Indicator Drop where there previously wasn't one and therefore assess them as harmful. If bringing milk into the picture produces the same Indicator Drop as weed killer, the therapeutic implications are obvious.

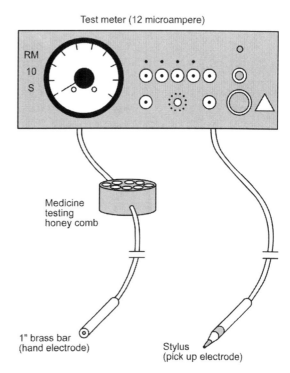

Test meter (12 microampere)

RM
10
S

Medicine testing honey comb

1" brass bar (hand electrode)

Stylus (pick up electrode)

Thus one of the applications of EAV is to look electronically for 'allergies'. After more than two decades of work in the allergy field I can add my own comment here. I have many times observed that patients can become ill without ingesting or breathing their allergens. Sometimes just close proximity to the reagent can do it.

In 1987 a young woman from Hong Kong flew over to see me in the UK. Her problem sounded bizarre; but she told it to the right person, because I believed her. Karen Rackham said she felt ill if she was merely in the same room as a cup of tea! It was indeed an allergy and subsequently we were able to help.

Providing the substance comes into the individual's L-Field, it can cause energy disturbance (remember the L-Field extends to infinity but in practice falls away very quickly, according to the inverse square law). Thus there have been many occasions when a highly-sensitive patient has had to be moved to the other side of the test room, away from the racks of testing substances.

I am now convinced that allergy is primarily an information field effect and not a biochemical or humoral one. The neutralizing solutions or vaccines of the Miller method, described in full in my earlier books, are simply another energy medicine dispensation and this explains why putting the neutralizing dose under the person's tongue sometimes works almost instantly. The relief can occur before there is any time for a humoral transfer via the circulatory system. This clinical observation accords very well with the theories of Jacques Benveniste, who holds that all molecules have an electromagnetic information signature which itself can produce the same clinical effect as the molecular substance, even when no chemical is present. He likens it to listening to Pavarotti or Elton John on CD, when the artiste is not actually present.

Naturally, this is highly controversial and regarded as little more than quackery by many doctors. But if one accepts the validity of the Indicator Drop and what it is telling us, this application of electronic allergy testing is at least consistent with the rest of the EAV system.

IS THERE ANY SUPPORTIVE PROOF?

Naturally any scientifically-orientated doctor would want to see some objective proof of what EAV can do. I am pleased therefore on two counts to report two small-scale studies by Julia J. Tsuei and others using EAV to evaluate food allergies and hypertension.

Tsuei received her medical education in China, Taiwan and the US and naturally has a strong affinity for TCM; acupuncture in particular. She has been engaged in several research programs to further the scientific credibility of acupuncture and Voll's electro-dermal technique.

The food allergy test was simple but sound. Thirty volunteers were used. Allergies identified by the Voll method described above were compared with findings from five other recognized allergy tests: history, skin tests, RAST, IgE levels, and food challenge testing. Voll testing correlated well, particularly with results from challenge tests which, logically at any rate, should tell us the most about food allergy (personally I have strong reservations about the use of food challenge tests as the benchmark in scientific trials).

Tsuei and her team carried out another study on hypertensive patients which is also worth reporting. There were 336 participants, 171 normal and 165 hypertensive individuals. Measurement points were selected based on either TCM or Voll's hypothesized correlations, totaling 56 points tested on each participant.

The 56 points could be divided into seven groups, of which two were measuring cardiovascular energy, three were not, and a further two groups measured both cardiovascular and non-cardiovascular points. The first group, measuring only cardiovascular energy, correlated extremely well with systolic and diastolic blood pressure, and the other cardiovascular group also correlated with left-ventricular mass (hypertrophy due to excess blood pressure). Indicator Drops (IDs) on these points gave the most accurate method of identifying the hypertensive patients; but there were also significant relationships between IDs and left-ventricular mass and either systolic or diastolic pressures among three of the five remaining groups.

CAUTION

It is very important for the reader or potential patient submitting to EAV to remember one thing, which is that what we are measuring with this system is energetic disturbance. It is not equivalent to a blood test or special x-ray, demonstrating gross pathology. We can find the energy signal of cancer of the colon and yet absolutely nothing can be detectable clinically. The energetic system is saying that trouble may be on its way and be able to characterize what the likely nature of it will be. Obviously there is great preventative potential here. But there are strictly no grounds for disputatious exchanges with conventional doctors or accusations of 'missing' the diagnosis.

This sometimes poses great difficulties for EAV practitioners (many of whom, it must be said, are not qualified doctors anyway). A natural desire is present to try to persuade conventional physicians to investigate what has been found energetically and see if there is confirmatory structural or biochemical evidence of disease. But one is inviting ridicule and hostility by revealing one's source of the diagnostic suspicion. Perhaps it is not conceited to hope that the publication of this book will prove helpful when these ticklish situations arise; it could be given to the un-informed physician as a primer.

Casebook: Female, 38 Years

Stan Richardson, a capable if medically-unqualified Voll practitioner in Heckmondwike, Yorkshire has the following remarkable story to tell:

> A woman telephoned one day, asking for help, saying she was sick and frightened she would die. Could Stan help?
>
> When she attended, she looked ghastly and even Stan was concerned.
>
> Without allowing her to explain anything, he sat her down and surveyed the initial points. It showed serious drops on the stomach, small intestine and large intestine meridians. Only then did he ask her, 'What's been happening?'
>
> She explained that for over three weeks she had been suffering from overwhelming diarrhea and vomiting. She could keep nothing down.
>
> Medicine from the family practitioner was ineffective. She had lost over 3 stone (40lb) in weight and was frightened but preferred to see an EAV specialist she trusted, rather than attend a hospital.
>
> Stan then resumed and stopped, quite puzzled, when he found a strong resonance that said rabies was present in the stressed organs. He didn't tell the patient this but asked the quite reasonable question: 'Have you been abroad lately?' The patient answered that she had just come back from India and been ill ever since she'd arrived home.
>
> 'Were you bitten by any animal?' Stan asked; again a very pertinent question. The woman insisted that she had not. Eventually, Stan had to reveal to the patient that the signal from her tissues was rabies. After discussion it emerged that this woman, in her misguided kindness, had been feeding dogs with kitchen scraps at the back door of her hotel in Delhi each night. Clearly what had happened is that she had been licked by a rabid animal and had swallowed the virus from her own fingers, resulting in the appalling intestinal symptoms.

Normally, rabies is spread by a bite which breaks the skin; the virus enters the nerves and travels backwards to the brain, where it is deadly. She had escaped a fatal disease by amazing good luck.

Stan supplied her with a mixture of homeopathic medicines which remedy-testing had said would be beneficial. Her symptoms ceased within 24 hours. By the end of the week she had gained back 10 pounds and eventually made a rapid and full recovery. She had fought, and won, a serious medical battle within her body, using nothing more than quantum energies.

The importance of this illustrative *Medicine Beyond* story is not merely that it is dramatic and life-saving. It is that no conventional doctor in his or her right mind would have diagnosed rabies in this situation, or even considered it. Yet the virtual energy signal showed quite clearly it was present, and with a suitable remedy led the patient back to safety.

Otherwise, she might well have died of severe 'gastroenteritis', without the hospital doctors ever suspecting what the cause was.

That's EAV for you!

CHAPTER 16

The Vegatest

Dans la nature rien ne se crée, rien ne se perd, tout change. (In nature nothing is created, nothing is lost, everything changes).

— Antoine Lavoisier, *Traité élémentaire de chimie*

It is said that Reinhold Voll submitted the last few additions to the EAV system a matter of days before his death. Whether this is whimsy or truth, it is clear that he achieved remarkable things despite the blight of a terminal illness. His life work completed; there was little point in going on suffering.

Two subsequent, related developments emerged during the 1970s. Both came into clinical use while Voll was still alive. We shall look at each in some detail in the next two chapters.

The basic problem with Voll's raw method was that it was complex and difficult to organize the data gleaned in a meaningful hierarchical manner. Many points had to be tested and he was gathering too much data. It was thus a very laborious and time-consuming procedure which made it exhausting for both the patient and the practitioner.

Starting in the early 1970s Helmut Schimmel hit upon a simple improvement which was to stay with only one testing reference point, usually on the hand for convenience, and introduce diagnostic test ampoules containing low-dose homeopathic extracts of different mammalian organs (usually pig). Applying the same logic to the meaning of an Indicator Drop, if the pathological reading appeared when the liver D4 ampoule was placed in the circuit this would infer problems with the patient's own liver. The test organ ampoule was energetically resonating with the distressed organ tissues within the body. Schimmel called his instrument the Vegetative Test Machine, or Vegatest for short (often just 'Vega').

Again, the core diagnostic indicator is the drop in energy (decrease in measured skin resistance), coupled with a musically falling electronic wail. As with all EAV devices, I find that practitioners tend to test 'by ear', not just by needle deflection. Schimmel named this cadence the 'disorder control' and it is calibrated at the start of testing by introducing some poison into the 'honeycomb' of the EAV, such as an ampoule of Paraquat or Lignocaine. It is not easy to master the use of this indicator, but those who can manage it have at their disposal a rapid and approximately accurate means of testing large numbers of organs, pathogens and likely treatments.

PRELIMINARIES

Vega testing is measuring extremely fine energy oscillations, either in the quantum realm or connected with spin phenomena described on page 199, or some unknown mechanism. This makes it highly susceptible to 'noise' and corruption of signals. Proper observance of start-up procedure is therefore important.

The test room must be free from geopathic stress (see chapter 25). Computers, x-ray machines and other electronic apparatus should be situated well away from the test zone (or at least switched off), making certain there is no interference from equipment in adjacent rooms or even above and below the test room. Electromagnetic fields travel through walls. Even electrical cables give off a substantial magnetic field, and for normal household and commercial voltages the patient must be seated at least 70 cm (2 feet 4 inches) from the nearest power source and at least 1.5 meters (5 feet) from any fluorescent lighting.

It is important that the tester is not personally geopathically stressed; otherwise he or she is likely to 'find' this condition on all patients. In fact if any condition keeps arising in consecutive cases, the first thing the astute BER (bio-energetic resonance) practitioners think of is that they are picking up their own disorder.

The practitioner needs to be in good shape health-wise, and well-rested. Sick patients are often in a predominantly yin phase and tend to drain the practitioner's energies (even lay-people may notice this effect with certain invalids). An exhausted tester cannot get good results. You may notice that the practitioner wears a peculiar magnetic belt. This is said to provide additional protection when testing. Nevertheless, it is unlikely that the practitioner can realistically test for more than a few hours per day without becoming substantially yin and unable to get meaningful results.

CHOOSING THE REFERENCE POINT

Just as in EAV, the Vega specialist tests on an acupuncture point. The tips of the fingers are readily accessible and are chosen by preference: the so-called 'Ting points' just at the corner of the nail bed. The allergy vessel, endocrine or connective tissue meridians are common preferences.

A point has no testing potential unless it can first be made to give off a disorder read, so the practitioner begins by establishing this important prerequisite. Gentle probing should give a reading around 100 and when a poison is introduced into the metal honeycomb the subsequent reading drops markedly. Ideally, the fall should be 20–30 points on the scale. If this is impossible to obtain, then amplifiers are introduced, in this case ampoules of Epiphysis D30 (30X), until the reading is sufficient to be useful (the homeopathic dilution scale is explained in Chapter 18). The amplifiers are left in the honeycomb throughout the testing session. Obviously, since the same point is being used over and over, it may well become traumatized and cease to give off any further disorder control. This is especially liable with a beginner using nervous, heavy-handed pressure. Another point has to be selected, but it must be checked for a disorder read before proceeding.

STRESSING THE BODY

It may seem surprising at first, but the body often needs stressing lightly in order to unmask energy disorders. The body's own bio-energetic compensatory mechanisms can be remarkably good at covering up a problem (a reason why normal medical diagnostic skills may be needed as well as an interest in these new methods).

Under normal circumstances the body will always endeavor to obtain a homeostatic balance of the energy flow within the body and the surrounding field. Sometimes only when an additional burden is imposed on the body do masked disturbances become noticeable. Ideally, we would like to choose a mild stressor that produces no harm and is soon rebalanced after testing.

In practice the best approach has been found to be a small electrical shock applied to Lymph 1 and Allergy 1 (points suggested by Voll). A piezo-electric device is generally used, which administers a mild charge of 4,000 volts per millisecond. It sounds scary but the current is mild and the patient rarely feels anything at all. Alternatively, the Vega machine also has a 13 Hz provocation output which can be used. This is a stressor frequency (low beta).

The body is thus required to make a compensatory response, which will divert the masking energies and expose real pathological readings which could otherwise be missed.

FINDING THE STRESSED ORGANS

As quickly as possible, the Vega tester wants to get to grips with the most stressed organs. This is where the key pathology lies and where the therapeutic response is going to be at maximum. This is done by testing a series of organ ampoules, usually at the D4 (4X) potency.

Testing can be speeded up by testing brackets or racks of test ampoules simultaneously. A bar connected by a wire to the honeycomb and laid across several ampoules at once gives a result which is referenced to all those ampoules. If a read appears, then one of the ampoules is active. This can be located by examining them one by one. If the whole bracket is negative, then all of them can be set aside and time has been saved.

The knowledgeable Vega tester will learn to relate what shows up to the patient's clinical condition. It is of course possible that he or she is unaware of any relevant subjective symptoms. Let me once again repeat that the search is for an energetically disturbed organ, which will not necessarily be 'diseased' by the criteria of Western laboratory medicine. We correct the disturbance, Nature does the rest. Only if the energy is left untreated may pathology ensue.

FILTERS

The range and sophistication of the Vega machine is greatly extended by the use of what Schimmel called 'filters'; that is, extra ampoules of test reagents introduced into the circuit which modify the response. Reagents have been chosen empirically, and supposedly give further information about organ status and the disease process. For example, here is a list of filters and what they tell us about a disturbed organ:

Zincum met D400	Severe organ stress
Zincum met D200	Most stressed organ
Zincum met D60	Critical organ stress
PhosphorousD32	Most damaged organ
Ars. Alba D60	This is the origin of the patient's complaint

I have already introduced the concept of a focus in the previous chapter. Filtering with the homeopathic remedy Thuja D30 will show a focus is present, and this can be related to the relevant organ. Causticum D60 shows a focus with a disturbance field. There is actually a certain logic to these potencies; thus Causticum D400 (more potent) shows a dominant focus with a disturbance field. Generally, the higher the potency that reacts, the more severe the disease.

If the clinical condition is caused by or associated with psychological disorder, a number of emotional filters can clarify matters further. Thalamus D4 will show a neurological disturbance based on autonomic dysfunction. Epiphysis D4 tells us that psychogenic stress is present. Mandragora radice D30 shows exogenous depression, and at the D60 potency tells us it is endogenous in nature. Hypothalamus D800 shows psychosomatic illness; Epiphysis D400 shows hypersensitivity.

Geopathic stress has become a matter of keen interest among alternative practitioners. The Vega system claims to have filters that can tell us more about a patient's problem:

Geopathic Stress Filters

Silica D60	Geopathic stress present
Iron filings	Geomagnetic stress
Quartz sand	Curry grid (Dr. Manfred Curry lines)
Cuprum met. D800	Double grid stress
Phosphorous D60	Electromagnetic field stress
Agate	Yin stress (discharging field)
Calc. carb. D1	Yang stress (charging field)
Radium bromide D1000	Ionizing radiation exposure
Silica D2000	Frequency stress

Other filters can tell us if the patient is yin- or yang-dominant (linseed oil and sugar water, respectively), mercury toxic (Merc sol. 30), vitamin-deficient (Manganum D200), enzyme-deficient (Zincum met. D200) or hormone-deficient (Molybdenum met. D200).

I have some problem with the nature and efficacy of these 'filters'. They were largely developed by Schimmel and seem very subjective, as well as empirical. However, I do accept that the Staufen pharmacy, which prepares the ampoules, manufactures strictly ethical products, using dilutions of real-time substances to create the filters. Something is going on, that is clear; I know a case where Radium bromide D1000 read on a woman patient—it emerged her husband worked in the Sellafield Nuclear Power Station. The tester knew nothing of this at the time. Did she carry minute traces of radioactive material? If not, what strange quantum ripple or 'etheric' message was picked up by the woman from her spouse and carried to the practitioner's clinic?

I find these matters fascinating and filled with the richness and luxurious mystery of Nature rather than an affront to my scientific training. I just think it is high time that proper evaluation studies were carried out and we got past the 'empirical' stage which has now dragged on until one could call it entrenched opinion.

The Vega machine manufacturers are fond of attacking other people's technology. It is time they applied the rules to themselves. What little material is published is mainly in German and this does not advance the international stature of this potentially enlightening test system.

STRESS INDEX

A novel and useful concept, introduced by Dr. Erwin Schramm with his Neo Bio-Electronic Test, is that of 'biological age'. It was taken up by Schimmel and also appears in a number of subsequent devices. This has nothing to do with calendar age (years) of the test patient but with the vitality and resistance of his or her tissues. The higher the biological age, the more prone the body is to decay and malignant processes. A more descriptive term might be 'stress index'.

Schimmel used potentized embryonic mesenchyme tissue as the reference test agent and gave a range arbitrarily calibrated from 1 to 21. A filter of Cuprum met. D400 is put into the honeycomb. Apart from amplifiers this is the only ampoule used, and it will set the 'indicator drop' (see page 258). One by one, starting with 21 and working down, the Mesenchyme ampoules are put in to test; if the Vega reading reverts to 100 (the reference point or prerequisite of Vega testing, indicating no disorder) this is positive.

Usually testing shows a high age (representing the pathology), a mid-range value (representing the body's present resistance capability) and a low value which is felt to be the 'optimum' biological age for that person.

Reference ranges are shown here:

1–6   Represent the range of normal cellular respiration and do not normally need treatment.

7–10   Indicate preclinical phases or functional disturbance with clinically manifest changes.

11–13   Usually clinically recognizable disease.

14–15   The beginning of chronic degenerative changes; Pre-malignant.

16–17   Possible micro-malignancies may be present.

18–21   Possible macro-malignancies which need to be tracked down.

Readings above 10 are usually a sign of clinically manifest disease.

The idea with therapy is to help the patient get down to his or her 'optimum biological age' value. But those who teach the Vega method explain that it is unwise to try to come down to the optimum age too quickly, otherwise unmanageable homeostatic stresses, which decrease the body's ability to recover rather than enhance it, may appear. Gradual improvement may take several sessions and a number of different remedies to drive out the disease signal and attain a suitable biological age.

REMEDY FILTERS

The Vega system obviously includes the capability of remedy testing, along the same lines as Voll's method. Possible remedies will give harmonious balanced readings; unsuitable remedies will create or increase the disorder control.

In fact we can be more refined in this. A number of filters introduced into the honeycomb prior to remedy testing will increase the success rate markedly. Thus, for example, filtering with the ampoule Ferrum metallicum D800 will eject remedies which are not going to be tolerated by the patient; Ferrum metallicum D26 shows it will be effective; and Manganum metallicum D26 shows it will be compatible with other remedies selected.

Homeopathic remedies, as you will read in Chapter 18, can sometimes have strong effects on the patient, even when ultimately beneficial. It is important to avoid causing too much unnecessary disturbance, since this rarely assists the true course of healing. This triple bracket of remedy filters is helpful in getting the balance just right.

ORGAN THERAPIES

Voll and Schimmel have given us the concept of 'the most stressed organ' and this has naturally led to new therapeutic regimes. Why treat a pain in the foot if the precipitating cause lies in the liver or adrenals? Obviously, medication to enhance organ function is the logical path.

Unfortunately, there is the stigma of patent medicines attached to such an approach (I still remember my mother's 'Little Liver Pills'). The fact is that centuries of herbal lore and specialist healing knowledge go into these compound formulas, which is more than can be said for most of the allopathic medicine range, where treatments come and go like fashions as they are found to be too toxic and then swept under the carpet.

The truth remains that there are considerable degrees of lowered function before gross pathology finally appears. It is right to give the body support at this stage, not when pathology has finally engulfed the organ. This is so elementary one wonders why the medical profession has such a struggle with the simple logic involved. Conventional tests for liver function require alterations in blood status or actual anatomical structure before a diagnosis of disease can be made. Yet these changes represent the final failure of the body to compensate. Long before that stage, Nature is working hard to keep everything going as it should, a nip here, a tuck there and a little bit of patch and mend. This is hardly optimal, and yet doctors will so often pronounce 'Your blood work is normal, therefore there is nothing wrong', when manifestly there is a problem and the patient feels unwell. It can be a question of degree.

Here is where energy medicine triumphs because it measures the electrical status of the organ and monitors its function as a whole. One might think of an 'organ gestalt' (whole composite). Subtle changes in this complete electrical field can reflect the fact that several different functions aren't working exactly as they should, while yet there is nothing majorly wrong.

Organ support could include a vitamin and mineral panel, such as my adrenal stress formula, digestive enzyme aids (to boost pancreatic insufficiency) or a liver nutrition formula. This can be combined with physical measures such as a coffee enema to stimulate the liver (common procedure with cancer cases), or colon cleanse where parasites and other bowel toxins are suspected.

PHENOLIC TESTING

A special and very useful application of the Vegatest is that of phenolic testing. I have written about this in my previous book *The Complete Guide to Food Allergy and Environmental Illness*.

In 1979 Dr. Robert Gardiner, Professor of Animal Science at Brigham Young University, Utah, began to speculate that his own allergies might be caused by a sensitivity to certain aromatic phenol-based compounds that are found naturally in plant foods and pollens. He acquired some of the pure compounds, made serial dilutions and began to experiment by taking sub-lingual (under the tongue) doses and noting the results.

Sure enough, he found that some phenolic substances reproduced his main symptoms. Not only that, but neutralizing these reactions with subsequent low-dose antidotes of the Miller-method type effectively solved his allergy problems. He was able to eat most foods without reactions. He experienced a major improvement in health.

In other words, allergy to coffee might really be an allergy to chlorogenic acid which is found in the coffee bean. Injecting the chemical produces the same allergic wheal and flare response as the food itself would. There are many such compounds in food. Milk contains 13; tomato has 14, soya 9. A little expertise in these phenol families leads to new allergy diagnostic skills. For example, someone reacting to beef, milk, banana, yeast, potato and tomato might actually be allergic to nicotinic acid. The table gives a number of common foods and their phenolic content.

PHENOLIC COMPOUNDS IN SOME COMMON FOODS

Compound	Found in
Apiol	almonds, beef, carrot, celery, cheese, milk, oranges, peas, rice, soya beans
Capsaicin	milk, onion, potato, tomato
Cinnamic acid	apple, banana, beet sugar, celery, cheese, grapes, lettuce, milk, onion, oranges, peas, tomato
Coumarin	apple, banana, beef, cane sugar, carrot, celery, cheese, chicken, egg, lamb, lettuce, oranges, peas, potato, rice, soya beans, tomato, wheat, yeast
Eugenol	almonds, beef, carrot, celery, cheese, milk, oranges, peas, soya beans, tomato

Gallic acid	almonds, apple, beet sugar, cabbage, cane sugar, carrot, celery, cheese, egg, grapes, lettuce, milk, onion, oranges, peas, potato, tomato, wheat
Malvin	apple, cabbage, carrot, celery, chicken, egg, grapes, lamb, lettuce, milk, onion, soya beans, tomato
Menadione	apple, celery, egg, grapes, lettuce, onion, peas
Nicotine	beef, milk, potato, tomato, yeast
Phenyl isothiocyanate	beef, cabbage, chicken, egg, lamb, milk, onion, peas, soya beans, tomato
Phlorizin or phloridzin	apple, beef, beet sugar, cheese, egg, grapes, lamb, lettuce, milk, orange, soya bean, yeast
Piperine	beef, beet sugar, cheese, chicken, grapes, lamb, milk, onion, peas, potato, soya beans, tomato, yeast
Piperonal	almond, beef, beet sugar, cabbage, lamb, lettuce, milk, tomato, yeast
Rutin (quercitin)	apple, beef, beet sugar, cane sugar, carrot, celery, cheese, chicken, egg, grapes, lamb, lettuce, milk, orange, pea, potato, rice, soya beans, tomato, wheat, yeast
Vanillylamine	almonds, apple, beef, cheese, grapes, lamb, lettuce, milk, onion, orange, potato, soya beans, tomato, yeast

The story was taken up by Dr. Abram Ber, who began testing patients for sensitivity of this type with a Dermatron. He was able to claim success with a wide diversity of complaints, particularly in infants and children, getting excellent results with autism, dyslexia, insomnia, enuresis, respiratory allergies, abdominal pains and asthma. In adults, remissions were achieved with many chronic problems such as migraine, fatigue, depression, asthma, arthritis, colitis, hypertension, menstrual problems, skin diseases, chronic constipation and cardiac arrhythmias.

People struggling against their allergies suddenly found a whole new dimension of management for their condition. This can rightly be ascribed as a major benefit of the Vegatest system, or any EAV derivative. Intradermal testing of these compounds would be slow, painful and time-consuming. The Vegatest is quicker, non-invasive and far cheaper to administer than hours of intradermal tests, though as someone who has done both, I believe it is not as accurate and is subject to the cautions discussed in the following section on objectivity ('Considerations', below).

Some phenolic compounds have been found to correlate well with certain diseases. Cinnamic acid (in fruits, cheese and nuts) is a major cause of skin irritation in eczema and other dermatological conditions; coumarin (wheat, rice, barley, corn, soya, cheese, beef and eggs) contributes significantly to arthritis; malvin (found in some 35 common foods, including chicken, egg, corn, milk and soya bean) may be associated with autism, dyslexia, learning difficulties, epilepsy and other neurological disorders in children[1].

There are many other phenol-based compounds which are crucial to our physiology, such as neurotransmitters (serotonin is one), hormones, co-enzymes and pharmacological food ingredients such as caffeine, enzyme inhibitors and anti-nutrients.

The Vegatest is used to establish neutralizing dilutions in just the same manner that any remedy testing is carried out. The ideal antidote would be that which eliminates the disorder read when an allergy filter is in the honeycomb. The patient takes these neutralizing dilutions sublingually for a month and then returns for retesting. The aim is to get down to the first dilution (5X), meaning that the patient has become fairly tolerant of the allergen. He or she can then use a weekly or twice-weekly maintenance dose.

IMPORTANT CONSIDERATIONS

Vega testing requires more skill than EAV but both are difficult to perform well. The clumsy Vega probe is certainly part of the problem. I myself learned to use this technique in the 1980s and it would not be right to withhold from the reader that the machine tends to give the practitioner what he or she expects. In other words, I liken it to 'electronic dowsing'. Those who watched Schimmel himself at work observed that he often varied his probe pressure and seemed to know what he was going to 'discover' before he found it.

This raises the question that the disorder control (or indeed Voll's Indicator Drop for that matter) are no more than subconscious muscle responses to a preconceived mental intuition. In a world of supposed objective science, this standard of testing may seem a little strange; it may not sit comfortably for some. Therefore it is vital to make clear to the reader that any such 'objectivity' is a myth. No scientific study has ever been devised which eliminates the element of operator intrusion. This is one of the main things that quantum physics has taught us.

This is a widespread problem in energy medicine and subjective practitioner "detection" techniques. I feel I need to warn the reader that many would-be health investigators are deluded. The late Dr. Hulda Reger Clark was notable in this respect. She played heavily on her PhD (not a medical qualification) and published a book entitled "The Cure for All Cancers"[2]. In it she describes tests in which she, the operator, "diagnoses" cancer in the patient and then, a week or two later, announces to the happy patient that he or she has been "cured". Even the most liberal alternative practitioner could not and should not accept this shabby standard of science.

That's not to say she is wrong in proposing organisms and substances have unique identification signatures. That's the whole premise of the *Medicine Beyond* model (see Chapter 19 for more).

But this good lady seems unable to understand that if she has a fixation that all cancers are caused by the parasite Fascioliasis buski and isopropyl alcohol, then that is what she will find when she "tests" for them. That doesn't make it true!

Her platform is ridiculous, in that the parasite in question is not found in any country in the Western world, where cancer statistics are highest. In fact it is confined to China, Vietnam and other south-east Asian countries.

Moreover cancer has been around for centuries more than isopropyl alcohol. The major discrepancies are, I think, sufficient to brand her as a crank, if not a crackpot.

It is not supporting evidence to point out that many patients get well with her treatment. Many patients get well anyway—patients recover from cancer if you do nothing[3]!

Nor is it enough to say more patients get well than with conventional anti-cancer therapy; because the population she deals with is highly motivated towards alternative survival strategies and self-help. Many of these will fight their way to a recovery, with or without her ideas.

If Clark gets positive results at all (and some people claim she had success), then I wager it is because of the adjuncts to her theories, namely that patients are encouraged to depollute, eat a good diet and take adequate nutritional supplements. There is ample proof that this helps the fight against cancer; so it does not mean her outlandish ideas hold water.

In the same way, practitioners who are constantly finding the same thing on their patients should try to be honest in self-appraisal and ask the question whether or not they are finding their own story all the time. This can mean pet obsessions and narrow thinking; or it could mean that the practitioner in question has the disease personally and is misinterpreting the findings to mean it is a signal from the patient!

Naturally, you may expect that this teaching isn't popular with would-be practitioners. But I can only tell it as I see it and encourage you to be cautious in evaluating the truth.

In fairness, leading Vegatest practitioner Dr. Julian Kenyon acknowledges the inevitable inclusion of the psychokinetic effect and defends it heavily. As he says, *'It is important to recognize the part played by the practitioner in bio-energetic regulatory techniques such as the Vegatest method. This does not detract from their validity but merely means that the Vegatest and similar methods are looked at for what they are, no more and no less. They are however easier to carry out than using a totally psychic effect such as in dowsing because an objective subtle electrical change is taking place.'*[4]

Dutch worker Van Wijk investigated this further in 1989[5]. He carried out studies on EAV performance. Voll's method of point testing was addressed in great detail and it was found that a pressure of 125 grams was optimum. At this level the variability of resistance was less than 5 per cent. The average recovery rate of refractory skin tissue at this optimum pressure was 10 seconds. Van Wijk really showed that changes in conductivity are pressure-sensitive and independent of electrical current which, on the face of it, undermines Voll's work.

However, in 1992 Van Wijk showed that trained practitioners could identify an 'active' ampoule among 19 blanks over 90 per cent of the time (1:20 probability).[6]

This is a far higher rate than chance and considerably better than conventional medicine recovery rates.

THE HUMAN DETECTOR

My own view is that the human organism is capable of operating as a sensitive quantum biomagnetic detector and that the results are at least in a degree objective. In other words the tests can be blind and the operator will sense something; that 'something' will lead to a subconscious alteration in probe pressure. I judge this valid scientifically. However, a great deal more investigative work needs to be done, otherwise all this is food for the critics. It does not serve the cause of advancement to duck the awkward issues. Instead we need to address them conscientiously and vigorously.

The necessary mind-brain link probably comes within known physics laws which at present remain hidden from view simply because of current practical limitations and gaps in our theoretical understanding (as was the case for so many centuries regarding the body's energy fields). All we can say with our present state of knowledge is that a thought potential somehow excites an electromagnetic response which can then act at a distance.

We have already seen that the human energy field can damage or disrupt computers, watches and other sensitive electronic equipment. I wrote about this in *The Allergy Handbook* (1988) and suggested that allergy sufferers seemed to have far more powerful electromagnetic 'auras' than most people. As a spectacular demonstration of this human energy charge, an experiment was conducted at the Menninger Foundation[7]. Exceptional subjects were suspended in front of a large wired copper wall and were shown to give off very substantial electromagnetic fields. These fields were easily capable of disrupting microelectronics and therefore capable of attracting reads on an EAV instrument.

A cadre of scientists has taken the view that if quantum theory is the best explanation of reality we have at present, then it should take account of mind and consciousness and the part these play in phenomena. Professor D. F. Lawden at Aston University, Birmingham, England, is among those who think that systems which are dependent on the observer state—that is, which include consciousness in the nature of the construct—are especially worthy of study.

Several of the diagnostic and therapeutic techniques I have detailed in this book are just such examples of psycho-physical states displaying quantum characteristics. Lawden has gone so far as to draw up modifications of the basic equations of quantum mechanics, to allow for possible disturbing psychic effects being introduced by the participants[8]. This has also helped to clarify what constraints to 'reality' there may be, when recognizing there is no absolute or autonomous state. In this, Lawden likens quantum science to the philosophy of Irish bishop George Berkeley (1685–1753), one of the so-called British Empiricists. Berkeley's basic premise was that all matter and material form has no meaning whatever outside the mind. It might be there, but how could we ever contact it without mind?

To accept Lawden's argument would put ideas and sensations as the primary events, and matter (particles, energy) as secondary participants; this is exactly where our Eastern forebears left our cosmos 4,000 years ago. We have gone through the convolutions of supposedly superior scientific method, right up to the minute and beyond, only to end up where intuitive gifts and metaphysical knowing took us a long time ago!

Casebook: Male, 40 Years

In case this review of objectivity should have suggested that the Vega test or any EAV is of doubtful worth, let me cite a case from the files of world-class EAV specialist Anthony Scott-Morley of Poole in Dorset.

The patient had complained of persistent discomfort in the region of the liver. Routine laboratory examinations by the family doctor had revealed no abnormality. Orthodox treatment including anxiolytic drugs had, not surprisingly, failed. The private opinion of the referring doctor was that the patient was neurotic and would benefit from psychotherapy.

Vega testing showed a stressed liver, which was balanced by the ampoule aflatoxin. Aflatoxin is a highly toxic fungus commonly growing on moldy nuts, especially peanuts. Scott-Morley asked the patient if peanuts had any significance for him. The patient expressed great surprise and started to cry.

It emerged that he had been employed as a truck driver and had some months earlier transported a truckload of peanuts to England. On arrival at Customs the consignment had been condemned as moldy and unfit for human consumption. Yet the driver had, not unnaturally, consumed many handfuls on his journey across Europe.

Treatment using the Aflatoxin nosode resulted in prompt and permanent relief of all symptoms.

CHAPTER 17

Bioresonance – The Substance of Things not Seen

 *If we knew what it was we were doing, it would not be called research, would it?*

— Albert Einstein

Everything in Nature gives out information, whether in the form of sound, light, smell or vibrations.

Cymatics, developed by Dr. Hans Jenny, is basically a method of visualizing sound. Vibrations can be transferred to a suitable medium, such as sand trays or water surfaces, where the sound appears as distinct visible patterns (remember the shaking water cup in the movie Jurassic Park?)

Sound has form and sound can create form within matter. Later in the book we shall visit the later work of Jacques Benveniste and see that he found a way to turn the electromagnetic "signature" of biologically active substances into sound patterns that could be transmitted over vast distances.

Cymatics could be said to be an early version of resonance in nature. Today it is often presented electronically, for convenience. But the same resonance patterns are there. Moreover complexity increases as frequencies rise. It proves once and for all just how critical vibrations are for living creatures. Heck, even non-living substances respond, as described in the notes about Jagadish Chandra Bose and his metal plates experiment (page 79).

Artist Evan Grant, in one of the TED talks, has likened Cymatics to an almost magical tool, to allow us to look into other physical realms than the obvious. The universe itself has resonated with complex frequencies since the dawn of time and, knowing Cymatics theory, we can state that resonance forms and frequencies are integral to the structure of reality.

It follows, therefore, that resonance forms and frequencies are integral to the makeup of living forms, not just the non-living. Grant calls it the "substance of things not seen".

We can take that as the theme for the rest of this important chapter.

RESONANT DISHARMONY

As I have hinted throughout, if resonance and harmony are good for health, it follows that disturbed, unharmonious resonances can initiate disease.

We have considered so far how the patient's energy field is paramount, and how disturbances in that field may give rise to disease. The field itself has the power to make changes, leading to decay and sickness.

A novel idea which evolved in the 1970s, piggy-backing new technological possibilities, was to use modifications of the patient's own energy emissions as a means of eliminating disharmony and morbidity. If we can somehow use electronic machines to strengthen the healthy energies and at the same time eliminate the unhealthy ones, whole new therapeutic possibilities open up. This was the line taken by Dr. Franz Morell and led along a parallel development sequence to the Vegatest.

The term 'bioresonance therapy' (BRT) has come to mean therapy with the patient's own oscillations, after being modified in a pro-health way.

This differs somewhat from the EAV approach on two main counts: first, that one need not identify the cause of pathological oscillations, and second that the counter-agent or means of eliminating the wrong energies need not be some exterior agent, such as a medicine, but can be accomplished by means of modulating or cancelling the unwanted signal, while at the same time strengthening the 'good' energies. We could introduce the term electronic homeopathy for this class of healing.

ELECTROMAGNETIC SIGNALS

Pathological electromagnetic oscillations are active alongside normal oscillations in the body of every patient. Indeed, even healthy individuals certainly have some element of such disharmony but, as Lakhovsky suggested, if the energies of the normal cells are stronger than the pathological energies, then health can be maintained. On the other hand, if Lakhovsky's 'war of energies' goes against the tissues and cells, the resulting disturbance of the dynamic equilibrium will lead to disease, even cancer and death. The important point is that the electromagnetic signals from a diseased patient contain all the information needed for therapy, if only we could successfully decode it.

Morell's idea was that we do not necessarily need to decode it, if only we can identify which signals are the problem. Ideally there would be some kind of filtering process to divert the pathological energies, which could then be altered and used to modulate the disease process. The problem is to know which are the bad energies among the huge volume of information traffic and 'noise' going on round a living organism such as a human body. Fortunately, harmonious energies do tend to be similar from person to person. These are the dynamic energies. Any impinging signal which is fixed is very likely to be non-biological in nature; in other words, harmful.

THE MORA MACHINE

Morell went to work, with his son-in-law Erich Rasche, and together they developed a device now known as the MORA machine (MO from Morell and RA from Rasche). Rasche, an electronics engineer, reports that it was some time during 1976 that Morell handed him over 500 small metal washers. These were color-coded and, according to Morell, had the 'information signal' imprinted in them of homeopathic potencies. The idea was to use these for remedy testing, along the lines of EAV.

Plexiglas sheets holding 100 washers each were made; 10 such sheets would store 1,000 remedy tests.

In fact, nothing directly came of this idea and it was not until the advent of computer technology a decade later that this dream of storing a large number of 'information signals' came to fruition[1]. However, this got the two men started on research and development, together with biophysicist Ludger Mersmann, and what they came up with in 1977 was a machine which certainly changed the face of future medicine. We are still only three decades into its development, and so it has far from fulfilled its potential yet. But, scientifically speaking, the principle is simple and sound; technologically it is straightforward; and therapeutically it has proved its usefulness time and time again. As the energy medicine paradigm advances, the MORA machine will grow in stature. Already there are a number of copycat and derivative devices, including the BICOM, which is discussed later.

What the MORA machine basically does is enhance harmonious oscillations to help the tissues overthrow the noxious process, and inverts pathological signals, which effectively cancels them out. *www.med-tronik.de*

A little more physics is needed here. A waveform has peaks and troughs, as the signal 'oscillates' or varies in intensity. To invert a signal means to put peaks where there were troughs, and vice versa; this effectively results in zero energy, since one cancels out the other (see illustration below). It is very simple to arrange this electronic process. In fact Rasche also arranged that all signals could be passed through to the patient, unaltered; the harmonious signals could be amplified (but would not, logically, be inverted), or the harmonious energy, combined with inverted pathological energy, could both be amplified if necessary.

The input signals from the patient are picked up directly from electrodes held in the hand, or from foot plates. These are delivered to the machine and modified in various ways. The resulting output or therapeutic signals can be 'played back' through the same electrodes, or via a probe. As in 'Basic Therapy' described below, the input signal may even be taken from a little of the patient's body fluid, such as saliva or blood.

In addition to the electronic apparatus necessary to make these arrangements, the MORA machine is also fitted with an EAV device, since practitioners of BRT are almost invariably involved with EAV, so close are the two disciplines.

However it should be pointed out that the MORA machine probably has more in common with Abrams' *Oscilloclast* and Boyd's *Emanometer* than with EAV[2]. Other possibilities offered by this family of machines include the use of low light frequencies, filtered and modulated, which are then played back electronically through skin electrodes, or the use of direct light enhancement (compare this with the machine described in Chapter 22).

For most people Bioresonance Therapy is very well tolerated. It has been in use for over 30 years and there have been no cases of anyone experiencing serious side effects as a result of treatment. It can be used to treat people of any age and in any state of health. In some cases people may experience mild side effects such as headache, nausea or tiredness for up to 24 hours after treatment. This is common in so-called "detoxing".

A USEFUL EXPERIMENT

Experiments on animals can be revealing. One uses animals not only because doing so throws up fewer moral implications, but also because in doing so one can exclude likely psychological factors.

In a 1985 study using Syrian hamsters, benefits from bioresonance were clearly seen which could have no placebo basis. One group of hamsters was treated with bioresonance, while the controls were left untreated. All other factors, such as food, heat and lighting were kept constant. Various parameters were studied, including red cell count, a differential leukocyte count (thus giving lymphocyte totals), weight and quantitative food hoarding.

The treated group became more lively, their defense and flight reactions were faster and their coats were smoother than those of the controls. Food hoarding, a species sign of health, was considerably higher in the treated group than in the controls.

Among the hematological parameters tested which were significant, the treated group showed a marked rise in lymphocytes, which is equivalent to an increase in immune function and longevity[3]. The protocol, though simple, was impeccable and the results convincing.

Veterinary bioresonance has since become a reality. Animals are said to be particularly rewarding and responsive subjects. It is just as effective with very large animals, as with smaller species. The only difficult group is that of very hairy patients!

BASIC THERAPY

The methodology of BRT is relatively simple. Before starting with a therapeutic regimen using a device such as the MORA machine, it is customary to carry out a pre-treatment or so-called 'Basic Therapy'. This means to enhance harmonious energies and invert pathological ones, so strengthening the patient's resources. This can be very important with chronically sick and weakened patients, who want to be in good shape to receive the main therapeutic energies without being knocked over by them!

The patient provides a little saliva which is put into the metal beaker on the input side. This beaker is in effect a receiving device, rather like a radio aerial; the signal is led away through a lead, to be amplified and modulated within the apparatus. Other 'input' samples could include skin scrapings, nasal secretions or vaginal and rectal swabs—in fact any bodily tissue or fluid.

Settings on the machine allow simple choices such as amplification, inversion and filtering. For children it may even be desirable to attenuate the signal somewhat. A few minutes of this pretreatment is all that is required.

VOLL MERIDIANS

The MORA specialist then goes on to test individual meridians, keeping a note of the readings at each Central Measurement Point (CMP). This is much in line with Voll's method; balance is taken to be anything between 45 and 55. Again, too high is inflammatory and too low means degeneration. Indicator Drops (IDs) are seen, exactly as you would expect.

But here is where bioresonance enters. With bioresonance it is possible to alter the emanations being collected by the probe at each main pathology point (most abnormal reading or biggest ID), using the amplification, inversion and broadcast principle. The modern MORA has various settings which allow the practitioner to focus on different bands or 'windows' of frequencies. He can then take the incoming signal and make three basic changes: amplify it; invert it and amplify it; or filter out the pathological signals. The way this is decided in practice is by playing each modulation in turn and seeing which brings the point back nearest to the ideal 50.

A treatment would then consist of playing the therapeutic signal through the patient for several minutes. The body cannot respond well to the intensity of a constant signal; it becomes refractory. Instead the therapeutic message is broken up into parcels. A fixed number of timed units can be spaced out with pauses between. Empirical tests indicate that 3 seconds of signal followed by 1 second of pause is probably the optimum. In this way the full treatment energy is received without resistance by the tissues.

ALLERGIES

One unusual aspect of the MORA machine, not shared by other EAV apparatus, is the ability to modify allergy signals. I have always argued that allergy is basically an information-field signal, rather than a simple biochemical process (based on antibodies). Because of this little-known fact there is the potential to modify the patient's receptivity to the harmful energy of an allergen.

This is also, incidentally, a good demonstration for those who remain skeptical about the whole process now being described. If the patient's allergen is placed in the beaker and the signal therefrom is played back electromagnetically through the output electrodes, the patient may experience symptoms. It is remarkable that the signal for wheat can provoke, say, an attack of wheezing in an asthmatic. If not, turning up the amplitude of the signal is very likely to do so. This verifies the existence of the allergy and proves that it is not a biochemical or immune process, whatever conventional medicine says. It allows us to show once and for all that every substance has a unique energetic signal and that this can harmfully interact with our endogenous energies. No chemical or fluid changes position or enters the patient's body, yet symptoms are triggered!

Treatment of allergies may be effectively carried out by inverting the input signal. It is not easy to see the logic of this but it does seem to work; indeed, in my opinion it is one of the best available uses of the MORA family of devices. Perhaps the body is being electromagnetically reprogrammed using the 'anti-allergy' signal, which can then be incorporated into the energetic dynamics. Treatment takes place weekly, with gradually increasing numbers of timed units, rather like the old immunological allergy protection known as hypo-sensitization, where the dose increases until the body can learn to tolerate it. From then on it protects the body in much the same way that any antidote would.

As an amusing aside, this process can be carried out on other substances. If cheap rough whisky or wine is placed into the tray, and then signals from it are inverted and played back into the bottle, the resulting drink is unquestionably enhanced. This claim never fails to attract laughter and disbelief from audiences; yet even the most incredulous of sceptics is usually impressed by the happy result. Blind tastings show that there is indeed a difference.

BAND PASS DEVICES

Certain improvements in the basic MORA procedure suggest themselves. A competitive device, developed by former US MORA representative Hans Brügemann, addresses some of the issues. It has taken advantage of available computer technology and is accordingly dubbed the BICOM (BI-ological COM-puter): *www.bicom.com*

It has around a thousand pre-programmed case handlings, with pre-set frequencies and timed units based on the pooled knowledge of many practitioners of the MORA school.

101 is the so-called 'basic program'. A BICOM practitioner is also offered the possibility of entering and storing their own favorite programs. This is certainly an advance over the 'manual programming' of the MORA machine and an obvious benefit of computer technology that lends itself to the situation.

But the chief technological advance the BICOM boasts is the use of a band pass, a cyclical passage of a narrow 'information window' up and down the scale from 10 Hz to 150,000 Hz. This innovation is based on the observation over many years that therapy works best if oscillations are returned in a relatively narrow range. Otherwise the cellular dynamics may be given too much to deal with.

Couple this with the discovery by Cyril Smith at Salford University, England that effective bioresonance therapy results in an immediate response, whereas less appropriate or detrimental energies take some time to develop the adverse effect. It makes sense to move rapidly over the ground and give short bursts of therapeutic signals, rather than linger as with the older method.

Thus we have a number of new options in the BICOM, over and above returning all frequencies simultaneously:

1. Only a small part of the frequency is returned, in a selected range, usually chosen by the operator.

2. A range of frequencies is swept just either side of a central set figure. Technically this is known as 'wobble'. The amount of deliberate wobble can be varied but still operates within a relatively narrow range.

3. The whole end-to-end range is swept automatically, concentrating on one part at a time, but covering every possible allowed frequency.

It will be seen that only option 3 actually covers all possible frequencies, though not all at once. It may be important to operate over the whole range; since no frequency is transmitted for long the chance of developing adverse effects is almost zero, whereas the benefits, as Smith showed, happen almost instantly. Furthermore, the patient may respond favorably to several different frequencies; in fact commonly does. This ensures these secondary beneficial zones will be visited too; and yet overall it saves the operator time.

A BRIEF CRITIQUE

Much controversy has surrounded the BICOM, some of which, if valid, should rightly be aimed at the MORA machine too. Part of the attack on the BICOM's performance has come from rival manufacturers, such as Vega. The latter claim to have special electronic sensing equipment which has examined the output from the BICOM and shown it to be worthless and not what is claimed. Perhaps this should be seen mainly in terms of a marketing offensive, rather than the purest of scientific motives.

You will need to read Chapter 23 for a sensational update on this particular story.

One thing is certainly true: BICOM comes under the anti-radionics legislation in the US and encountered hostility from the authorities. The American public, it seems, needs protecting from funny waves, even though the US Food and Drug Administration claims these waves do not exist!

The EAV device incorporated in the BICOM is perfectly straightforward and cannot be challenged legitimately by Vega. It is a simple resistance measuring device, a Wheatstone bridge, known to every schoolboy (do I have to say every schoolgirl too these days?)

Also the inversion and amplification channels are simple and unarguable electronic manipulations.

The logic and empirical science behind the band pass is perfectly cogent to me. It is notable in this respect that the MORA people have responded by introducing the band-pass facility into their own latest machine.

It is only the pre-program facility of the BICOM that can be separated from the other aspects and targeted for special criticism. I doubt it is so important, since most BRT practitioners have their own views on suitable treatment programs.

My own unease comes from the performance of the filter or separator, which is absolutely critical to BRT. If your filter lets through the harmful oscillations, the theory is lost. We have no standard against which to judge what is a pathological signal. I indicated above that any fixed vibration is unlikely to be physiological in nature, but other than that it is little more than speculation what a disease oscillation behaves like.

Brügemann defends his separator vociferously by pointing to an experiment which showed that temperature drop in healthy patients, caused by subjecting them to the information signal of mercury in the input beaker, was effectively blocked by it. Without the protection of first passing the signal through the separator, subjects experienced an alarming fall in temperature of almost 2 degrees Centigrade within 30 seconds; the experiment had to be discontinued because of heart fibrillations[4].

My view is that such an experiment is rather unethical if you believe your own story about negative oscillations. But it also seems to me that Brügemann fails to make his scientific point, since this only shows that the machine can single out mercury signals. It does not show it is capable of discerning all good from all bad among the huge totality of ultrafine oscillations of the body, as is claimed. What it does show, which is helpful for my text, is that energy signature oscillations of toxic substances have great impact on biological systems, exactly as Jacques Benveniste demonstrated (see chapter 10).

Until Regumed, the manufacturer, stops hiding behind proprietary secrets and tells us what they are using in the separator, we cannot properly evaluate their ideas. Perhaps time and further research will clarify matters for us all.

Noteworthy: the current MRSP for the new Bicom Optima is $30,000 or more. That's the price of a brand-new typical family car. The MORA machine remains around $20,000. My suspicion of claims (in any commercial venture) rises as the square of the profits to be made!

SMOKING CESSATION

One very useful application of bioresonance that has emerged in recent years is to use it to aid patients in their fight to stop smoking.

Inverting the nicotine signature helps eliminate the toxin from the body and simultaneously helps the body overcome any addiction. The cravings are dramatically reduced. Proponents of the method claim a 90% success rate, which is far ahead of anything that nicotine patches or SSRIs (like Chantix) can achieve. In fact patches and drugs achieve only a miserable 10 - 11% quit rate, when measured at half a year (26 weeks); this drops to around 5% at the 12-month mark.

The much-vaunted drug varenicline (Chantix) by Pfizer was really no better than nicotine patches, despite all the hype that went into its initial marketing[5]. The joke is that quitting on your own, just with willpower, can achieve an 11.5% quit rate. - In other words, no real difference.

Moreover, high quality local clinic programs around the world were achieving 25 to 40% quit rates at the 24-week mark. Some really good ones achieve 24-week rates in excess of 50%. Programs like Joel Spitzer's abrupt cessation Chicago two week clinic has consistently generated one year rates near 52%, and the Ohbayashi program in Japan generated a 58% one year rate. These are sudden-quit methods; not attractive to the marketers peddling "slow withdrawal" using their expensive OTC nicotine patches.

Compared with other methods, bioresonance substance-free quitting has a lot to offer.

PARASITES

Bioresonance may come into its own in respect of parasites. These critters are notorious at hiding and evading detection. They have even been accused of shape shifting or, to use a more prosaic word, *pleomorphism*.

Recently Jane Andrews, arguably Australia's leading bioresonance expert, stayed at my home and I had the opportunity to grill her on the use of her BICOM device for dealing with parasites.

Without prompting from Jane I knew, of course, of the many and varied symptoms that can be traced by the astute clinician to the presence of hidden parasites. Even so, I was surprised that Jane was finding parasites quite often as a contributory cause of unlikely conditions such as menstrual pains and bladder symptoms.

The BICOM (or MORA, etc.) scores heavily when compared against laboratory testing, which is very unreliable for finding and confirming parasite burdens. Not only can such a device detect parasites, by virtue of their "resonating" presence, but it can also help to indicate where the parasites are hiding. Jane had found worms in the uterus, bladder and other pelvic organs, hence the surprise effect on gynecological symptoms.

Parasites can move too, once they are being hit by effective treatment. So they retreat into other tissues, to escape being killed. But testing the stressed meridian points, as described in Chapter 15, will still locate them, without needing a whole new lab work up—a further advantage of this approach.

What Jane especially emphasized to me was the need to couple parasite roundup raids with heavy metal detection. Parasites seem to especially flourish where heavy metals are present; they almost seem to "feed" on such substances. In any event, metals like lead and mercury poison the immune system and render it less effective at shrugging off cunning parasites.

She starts her investigations with a "mix" of heavy metals test ampoules. If these reads positive, she then does individual heavy metals, to establish which one is the main burden. With that filter in place, she can then go after parasites with their natural cover shield in place.

A neat trick.

Several treatments may be needed, the first to stun the parasites and inhibit their ability to reproduce. Later treatments come down and down in frequency, until all residues are gone. Subsequent attempts to provoke a parasite resonance response should be negative.

Now in case you may be thinking that this is all nonsense or, at best, speculation, let me tell you my working rule: *he gets to make the diagnosis who effects the cure*. Meaning: if you can produce successful recovery results, or even a cure, your version of the diagnosis is probably correct.

In this instance, Jane has been getting exemplary results, whether or not her electro-acupuncture skills are just average or above.

MERCURY AMALGAM

Mention of heavy metal poisoning prompts me to write about mercury overload. So much has been said about mercury toxicity from dental amalgams that it would be superfluous to debate the issue here. More is said about it in Chapter 24, along with other more important and up-to-the-minute theories.

Bioresonance therapy does offer a new approach to this problem. Whereas one should remove fillings and so eliminate the source of contamination, this does not remove established tissue deposits, which are often considerable. One can try to use chelation agents such as DMPS (dimercapto-propane sulphonic acid) and DMSA (dimercapto succinic acid), which bind with the mercury and so eliminate it through the kidneys. But even this has potential dangers, since DMPS actually binds with neurological tissue and so cannot eliminate brain deposits. A better plan is to use the MORA playback facility to invert and counter the mercury signal, in much the same way as is done with an allergen. Rasche claims that this actually enhances the excretion of amalgam compounds.

The EAV part of the device can be used to establish exactly what heavy metal burden is present in the patient's body. This can then be used in the input beaker and the signal inverted, amplified and thus neutralized. Generally, Rasche recommends that the heavier the mercury burden, the higher the amplification needed. This seems to be logically sound.

Treatments are carried out twice a week for 3 to 4 weeks. Drinking copious soft water helps the ion elimination process and this is mainly effective at the time of therapy. In Rasche's words,

'The excretion process continues until the earth's natural magnetic field realigns the elementary particles of the remaining amalgam.' He offers no evidence for this claim[6].

AGENT ORANGE

Jane Andrews shared with me a particular case of a man in his late sixties. He had been exposed to Agent Orange, a herbicide manufactured by Monsanto (yes, them!)

Numerous studies have examined health effects linked to Agent Orange, its component compounds, and its manufacturing byproducts. I repeat my frequent warning that the term "herbicide" is a misleading one; the correct term is *biocide* (kills all life). To suggest it works only on plants is a deliberate misdirector.

In 1969 it was revealed to the public that the 2,4,5-T was contaminated with a dioxin (tetrachlorodibenzodioxin or TCDD), and that the TCDD was causing many of the previously unexplained adverse health effects which were correlated with Agent Orange exposure.

TCDD has been described as "perhaps the most toxic molecule ever synthesized by man". Internal memoranda revealed that Monsanto had, in fact, informed the U.S. government in 1952 that its 2,4,5-T was contaminated with this deadly substance. But no precautions were taken against this unintended side reaction, which also incidentally caused the Seveso disaster in Italy in 1976.

Predictably, Monsanto denied any responsibility (as they do) and in 2004, spokesman Jill Montgomery said Monsanto should not be liable at all for injuries or deaths caused by Agent Orange, saying: "We are sympathetic with people who believe they have been injured and understand their concern to find the cause, but reliable scientific evidence indicates that Agent Orange is not the cause of serious long-term health effects."[7]

Jane Andrew's patient, by the time he presented to her, was majorly deaf in both ears, needing hearing aids, had a tremor and suffered disabling dizziness. Agent Orange was reading clearly on the BICOM.

She started gently enough with a program to reduce heavy metals and chemicals, as part of a plan to eliminate the body's overall burden of toxins. But the patient's response was so severe, it resulting in him being bedridden for many days. Nevertheless, his hearing had returned in the left ear.

Despite the patient's pleas for more, Jane felt she could not risk incapacitating him further and subsequently gave a much-reduced "dose". The result was that his hearing returned to normal in both ears and his tremor and dizziness were much improved[8].

It's debatable whether there may have been Agent Orange residues in the man's body (very probable). What was certainly present was an Agent Orange energy and information "field" lodged in the man's nervous system. Bioresonance was able to shift that field off, to the great benefit of the patient.

OTHER APPLICATIONS

There are clearly very many possible applications for this energetic approach to health. Some which have had particularly gratifying results include infertility, where sperm count and motility have been seen to increase markedly after BRT; extensive burns, where non-invasiveness is a strong point; healing of bones; eye problems; tinnitus and gynecological problems. Children appreciate this treatment modality, since no pain is felt and their natural apprehensiveness is soon appeased. The child or infant can sit happily on his or her parent's lap while therapy is administered. ECG electrodes (the kind with rubber elastic straps) can be adapted as electrodes for very small babies.

Bioresonance therapy is especially useful in the management of substance addictions, such as heroin and cocaine. It is very helpful to an individual going through the unpleasant withdrawal phase to have harmful energies filtered out and the natural, health-boosting frequencies amplified. Obviously this does not eliminate the need for the patient to make a clear and determined decision to stop indulging their addiction. But by forcing the excretion of toxins and balancing yin-yang energies, the misery is much reduced.

Thus, after a general Basic Therapy, the addictive substance is placed in the input beaker and passed to the patient inverted and amplified, exactly as described for allergens and toxins above. It is essential to prescribe a simultaneous forced excretion therapy, including copious amounts of water, teas, enemas and liver cleansing. Vigorous exercise, lymph massage and depuration saunas are also helpful where possible. Homeopathic drainage support and organ stimulants may also be indicated (see Chapter 18).

Finally, an aggressive vitamin and mineral program is required, to help the body nutritionally overcome the toxins present and to ensure renewed healing and tissue repair. Withdrawal symptoms are very stressful to the organism and adrenal cortical function is often at maximum revs. High doses of vitamin C in the 10–20 grams range are also useful as a short-term detoxicant.

Even where the regime proves quickly successful, it is recommended that the patient attends regularly for many months, to reinforce the determination to quit.

PAIN

'Pain is the cry of connective tissue caused by blocked energy'; so the saying goes. This maxim of Dr. Weichel was often quoted by Voll. It emphasizes that pain is not really a local manifestation, even though the triggers may appear to be. Morell found benefit from treating the ends of those meridians (Ting points) which pass through the pain area, starting with the mirror-image points on the side opposite the painful area.

This can be followed by picking up signals from the pain area and, after inversion, playing these back to the tissues somewhat distal to the disease area. Increasing the amplitude of the inverted signal effectively pushes it deeper and deeper into the tissues. If pain is intensified during the treatment, this may not be a reason to stop the therapy. The practitioner must decide each case individually, but there can be a degree of beneficial intensification before the pain finally eases off. Sometimes physiological changes can be seen in the skin, such as a white patch becoming visible. This area should be made the target of output therapeutic energies. Treatment is continued until the skin resumes normal coloration.

Casebook: Male, 6 Years

This boy developed an astrocytoma, which has a very bleak prognosis. The consultant neurosurgeon had recommended chemotherapy. The parents, who were Buddhists, had rejected the idea and decided their child would die gently and with dignity, if that was to be. They prayed. Even better, they also took him to see a MORA therapist!

By this time the boy was in a desperate state and was so weak and wasted he had to be helped to walk into the clinic. The practitioner took blood and subjected it to the inversion and amplification process described; just a few minutes for the first visit. The child was sent home with homeopathic support therapy along the lines described for mesenchyme therapy in Chapter 18. Then, by gradually building up the timed units of treatment, once a week and then, eventually, once a fortnight, the lad was soon feeling well. A few months later he was able to resume athletics and playing rugby football.

The practitioner, who could also use a Vega machine, tested and found no remaining tumor signal, but there was a focus which was cystic. At about this time, the parents (without telling the MORA practitioner) took their son back to the original consultant. He was surprised to even see the boy alive. As is often the case, his attitude was dismissive and he said 'We must have been mistaken in our diagnosis.' This angered the parents, who were naturally incensed at the idea of their son being subject to chemotherapy based on a shaky diagnosis. But the old scans were brought out and re-examined: there could be no doubt... It was a tumor all right. With persuasion, the parents allowed a re-scan which showed that only a cyst now remained where once the tumor had been. The MORA practitioner has a copy of the letter from the hospital confirming this in his files.

This was a very satisfactory result for bioresonance medicine. Incidentally, the specialist never asked what the miraculous treatment was or showed the slightest interest in learning about it. He goes on giving chemotherapy to his patients.

RESISTANCE TO BRT

A number of factors are recognized to impair or block the benefits of BRT. These have been observed empirically over the years and form a basic list of resistance factors to any kind of therapy.

1. The place of therapy is geopathically stressed.

2. The patient's home or workplace is geopathically stressed.

3. There is a tooth focus or strong amalgam stress (see Chapter 24).

4. There are hidden psychological factors preventing success, which would include the practitioner's own doubts or skepticism.

5. There is a nutritional deficiency (no therapy works well in the present of nutrient deficiency).

6. There are hidden toxins, parasites or allergies present.

7. Allopathic drugs have a blocking effect. Even alternative therapies can sometimes interfere with each other.

8. The cables are damaged or the electrodes are not cleaned properly (energy disturbance can be carried over from the previous patient).

9. There is interfering scar tissue.

10. The therapist is insufficiently skilled or knowledgeable at what he or she is attempting.

COMPETING DEVICES

As is usual in any burgeoning field, there are many me-too products, some of which are very good and some of which are… well, not so good.

I have no intention of attempting a review of all available devices. Suffice it to say that you can find other models to consider by questioning at health shows or searching the Internet and these include:

- Bioresonance-LaesEr
- BIT 2012
- Holimed Bioswing
- Meritest
- AMS
- Kindling
- Rayonex

I have not given URLs because these seem to go out of date so quickly.

The Psi Sensor, also known as KPS, is a little different. About the same size as a VHS video, when linked to a PC with special software, the Psi Sensor is able to decode the electromagnetic frequencies between 0.5 and 80 Hz transmitted by the human brain. All this at a distance of just 1-2 meters and without connecting electrodes to the head or body of the patient.

SUMMARY OF BIORESONANCE THERAPY

Hans Brügemann of the Brügemann Institute, which manufactures the BICOM machine, has nicely summarized the chief precepts for understanding bioresonance therapy. In conclusion I give here a modified description of his bullet points:

1. In and around the human body there are electromagnetic oscillations. These oscillations are superordinate to the biochemical processes going on in the tissues and are the real control mechanism of tissue function.

2. As well as physiological oscillations there are also pathological interfering oscillations in every person, caused by toxin overload, injury, infection, unresolved disease processes and psychologically negative states (so-called emotional toxins).

3. Both natural and pathological oscillations can be picked up from the skin surface (antenna effect) and led to a suitably tuned therapeutic device.

4. The mixed oscillations from the patient can be modulated in three main ways:

    i. healthy signals amplified;

    ii. pathological signals inverted (and thus cancelled out); and

    iii. filtered, to separate the desirable frequencies from the pathological ones (the latter are, of course, eliminated in this process).

5. No technologically-generated artificial frequencies are needed; only oscillations from the patient which have been modified, as given in 4. The basic aim is to strengthen the good oscillations and eliminate the unwanted ones.

6. The body takes its cue from the modulated therapeutic signals and continues to produce enhanced physiological signals and appears to reprogram itself, so that in future a renewal of the pathological signals is guarded against. Thus the treated harmonious levels of electro-magnetic energy go beyond the merely temporary stage of treatment sessions.

7. Beneficial changes in the energy field are followed by a subsequent modification and improvement in biochemical function and physical structure.

8. BRT is successful when the body's own endogenous regulatory forces reassert control and lead to normalization and maintained health. Note that there is the possibility that merely wiring up a patient to devices and connecting their personal energy field to substances may be the crucial mode of operation, rather than resonance broadcasting as I have described here. The surprising secret is revealed in chapter 23!

CHAPTER 18

Basic Treatment Modalities

 Following a curious dogma that what we don't understand can't exist, mainstream science has dismissed psychic phenomena as delusions or hoaxes, simply because they are rarer than sleep, dreams, memory, growth, pain, or consciousness, which are all inexplicable in traditional terms but are too common to be denied.

—Robert O. Becker

I have already mentioned the idea of healing by strengthening chakras and, in acupuncture, releasing a healthy flow of Ch'i in the meridians, which can be done by electrical stimulation of appropriate acupuncture points.

It is time now to consider the medicinal therapy and remedies which are integral with EAV and its derivative, computer electro-dermal screening technology (see Chapter 19). In general this type of therapy is based on bio-information and energy; these therapeutic substances could therefore be termed 'virtual' medicines, in line with our overall theme and therefore beyond the ordinary laws of physics, biology and medicine.

To understand the place of this remarkable form of treatment it is useful to look at a categorization of different forms of therapy:

1. Invasive Methods

    a. Surgery, lasers, acupuncture, moxa therapy

2. Biochemical Methods

    a. Inorganic (e.g. minerals)

    b. Organic (e.g. herbs, drugs, vitamins)

3. Energy Methods

    a. Electro-magnetic waves, Reiki, acupuncture, bio-magnetism, sound, music, color therapy, homaccords

4. Information Methods

    a. High-potency homeopathy, Bach flower remedies, gem therapy, electrical bio-resonance, nosodes and sarcodes.

There are elements of all these modalities mixed in with what follows. Note that Robert O. Becker was particularly concerned with energy methods that might be too strong for body wisdom. In general, he would have liked homeopathy.

COMPLEX (GERMAN) HOMEOPATHY

Almost all practitioners of EAV use what is known as complex homeopathy. To understand its precise advantages it is necessary first to clarify the basic nature of homeopathy. Today it is largely forgotten that this was once a major system of treatment taught in over 25 per cent of US medical schools and that, until the arrival earlier this century of patentable allopathic drugs which could be marketed for huge profits, it enjoyed a sound reputation and was widely practiced, both in Europe and the New World.

With the coming of the drug boom, however, there emerged a new supposedly scientific paradigm based on laboratory testing on animals and clinical trials, particularly the double-blind sort. Alternative methods, or more traditional (older) approaches, were re-evaluated as 'not scientific'. Even simple remedies such as good food and rest were more or less rubbished in the stampede for newer and better 'magic bullets'. The attitude which today pervades conventional medicine is that what the treatment of disease needs is something to oppose or crush the unruly process. There is no concept of nurture or helping Nature to perform the cure. Indeed, Nature's generous wisdom is often abused or over-ridden, as in the case of chemotherapy or commando surgery for cancer.

Even less do many modern doctors understand that the disease process is necessary; it is a natural complement to the exigencies of life. Without the fight-back response, or what Hippocrates called *ponos* (the bit that hurts!), we would be overwhelmed by our hostile environment. Acute disease is actually the process of throwing off unwanted challenges. Usually this is successful. But by untimely interference with the process of resolution—by administering chemical suppression therapy, for example—we are simply driving the toxins or insult underground, where they will emerge later as a more chronic illness.

Homeopathy does the opposite. Far from being a powerful antagonist of disease, it actually mimics and uses the disease process to get the cure!

The name homeopathy comes from 'homo-' (same) and 'pathos' (disease, as in pathology). There is a famous Latin maxim: *'Similia Similibus Curentur'*, which translated means *'Like cures like.'* Although the idea has been in use since Hippocrates' time, and the great Paracelsus also wrote comprehensively of it, it fell to German physician Samuel Hahnemann to organize the key principles of homeopathy into a cogent scientific thesis, which he did in his great work *The Organon of Rational Medicine*, published in 1810 (he was 55 at the time)[1].

An example of this so-called 'law of similars' is that substantial doses of deadly nightshade (Belladonna) produce a clinical picture almost identical with scarlet fever (a once-common form of streptococcal tonsillitis which doctors hardly ever see these days). The scarlet fever patient has a bright red rash (hence the name), burning hot, dry, headachy, maybe even delirious, with wide staring eyes and extreme restlessness. Hahnemann found that if he administered Belladonna to a case of scarlet fever, the results were quite beneficial, sometimes even dramatic.

POTENTIZATION

But Hahnemann didn't stop there, and this is where homeopathy indeed seems strange. Hahnemann found that if you dilute the active substance, the treatment becomes more effective. The more dilute it is, the more powerful the remedy seems to be. This applies even when the original substance is so dilute there can be no chemical molecules left. Hahnemann called the dilution process *potentization*, since it manifestly made the treatment more powerful.

The apparent illogicality of intensification-by-dilution is what excites so much hostility from conventional doctors. They seem to have a silly fallback logic which argues: 'It can't work, and therefore it doesn't'. In fact the results show otherwise. There are an ever-increasing number of scientific trials being published that show homeopathy is an effective and safe alternative to drugs for many conditions. Even so, an editorial in the Lancet, which accompanied a paper showing that homeopathy worked, could not resist sniping with the comment that Hahnemann's theories were 'inherently implausible'.

In fact there is nothing implausible whatever about potentization. It merely requires that one finds the right model. Instead of thinking in terms of the concentration of biochemical substances, one has only to think in terms of an information field and realize that this is how homeopathy works. The medicine is carrying a message which knocks out the disease 'similar'. The medicine gets better through dilution, simply because we are diluting out what the technical people call 'noise', meaning the extraneous and unnecessary information which interferes with the message we want carried to the tissues.

CLASSICAL vs. COMPLEX HOMEOPATHY

It is sad to report that controversy has broken out even among homeopathic practitioners. There are two factions: the classic homeopaths, practicing in the manner of Hahnemann and those who use what is known as 'complex homeopathy'. I will briefly address the arguments which seem to be creating the rift so that, in looking at the issues, the reader may learn more about both disciplines.

The major difference is that classical homeopathy argues that there must be only one correct remedy for a patient at any one time. It has to be said that there is no scientific or logical basis for this supposition; merely that 'Hahnemann said so' but to insist upon it as doctrine risks becoming inflexible and out of step with newer developments. Complex homeopathy on the other hand, as you may suppose from its name, means giving multiple remedies at the same time; or only one remedy, but in a range of several different potencies (called a Homaccord).

But there are more subtle differences in philosophy and method between the two fields.

In general, the complex homeopaths use far lower dilutions, closer to what one might call biological values. Classical homeopathy, on the other hand, hots up at around the 30th centesimal, which means a substance diluted 100-fold repeated 30 times (10030); it can go to MM, meaning diluted 500-fold repeated 500 times (500500). To put this into perspective, from 24C (24th centesimal) onwards the dilutions are so enormous there can be no physical substance left.

Complex homeopaths, on the other hand, are quite happy with mixtures that contain 2X, 3X, 6X, etc., meaning a 10-fold dilution repeated 2, 3 and 6 times respectively. Complex homeopaths also tend to use a great deal more of diluted tissues and disease material, which we might call 'isopathy' though this word has little real impact. What this means is not so much 'treating like with like' as using 'same to heal same' (for example, healthy pig pancreas for pancreatic disease, Tonsilla for tonsillitis, Carcinomium for a lung cancer, and so on). This will be explained more fully below.

BUCKSHOT

The result is that complex homeopathy tends to be less of a one-hit miracle and more of a gradual attrition of the disease process, over a space of several months. Whereas a classical homeopath will stop the remedy the moment it is seen to produce a significant result, a complex homeopath smiles with satisfaction and adds another two months' prescription to the therapy program.

I bring up this controversy in some detail simply because it strikes at the heart of what we mean (or believe we mean) when we talk about homeopathy as being an 'energy medicine' or based on resonance and information fields.

If we believe our own explanation, then complex homeopathy ought to make the more sense of the two. We are talking about energy signals or information patterns resonating or interacting with sympathetic frequencies in the diseased patient. Therefore if there are a number of frequencies or a 'spread' of energies (like buckshot) at around the right magnitude, there will be more chance of successfully hitting the target. The unwanted resonances, which find no counterpart in the body, should have no interactive effect whatever. They just go away.

Classical homeopathy, one remedy at a time, it is true can produce very impressive results. But if the practitioner is mistaken in the choice of remedy, or chooses an unsuitable potency, there may be little or no result. This means added delays and suffering for the patient, while the practitioner tries something new.

There is another simple, all-too-human appeal in complex remedies. If we doctors are honest with ourselves and others, the reality of daily clinical practice reveals that we are far from perfect. With the exception of those individuals with outstanding memories it isn't possible to carry a full working knowledge of all potential remedies. A busy homeopath will often settle for a similar (near enough) rather than a true 'similimum' (exact remedy).

This lack of precision in choosing the similimum results in less effective therapy. Complex remedies are designed, at least in part, to accommodate for this lack of precision.

Complex homeopathy is sometimes called the 'German system', though in view of Hahnemann's nationality one could argue that both are the property of that great intellectual and cultured race.

In conclusion, it must be pointed out that all complex homeopaths are flexible enough to use classical remedies in the classical manner when these seem appropriate. We accord great respect to Hahnemann's teachings; but are not restricted needlessly by them.

MESENCHYME THERAPY AND THE MATRIX

In the absence of any objective measurable change at the structural or chemical pathological level, doctors are reluctant to consider 'real' disease and think instead of psychiatric or functional disorder (meaning disordered function of the mind; a euphemism for madness or delusion).

But there is another domain or theatre of disease, which, although ignored by the powerful financial lobby which controls modern medicine, has continued to be researched quietly in Europe and the former Soviet bloc for most of this century. We may term it the 'humoral' nature of disease—that is, disease manifested as a result of disruptive imbalances in the quality and content of the fluid medium in which our organs and cells are suspended. Two central figures in the development of this model, which is also sometimes called Homotoxicology, are the clinician Dr. Hans-Heinrich Reckeweg and Professor Alfred Pischinger, the father of modern histochemistry.

The fundamental concept is that of homo- (auto) toxins accumulating in the interstitial (support) fluid and tissues which we call the mesenchyme or 'matrix'[2].

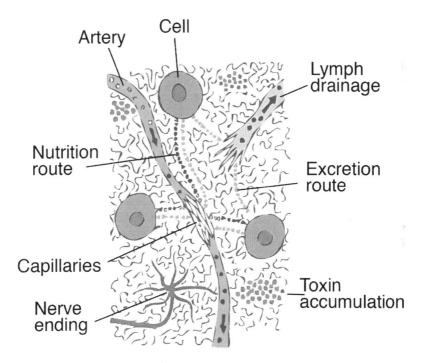

Toxin here does not simply mean pollution or waste matter from cells, but includes the 'memory' of disease and the residues of malfunction and stasis. But I would like to challenge the perceived wisdom. I suggest that the importance of the biochemistry of these toxins is secondary to the deterioration in the ionic energy-conductive properties of the collagen matrix.

Remember from Chapter 7 that Georges Lakhovsky predicted that the accumulation of interstitial toxins would cause alterations in electromagnetic oscillation potential, which would alter conductance and resistivity and mean that cells could no longer vibrate at their inherent healthy frequencies.

I have already reported on the concept of the intercellular matrix as a variable dielectric in Chapter 11. What is clear is that there is far more interstitial matter than cells which comprise organs. Thus, in terms of volume alone it makes a great deal of sense to pay attention to this fluid matrix. Yet it is barely mentioned in the medical school curriculum and doctors continue to graduate with no more than a passing knowledge of this vital energetic domain of our bodies. Far from being what is left when you take away the 'important' structures, the connective tissue matrix is the basic regulation system of the entire organism. Without it the organs could not function in a concerted whole. The matrix is to the organs of the body what the engine, gears and wheels are to the body of a car. A harmonious and well-functioning matrix is synonymous with good health.

This matrix has three obvious functions: nutrition, defense and repair. It carries out these functions in response to a whole gamut of input stimuli, whether energy, hormones, osmotic gradients, electrical impulses, immunological signals, neurotransmitters and, of course, any toxin-irritating presence.

What Reckeweg correctly perceived was that if Pischinger's matrix becomes clouded and sludged up with toxins, then there is a cumulative process of degeneration and decay, leading towards advanced pathological conditions, notably malignancy; the same message as Lakhovsky's. The organism works less and less efficiently until resistance is overcome. Finally the processes of pathology take over and run down the machinery towards death. By the time cancer growths appear, the end may well be close. Reckeweg coined the term 'homotoxicosis' for this sequence.

What Homotoxicology does is best thought of as de-polluting the matrix. The skilled use of appropriate complex homeopathic remedies can cleanse or reverse the decay process. It often means using toxin signals, presented homeopathically in the form we call nosodes. This drives out the disease process, though unpleasant reactions can appear as the reversal process gets under way. To prevent this we use drainage remedies which speed the elimination of toxins, as described below.

Reckeweg called this cleansing of the matrix and reversal towards a healthy state 'regressive vicariation'. I regard it as a potentially misleading term; I would prefer 'progressive vicariation', since it gives the idea of improvement. But Reckeweg's chosen expression calls attention to the fact that we are rolling disease backwards, reversing into earlier and better levels of health.

HERING'S LAW

This reversal of the disease process described by Reckeweg is associated with an older and well-established healing law. It was formulated by the 19th-century American homeopath Constantine Hering, but it applies to many healing disciplines, not just homeopathy. It is a truly great insight into the healing of disease and should be taught in letters of fire to all who aspire to comfort and mend our fellows.

Hering's Law states that, in the course of healing a disease, recovery takes place in three clearly defined ways and that these are signs of meaningful recovery:

1. Healing is from inside to outside. Thus a runny nose is an improvement on colitis or asthma. Do not diagnose 'rhinitis' and try to prevent the nasal mucus! The response is a healing process and not a new disease.

2. Healing is from top to bottom. Thus a skin rash will clear from the head first and lower limbs last. Keep going!

3. Healing takes place from the most important organs towards the least important. Thus irritable bowel could be a sign of therapeutic response from mental illness. You are drawing the disease from the mind into the body.

There is another very important and related aspect to this, which is that during the process of recovery the disease sometimes 'rolls back' through time: symptoms that came last go first; symptoms that preceded those may reappear for a time before they in turn vanish. A child who developed asthma and then migraine may well go temporarily back to asthma when put on an effective remedial program (this also fits rule 2). It's like putting the mesenchyme 'car' into reverse; you have to go back through all the old familiar landmarks you passed on your way to 'Disease-Ville'.

This observation is often tacked onto Hering's Law, though Hering himself did not phrase it so. Reckeweg may not be the first person to recognize the back-track phenomenon, but he was the first to give it a name, albeit the rather clumsy 'regressive vicariation'!

I myself have sometimes speculated that this order of healing is a sort of time-reversal (page 96).

NOSODES

I have hinted that probably the key therapeutic agent of mesenchyme therapy is the nosode. A nosode is a homeopathically-prepared sample of disease tissue or biological toxins. These samples are negative energy signals of substances which hurt or poison the body, or dangerous tissue. For example Carcinomium, made from cancer tissue, is very hostile to the body, as you would expect. Any disease-producing virus, bacteria or parasite would automatically make a nosode; Dr. Edward Bach, famous for his flower remedies discussed shortly, actually made some of the first-ever bacterial nosodes by potentizing vaccines, still known as the Seven Bach Nosodes[3]. Modern advances in the field of EAV and beyond have made it quite clear that pesticides, heavy metal poisons, electropathic stress, medicines and numerous other stressors all have the essential character of nosodes.

Nosodes are potentially strong remedies and may provoke an illness in response to their administration. Even though measles or TB may not be present, except as a virtual signal, the body still reacts as if the disease was in progress. The tissues fight back. The patient feels bad once again; we call this a 'healing crisis'.

DRAINAGE REMEDIES

Notwithstanding Hering's law, we solve this problem with the use of what are known as 'drainage remedies'. As the name implies, drainage remedies are substances which can provoke speedier toxin removal, whether by stimulating the kidneys, liver or other excretion pathways (diarrhea is seen by holistic practitioners as nothing more than toxin-flushing and often comes on in response to a treatment). We can categorize drainage according to organ: pancreas, liver, gut, etc. Or we can grade it according to power: mild, gentle, medium, forte and 'ultra' preparations.

It is said that almost any pathological or nosode preparation is capable of working as a drainage remedy, if the dilution is right. This will happen if it is not too forceful (lower potencies) and does not provoke more quickly than it cleanses. One of my patients joked about 'taking her diseases in water'!

It might seem tempting to administer the strongest drainage remedy possible, to give a good flushing to the system. But that is to think like a drug-prescribing physician. All energy medicine is conceptualized on the principle of the so-called 'minimum dose'.

SPECIFICITY

It is important to note that nosodes are not necessarily given only for the disease to which they relate (for example giving a 'flu nosode in a case of 'flu). In fact that is to underestimate and miss the importance and applicability of this new therapeutic range. Empirically it has been found by Voll, Schimmel and others that certain diseases associate with particular nosodes. Conversely, some nosodes come up time and again as trouble-makers in many different conditions. Childhood vaccines are particularly notorious in this respect. I think we can go some way towards answering the mystery about where the present post-war epidemic of allergies has come from. At least part of the reason is the childhood vaccination program, dropping toxins on the immune system, spleen, etc., which then results in malfunction. The child may avoid the whooping cough or diphtheria, only to suffer with many more obscure and difficult-to-treat symptoms later in life.

I myself prefer to use homeopathic 'vaccination' in which the body is accustomed to the noxious agent, using very small safe doses. It is safer, painless, and cheaper and does not have the same side-effects as true vaccination. (Lest you fear it won't work, it is interesting to note that in the last great diphtheria epidemic in Glasgow, just before the advent of antibiotics, over 50 per cent of the children died with conventional therapy, yet not one fatality occurred at the city's homeopathic hospital)[4].

Here are some examples of the diversity of effects of nosodes, though the full reference range of many hundreds of items is a matter of considerable learning and remains the intellectual property of a well-trained practitioner.

Disease Condition	Nosode Indication
Acne	tuberculinum, bacillinum, psorinum
Arthritis	streptococcinum, staphylococcinum, apis melifica, variolinum, vaccinium, influenzinum

Disease Condition	Nosode Indication
Breast cancer	tuberculinum, medorrhinum, carcinosin, syphilinum, variolinum
Diabetes	parotidinum, diphtherinum, tuberculinum, bacillinum
Migraine	diphtherinum, variolinum, vaccinium
Prostatitis	tuberculinum, diphtherinum, pertussin
Sciatica	influenzinum, staphylococcinum, streptococcinum
Warts	medorrhinum

One can reverse the starting place and view each nosode as a polyvalent remedy—that is, capable of reaching out and de-energizing many different disease conditions. Thus:

Herpes (all)	arthritis, canker sores, spleen, shingles, heart, nerve, pancreas
Morbillinum	hypertension, multiple sclerosis, neurological disorders
Syphilinum	swollen knees (especially in women), brain cancer, heart valve disorders, prostatitis, chronic gynecological problems
Typhoidinum	intestinal complaints, liver, gall bladder, spleen, heart
Varicellinum	arthritis, myocardial disease, multiple sclerosis, cranial nerve palsies, shingles

MIASMS

A miasm is one of the most powerful influences in health and disease I know, yet the least acknowledged or understood. The word was introduced by Hahnemann, but I prefer to think of it as a 'genetic toxin', since this term gives a far clearer idea of what we think we are dealing with. Basically a miasm means a shadow or disease 'imprint' which is inherited down the generations.

All observant doctors are aware that disease and disturbance tend to run in families, and can be likened to a kind of family blight. This is not to mean a specific replicated genetic disorder carried by the genes such as, for example, hemophilia or Freidrich's ataxia. The sickliness can manifest itself in many different ways, each individual suffering differently from the others in his or her family tree but all bound by the commonality of being a somewhat weakened or unhealthy bunch.

This idea may seem to be an attempt to revive Lamarck's discredited theory of evolution, which said that an organism's responses to environmental stressors could be passed on to offspring. This is now held not to be true; the Darwinian/Mendelian dogma reigns, which states that only the factors carried in the genes can be inherited. Rigidity of this degree sounds suspiciously like yet another road-block in scientific thinking; a fashion that will one day have to be exposed to common sense and revised.

To Hahnemann a miasm was something more in the nature of a primitive illness, a throwback. He named three in particular: Syphilis (or Luesinum), Sycosis, and Psora. Briefly, syphilis has ulcerating tendencies; sycosis (meaning from gonorrhea) is congestive, leading to deposits and tumor formation; while psora is a protean disturbance which relates to functional imbalances of all kinds.

Psora is said to have formed in the time of the Plague (the Black Death).

Antoine Nebel and Henry C. Allen added Tuberculinum, which many practitioners now regard as the pre-eminent miasm, presumably since it is but one generation removed from today's population stock[5]. Among the fall-out diseases from this inherited toxin one can list asthma, eczema, hay fever, food allergies, chronic sinusitis, migraines, mental illness of various kinds including retardation and sub-normality, irritable bowel, colitis, heart trouble, diabetes, Hodgkin's disease and even leukemia.

Leon Vannier added a fifth, which is the Oncotic (cancer) miasm. It is characterized by changes in body odor, warts, excrescences, sores that refuse to heal and a sallow skin, somewhat like that of malignant cachexia.

It is also fashionable to consider the emergence of at least two new miasms: Candida and Chemical Sensitivity; Sugar Glut may very likely become a third modern miasm. I suggest we call the Candida miasm, if we can agree there is one, 'Moldy'.

I introduced the term 'moldy patient' in my book *The Allergy Handbook*[6] and it seems to me a far bigger issue than just Candida; the patient becomes sensitized to a wide variety of molds and yeasts. Unquestionably it is brought about by overuse of antibiotics, made worse by our obsession for refined carbohydrate and sugar, which results in a great deal of unnatural fermentable matter in the gut.

May we say then what a miasm is? I think in the light of modern understanding of energetic medicine it is possible to go beyond Hahnemann's hypothesis and say we are surely dealing with some kind of transmittable information field with its accompanying energetic disturbance. It appears 'etheric' or non-material in quality, but that is because hitherto we have not had the electronic means to search in the outer energy shell, except by dowsing. The fact is, miasms show up repeatedly on comprehensive testing of the electro-dermal screening (EDS) sort (see Chapter 19). We know they are there. Treatment consists of giving the homeopathic similar most exactly pertaining to the shadow. EAV and remedy testing can help us to identify and treat miasms with greater accuracy than ever before.

Casebook: Male, 10 Years

From the age of three the patient suffered from repeated vexatious sore throats and ear trouble. He fell steadily behind other children his age in scholastic performance. His tonsils and adenoids had been removed (no improvement) and finally his parents were told by an ear nose and throat (ENT) surgeon that the trouble was caused by allergies and the boy would suffer from this all his life.

Analysis showed that the predominant stressor was TB miasm and an acquired measles toxin. The indicated miasm and nosode were started and continued at appropriate repeat intervals over several months.

The ear and throat condition cleared up rapidly and has never reappeared. The boy's mental and physical slowness, which had been such a worry to his parents and teachers, soon abated and he was able to hold his own with his peers.

THE STUDIOUS MONK

Former head of a monastic order, Simon Goodrich, now an alternative practitioner in Oxford, has worked extensively on historic miasms. Goodrich has identified a number of obscure miasmata and post-infective dyscrasias, along with recommended treatments, which I find most helpful (dyscrasia is a general term for a body disorder, which derives from the old theory of mixed "humors": Greek krasis, mixture, hence bad mixture). Here the theory is of an old (but not necessarily ancestral) infective disease process which lingers. A list of the fifteen predispositions, with an historical estimation as to when the particular strain of this condition was prevalent, and in which society, follows here:

Goodrich's List of Historic Miasmata

15) Cytomegalo-virus (ME): Spread via cotton trade from USA; Emergence in approximately 1900. Immunity acquired around 1990.

14) Tuberculinum Kent. (Tuberculosis): Spread through shipping routes in British Empire; Emergence in approximately 1650. Immunity acquired around 1800.

13) Baryata Acet. (gonorrhea): Spread through silk trade with Iranian civilization (Arabia); Emergence in approximately 1600. Immunity acquired around 1750.

12) Endorid (cholera): Spread through spice trade from Ceylon, the Ceylonese civilization; Emergence in approximately 1500. Immunity acquired around 1650.

11) Arsen. Sulph. Rub. (Syphilis): Spread through the jute trade with Bangladesh, The Mughal Empire; Emergence in approximately 1500. Immunity acquired around 1650.

10) Lycopus Eur. (The Black Death): Spread through the fur trade with Turkestan, The Ottoman Empire; Emergence in approximately 1400. Immunity acquired around 1600.

9) Cobaltum Nit. (The Plague): Spread through the porcelain trade with Ming China; Emergence in approximately 1200. Immunity acquired around 1400.

8) Aesclepias Inc. (pneumonia): Originated in Europe, and prevalent within the Frankish Empire; Emergence in approximately 600. Immunity acquired around 750.

7) Droleptan (typhoid): Originated in Babylonian Empire; Emergence in approximately 900 BC. Immunity acquired around 800 BC.

6) Apium Grav. (fungal infections): Originated in Egyptian Empire; Emergence in approximately 1200 BC. Immunity acquired around 1100 BC.

5) Urinum (leprosy): Originated in Hebrew society; Emergence in approximately 1400 BC. Immunity acquired around 1300 BC.

4. Cornus Flor. (impetigo or scall): originated in Canaanite society; Emergence in approximately 2200 BC. Immunity acquired around 2000 BC.

3) Pectinum (uteritis, inflammation of the womb): Originated in Phoenician civilization; Emergence in approximately 2600 BC. Immunity acquired around 2400 BC.

2) Ornithogalum (meningitis, cerebral palsy): Originated in Sumerian civilization; Emergence in approximately 3200 BC. Immunity acquired around 3000 BC.

1) Cuprum Met (genital herpes): era unknown

Goodrich's remedy is shown with each condition.

Controversially, Simon told me his researches led him to believe that we each carry a number of miasms and this impacts our survival. The body's energies can become locked up in fighting the miasms, with adverse consequences for long- term health. With four miasms present, the individual is unlikely to survive (succumbs in infancy to childhood illnesses or teen disasters, such as leukemia); a person with three miasms will make it to adult life but die early (heart attack at 40-50 for men, breast cancer same age range for women); with two miasms, that's good for survival to 60-70 years; the lucky person with only one miasm should make it through to 70-80 and beyond[7].

All this, unless you are lucky enough to meet a skilled homeopath or good EAV specialist!

BACH FLOWER REMEDIES

One cannot consider energy medicine, particularly the information-in-water-alcohol kind, without giving some consideration to Bach's flower remedies. These are superb information medicines of the virtual sort and a great gift to the healer from a humanistic but strange man.

Despite the Germanic sounding name, Bach (pronounced like batch) was actually of Welsh origin, born near Birmingham in 1886. He practiced homeopathy in fashionable Harley Street in the 1920s. After 1930 he gave up his successful practice to study plants and trees and their psychological effects, culminating in the publication of the book *The Twelve Healers and Other Remedies*[8]. Today there are 38 remedies in all, ranging from gentian, through wild oat, to oak.

One outstanding remedy called 'Rescue Remedy' (a mixture of Cherry Plum, Clematis, Impatiens, Rock Rose and Star of Bethlehem) seems to have a special place. I have seen it effective against shock, trauma, children's hysteria, travel sickness, rashes and even bees refusing to pollinate. It is one of medicine's truly great remedies and should be in the emergency cupboard in every home: A word of caution, however: it is a shock remedy and if you take it when not in shock it can predispose unpleasant shock-like reactions. Never use Rescue Remedy prophylactically (as a preventative).

Bach was what is sometimes called a 'sensitive', that is, a person who has the gift for unusual psychic perceptions. I have noticed that surprisingly many of these people, for all their gifts, are not very healthy. Bach was no exception and died tragically young. Maybe their gifts are the result of being out of focus with the rest of us. I have seen this effect so often in my allergy patients; I soon became aware that feeling unreal and depersonalized has a certain transcendent aspect.

What Bach came to investigate was the way in which psychological attitudes prevented the normal healing and recovery process. It is usually forgotten today, when his remedies are in fashion for every kind of psychological hang-up, that what he originally proposed to treat were merely the barriers to healing.

He carried out his investigations by touching plants or the dew which settled on flowers and noting the emotional feeling it gave to him. He collected the coded botanical information by shining sunlight through the petals onto a brandy and water stock (sunlight method); or by boiling down the plant to create a concentrated extract or tincture (boiling method). Only one remedy, Rock Water, is not botanical in origin but is exactly what its name suggests and comes from mountain streams.

Bach remedies are unquestionably bio-informational in character, which is why they are reviewed here. They work mainly at the etheric or trans-dimensional level, and are in every sense a 'virtual remedy'. A person sometimes has only to touch or hold the bottle to get an emotional release. Your author actually burst into tears on picking up a book describing these remedies; I tell this only because I think it says more about the remedies than about me! Make of this strange occurrence what you will.

One theoretical objection might be the concern that what applied to Bach and his other-worldly persona would not necessarily apply to the rest of us, or at least not in the same manner. However, this hypothetical problem has largely been taken care of with the passage of time; the remedies today enjoy enormous popularity, and world-wide sales attest to their astonishing efficacy.

CLINICAL APPLICATIONS

I can only echo Bach's original view and say that, in my own electronic diagnosis and therapy system called the Acupro (see Chapter 19), I find I sometimes need to add one or more flower essences to the treatment tanks before the Indicator Drop will vanish and we know that the therapy program will succeed. It is axiomatic that much disease has a psychological element and that unless this is addressed, even by something as gentle as a coded flower message, the patient may have limited recovery.

Casebook: Female, 37 years

Dr. Sam Williams told me the remarkable story of a woman patient who had been severely traumatized by a road traffic accident several years before. The emotional impact was, to say the least, unnerving. Ever since, she had been unable to leave her home without being wrapped in heavy blankets against traffic noise and blindfolded, so that she could not see anything connected with cars or roads.

In this pathetic state she was driven to his office and unwrapped, looking very miserable and disheveled. His Acupro system sang out the flower remedies, including Mimulus, which is 'fear of known things' and the patient went home with her formula, unconvinced.

Despite two decades of EAV experience, no-one was more surprised than Sam when, next morning, the woman drove herself to his office alone, dressed to the nines, and handed him the bottle back in person, saying 'I don't think I need these any more Doc, but thanks!'

She was on her way to her first shopping spree.

In conclusion, Bach has given rise to a whole culture based on flower essences. At least two additional schools have emerged, one in Australia using Pacific Flower Remedies, and the other from the West Coast of the US, the so-called California Essences. Notable is the Flower Essence Society founded in 1979 by Richard Katz. Doubtless there will be more and more expansion as other adepts add their own contributions.

IMPRINTING

This review of the main available remedy modalities for EDS and Medicine Beyond practitioners would be incomplete without describing a sort of trade secret called 'imprinting'.

Dr. Franz Morell, the MO- of MORA (Chapter 17), discovered that sometimes during the course of bioresonace medicine, the patient would actually recover if the remedy was 'played back', like a recording, into the patient's tissues, either through the bar electrode or directly via the acupuncture point through which the necessary data was accessed. Very occasionally just being exposed briefly to the remedy while it was being tested was sufficient to produce a therapeutic result. Although the benefit could sometimes last a considerable time, these responses were usually of short duration, often disappearing as soon as the remedy signal was removed from the circuit and the point retested.

But Morell discovered in his experiments that if the chosen remedy oscillation was amplified 8–10 times and then played back, the result could last for weeks, months or even indefinitely[9].

This is basically what the MORA machine does. The rest of us, who don't use one, have to adopt some other means of attaining the same result. This leads almost naturally to the idea of imprinted medicines, which can extend the electronically-derived treatment process once the patient has gone home.

An imprinted medicine is one in which the supposed therapeutic electromagnetic message, derived from the Acupro library or similar sources, or a real sample on the input honeycomb, is transferred into a mixture of water and brandy. In other words, instead of giving the patient Echinacea, we play the information signature of Echinacea into the remedy bottle and give the patient that instead.

Lest you think the whole idea absurd, let me tell you that many of the cases reviewed in this book were treated in this way. The very dramatic story of Ed Butler of the Platters (page 339) was treated with only imprinted remedies, since I carry no nosodes of 'flu virus. The machine detected the disease and told me what would eliminate it.

We talk about the individual 'vibrational signature' of substances, herbs, homeopathics, enzymes and other beneficial substances. It ought to be quite logical and indeed scientific, if we really are dealing with nothing other than energy signals, to be able to transfer the energetic signal to a carrier fluid or other medium. I have already explained that the peculiar properties of water and brandy mean that these are especially suited to carrying transferred electromagnetic signals.

We can call this electro-homeopathy.

CAUTION

In view of what has just been stated, it would be remiss of me not to point out a potential danger. If we can imprint the 'signature' of a substance in liquid, it follows that the same would apply even regarding unfriendly or toxic material. Many years ago at an advanced think tank, I heard a proposal that boiling water in an electric kettle or using electric heating rings to cook our food might impart what we ate or drank with hostile electromagnetic energies (bear in the mind that mains frequency of around 50–60 Hz is particularly damaging to biological systems).

I am sorry to say that I somewhat scorned this possibility at the time (1982). At least I should have kept an open mind. More than two decades on I have learned enough to know that this is more than a theoretical possibility. We certainly do imprint liquids with unintended energy codes. A beer on the top of the TV may have a little of your favorite (or most hated) program in it! The question which remains unanswered is can imbibing these imprinted substances have detrimental effects on health?

I have no idea of the answer. But I would say this: keep all medicines and remedies, even vitamins and minerals, well away from any source of electromagnetic radiation, such as computers, TVs and microwaves. Otherwise they will almost certainly be spoiled.

THAT MAN BENVENISTE AGAIN

I have elsewhere referred to the way in which Jacques Benveniste caused a scandal when he published proof of what came to be known as 'the memory of water' in the scientific journal *Nature*. In fact, in the true nature of science, his work has now been reproduced at different study centers[10].

He is vindicated (but he didn't get an apology).

His more recent work suggests that it will be possible to record electronically the specific characteristics of a remedy or any other substance, such as adrenalin, nicotine and caffeine, or the immunological pattern of viruses or other pathogens. These recordings can subsequently be played back and even transmitted through telephone cables and thus on to the Internet and will have a measurable physiological or remedial effect.

His researches, as before, are meticulously controlled, comparing the effects of a "digitized remedy" with the authentic substance, using digitized water (no specific imprint) as a control. By the time of his death, Benveniste had only got as far as recording and playing back substance signatures. So far, no-one is able to recognize patterns or identify unknown substances from a recording made of their presence.

But I am confident that will come eventually.

One exciting aspect of the digital substance hypothesis is that it explains the manner in which many remedies or physiological substances have an almost instantaneous effect throughout the organism. This can be much too fast to be explained by humoral or biochemical means. The usual proposed mechanism is a neurological one. But Benveniste's model makes more sense. It also sheds light on the phenomenon of specific biological receptors. The usual explanation is one of a 'lock and key' mechanism; that is, the receptor site has a physical shape which admits only the correct trigger molecule. I have always viewed this as specious and remarked earlier in the book that allergic reactions, or recoveries due to therapy, can be so instantaneous as to beggar the normal pathways. Benveniste's proposal of transmitting molecules and 'tuned' receptor sites (like a radio aerial) fits these clinical observations far better. In his view, it would take only a tiny alteration of the receptor to de-tune it, so that it no longer responds.

I am grateful to Benveniste for progress with understanding one of the last major building blocks of the *Medicine Beyond* paradigm. It accords well with my view that DNA and other cell molecules 'transmitting' the body's genetic message, resulting in species-specific growth.

Western energy medicine, I believe, is this kind of revelation, not a makeover of oriental thinking!

PRINT YOUR OWN REPLACEMENT ORGANS

Right on time for the final proof edition of this book comes a fascinating article which plays right to the theme of Western technological brilliance! OK, not exactly beyond the laws of physics but way beyond what anyone could have dreamed of, even a mere ten years ago.

Using energy and information, we can now actually "print" organs, such as a replacement kidney, using 3-D printer technology. Sound mad? Read on...

Creating new organs, using a patient's own stem cells attached to a biological matrix with the shape of a required organ is not even new anymore, though it's still very exciting indeed. We can grow baby hearts, baby kidneys and baby livers by the trayful. But the idea of being able to do it with 3-D printing technology (as for example car parts or buildings), has been dogged by the problem of finding a suitable bio-compatible matrix that will hold the organ-forming cells while they do their work.

Now teams led by Dongsheng Liu (Tsinghua University) and Will Shu (Heriot-Watt University) have solved the main challenge, by developing a "printable" gel to act as a matrix or scaffold to support the live cells in 3D, and which is not rejected by transplant recipients.

The gel, rather like some proprietary glues, comes as two separate liquids into which cells can be added. These do not turn into a gel until the two liquids are actually mixed together during the printing process.

The formation of the new DNA gel does not involve heat, UV, salt or other harsh conditions. In combination with Shu's delicate 3D printing system, they have been able to demonstrate they can produce a three-dimensional matrix containing fully viable live cells.[11]

The eventual aim of the Chinese researchers is to 3D print organs for transplant, as well as producing alternatives to the testing of drugs on animals. This new gel in combination with a 3D live-cell printer is a huge step forward towards these potential long-term medical benefits.

It's really rather amazing and certainly medicine way "beyond" for the moment.

CHAPTER 19

Electro-Dermal Computer Screening

> *Energy is liberated matter, matter is energy waiting to happen.*
>
> — Bill Bryson, *A Short History of Nearly Everything*

We now come to the moment when the promise of this book's title is close to fulfilment. Picture the scene in a 21st century doctor's surgery. After the preliminaries, the patient sits down in front of a computer display, picks up the passive electrode and the doctor begins to touch the patient's skin at certain of Voll's electro-acupuncture points which we call the central measurement points (CMPs), one on each vessel or meridian. The sensor is similar to the Dermatron but is now hitched to a high-powered desktop PC and the two talk to each other electronically. There is a picture of a hand skeleton; a bright red dot wanders across each digit, beep-beep-beep. After every measurement the doctor clicks a button and the reading goes into the computer's memory to be stored. We now have an electronic file which can be called up any time in the future and printed out for study or even for the patient to take home a personal copy. Times have changed!

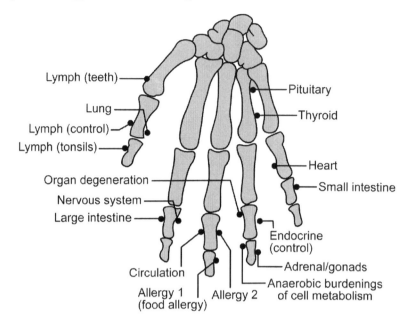

Lymph (teeth)
Lung
Lymph (control)
Lymph (tonsils)
Organ degeneration
Nervous system
Large intestine
Circulation
Allergy 1
(food allergy)
Allergy 2
Pituitary
Thyroid
Heart
Small intestine
Endocrine
(control)
Adrenal/gonads
Anaerobic burdenings
of cell metabolism

Some things are the same, however. This is still electro-acupuncture according to Voll (EAV): there are two meridians to each finger digit and two to each toe, making a total of 40 readings in all. But when this preliminary stage is complete, by pressing a key the doctor brings up on the screen an attractive colored graph. It shows all the CMP measurement values; right and left sides are in different colors for ease of identification; Indicator Drops (IDs) are marked as white bands and stand out clearly.

The doctor pauses and looks deep in thought for a few moments. He taps the white marks on the screen and announces: 'Your spleen meridian is down, the endocrine is not so good and something is disturbing the large intestine. The liver is high, which means it's having to detox hard; but there is no drop so no liver damage so far.' He then presses a couple of keys and goes into 'branching', which means that he now studies the spleen meridian in more detail, passing along it point by point, recording all the values and IDs.

You are watching what it says on the screen out of the corner of your eye: lymphocyte function of the upper body—click; serous coating

330

of the spleen (what's that, for goodness sake?)—click; lymphocyte function of the lower body—click; erythrocyte function (that's the red blood cells)—click; reticulo-endothelial system ... the what? You decide this is all very high tech: but the doctor touches a spot just above your left ankle—click, and announces he has finished that step.

Once again, due to the power of the computer, he taps in a key-code and the sequence of measurements is displayed for review as a table showing highs and lows and the size of the Indicator Drops. The 12-point ID which was found on the CMP reappears on SP2, the reference point for 'lower body leukocyte function'. The doctor is satisfied that this is probably what was disturbing the spleen meridian. Something in the lower body is producing an energetic disturbance that upsets or overstresses the lymphocyte function down there. This could cause a chain reaction, since we need our lymphocytes for defense.

Really upset lymphocytes could even mean leukemia. There is a problem; but what?

DATABASE

Next, as I think of it, comes *Dr. Kildare Meets Chinese Traditional Medicine in Cyberspace*. The doctor calls up a comprehensive database of disease entities and possible cures. On my own system there are over 25,000 entries. This is fairly typical for software packages of this type.

By highlighting an entry and pressing the return key, the doctor can access the energy signal named there on the screen. He can then compare it with what is coming from the disease zone; he does this by touching Spleen 2 with the probe, where he found the biggest drop. He no longer looks for IDs but is probing to see if there is a resonance. This is shown by a reading at or very close to Voll's balanced reading of 50. This means a 'yes' from the body.

But the doctor still has to make choices: could it be a virus? A parasite? Malaria maybe... that's likely for spleen for anyone who has been to the tropics; and so on. But he can check his theories very quickly and begin to establish the likely cause of the trouble.

The software programmer, if he is good, will already have programmed in some suggestions which relate to that meridian. For the spleen one would give high priority to testing infectious mono-nucleosis, 'flu, Tuberculinum, Diphtherinum, pertussis, tetanus, malaria, Variolinum (smallpox) and hepatitis A, B and C. These would accordingly come at the top of the list.

Gall-bladder would give a different range of suggestions. On my system the first 10 offers (in order) are: cholelithiasis (gall-stone), amoeba, streptococcus, staphylococcus, 'flu, Diphtherinum, Variolinum, TB and hepatitis A and B.

The nerve-degeneration channel would put measles and rubella in the first 10; also probably *Syphilinum* and *Medorrhinum* (gonorrhea code), which may be less obvious.

This is a good moment to reiterate that EAV gives one a completely different perspective on the origins and nature of disease. Remember that we are testing an energetic signal. This is not looking for antibodies to the micro-organism or a sample culture to 'prove' that this is what the patient has right now. Indeed, it generally turns out to be something from long ago. Time and again, when we question the patient, he or she can remember the problem that the machine has unearthed and says is still causing trouble. Sometimes the patient will telephone next day, excited, to say that a parent or some other relative confirms the diagnosis which the patient was unable to remember personally at the screening session. Childhood diseases and vaccinations come up over and over again as underpinning disease in later life. The energy disturbance is still around, provoking trouble years later. The proof of such a contentious remark, of course, is that when you eliminate the signal, the patient begins to improve!

We call this Voll investigative process with computer-based technology electro-dermal screening (EDS). With necessary caution, I can state that it holds great promise for the future. Considering that we are merely in the first decade or two of its development, it already surpasses expectation. As more is learned and scientific studies using this approach give us even more insight and understanding into what is happening in disease, then I think we may soon see a time when it is the basis of any sensible medical practice. EDS is a quick, non-invasive and painless method of health screening.

THE PRODUCT LIBRARY

We can think in terms of a 'library' of signals available to the practitioner to check against. Among the likely categories found in a computer database for this sort of testing are signals of:

- Alcohol products

- Amino acids

- Ayurvedic herbs

- Bacteria nosodes

- Chemicals

- Biological age

- Geopathic stress

- Color therapies

- Chakras

- Dental materials

- Enzymes

- Flower remedies

- Herbal remedies

- Gems and crystals

- Hormones

- Environmentals

- Essential oils

- Food allergies

- Grass pollens

- Habit drugs

- Heavy metals

- Homeopathics: combinations, drainage, singles

- Polychrests - (a subdivision of homeopathics, polychrests are major remedies with great impact and many ramifications)

- Miasms

- Minerals

- Parasites

- Pesticides

- Phenolics

- Pollens

- Sarcodes (healthy tissue signals used as support)

- Scheussler tissue salts

- Tree pollens

- Vaccines

- Venoms

- Viruses

- Vitamins

At first such a huge database can seem very overwhelming, there are so many choices; how is it possible for one brain to take it all in? Actually, it isn't too daunting.

First, it has to be said that no one individual does or possibly could use and come to grips with all of it; I mean understand all the possibilities to a professional level. There have to be selections and generally we work to our strengths. My system has chakras listed: I've never even opened this section for a patient, since in all honesty I wouldn't know what to do with a chakra that was out of balance. But I understand nosodes, such as bacteria, viruses, parasites, chemical toxins, vaccines and allopathic drugs, and I 'find' these a great deal, since I am looking for them. As with all EAV systems, allergies and nutritional guidance is a strong point.

The second vital point which brings it within human capability is that computers by their very nature can help a lot when searching, namely breaking things down relentlessly with either-or logic. It is possible to test a hundred possibilities, and then halve it and test that; then halve again, and so on. There is a mathematical principle that you can get down to one item with just six, or at the most seven, decisions using this split logic. Thus if there is a single item you want buried somewhere in a hundred possibilities, it can take less than 20 seconds to find it; such is the power of computers.

The really great thing about these computer programs is that they will tell you first: 'Yes there is something in this list of test substances'. You don't have to waste time searching fruitlessly in sub-folders that are not relevant to the case.

A refinement which is added to the LISTEN system—one of the first such software packages; the name stands for Life Information Systems Ten, and was developed by James Hoyte Clark of Orem, Utah—is that the search is made 'blind': the items on the list are kept hidden from the practitioner until after he has decided which agent is the real culprit or the desired remedy. This eliminates any prejudgment by the practitioner, which can bedevil objective results and is a good answer to criticism that EAV is really just sophisticated 'dowsing'.

But there are numerous EDS systems on the market today. As Julia Tsuei tells us, all share the same basic design and functional use. The core is an ohm-meter which delivers 10-12 microamperes of direct current at 1-1.25 volts. Since the ionization potential of hydrogen atoms is 1.36 volts, this is perfectly safe. In most devices the meter is calibrated to read from 0 to 100 so that the standard skin resistance of 100 kilo-ohms reads 50. Zero represents infinite resistance and 100 indicates zero resistance at this electrical potential. Some devices read from 0 to 200 and 100 indicates normal skin resistance.

The testing probe has an insulated body with a tip of brass or silver connected to the positive side of the circuit. This, held by the operator, is pressed firmly on the patient's skin at the measurement point. A brass hand electrode is held by the patient and connected to the negative side of the circuit. Just like EAV, a metal plate, for medicine testing, is inserted between the EDS device and the patient's hand electrode[1].

However, it needs to be said that in these database systems, nothing can take the place of clinical experience on the part of the practitioner. The machine does not (yet) think for us. It does not 'know', for example, that a large bowel ID, with intestinal lymphatic stress and toxic liver burdenings, would suggest a parasite high in the probable list, or that a head focus is likely to be tonsils, teeth and then sinuses, in that order.

ELECTRO-DERMAL SCREENING

There are a number of systems you might run into, all much of a muchness. I do not wish to become involved in arguing the relative merits of each; cost, software facilities and back-up service would all be part of such an evaluation. But of the ones I have heard of, I can suggest good results from the following: the BEST (bio-energetic stress test) system, LISTEN, Acupro, Avatar and the Limbic Ark. Now the MORA firm and BICOM manufacturers have put together adaptations of their machines which have a "diagnostic library" and could, fairly, be said to have joined this group of devices. Since these also combine the facility of Bioresonance with EAV and a database, it is perhaps the best class of machine on the market at this time.

For medico-legal reasons, in the US these devices are considered a 'new device' to be used for investigational purposes only. This is a good description. But actually I have found them also educational. One does learn about illness in a totally new way by exploring each case for the consequences which finally led to the onset of disease.

The really critical factor in getting results is not the software but the operator's ability. The most sophisticated device in the world is less than useful if not backed up by the knowledge and skill requisite for using it. It is still fundamentally EAV and is subject to all the difficulties in objectivity found with this approach. We have to be honest and recognize the drawbacks, as well as the strengths.

Of course I cannot comment on their legal status in each individual country. That is for the reader to determine. However I would warn readers against the vile postings and rabid ranting found at QuackWatch, where they seem to take the posture that anything they don't like, or the FDA disapproves of, is somehow criminal. It is offensive and stupid to suppose that the USA, with all its financial corruption and scientific demerits, should be sole arbiter of what is ethical and effective in the field of healing and medicine.

TANKS

There are many advantages to using a computer, not the least of which is what we call 'the holding tanks'. These are somewhat akin to "folders" on a computer and can store diagnostic information and useful remedies and return the signal of their contents to the site being skin-tested. My system has eight holding tanks in all. Remedies can be directed into any

336

one of the eight and stored there, to be played back and tested against the tissue, in company with later choices.

These tanks can be switched in and out, which gives us a number of potential refinements. Thus we sometimes see that a remedy is effective on a particular meridian but when later treatments, especially nosodes or stressors are introduced for treating other organs, that the first point becomes unsettled. We can switch tanks or substances in or out until we find which is the culprit. We can test the whole planned treatment regimen against several points consecutively.

A tank behaves just like a honeycomb on the Dermatron or Vega machine. Filters can be put into the tanks and held there for subsequent testing. They also allow us to organize our thinking a little: I prefer to put my flower remedies in one tank, allergy results in another, homeopathics in a third, biological age in a fourth, and so on.

Most systems will allow one to imprint individual tanks to make individualized remedies.

FILTERS

A wise EDS specialist will take a leaf out of Schimmel's book and call up the Vega filters for tolerance (Ferrum metallicum D800), compatibility (Manganum metallicum D26) and effectiveness (Ferrum metallicum D26). These can be put into tank 1 and remain there as a background filtering process. This ensures that any remedies chosen are likely to be not only effective but well tolerated by the patient and compatible with other aspects of therapy.

Once a reading-stressed area is found, then a remedy program needs to be found which will relieve the problem. Obviously an effective remedy must be able to eliminate the ID. We are, in effect, interviewing the body's cells and asking the tissues what they want. Operator knowledge is important, but with such a vast database on tap what he knows becomes less of an issue.

At first the budding EDS practitioner will tend to go along with nosodes and other suggestions put forward by the software. But gradually the practitioner learns his or her own path through this database.

As a comment, I have started to use Bach's flower remedies simply because, on many occasions, I could not get rid of the ID until I included these; often more than one at a time, which will incense the purists. The inference is, of course, that all disease has some psychological component. Unless that is addressed there is resistance to treatment, as Bach postulated. Time and again the patient will recognize themselves in the description of the flower remedy or, if not, a close relative will speak for them and confirm how uncannily accurate EDS can be.

ELECTRO-DERMAL COMPUTER SCREENING

A typical EDS machine is capable of potentizing energy signals. Thus if Candida albicans is a reading pathogen, as part of its software capability the machine is able to offer for testing a Candida 4X, 6X, 8X, 12X, 24X and so on. The centesimal scale is also represented (see Chapter 18). Generally these are 'softer' in nature. They are more applicable to chronic or constitutional conditions. My system, the Acupro, even allows testing of a range of 5X potencies, which can be used in correlation with the allergy testing and neutralization system known as Miller's method[2].

Thus the practitioner can make up his or her own remedy formulas by combining different strengths of different substances (which can be imprinted, as described on page 325). Also supplied are what we call accompanying remedies, which are selected for each organ concerned. These give lift and support for the organ and help to eliminate toxins. They are in fact specially chosen drainage remedies (see page 339).

Many proprietary remedy brands are included with these machines, such as Heel products, Guna, Reckeweg, Pascoe and Futureplex, to name a few. Here in the USA one could cite the Deseret Biologicals range. Again, practitioners tend to develop prescribing favorites, but it often happens that only one remedy reads 'OK' and this is what the body is saying it really wants, regardless of preferences.

ACCURACY

Most EDS systems take advantage of the computer modality to allow the practitioner to set a definition of 'yes' or 'no' when choosing a remedy. Voll's classic 50 is a theoretical mean. Some practitioners will take anything between 45 and 55 as a positive acceptance by the tissues. I prefer to tune mine at 48 – 52, but since the Acupro takes anything borderline as a 'yes' this degree of accuracy can be very inconvenient at times.

The difficult part is getting the probe pressure just right. Too much or too little pressure will markedly alter the reading. I would say that the touch required is every bit as fine as getting a correct note on a violin string.

The Avatar claims to have the advantage that a feather touch is what the system is set up to operate on. This is supposed to be more reproducible, though I do not know on what premise.

Casebook: Male, 57 Years

I was called to see Ed Butler of the Platters singing group. He had just had a massive right-sided stroke, a few days after completing his last recording session. He was now severely incapacitated and sitting disconsolately in a wheelchair. EDS screening showed a major drop on the nervous channel, which was hardly surprising. But what surprised me was that the read was on the right. Yet, as everyone knows, the motor nerves cross over before leaving the cranium and the left brain controls the right-sided musculature.

Notwithstanding, I chose to believe what the machine was telling me. I used the right-side as a reference zone. A search for pathogens revealed a loud and unmistakable signal for 1975 'flu. I checked with Ed who, even though it was 23 years previously, remembered clearly having a bad attack and being confined to bed for two weeks. 'That was the start of your stroke,' I told him. In my earlier *Allergy Handbook* I have already pointed out the great potential of 'flu virus to cause considerable neurological damage.

I made up some X-potencies of this pathogen and offered it to the Voll point; it showed a big improvement but the reading was still dropping to a degree. I added some gentle drainage and homeopathic Co-enzyme compositum (a Heel product), to reinvigorate the metabolic process. The read had almost disappeared. Finally, I decided to try flower remedies; including one or two of these did the trick. I gave Ed the remedy the machine had selected for him. In the meantime he was having energetic healing of the 'hands of light' type.

The very next day I had a call that he could move his thumb. Only six weeks into a massive cerebro-vascular accident this was indeed startling. Good recoveries are possible, but we think in terms of 12

– 18 months, not just a few weeks. In any case this was less than 24 hours after starting the 'virtual' remedy.

Over the next few weeks he improved steadily but then pegged. At this point I recognized the remedy was exhausted due to the heat of our Spanish summer, because it had begun to happen with several other patients. I refreshed his remedy, taking the chance to add a couple of items suggested by the repeat test. Once again, the next day, I had a call that he was now able to stand on his legs, provided he kept his weight off the weak side. He soon learned to walk and within six months he was back singing in public; an altogether remarkable recovery from a potentially disastrous episode.

I give due credit to the energetic healers, but the immediate response to the remedy indicated by the Acupro is unarguable. Ed's grit and determination were also, of course, major factors.

OTHER REMEDIES

Yet another advantage of the flexible complex homeopathy approach emerges in the EDS domain. It is possible to give 'remedies' of a non-disease modality. For example, we can intervene in metabolic pathways by giving potentized enzyme similimums. Often I find that a person is loaded with toxins and quite sick, with low personal and metabolic energies. It takes quite a lot of internal cellular energy to push out toxins, maybe against a chemical gradient. Thus a vicious circle is established. It may require the use of enzymes of the Krebs cycle to bring metabolism back up to speed, before the patient can recover. Mixtures such as Heel's 'Co-enzyme compositum' can really help any detox program by stimulating chemical energy pathways. The patient usually reports subjective increases in energy levels.

We can also administer homeopathically-potentized support signals of substances like essential fatty acids (GLA and EPA), vitamins or minerals. This is not the same as supplementation, which I would always give 'in the physical' as we say. But often the process of uptake and utilization of such nutrient substances is enhanced by the signal 'in the etheric'! It comes back to the subject of resonance; if the body meets something with which it resonates, a new level of energy can be created. The lithium experiment described on page 138 demonstrates this vital principle.

340

We can beneficially intervene in hormone secretion and response to hormones, either by giving potentized hormones or endocrine gland similimums. If the relevant organ can be stimulated, supplementation may indeed be unnecessary. Thyroidea comp. (HEEL or BHI) is a remedy I have frequent recourse to for treating low energy states, weight problems, putative low thyroid and, surprisingly, it has strong anti-tumor potentiality, since there is a correlation between thyroid disease and cancer. The thyroid has important and generally little-regarded effects in maintaining strong immunity. This is quite logical if you consider that the thyroid is responsible for setting the basal metabolic rate. Often the patient does not need to take thyroxine.

Other possibilities include balancing neuro-transmitters, such as dopamine and serotonin, with consequent benefit to the patient's mental well-being, anti-parasitic programs and resonance with personal chemical pollution, such as organophosphates or heavy metals.

With the benefits of a data file record it is nice to be able to revisit earlier diagnostic discoveries and compare them graphically or numerically with later progress.

SO-CALLED IMPONDERABLES

Given the essentially informational nature of the VIRTUAL MEDICINE paradigm, it would be hardly surprising that almost any substance can be encoded and checked against the patient's energy body, to see if it is a help or a hindrance to health.

It is possible to check the chakras and balance those which need it; to test colors and use those which suggest themselves as treatments; relationships; even moonlight!

We call these intangible elements imponderables (meaning have no substance and cannot be weighed).

Taking the information idea one step further, Dr. Vaughn Cook has told me informally that he has carried out tests in which data sets (such as a language vocabulary) were imprinted into liquid as an oscillating signal and then transferred to the subject, using laser therapy; with the result that the individual scored significantly higher after study than controls which had not been so treated. Cook was keen to point out that the individual must still study the topic. Information imprinting did not avert the need to learn but did seem to improve scores.

We are both eager to repeat this in a formal clinical trial.

I must say this revelation put me in mind of Edgar Cayce's claim that he need only to sleep with a book beneath his pillow to absorb details of what was said in the print. A remarkable claim; but then, Cayce was a very remarkable man.

Apart from being a gifted psychic, Cayce also devised the "bio-battery". It contains no battery but is a kind of mind enhancement machine that creates subtle improvements of mood and definite improvements of memory. The bio-battery is perhaps a kind of "virtual information machine", working on the body's energetic aura. According to Cayce, "It can almost build a new brain"! He said the device could help amnesia, senility, dementia, brain damage or retardation[3]. This is impossible according to the currently-fashionable mechanistic model of consciousness. Memory lost is irretrievable.

But "Memory is never lost," said Cayce. In his view memory was stored outside of the body. In the 1930s this claim was absurd or at best mystical. Now we can see that he understood over half a century ago that the living being was an information and energy field.

CAUSAL CHAINS UNDERSTOOD

I made my reputation as the Number One 'Allergy Detective' (Sunday Mail, 1990). I've found pathological reactions to all kinds of strange substances, from herbicide on a bowling ball to a husband's semen, via food, chemicals, electromagnetic fields and meteorological phenomena. The recoveries have been very gratifying. I hope I will never lose my knack for this.

But there has always been the nagging question in the background: why has this person got allergies or intolerances in the first place? Part of the ongoing controversy over 25 years of my clinical ecology practice has been that it is comparatively rare that these reactions are what I was taught characterized an allergy (IgE-mediated acute hypersensitivity response) when I was at medical school. It has sometimes been a considerable mystery why the patient should react as he does. A type of antibody serum sickness has been proposed, but this is still within the biochemical hypersensitivity domain.

Now at last, since learning EDS, I have begun to find real solutions to this riddle. The answers that come up are enlightening, fascinating, almost unbelievable and, sometimes, rather scary (see Chapter 26). I have long thought that allergy was really the final result in the patient's problem, rather than the true cause. Now I can see that this suspicion is not only well-founded, but I can get an idea of just how much the patient has suffered, often without realizing it, to arrive at the doorway marked 'Allergy–Enter'.

We speak today of 'causal chains'; that is, the true sequence of events which led up to the patient's current predicament. The all-important question, naturally, is where did this sequence start? This often opens the door to a new therapeutic plan which, after all the years of distress and illness, has a good chance of succeeding. It can seem like lateral thinking gone mad sometimes, but there is always an understandable logic behind the events, once they are put into some kind of sequence and perspective.

Nearly always, the problem starts in an unsuspected way with an earlier illness which does not properly resolve. Ed Butler's 'flu of 23 years earlier is just one of many examples. The energetic shadow or disturbance remains in or around the body, sometimes for life, unless it is found and eradicated. One is wise to accept what is found and, time and again, the results speak for the veracity of the hypothesis.

I can only say that I have seen childhood illnesses and especially vaccines initiate disease sequences so many times that I am left with a sense of great unease. What can we do to stop our kids getting ill? I don't think we should abandon the vaccination programs; we don't want a renewal of the epidemics of old. But how can we get round this difficulty of causing chronic health hazards?

I am not sure. But I do know that my concern is shared by many other doctors who have stumbled across this unpleasant truth while performing routine EAV and EDS. I think that part of the problem is that we treat the disease when it manifests and thereby block its proper resolution.

A wise old Chinese doctor, Yang Tschau, once said 'Beware of treating the symptoms of a disease.' Yet in Western biochemically-based medicine that is almost all that is done; no attention is paid to the true causes of disease, only the causes of manifestations of disease. Yet so often the actual disease is the person's habits and lifestyle; the illness itself is only an outward symptom of what went wrong.

It may emerge in time that it is better to leave most illnesses untreated, especially avoiding the use of allopathic medicines, rather than block natural recovery. I firmly believe from my studies to date that to block an acute illness is to risk driving it underground, from where it may emerge years later to cause a more chronic illness.

Another very worrying concern and challenging management problem is the focus. I already mentioned this phenomenon in Chapter 15; dental foci are discussed further in Chapter 24. It is quite clear to the unprejudiced observer that foci can generate problems far from where they are found. There is compelling evidence that toxic and infective matter can travel along nerve channels, as well as along the more obvious blood route. In one case the bacterium Pseudomonas was recovered from a cervical spinal osteitis in a man who had the same organism in his urine. The likely mode of travel was along the venous plexus of the spinal column. If this can happen at all, it can happen any time!

I become worried if I think of the bigger implications.

A focus may also pose dangers by initiating pathological changes locally that is without spreading to a remote site. It is highly likely that an infective focus can give origin to a tumor, possibly due to synthesis of carcinogens by bacterial and fungal micro-organisms. We know that *Aspergillus flavus* (Aflatoxin) and common bacteria, such as E. coli, can do this. Late Professor of Neurology in Stockholm Dr. Patrick Stortebecker makes it clear that a periapical abscess is a very typical finding in close proximity to a jaw cancer[4].

NEW CLINICAL PERSPECTIVES

It is right to talk about new clinical perspectives with EDS: the whole view of disease changes. Indeed, it is a paradigm shift, no less: even the language of healing changes. It is proverbial that Eskimos have around 50 words for snow, since their technical knowledge of its form, texture and properties is so much more detailed than ours. It is the same with the new medicine. Focus, energetic masking, homotoxins and mesenchyme become the new rhetoric, instead of the names of obscure pathogens and weird little eponymous syndromes which most doctors would have to look up in a textbook to remind themselves what form it took.

One becomes confident, I believe, in viewing disease as non-random but operating to probabilistic laws, governed by energetic phenomena which impact on our physical systems and control them. We are controlled by biological information fields through an energy system; surely this is the way to start looking at disease? Why just mop the floor when you can go back to the leaking tap and turn it off?

Perhaps I can illustrate some of these newer orientations by featuring cases from the files of EDS specialist Ann Smithells, director of the Bio-Tech Health and Nutrition Centre in Petersfield, UK. Ann was a LIS-TEN user for many years but later upgraded to the BEST (bio-energetic stress test) system.

Casebook: Male, 53 Years

The patient first attended because of a chemical taste he was experiencing and excreting. His medical history revealed he was taking the medication Sotol for cardiac arrhythmias; he had high stress levels, nausea, headaches, fatigue and lack of concentration.

Ann's initial screening identified Candida, adrenal exhaustion, low zinc and digestive enzymes, plus high levels of toxins in the gall-bladder, prostate, liver, lung and connective tissues. These toxins were mainly heavy metals, probably due to current dental amalgam removal, and very high levels of benzene. The latter was the putative cause of the bad taste.

The patient was given homeopathics and a high dose antioxidant formula to deal with the heavy metal overload and a homeopathic nosode of benzene at 10M and 20X. Four months later he was much improved but there were still high levels of benzene. This forced an investigation into the cause and it turned out to be a leaking fuel pipe in his car, which shunted petrol into the vehicle's ventilation system whenever he pressed the accelerator.

Casebook: Male, 23 Years

The patient attended a year and half after a lengthy tour of the North Vietnam jungle in search of biological specimens. He complained of hunger, significant weight loss, and occasional abdominal pain after eating and insufficient energy to participate in sports, despite being a former county tennis player.

Ann identified inflammation of the stomach, liver, lymph meridians (suggesting parasites) and pituitary gland. He also had a high chemical intolerance. A number of exotic parasites were found, together with bacterial encephalitis and high levels of DDT.

The LISTEN system identified the need for 20 different remedies, including nosodes and the miasm Medorrhinum at 10M, and high-dose antioxidants. To complement these therapies the patient was put on a whole-food diet, with lots of organic fruit and vegetables. He was also given a liver support formula, HEP 194 from Biocare, UK.

Within 8 weeks the patient had gained more than a stone (14lb) in weight and reported his energy was returning to its former levels. Most of the meridians had rebalanced. The liver, which characteristically produces a high reading when detoxing, gradually came down to normal.

This is a patient who had been let down by conventional medicine. It needed a complete rethink from within a different paradigm.

SIMPLE LIVER CLEANSE

If you are not getting any results on therapy after three weeks; if you had an initial good result but have started feeling unwell again; or if you have had many years of toxic build-up (drugs, alcohol, tobacco, etc.), you may benefit from a detox program and a simple liver cleanse.

If you have started a detox program, this may release further toxins from the fatty and connective tissue where they have been lurking. Sometimes body metabolism can't cope properly at these times and you may go into an overload crisis. Typical signs would include:

- feeling heavily hung-over in the morning (even when you've not been drinking)

- slow getting started in the morning

- feeling unduly tired or drained, even when rested fully or sleeping a lot

- having a very low tolerance of alcohol.

There is no need to attempt the extremely heroic 'liver flushes' sometimes in vogue in the alternative field. There are claims that you will release showers of gallstone gravel but this is nonsense. What actually happens is that you pass granules or pellets of saponified olive oil, which you are supposed to swallow in huge amounts (a liter at a time) in these misguided procedures. It's a hoax, basically. The give-away clue is that these "stones" float in the toilet pan. Only fat is lighter than water!

Instead try the simple formula overleaf for 10 days (you can then repeat it a few days each month):

Recipe

- 6 tablespoons of lemon juice

- 3 tablespoons of virgin olive oil (cold pressed)

- 1 small garlic clove, crushed

- Pinch of grated ginger

- Pinch of cayenne pepper

Whisk in a blender and drink immediately. Do not eat for at least 1 hour afterwards.

The acid test, of course, is treating the energetically ailing organ and being able to observe the resultant recovery in health. Whereas no method of testing and treatment is foolproof, the EDS approach gives successes often enough to be considered a very valuable attack on the disease process.

CANCER

It is possible to see cancer coming with good EAV, while it is still just an energy disturbance and sometimes years before the actual disease is manifest. Occasionally the EAV cancer-predictive low readings (30 on down) do not show up as expected. I believe this is because the tumor may be surrounded by an inflammatory process, which causes paradoxically high readings. However there are a number of warning signs in EDS that would require a high degree of suspicion of cancer, either established or developing imminently. These include readings below 30 on any meridian, multiple large ID drops, high biological age, low immune performance, chronic toxic overload, dangerous foci in the teeth and anaerobic burdenings (meaning that the general cell chemistry is running too slowly and not burning up molecular fuel properly, creating toxins).

Probably there is no better way of summarizing the difference between the methods of the EDS prescriber and the conventional doctor than to review cancer therapy. Western scientific doctors look upon cancer as an invasion; cancer cells are 'the enemy'. Their response is to fight back with as much fire power as possible, in an attempt to slaughter every last cancer cell. The patient's body becomes the battlefield and is otherwise ignored. Yet anyone who has seen pictures of the blasted wastelands around the trenches of the First World War will know that the battlefield comes off worse than either army.

The EDS specialist looks at cancer as the final result of many disease pathways. We are used to thinking of it as a tissue ageing process, where toxins and pathogens have accumulated to such an extent that the body defenses can no longer cope. We try to undo the ill-effects of years of negative health, thread by thread.

Here are seven main factors contributing to deterioration in health and leading, if untreated, ultimately to system breakdown and the threat of cancer. These are:

1. geopathic stress, centered especially around the patient's bed or daytime chair

2. parasites of many types present in the body

3. degenerative toxic focus, most commonly in the teeth or jaws but also often in the tonsils or pelvic abdominal areas

4. unresolved emotional trauma

5. miasmic influences, from parent to child, passed through the generations

6. radiation and/or electromagnetic exposure

7. personal chemical pollution with toxins such as nickel, cadmium, mercury, aflatoxins (from molds and fungi), pesticides, benzene, toluene, xylene, formaldehyde, isopropyl alcohol and 'autotoxins', chiefly from the patient's own intestines[5].

EDS specialists make no attempts to treat the cancer, only to treat the patient. If he or she is going to survive the intruder, the patient will need a fortified immune system that is capable of closing down the attack. This can only be achieved by detoxing, removing coincidental and distracting pathology, pumping up nutrition and taking remedies known to stimulate immunity. Of course this cannot all be done with homeopathy. I myself give intravenous drips containing high-key nutritional supplements, especially high-dose vitamin C which is a proven safe cytotoxic agent. Dental work and other physical intervention may be indicated.

Most important of all, the patient must change his or her life, radically. Cancer is a wake-up call; it means the patient is badly off-balance in respect of all or part of his or her life. Unless steps are taken to remedy toxic relationships, unhappy work conditions and low self-image, then no therapy is going to be effective against cancer.

It is hardly necessary to point out that these are good universal health measures and apply to any chronic disease process. I call it my ortho-immune program; ortho meaning good or best, as in orthopedics.

Suitable complex homeopathic remedies that can be considered are:

1. Viscum (Mistletoe) in various combinations. Iscador is Rudolph Steiner's formula. HEEL (BHI) do Viscum compositum.

2. Echinacea compounds, alternating as immune boosters.

3. Glyoxal (very powerful and for intermittent use only)

4. Causticum

5. Carcinominum (nosode)

6. Drainage remedies, e.g. lymphomyosot (HEEL), galium

7. Detoxing compounds (Berberis, Nux vom, etc.)

8. Defense remedies e.g. Tonsilla comp., Discus comp. (HEEL)

9. Miasms, individually or composite, as in Psorino-HEEL.

10. Specific tumor nosodes, bronchus, uterus, cervical cancer etc.

Dental and other foci will need to be eliminated. In truth, it comes back to my old saw that all good health measures are anti-cancer measures.

CHAPTER 20

Star Trek Medicine is Here

Star Trek Medicine is a term I invented in the late 1990s, to describe the SCENAR device here featured. I notice this term has been stolen without attribution by hack writer Mark Sircus. This is ironic, in view of his vitriolic online attack on me, in which he called me a "madman". He feels safe in doing this since he lives in Brazil and thinks he's above any libel suit.

Sircus likes to be called doctor though he has no formal medical training; just a few "paper mill" diplomas that anyone can buy for a few dollars. His output as a writer seems to be no more than copying other sources and pretending them as his own.

Google "Star Trek medicine" and my name and you will get thousands of returns that put this plagiarism beyond question.

As I said in the first edition of *Virtual Medicine* (1999), a pocket-sized device to defibrillate hearts, rapidly heal sports injuries, strokes, angina, back pains and irritable bowel disease (as well as pre-menstrual tension and post-surgical complications) sounds like a large claim. Yet by the late 1990s this was what was being asserted for a family of medical devices called the SCENAR.

S.C.E.N.A.R. is an acronym for self-controlled energo-neuro-adaptive regulation (you may also search SKENAR on the Net, since some people spell it that way, but which makes nonsense of the acronym).

There were very few diseases, it was said, that these devices could not treat and often cure, cancer being one of them, though it may be used for painful malignant conditions, avoiding stimulating the tumor itself.

Having obtained and experimented with one, I was very impressed and enthusiastically gave it my support. This new system is a revolutionary approach which again combines the technology of orthodox Western medical practice with ancient knowledge of the East.

The promise of a small hand-held device that seemed capable of curing most illnesses such as was portrayed in the cult 1960s TV series 'Star Trek' had in less than twenty years almost become a reality. I am pleased and amused that my book launched the phrase "Star Trek Medicine" and it has now passed into wide usage.

I remain satisfied that this is a major new advance but I have become aware that there have been outrageous claims, lies told and ugly politics surfaced. Suppliers and teachers of the method vie with one another economically and are not beyond attempting to trash each other's reputation. One supplier is even reputed to be in league with the Russian mafia and other dealers claim to have been threatened. Greed has surfaced in a big way and there are many individuals and companies involved in the "boom" who have little holistic health skill or experience.

I have cynically posted two typical threads of development below. You may hear more; believe what you will! When I spoke to one of the Russian developers on their first UK visit, he even muttered something about the origin of the instrument being the deliberate creation of pain (torture). It sounded rather dark and sinister, given the murky political background of 20th century Russian science. Trouble is, you don't know who to believe.

The original inventor of the SCENAR is said to be A.A. Karasev an electronics engineer back in 1973, who made one for himself after some of his family members died and the conventional medicine of the day could not help[1]. Karasev later worked for the Russian Cosmonaut program and showed his invention to his superiors who were very interested, so much so that a team was set up with funding to develop the idea further.

When the Soviet Union decided to send cosmonauts into orbit for prolonged periods, it was clear that they needed to have a means of treating any illnesses that could befall them. Unlike the American system, there had no convenient reusable shuttle craft to bring an ailing cosmonaut back to Earth, should the need have arisen. The possibility of incapacitating disease was a major worry.

The pharmaceutical approach was not tenable, bearing in mind the rigorous weight and space limitations and the fact that drug-oriented medicine is based on the principle of one substance for each (potential) condition. Even a very modest pharmaceutical range would be weighty. Also, an environment where recycling of water is such an essential feature, any drug entering the water circulation system would persist, passing through fellow cosmonauts many times.

This was when the Russian space program was being watched by the rest of the world and maintaining national prestige was of paramount concern to the Soviet government. It was essential to come up with something radically new. It had to be light, easy to use and, of course, really effective.

Bioresonance technology was the only extant medical paradigm capable of delivering these stringent requirements. By expanding on the theoretical work of P K Anokhin[2], particularly in connection with non-anatomical "functional systems", the team developed elegant new physiological models, which led to the current range of electronic interactive devices.

Ironically, no SCENAR device has been used in space to date. There were delays caused by the authorities insisting on a waterproofing process. Before this matter was resolved, funds were suddenly stopped at the time of *perestroika*, the so-called space race was called off and the team disbanded. The US began working on combined space projects with the Russians and this introduced the capability of evacuating sick cosmonauts on the shuttle, which meant there was no further need for on-board therapy.

The end of the communist era led to a cessation of funding but some of the members of the team decided to continue and formed the OKB RITM Company in 1983. Names you repeatedly come across are A.N. Revenko, Y. Grinberg, and Y. Gorfinkel as well as Karasev. They managed to get approval in 1986 from the Russian Ministry of Health for the device to be used in health clinics.

BACKGROUND STORY NUMBER TWO

The SCENAR devices arose from a study of an Eastern therapy known as 'zonal contact massage'. The intention had been to develop some way of altering the pressure of the massage, according to skin response (readers will recall that in Chapter 7 I described how the dielectric potential of collagen tissue is stimulated by pressure). Equipment was developed to tap magnetic effects from the skin and use these to modulate changes in pressure of the massage. A team of scientists, including five research doctors, was involved in the original studies, based in Sochi and Krasnodar.

The establishment of a biofeedback mechanism led to the creation of a device whose output would depend on skin energetic response. The term SCENAR was born. It is yet another brilliant marriage of Western electronic technology and Eastern energetic healing skills.

The aim is to stimulate the body's own endogenous energies to effect the cure, using as a mediator the brain's own internal pharmacy of neuropeptides. This allows the body its own choice of healing ingredients. Through biofeedback a dialogue is formed between the tissues and the instrument, each new signal evolves as a new output. No two consecutive signals from the device are the same. This allows the treatment to be truly dynamic, adjusting for changes in the body through time and in different physiological conditions.

Certainly, when you learn the SCENAR method properly, you will be impressed that it overlaps well with acupuncture and zonal therapies. You can stimulate acupuncture points and work on meridians. Perhaps this, really, is the true story.

WHAT ACTUALLY HAPPENS?

The Russians make a great deal out of the chemical model and the "on-board" natural pharmacy of the brain. Stimulating the nerve pathways externally with the SCENAR feeds back to the brain and causes the release of case-suitable neuropeptides. The operator does not have to know what these chemical compounds are; just leave it to Nature to select what is best.

Whereas it is nice for some to have the credibility-factor of invoking reticulo-endothelial pathways and neuropeptides, I have never seen any hard evidence adduced for this often-repeated claim.

I think what is much more important and tends to be glossed over is that the SCENAR is an electronic energy healing device. It belongs firmly in the bioresonance model referred to in Chapter 17. I discussed this at length with Professor Revenko and his colleagues at the first launch in Europe (Marlow, 1999) and that is what he propounded.

Liken it, if you will, to throwing a grenade into the enemy bunker. Fixed energies, we know, are the pathological ones. Anything which disrupts these will lead to a realignment and transformation to something healthier. Thus, strongly overwriting fixed energy patterns with the SCENAR will move things out of status quo and the rest is done by Nature herself.

I brought Morell and Rasche into the conversation (see Chapter 17); Ravenko was indignant that the real founder of bioresonance was Alexander Gurwitsch, whose discovery of ultra-weak photon emission from the living systems I describe on page 371. This gave rise to biophotonics, showing that light (electro-magnetic radiation) was the principle means of communication between cells. You will hear me remark through and through this book that the Russians are much more open to broad-minded and revolutionary concepts than their Western counterparts.

Gurwitsch, incidentally, was also a founder of morphogenetic field theory, long before Rupert Sheldrake made this model very popular (page 61).

OPERATION

The impressive technology, though dogged initially by Russian low build-quality, allows modulation of wave forms, frequencies, pulses, damping and intensity, as well as the current strength or "force" settings.

One general mode allows the operator to choose the signal qualities; the other is adapted from the body's own energies, which are altered to a pre-set algorithm and returned to the tissues. I explain this to patients as being rather like two radio programs: on one channel the DJ chooses all the tunes; the other is rather like a request program and incoming calls dictate what is broadcast out!

Essentially, SCENAR is using the patient's own endogenous signals on a cybernetic feedback basis, scanning and retransmitting many times a second. As described to me, the device 'evolves' a new signal pattern for the disordered tissues, the machine literally entering into an information dialogue with the body. New frequencies and energy patterns are established, which in turn become fresh input signals, to be further modified, and so on. This output-equals-new-input is much the way that fractals are generated and thus, biologically speaking, we seem to be on good ground here.

A word of warning, if you get involved: the Russian fashion is to turn up the current and zap the patient; a crude "Give 'em a good whack" attitude. This does not truly accord with the principles of energy medicine, which is that it is not the quantity of energy but its nurturing quality that counts. The more-is-better approach is what blights conventional medicine and so often makes it dangerous.

Casebook: Male, 69 years

This patient was a gardener with suppurating osteomyelitis of the foot which could not be controlled. He was scheduled for an amputation of the lower leg in four days' time, largely because of the intractable pain. At the last moment a British SCENAR practitioner was called in to attempt a treatment. The device was used bilaterally for around 30 minutes on the first day.

Next day, the leg was pain-free for the first time in eight months. Later that day another 30-minute treatment was given. By next morning the recovery was so dramatic the amputation was called off. A third treatment was given and seven days after the first SCENAR this man was back at work, digging in the garden. His leg has completely recovered.

CLINICAL ASPECTS

No pain should be felt but the patient is usually aware of a tingling sensation while it works and some people are very uncomfortable with this.

The practitioner seeks for what the Russians term asymmetry, meaning something different about the tissue characteristics in the vicinity.

There are five main criteria:

- Color difference (reddening or pallor)

- Sensation (numbness or the opposite: hyper-aesthesia)

- 'Stickiness' in which the machine drags with a magnet like quality as it is drawn over certain tracts of the skin

- Sound changes (the machine begins to chatter electronically when it hits the right zone)

- Numerical display readings alter and can be interpreted

Even though it may not coincide with the obvious area of symptoms or pathology, the important point is to *treat the asymmetry*. For reasons we do not fully understand, when the asymmetry is eliminated, recovery will rapidly follow.

For treatment of cases where direct application of a SCENAR device is not possible, a number of external electrodes have been developed and successfully used for treatment of various pathologies.

For the treatment of periodontal diseases, a special toothbrush electrode, with parallel silver electrodes installed below the bristle line has been developed. The importance of treating periodontal disease will be apparent, once you have read Chapter 24.[3]

There are few contra-indications, notably heart pacemakers and, after 30 years in widespread use, a remarkable absence of negative side-effects. One of the complications of therapy, however, is that the instrument battery can (and does) pick up energies from the previous patient and can transfer them adversely to a subsequent person. This "memory" effect affects most energetic healing devices I have written about.

As a further note, it is unwise to treat a tumor or work in the region of a known tumor. The energy modifications are random, as explained, and could have an unfortunate consequence. However the SCENAR is good for revitalizing the sagging energies of a seriously ill cancer case and that has tremendous healing value. Ultimately, as Lakhovsky told us, cancer is a "battle of radiations" and the stronger the body's own energies, the better. So use the SCENAR generally on the body, away from any known tumor sites, to ginger up the body's own defenses.

FULL AND FINAL HEALING

One of the reasons I am confident that the SCENAR is more an energy healing device than a neuro-physiological one is the characteristic way that a so-called "healing crisis" or past shock may come to the surface.

It is not uncommon while treating some chronic condition for the body to suddenly erupt in the manifestation of some old but clearly discernible disease. The patient seems to be carried back years in time and experiences a cleansing and revival by re-experiencing the former condition. The ensuing illness can be severe and shocking to the patient but the recovery more than justifies the process.

This goes to the very heart of the *Medicine Beyond* healing model I have described all through these pages, where an old pathological energy "imprint" is attached to the body and when this is dislodged the disease will fade and vanish. Unfortunately, sometimes it may induce a temporary reversion to the disease of old, as I described under Hering's Law in page 315. Very likely in these cases the proper natural process of resolution has been interrupted by antibiotics or some other drug intervention which left the acute illness suspended, only to emerge years later as a chronic disease or condition.

Properly conducted, energy healing modalities do not have this hang up liability. Healing is full and final.

OPERATING WITH OTHER MODALITIES

One of the appealing aspects of the SCENAR I have found is the easy interaction with other healing modalities. For examples, SCENAR stimulation can be applied to acupuncture points. The results may enhance both modalities.

Thus pressure on the point Colon #4 at the base of the thumb can bring deeply buried old emotions to the surface and a resolution. On one occasion I applied a SCENAR to my own lung #7 and that brought a burst of tears; this is also a notorious emotional point! We have the expression "getting it off one's chest" for emotional release, don't we?

Other points worth considering are:

- Bladder #47 - helps to release repressed fear and encourages feelings of strength and resolution.

- Kidney #6 - this point may be used for stage fright or fears about any performance.

- Triple Heater #15 - this point helps relax nervous tension associated with worry.

- Stomach # 36 - helps to reduce anxiety by strengthening the entire energetic and physical body.

SCENARs also adapt very well with the auriculo-acupuncture method of Nogier, described on page 195. I have no doubt this kind of device can integrate well with other micro-acupuncture systems.

SCENARs can be skillfully combined with knowledge of myofascial trigger points. These are described as hyperirritable spots in skeletal muscle that are often palpable as nodules in taut bands of muscle fibers. These are said to be the origin of a great deal of soft-tissue pain. The trigger point may not be where the pain is felt (referred pain) so it took a little time for this phenomenon to come to light.

The trigger point concept still remains unknown to most doctors and is not generally taught in medical school curricula. The most recent definitive work is by Janet G. Travell and David Simons (*The Trigger Point Manual*).[4] Travell was so successful at treating John F. Kennedy's back pain that she became the first female Personal Physician to the President.

Because of this versatility the SCENAR is exceptional for sports injuries and has kept many a professional athlete on the field, instead of being laid up in bed.

In fact for pain relief, it is quite exceptional. I have seen it dispel severe biliary colic, toothache and the pain of a fracture through the ankle in a matter of minutes (biliary colic—gallstones—is one of medicine's two worst pains; the other is a kidney stone).

COSMETICS AND EYE BENEFITS

One of the surprising additional benefits of the SCENAR has been its use as a cosmetic device. It is excellent for toning muscles and can thus be used to reverse some of the facial damage of aging, removing skin wrinkles and the sag of flesh by toning up tissues. Special electrodes are available with which to target particular muscle groups and, by stimulating them selectively, you can go through a process of what actors and actresses call "facial gymnastics".

Remember, the SCENAR is capable of revitalizing the whole body and good energies always benefit the complexion!

It can even reduce scars or at least cause them to fade and become less visible.

One available attachment for the DENAS range is the DENS-glasses. The main device is connected to a set of goggles which contain metal stimulus probes. These deliver the Bioresonance field right to the eyes and optic pathways and are said to benefit visual acuity, as well as ocular conditions.

WHERE TO GET THE DEVICES

The OKB RITM company produced several models using names such as Scenar 97, Scenar NT, Scenar 2003, Autoscenar, Kosmed and, lately, the SCENAR Pro. (http://www.scenar.com.ru/index_eng.html) At the risk of offending other manufacturers I have always held that the RITM models were the best built SCENARs, the best performing, with the European CE approval mark and the models with the best training and after service, thanks largely to Jan de Jong of Kosmed International.

Unfortunately, Russian business ethics and European standards don't really mix. This has been a long-term problem for suppliers and end-users. With the passing of Jan de Jong, co-founder of Kosmed International, who left us in 2013, things seem to have gone from bad to worse. I can no longer wholeheartedly recommend anyone trying to deal with a Russian-made device. With the added problem of an international trade embargo against Russia, the OKB hegemony is at an end.

PacificHealthOptions.com, managed by John Haché and his wife Lorraine Ann Vanbergen-Haché is a good place to look for alternatives. They now recommend the US-manufactured equivalent micro-current device called the Avazzia.

It has a number of advantages, including one I like, which is to pre-set your favorite programs and then call them up quickly, without having to dial in the details every time.

I traded in my RITM Pro and got an Avazzia Pro Sport III instead!

OTHER BRANDS

Karasev decided to go his own way in 1990 and set up the LET Medical company which produces a range of models under the SCENAR and Cosmodic brands. (http://www.scenar.ru/en/) His website is still active, I note.

The Rema company in Belorussia started producing Prologue and Enart models in 1993. (http://rema.by/) Check out their English PowerPoint presentation where it says 'English version' (http://rema.by/?module=about) The ENART manual, by the way, is one of the best out there.

CCC Invet is a reseller of several of the above companies' products and has an English website. (http://www.invet.net/32/e/ about_e. shtml)

Another company RTS ART was set up in 1995 and now trades as Denas MS producing the Denas and DiaDens models. (http://www. denascorp.ru/) They have many resellers, some with English websites. Denas themselves don't seem to have an English page.

The Pervade Wave company in Hong Kong has a regional (Asia) license to produce the Space Healer model. These are sold in HK. (http://www.naturalhealing.com.hk/spacehealer.php) and in Australia (http://www.enlightenedtherapies.com/index.htm)

Let Medical has a website: http://www.scenar.ru/en/about_scenar/ history/1972/

Note that I do not support any of this rash of providers, since it is beyond my ability to vouch for the technical performance of each device or the integrity of each of the companies or individuals concerned.

PRACTITIONER DIRECTORIES

If you want to know more, the following group of websites list local practitioners in each of the territories mentioned (at the time of writing). You can get treatment, help in buying and some training, one way or another.

- http://www.vitalitylink.com/modality-Scenar-Therapy-184

- http://www.scenar-therapy.com/therapy/scenar-therapists/

- UK - http://www.scenartherapist.co.uk/INFO-+-ADVICE/Scenar-Therapists.html

- Ireland - http://www.irishcollegeofscenar.com

- AU/NZ - http://scenar.org.au/

- Canada - http://www.ns-health.ca/Scenar-Therapists.html

- Mexico - http://pain-relief-therapy.com/scenar_therapist_directory.html

- South Africa - http://www.scenar-sa.co.za

- Switzerland - http://scenar.ch

There were, upon a time, a large number of online SCENAR user forums. However I can find none that are current. It might be a good idea to do a search from time to time, if you are interested in this particular technology.

MUDSLINGING

It seems that RITM was originally happy to license the SCENAR idea to other companies, but then, when they started to make their own variants, disputes arose as to who could use the brand name SCENAR and whose model was better etc. Hence there has been quite a lot of mudslinging.

I note that in 2013 the Supreme Commercial Court of the Russian Federation restored the trademark "SCENAR" to RITM OKB.

Most of the companies originally targeted the health care market with expensive products although there are now some cheaper home-use models with reduced features. They also tended to sell training courses to their customers and provided little written documentation.

The exception seems to be the Denas Company, which decided to go down the network marketing route with large numbers of resellers and reasonable prices. They have four current models including a Euro Denas one with CE certification and an English version of their printed 240 page Denas Therapy Manual and its accompanying 2 hour video, although the English translation could be much improved. Their latest model the Diadens-DT even includes two electro acupuncture modes.

This gives it Voll's EAV capabilities, which we met in Chapter 15 (http://www.scott-mumby-scenar.com/).

There is now also a PC-compatible model, which will supply a print-out suitable to give the patient and file a copy in his or her records for reference.

I also discovered that there is a wealth of SCENAR related information on the internet but unsurprisingly mostly in Russian. However you can use the free online translation engine WorldLingo.

http://www.worldlingo.com/en/products_services/worldlingo_translator.html)

My own take on this is that every home should have one of these devices in the medicine cupboard. The simple Avazzia home use model requires very little knowledge to use and, although they lack the sophistication of the more elaborate devices, will be very useful for sudden toothaches, sore throats, minor physical injuries and fevers. It has even helped MS sufferers and restored some degree of muscular function and strength.

MICROCURRENT ELECTROTHERAPY

Things have come on a long way since I first wrote about the SCENAR for the original edition of *Virtual Medicine*. Microcurrent therapy for healing (MCT) is now definitely on the radar of orthodox medicine.

A paper I found from the School of Health and Emergency Professions, University of Hertfordshire, UK, concluded that the evidence in support of MCT is convincing enough to justify its inclusion in the clinician's repertoire for treatment of several examples of recalcitrant bone and skin lesions.

Indeed, as the authors pointed out, federal and private health insurance providers in the USA have accepted its use for spinal fusions and hard to heal skin ulcers for some years.

In contrast, the authors complained, the lack of substantial and robust human trial evidence for the use of MCT with musculoskeletal soft tissue lesions is frustrating.

Or more exactly, they stated: Microcurrent appears to play a significant role in the healing process, and MCT can promote healing in a variety of bone and skin lesions. The evidence for other tissues *is encouraging* but presently scant.

Yet MCT has several significant features in its favor: there is already substantial evidence that it can work where other approaches have failed; it may help redress an underlying physiological dysfunction as well as reducing its symptoms. The mechanism of action appears to be as a trigger or facilitator of the whole healing process, unlike some new approaches such as exogenous growth factors, which have specific targets in the healing cascade.

MCT can be provided by a small, portable generator, over an extended period where necessary, requiring minimal practitioner supervision once initiated. The therapy has been shown to be most beneficial when it is used as part of a broader management strategy.

Reported side-effects of MCT are few and minor. Given these characteristics, the potential for MCT in a range of recalcitrant musculoskeletal disorders is worthy of closer attention by both research and clinical communities[5].

Yet another paper was effusively positive and said: the correct form of electromedical intervention will often have a profound and usually immediate effect on pain. ... Even at its present state of evolution, electromedicine offers an unprecedented conservative, cost-effective, fast, safe and powerful tool in the management of the pain patient. As such it should be the first priority on the list of treatment options[6].

CONTROLLING INFLAMMATION WITH ELECTRO-STIMULATION

Another paper I found from right here in Las Vegas, my home city, summed up the present state of play nicely: "...pharmaceuticals have a tendency to overwhelm biosystems, a very unnatural progression as evidenced by the side effect profiles. Electro-Stimulation Therapy (EST) works through biosystems and their controls. We have presented multiple mechanisms, most documented and one postulated, which demonstrate initial facilitation and then quick resolution of the inflammatory process to prevent it from leading to chronic inflammation and chronic pain...

"A paradigm shift in our approach should begin soon. Many patients in chronic pain are simply being undertreated for various reasons. Narcotic medications are being diverted in increasing numbers. Most importantly, a recent study on adverse drug events based on the FDA voluntary reporting system has found the death rate has increased out of proportion to the increase in the number of prescriptions written, and the greatest culprits are pain medications and immune modulating drugs. The authors emphasized that these findings "show that the existing system is not adequately protecting patients and underscores the importance of recent reports urging far-reaching legislative, policy and institutional changes."

The authors emphasized the physics approach, over and above the pharmacological approach and concluded that, while additional studies involving the treatment of inflammatory processes with EST are important, there appears to be enough evidence to encourage the primary or adjuvant use of EST for inflammatory conditions and for the potential replacement of chemical steroids. EST and the evidence presented have placed us on a threshold of discovery; it is time to apply this knowledge in the clinical setting. The alternative role of EST will depend on the outcomes of well-conducted clinical trials which utilize this reasonable and safe approach[7].

This is very satisfactory progress for what was a pretty "off the wall" treatment modality when I first espoused and wrote about it in 1999!

THE NEW GENERATION

Now we have more recent devices, notably the Avazzia range, manufactured and supplied by a US company, Avazzia Inc. Their top model, the new *Avazzia Pro Sport III* has a large number of programs or algorithms (53 in total) which includes everything from anti–inflammatory programs to vasodilatation, repetitive strain injury, the Schumann resonance frequencies, the major acupuncture point frequencies as well as the chakra frequencies, the cosmetic frequencies, toning frequencies, the brainwave frequencies of alpha, beta, theta, delta, and gamma, etc.

The SCENARs have nothing like this.

Take, for example, the VASO program (from vascular). This works well on the vascular system, which has implications for dementia (cerebral blood flow), to heart disease (coronary artery health), to diabetes (gangrene of the extremities, sometimes requiring amputation). In fact the health of blood vessels is critical to all parts of the body; blood brings oxygen and nutrients and removes metabolites and toxins.

John Haché remarked on a case of severe frostbite. A young military medic on a training mission to northern Alberta was trying for an elite search and rescue position. But he contracted extreme frostbite of the toes and feet. Death of the toes in question is usual, indeed a given in this situation.

The young man was placed on the critical list, pending surgical removal of the non-viable toes. However, it never came to that. Three weeks of use of the Avazzia Sport Pro unit, using mainly VASO to get blood flow back to the feet, saved all the man's toes.

OPERATOR PROGRAMMING

This Avazzia can also be programmed by the operator, using frequencies from ½ Hz to 1560 Hz. The ½ Hz is for deep depression transcranially, etc. Once you have selected the frequency of choice, then you can add such things as (pulses) for better pain control, damping, modulation, z interval (gap width between your pulses) Once completed you can now put your created program into one of 4 banks that you would keep for your favorite set of newly created programs.

In other words, there are also SCENAR modulations available, plus many other capabilities. The power output can be adjusted for normal, sensitive, soft, ultra-soft and gentle.

The Sport Pro III is FDA approved for pain control. It weighs 6 ounces (173 grams).

I do believe that Avazzia have really outdone the Russians, with their wide range of features and superb build quality. The port on the side of the device accepts options such as a SCALAR wave device or a PEMF device or, soon to come, an LED device.

If cost is an issue, there is the Avazzia Pro Sport Ultra: same basic device but with fewer programs for less money.

My friends at Pacific Health Options (John Haché and Dr. Lorraine Vanbergen-Haché, already mentioned) sell this device and run courses. You could do worse than contract them and enroll: www.AvazziaLife.com

John and Lorraine have founded the Academy of Applied Electro-Physiology (www.academyofappliedelectrophysiology.com) and are currently delivering courses in MCT, recognized in Texas.

As usual, there are caveats. The Avazzia is not to be used on those with a pacemaker or other implantable electronic devices; not to be used by pregnant or nursing women; definitely not to be used over the carotid artery, or to cause a current to run transcranially (through the skull).

Neither a SCENAR nor Avazzia should also be used directly on open wounds; too painful to bear! Just treat the immediate surroundings. Once the wound has closed, then you can work on it direct.

FAME AND INFAMY

I'd like to conclude this chapter with what must be the most dramatic SCENAR case history ever told!

My friend Dr. Lorraine Ann Vanbergen-Haché was walking down a city street in the UK a few years ago. Lorraine is a leading expert with the SCENAR. She was with a friend. It was down time. Suddenly, a running man burst between them, followed closely behind by another man in pursuit, wielding an axe!

To the horror of the two women, right in front of them, the assailant buried the axe in the skull of the man he was chasing, threw away the weapon and ran off.

The victim collapsed to the ground, his skull cleaved open, revealing the meninges and brain. Yet, remarkably, he remained conscious.

Now Lorraine is a very calming individual and quickly took charge of the scene; she asked someone to call an ambulance; demanded all the spectators be removed to a distance; and set to work. Her only tool was her SCENAR, which she carries in her purse at all times.

Lorraine worked around the wound, hoping to minimize the bleeding and damage, possibly also to sooth the energy field of a murder attack and the "information" imprint of violent damage to one of the body's most critical areas.

In due course the ambulance arrived. The paramedics could not believe the victim was even alive, never mind conscious, given the savage wound he had sustained. There had been almost no blood loss. The paramedics initiated standard procedure and whisked the wounded man off to the ER.

Lorraine later visited the hospital to see the man she had saved and found him fully conscious. He was in some pain, not surprisingly, but filled with gratitude.

Just a story? Not at all: the entire event had been captured by a street surveillance video camera and everyone in the country was startled to see the tape replayed, showing the whole murderous attack and the strange woman who produced what looked like a TV remote from her purse and started rubbing it over the victim's head!

Lorraine was welcomed home that evening as a heroine, before she even realized that her quick-thinking action had been televised for the whole nation to see[8].

Dr. McCoy ("Bones") would have been proud of her.

CHAPTER 21

We are Frozen Light

Consciousness cannot be accounted for in physical terms. For consciousness is absolutely fundamental. It cannot be accounted for in terms of anything else.

— Erwin Schrödinger

Light seems to have a very special relationship with living creatures.

It has always been curious to me that the whole of the electromagnetic spectrum is hostile to biological life... except light and heat (and even heat can be damaging to life).

But not light!

Specifically, the band of waves that we call visible light: once into the shorter wavelengths we call "ultraviolet", then it's not friendly at all. But then it's not light either, in the sense I am using the term. The very name "ultra' violet means beyond visible violet light.

Light has other surprising beneficial health properties. We already saw in Chapter 2 that it is the source of unusual nutrition, never before suspected in animals: human photosynthesis.

UV light we know is antiseptic. In fact plain blue light (in the visible range) is also useful as a sterilizing agent. It can even help cure infections when shone on the skin: the so-called Florence Nightingale effect. She showed that fresh air and sunlight were crucial to the management of infectious diseases in hospitals everywhere. Now scientists have discovered a "fresh air factor", some unknown property of air and sunlight that tests show is capable of wiping out microbes.

This chapter explores some more sensational uses of light that come under the banner of *Medicine Beyond*.

WE ARE FROZEN LIGHT

Robert Grosseteste, a medieval scholar (1175-1253) who is widely regarded to be one of the first true scientists, wrote a tract entitled *De Luce* (of light). In it, he describes the story of creation in terms of the modification of light. To Grosseteste, light possessed two aspects: one aspect was the light of our physical existence condensed into matter, and the other aspect was a light of intelligence embodied in the purely spiritual realms of the Godhead.

Grosseteste may have been close to modern quantum science. He presaged David Bohm's famous aphorism: that we are made of "frozen light".

In an interview Bohm gave with Renée Weber, Professor of Philosophy at Rutgers University, we learn more…

> *"When we come to light we are coming to the fundamental activity in which existence has its ground, or at least coming close to it. … Light is what enfolds all the universe … Light in its generalized sense (not just ordinary light) is the means by which the entire universe unfolds into itself. … It's energy and also it's information–content, form and structure. It's the potential of everything. … Light can carry information about the entire universe. The other point is that light, by interactions of different rays, can produce particles and all the diverse structures of matter."* [1]

These ideas incidentally are in striking accord with Helena Blavatsky's mystical statements in *The Secret Doctrine* of 1888: "… pure light condensed gradually into form, hence becoming matter:" further, "light is the great magician ... its multifarious, omnipotent waves give birth to every form as well as to every living being."[2]

QUANTUM HYMN

Maybe you thought all this was just New Age whimsy? Not at all. In fact the latest research has proven that we can make matter from light. It's the reverse, in a way, of Einstein's e=mc² leading to changes from matter to energy (the c is a constant, the speed of light).

The theory underpinning the idea of making matter from pure light was described 80 years ago by two physicists who later worked on the first atomic bomb. At the time they considered the conversion of light into matter impossible in a laboratory.

But a 2014 report published by physicists at Imperial College London claims to have cracked the problem using high-powered lasers and other equipment now available to scientists.

Not that we are ready to focus a laser blast and make a table or motorcar... yet! But indeed that time may come. Meantime, the kind of matter they aim to make comes in the form of subatomic particles invisible to the naked eye.

The two US physicists with the original idea were Gregory Breit and John Wheeler, in 1934. They worked out that two particles of light, or photons, could combine to produce an electron and its antimatter equivalent, a positron. Electrons are particles of matter; so... matter from light.

But Breit and Wheeler considered the process was so rare and hard to produce that it would be "hopeless to try to observe the pair formation in laboratory experiments".

Now, writing in the journal *Nature Photonics*, today's scientists describe how they could turn light into matter through a number of separate steps. The first step fires electrons at a slab of gold to produce a beam of high-energy photons. Next, they fire a high-energy laser into a tiny gold capsule called a hohlraum, from the German for "empty room". This produces light as bright as that emitted from stars. In the final stage, they send the first beam of photons into the hohlraum where the two streams of photons collide.

This squeezes enough high-energy photons into a small enough volume to create around 100,000 electron-positron pairs. There are a number of sites around the world that have the technology. One is the huge Omega laser in Rochester, New York. Another is the Orion laser at Aldermaston, the infamous atomic weapons facility in Berkshire[3].

It's no longer a new Age hallelujah to sing, "We are beings of light!" It's a quantum hymn too.

Not surprisingly then, we all emit photons. It's like spilling our material nature out into the cosmos! We leak light! Take a moment to revisit again the "Luminous Woman of Pirano", Anna Morano, described in Chapter 3. The human body literally glimmers, though not typically as strongly as Morano's did for a time.

That's what this chapter is about.

BIOPHOTONS

It's another extension of my concept of biology outside the skin, calling attention to the theory of ultra-weak luminescence or photon emission by living tissues, usually called "biophotons". This extends the work of Albert Nodon (page 116), cited by Lakhovsky.

In fact biophotons were first postulated in 1923 by Russian medical scientist Professor Alexander G. Gurwitsch. He placed the roots of two onion shoots very close together and noted that they had a positive effect on each other's growth. If he separated them by means of a glass partition, this mutual synergy did not take place; however, if the dividing screen was made of quartz, the original mutual benefit was once again manifest. Gurwitsch concluded therefore that the growth influence had something to do with ultra-violet light emitted by the roots[4].

In 1974 German biophysicist Fritz-Albert Popp proved the existence of biophotons, using sensitive photomultipliers, at the Max Planck Institute of Astronomy in Heidelberg. Popp later became an Invited Member of the New York Academy of Sciences and an Invited Foreign Member of the Russian Academy of Natural Sciences (RANS).

What Popp showed was that clearer and more vigorous light emissions are associated with rapid growth, whereas this falls away with cell ageing. Perhaps most remarkable of all was the discovery that when an organism dies almost all its cells give up their photons simultaneously in a 'death flash', some eight hours after the apparent cessation of life[5].

Popp also showed that stress increases the release of photons. Different disease states have different influences on the photon count: in cancer cases, the photons lost their coherence and diminished towards zero; as Lynne McTaggart quipped her best-selling book *The Field*, it seemed as if the patients' lights were going out. With multiple sclerosis, on the other hand, the photon count increased, perhaps oversaturating and diminishing the ability of cells to function normally.

In a series of fascinating investigations, Popp showed that free-range chicken eggs had far more coherent photons than the eggs of battery-farmed chickens. In general, the healthiest foods have the most coherent photons and the lowest "leakage" rate. This ties in cleanly with the fact that a stressed organism gives off more bio-photons - the less the better (healthier).

Most fascinating of all, tests showed that all living creatures trade photons, some sucking them up, like hungry vacuum cleaners. It can be postulated that this exchange of biophotons is a kind of hitherto undiscovered means of communication between all beings in the physical plane. Furthermore, it can take place over vast distances almost instantaneously; the speed of light is 186,000 miles (almost 3,000 km.) per second[6].

It's fascinating to learn how close light is to our very nature.

PHOTOGRAPHING BIOPHOTON EMISSIONS

Writing in the online journal PLoS ONE, researchers describe how they imaged light from volunteers' upper bodies using ultra-sensitive cameras over a period of several days. Their results show that the amount of light emitted follows a 24-hour cycle, at its highest in late afternoon and lowest late at night, and that the brightest light is emitted from the cheeks, forehead, and neck.

Strangely, the areas of the body that produced the brightest light did not correspond with the brightest areas on thermal images of the volunteers' bodies[7].

Actually, all objects, living or dead, emit a characteristic radiation, which is qualitatively and quantitatively related to temperature. This goes back to Max Planck and his original "black body" studies that laid the foundations of quantum theory. But it also includes cells individually and the body as a whole.

The point is that, after compensating for the expected emanations predicted by Planck's model, a significant number of photons (on the order of as many as 100 photons/cm^2/sec) are given off from living organisms. These surprise biophoton radiations have been detected over a range of wavelengths in the radio and microwave to ultraviolet range; that includes visible light.

The amount of light emitted is quite small; comparable to that observed from a candle viewed at a distance of 10 kilometers. Given the extremely small number of photons produced, for many years the predominant theory was that these photons were just a random by-product of cellular metabolism.

COHERENCE OF LIGHT

While science was underplaying the quantitative aspect, the qualitative nature of this light was being overlooked. It is phase coherent; that is to say, extremely highly organized. Given the random chaotic nature of the natural (physical) universe, it may be said that long-range organization is peculiar to life. Coherence is a defining quality of biophotons. By its very nature, it has the power to hold information; information about living systems, enzymes, structures, dynamic processes, and, of course, disease!

Extending Popp's work, Herbert Fröhlich went on to study coherence and oscillations in biological systems. The fact that such oscillations are inherent in any living system means the resonance effect discovered by Abrams is based on solid science; indeed it is inevitable.

As early as 1938 Fröhlich had become aware that a biological membrane supported an electrical field of 10 MV/m, which was way beyond synthetic materials of the time[8]. By 1974 Fröhlich had progressed to the point of showing that moist proteins behaved like moist ferroelectrics. Not only that, but tissues had super-conductance properties, even at room temperature. In physics this state could only be reached at temperatures just a little above absolute zero. Life was proving truly amazing.

Dr. Cyril Smith, from the Department of Electronic and Electrical Engineering of Salford University in the UK (who introduced a remarkable degree course in holistic biomedical electronics) has gone further and avers that the living body is intrinsically a macroscopic quantum system and has adduced plenty of evidence for his hypothesis[9].

Essentially, that means we are a field phenomenon, extending to infinity, containing vast repositories of data, from past present and future, that define the organism as an integrated whole, interrelated as a system to all other aspects of the quantum field.

This is what we may be talking about when we use terms like *Ch'i, prana* or the "Cosmic Web".

BIOLUMINESCENCE

Actually, we must distinguish bioluminescence from so-called ultra-weak photon emissions.

Bioluminescence, or phosphorescence, is weak but certainly visible. It is produced sometimes in living organisms, such as plankton, fireflies (glow bugs) or jellyfish.

Author naturalist Gerald Durrell gives a particularly vivid account of a memorable occasion, witnessing this beautiful phenomenon on the Greek island of Corfu:

> The phosphorescence was particularly good that night. By plunging your hand into the water and dragging it along you could draw a wide golden-green ribbon of cold fire across the sea, and when you dived as you hit the surface it seemed as though you had plunged into a frosty furnace of glinting light. When we were tired we waded out of the sea, the water running off our bodies so that we seemed to be on fire, and lay on the sand to eat. Then, as the wine was opened at the end of the meal, as if by arrangement, a few fireflies appeared in the olives behind us—a sort of overture to the show.
>
> First of all there were just two or three green specks, sliding smoothly through the trees, winking regularly; but gradually more and more appeared, until parts of the olive grove were lit with a weird green glow. Never had we seen so many fireflies congregated in one spot; they flicked through the trees in swarms, they crawled on the grass, the bushes and the olive-trunks, they drifted in swarms over our heads and landed on the rugs, like green embers. Glittering streams of them flew out over the bay,

swirling over the water, and then, right on cue, the porpoises appeared, swimming in line into the bay, rocking rhythmically through the water, their backs as if painted with phosphorus.

(From *My Family and Other Animals*, Penguin, London, 1956)

Such biological light is believed to be generated as the result of specialized enzymatic reactions that require adenosine triphosphate, i.e. luceferin–luciferase. Plankton produces the effect known as phosphorescence in seawater, when the tide and season is right. Light absorbed during the day is slowly released again at night, giving the sea a greenish glow. This phenomenon is also known as luminescence.

However, virtually all living organisms emit a different extremely weak light, spontaneously without external photoexcitation, at about 1000 photons per second per cm^2, several orders of magnitude below visible levels[10].

By using a sensitive charge-coupled-device (CCD) camera with the ability to detect light at the level of a single photon, scientists in Japan were able to image this spontaneous photon emission from human bodies[11].

Previously, for obtaining an image, it took more than 1 hour of acquisition, which is practically impossible for the analysis of physiologically relevant biophoton emission. By improving the CCD camera and lens system, it proved possible to obtain clear images using a short exposure time, comparable with the analysis of physiological phenomena.

Since metabolic rates are known to change in a circadian fashion[12], the scientists investigated the temporal variations of biophoton emission across the day from healthy human body. They found that the human body directly and rhythmically emits light. The diurnal changes in photon emission are presumably linked to changes in energy metabolism and reactive oxygen species (ROS) released thereby.

To further support this conclusion, immediately following the end of the previous experiment three volunteers were kept awake in a lighted environment and photon emission was measured at 1:00, 4:00 and 7:00 AM. Photon emission formed a peak at late afternoon, then gradually decreased and stayed low right through the night in a constantly exposed light condition (400 lux), indicating the diurnal rhythm of photon was almost certainly caused by endogenous circadian rhythms.

They also found no significant correlation of daily photon intensity and body temperature. This would suggest that the diurnal rhythm of photon emission is not a consequence of a change of temperature or microcirculation. But it also clearly points to the fact that these are living biological effects, not merely background radiation such as found by Max Planck (which is constant).

One other interesting point to note: certain areas of the skin (such as face and chest), had different photon emission rates, when compared with the rest of the body. The researchers suggested that different melanin content of different skin areas might be the explanation (see page 32 for revelations about melanin).

LOW INTENSITY LASERS

It is no longer surprising therefore that low-intensity laser therapy (LILT)—cold lasers—should have important clinical healing benefits. Currently, there is excitement generated by these devices, as a means of healing varied conditions, such as osteoarthritis, myofascial pain, carpal tunnel syndrome, wound healing and acute stroke.

Research into the use of LILT in the treatment of cardiac and cerebral ischemia has shown beneficial increase in improvements in tissue survival and function as compared to control conditions. LILT-induced improvements in these conditions have been attributed to rapid elevation of ATP content, increased angiogenesis, and several other mechanisms, including the mitigation of oxidative stress.

In a clinical setting, however, patients will vary puzzlingly in their response to LILT. It appears that cellular reduction/oxidation potential (redox) state may play a central role in determining sensitivity to LILT and may help explain variability in patient responsiveness.

Conditions associated with elevated reactive oxygen species (ROS) production, such as diabetic hyperglycemia, demonstrate increased sensitivity to LILT. Scientists are hoping therefore to find a convenient, non-invasive way of assessing redox potential.

The detection of biophotons may turn out to be just the thing. Biophoton release is associated with cellular redox state and the generation of ROS. In this review, we will present the case for pursuing further investigation into the potential clinical partnership between biophoton detection and LILT[13].

SEEING RED

What is perhaps the most fascinating aspect of laser healing is the recognition of the very powerful healing stimulus from one specific red light frequency: 632.8 nanometers (often rounded off to 635nm). It rose to prominence in China and Russia, where is has been extensively studied and used therapeutically. Needless to say, Western medicine ignores it disdainfully.

Meanwhile, the science has started to roll in.

In one paper published in 2012, researchers evaluated 90 subjects. All of them had either coronary artery disease or a history of stroke. They divided the participants into a treatment group of 60 and a control group of 30. They gave the treatment group low level laser red light for just 30 minutes daily for 10 days, three days off and another session of 10 days. They exposed the control group to a normal, non-healing light.

The age range of the treatment and control group was similar (older demographic). The researchers evaluated their blood for blood viscosity and lipid changes. The two key blood viscosity measurements decreased significantly. That means their blood became less "thick" and easier to flow. That's extremely important for vascular diseases and also the ability to clean up the tissues and "detox".

Blood fats improved too. Total cholesterol fell from 173 mg/dl to 147. LDL fell from 107 mg/dl to 97; "good" HDL cholesterol rose from 42 mg/dl to 47; and, triglycerides (bad) fell from 161 mg/dl to 151.

Red light can help stroke. A 2005 China study on 21 patients utilized the sophisticated SPECT scan, which actually determines blood flow to various areas of the brain. The therapeutic light improved brain perfusion on the treated side! Other studies showed improvement in stroke symptoms with this treatment.

In another study conducted in 2003, Dou et al randomly divided 60 patients who had suffered a stroke to the brain (cerebral infarction) and 36 patients with traumatic brain injury into 2 groups (total of 96 patients). 50 of these patients were treated with intranasal light therapy (low level laser) and 46 with intravenous low level laser blood irradiation. Both were treated once a day for 5 consecutive days, given a 2-day break and resumed for another 5 days, adding to a total of 12 days in the study.

They found that total cholesterol, LDL cholesterol, triglyceride levels, erythrocyte sedimentation rate and the hematocrit (red blood cell level) were significantly reduced. Fugi Meyer movement scale (assessment of motor recovery after a stroke) and Barthel index scores (measurement of a person's daily functioning specifically the activities of daily living and mobility) were significantly increased. The damaged areas of the brain were reduced in both groups.

There was also no significant difference in whether the patients were being treated with Intranasal Light Therapy or intravenous blood irradiation therapy[14].

In another (admittedly small) study, red light therapy was shown to cut cosmetic surgery wound healing time by half or one third, according to the researchers. They treated one half of the body and used the opposite side as its own "control". Their conclusion was clear: "In all instances, the LED therapy-treated side was statistically significantly superior to the unirradiated control by a factor of two to three."[15]

It even works for allergic rhinitis; go figure! In a double-blind placebo-controlled study reported in the *Annals of Allergy, Asthma and Immunology* in April 1997, 72% of those receiving the "medical light" showed marked improvement, compared to 24% in the placebo group. The improvements were confirmed endoscopically, in 70% and 3% of cases, respectively, meaning that most of the placebo group believed they felt better but actually didn't show any physical improvements[16].

These devices have already benefitted Parkinson's disease patients, those with sleep disorder and there is talk it may help to release growth hormone, which would be very valuable.

CYTOCHROME OXIDASE

Then, in 2013, a paper was published that is very important to us Boomers. It showed red light can beat senility; it can enhance cognitive function meaning, you hang onto your marbles a lot longer! This is hot stuff!

The use of transcranial lasers and LEDs at around 630nm enhances cognitive function, by lighting up your mitochondria, which are the tiny organelles in our cells which work like little engines: they take fuel and burn it to create energy!

The conclusion of researchers from the Departments of Psychology, Pharmacology and Toxicology, University of Texas at Austin and the Department of Neurology and Neurotherapeutics, University of Texas Southwestern Medical Center, Dallas, is transcranial brain stimulation with low-level light/laser therapy (LLLT) using the red-to-near-infrared wavelengths is able to modulate neurobiological function.

Transcranial means shone *through the skull*. Unlike microwaves and cell phones, it does this in a nondestructive and non-thermal manner. Tissues are completely unharmed by the "radiation". It's only light, after all.

The paper speculated that the mechanism of this action of cold lasers is based on photon energy absorption by cytochrome oxidase, the terminal enzyme in the mitochondrial respiratory chain. This enzyme has a key role in neuronal physiology, as it serves as an interface between oxidative energy metabolism and cell survival signaling pathways. Cytochrome oxidase is an ideal target for cognitive enhancement, as its expression reflects the changes in metabolic capacity underlying higher-order brain functions[17].

What's important for us is that you can grow new nerve cells, renew and invigorate the ones you've got, improve your arteries' structure and their function, diminish inflammation and turn on half-asleep energy modules called mitochondria.

Does that sound like anti-aging goodness? Or is it just good? It's something we should all be doing.

RIGHT UP YOUR NOSE

Now the great news is that it's been found that ordinary red light of the same wavelength is *almost* as good as laser light: so no worry about safety issues. No electrical power supply needed. That means it's possible to get a real therapeutic effect just using a low-intensity battery-powered device. These come fairly cheap, so this is a therapeutic breakthrough!

Now for the really fun part! The best way to administer magic "light food" is to shine it up your snout! I'm not kidding; intranasal light, as it's really called, has several advantages:

1. It's easy to do yourself

2. There is a rich capillary blood supply in the nasal cavities (once the blood is treated, that gets all round the body)

3. The whole area is just millimeters away from the brain itself!

So, intranasal red light power has arrived (see illustration). Scientific studies show that the nasal route gives just as good results as IV treatment.

Now you can buy one of these devices for just a hair under $400[18]. They last more or less indefinitely and you should use them daily, or at least several times a week. If you work it out over say a 5-year period, that's less than 2 cents a day.

I'd say that's a pretty good bargain for helping your body stay energized and your thinking on a clearer plane, for possibly years longer than otherwise!

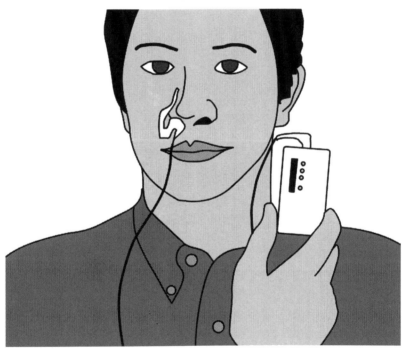

FAR INFRARED LIGHT

There are other devices using far infrared, instead of visible light (longer wavelength of 810nm and some are pulsed at 10 Hz, which is believed to make them more efficacious.

The pulsed mode of 10 Hz is most interesting. Based on studies with mice by Michael Hamblin of Harvard Medical School and other researchers, exposure to light at 810nm and pulsing at 10 Hz, draws the greatest neurological healing in the brain that has suffered traumatic brain injury. This may be because of its closeness to alpha brainwave frequency (when our brain is at rest or in meditative state) or in hippocampal theta state (which may help us with behavior inhibition). There is some claim that serotonin is released in this state, which would help in depression.

Using the wavelength of 810 nm gives deeper tissue penetration (reaching the deeper areas of the brain) without being outside the range that draws mitochondrial response. It just makes sense that this would help cover more areas of the brain, particularly the more ancient parts of the brain which happen to reside in the bottom sections and close to the nasal cavity. However, at this wavelength, the light is invisible to the naked eye—just be aware that the device is not broken, just invisible.

LIGHT HELMETS

This one is not quite ready for the market, as of the date of writing. But these devices will surely become available during the life of this book.

This too is not "red light" but near infrared. It can be supplied by helmets which were developed to help people with Alzheimer's disease make mental improvements. In some trials with senior citizens, it has actually fully reversed their Alzheimer's disease condition. Although this is a relatively new treatment for Alzheimer's the designer of the infrared light helmets named Dr. Gordon Dougal (a GP in the UK) has talked about the fact that these helmets promote neurogenesis in the brain as a result of treatment.

According to Dr. Dougal, these helmets work by directing intense bursts of infrared light into the brain to stimulate growth of brain cells. The reason he developed the helmet is because low-level infrared light is hypothesized to encourage brain cell growth and encourage tissue repair in the brain.

Allegedly, this infrared light helmet is able to reverse dementia symptoms like memory loss in just 30 days of treatment. Dementia sufferer the late Sir Terry Pratchett (the writer) had some success with the helmet and helped to promote the concept.

The important point to grasp is the skull is not impenetrable to light but that, by shining infrared light onto a person's skin, the light goes into the frontal part of the brain as well as onto the side of the brain. The light penetrates brain tissue and is able to repair damaged tissue and help people grow new brain cells.

LASER GUN HOMEOPATHY

Here would be a good place to report on a very interesting therapeutic approach using a combination of laser light and homeopathy by my friend Ken West. I first described it in *Virtual Medicine*. Here is that description in full...

Ken is an American performance scientist (sports) but I met him living and working in the UK. He told me of studies by Prof. Yoshito Mukaino, of Fukuoka University, showing a 20% increase in ball speed of athletes, as a result of checking and balancing acupuncture meridians[19]. That should come as no surprise to the reader.

Mukaino's work has now become widely accepted and many athletes around the world use his "Meridian Test". In conjunction with Dr. Dane Oosthuizen, Ken has developed a system called "Paradox Medicine" and he's now back in the US (last met him in New Mexico) getting great results with it.

Ken deals a lot with various injuries to athletes, knows the Reckeweg remedies, and has been experimenting with a hand-held laser gun, for both performance enhancement and healing of injuries. He simply shines light through the remedy onto the skin, at suitable sites. The laser light carries the remedy into the body, just as surely as if it had been swallowed—but perhaps with even more dynamic effect.

For reasons that are not quite clear, this seems to work better if Japanese acupuncture or *Jin Shan* points are used. These are fewer in number than the Chinese points and, although there is some overlap, they are rather different. Ken describes the Japanese points as "deeper" and reverts to Chinese points if the patient is young, old or weak, in order not to stress the system too much.

Ken's work is also interesting to me in that he has boiled the entire HEEL* repertory of remedies down to about a dozen items. By examining diligently each of the compounded remedies, he found many contained the same substances, grouped in different ways; by using this much narrower range of products, he was able to administer to his patients almost the complete repertory.

Ken has identified three main groups of remedies: Galium- HEEL® group (drainage), Traumeel® group (immune defense) and Coenzyme compositum® group (metabolic support). Each of these is connected to 3 others, making a list of 12 in all.

[*the full HEEL range, by the way, is reproduced by Biological Homeopathic Industries (BHI) in Albuquerque, New Mexico].

MASTER REMEDY	RELATED REMEDIES
Galium group	Thyroidea comp.
	Cerebrum comp.
	Mucosa comp.
Traumeel group	Echinacea comp.
	Engystol comp.
	Lymphomyosot
Coenzyme compositum group	Ubichinon comp.
	Hepar comp.
	Zeel comp.

Very interesting. However Ken added another remedy which he described as the hand grenade you lob (into the tissues) and cover your ears for the bang! I knew instantly he was talking about HEEL's Glyoxal compositum®.

I myself would add one other super-defense and strengthening remedy and Ken agreed: Discus compositum®, making 14 in all. This sounds like a plug for HEEL, I know, but they are good.

Given that laser light is so intense, Ken and I discussed the possibility of overloading the tissues with too much information. In fact this is only theoretical since, if we believe our (*Medicine Beyond*) model, only those substances the body actually needs will resonate with it. The rest will have no effect (much like a piano will hum or sing with certain notes near it, but will "ignore" the rest of the musical scale).

Ken extended this model usefully, by saying that perhaps the body cycled through levels. On the first round it would take certain remedies or oscillations. Others that were ignored at first will have an effect later on, as the system dynamics of the living organism change.

He offered a useful tip, anyway, for those practitioners who feel they may be encountering tissue stress, as a result of heavy detoxing: the use of homeopathically potentized vitamin B3 (niacin; don't use niacinamide). This makes sense to me since, as I explained in my last allergy book, niacin is a key precursor to NADH detox pathways; a strong reducing agent.

CHAPTER 22

Light as Therapy

*The release of atomic power has changed every-
thing except our way of thinking ... the solution to
this problem lies in the heart of mankind. If only I
had known, I should have become a watchmaker.*

— Albert Einstein

Among the earliest writers to advocate the healing use of light were Herodotus, Galen and the great Arabian physician Avicenna. The ancient Egyptians used a type of color therapy. But the Greeks went further in both the theory and practice of light medicine, using the sun's rays to treat disease in the famous healing temples of Heliopolis (Sun City).

In our own century, Nobel Laureate Albert Szent-Gyorgyi, who discovered vitamin C, acknowledges the profound influence of light on our health and states 'all the energy we take into our bodies is derived from the sun.'[1] By this he means that light is turned from electromagnetic sun energy into energized chemicals by the process of photosynthesis in plants. These plant energy substances (food) are subsequently taken in by leaf-eating animals, which are then in turn devoured by carnivorous species.

As I told you in Chapter 2, it is now beyond question that animals too, including humans, are able to process sunlight via the pigment melanin and create complex nutrients. Ultimately, all life energy derives from the sun. It is correct to speak of light itself as a nutrient.

Szent-Gyorgyi took his point further. His research concluded that many of the body's enzymes and hormones are functionally sensitive to light. Color changes can significantly affect the power and effectiveness of these enzymes and hormones. His findings were subsequently verified by researchers Martinek and Berezin in 1979. They found that some colors can increase the activity of enzymes by up to 500 per cent and markedly affect the transport of chemicals across cell membranes.[2]

It has even been found that the absence of certain wavelengths in light results in the body being unable to absorb fully all dietary nutrients. We can talk therefore of color starvation; and color therapy, visited in this chapter, can be seen as crucial to correcting deficiencies in the body's metabolic pathways.

Little wonder, then, that lack of light can have severely destructive health consequences. Few people today have not heard of the unfortunate condition SAD, or Seasonal Affective Disorder. This is a condition in which the shortage of adequate sunlight during the winter months of a northern climate causes gradual loss of vitality and even suicidal depression. The cure, quite naturally, is to enhance ambient light levels, either by judiciously taken winter holidays in sunnier climes, or the artificial simulation of daylight. The latter can be supplied by means of lamps with an adjusted output that has the correct natural daylight spectrum of colors (normal electric lighting has far too much of the yellow frequencies and is lacking in red and blue-violet).

MAL-ILLUMINATION

The study of light adaptation in humans and the attendant ills caused by deficiencies or incorrect balance in color frequencies has gone on apace in the last few decades. We now have the term *mal-illumination*, a concept proposed by John Nash Ott, who works with therapeutic full-spectrum lighting[3]. He compares this term with our existing term 'malnutrition'. Windows, windscreens, eyeglasses and urban pollution are among the many factors which alter the nature of the light our bodies receive, by filtering out some of the wavelengths. Mal-illumination is said to contribute to fatigue, tooth decay, depression, hostility, suppressed immune function, strokes, and loss of hair, skin damage and even cancer.

Sunlight is therefore vital to our well-being and, in the current climate of ultraviolet scares this should not be lost sight of (no pun intended). Despite the medical fad for claiming that skin cancer is caused by sunlight, the evidence points in exactly the opposite direction. A paper published in the 7th August 1982 edition of the British medical journal the Lancet, based on a study carried out jointly between the London School of Hygiene and Tropical Medicine and the University of Sydney's Melanoma Clinic, found that the incidence of malignant melanoma was far higher in office workers than in those who were regularly exposed to sunlight due to lifestyle or occupation[4].

When scientific opinion departs from common sense, it is nearly always science that is found wrong in the end. In this case it is dangerously wrong! Light simply cannot be both a nutrient and a poison at normal ambient levels.

PINK MEDICINE ANYONE?

White full-spectrum light is now being used in the treatment of cancers, anorexia, bulimia, insomnia, jet lag, shift-working, alcohol and drug dependency, as well as SAD.

Different colored light has a profound effect on how we feel, how a space feels (room lighting) and has important symbolic meaning, such as in art.

Experimental research lends support to these observations. Viewing red light has been found to increase subjects' physical strength by 13.5 percent and to elicit 5.8 percent more electrical activity in the arm muscles. For this reason it is now used to improve the performance of athletes. Whereas red light appears to help athletes who need short, quick bursts of energy, blue light assists in performances requiring a more steady energy output.

By comparison, pink has been found to have a tranquilizing and calming effect within minutes of exposure. It suppresses hostile, aggressive, and anxious behavior—interesting given its traditional association with women in Western culture. Pink holding cells are now widely used to reduce violent and aggressive behavior among prisoners, and some sources have reported a reduction of muscle strength in inmates within 2.7 seconds. It appears that when in pink surroundings people cannot be aggressive even if they want to, because the color saps their energy.

It is said that pink is the color of love! In a forthcoming chapter we will look at fascinating work in which singing a specific musical note to tissue cells causes them to glow Indian pink! Cancer cells also glow pink... and then explode! It would be absurd to dismiss connections like this, instead of asking ourselves the ultimate scientific question: what does it all mean?

COLOR THERAPY (CHROMATHERAPY)

A special application of light energies we call chromatherapy or color therapy. Briefly, different colors have different energetic qualities and each is healing in its own way.

In 1990, scientists reported to the annual conference of the American Association for the Advancement of Science on the successful use of blue light in the treatment of a wide variety of psychological problems, including addictions, eating disorders, impotence, and depression.

Blue light has also been shown to be effective in the treatment of arthritis pain. In studies by S. F. McDonald, most of those exposed to blue light for variable periods up to fifteen minutes experienced a significant degree of pain relief. It was concluded that the pain reduction was directly related both to the blue light and the length of exposure to it.[5]

In fact blue light can heal injured tissue and prevent scar tissue, in the treatment of cancers and nonmalignant tumors, as well as skin and lung conditions.

American Civil War General Augustus Pleasonton (1801-1894) conducted his own experiments and in 1876 published his book *The Influence of the Blue Ray of the Sunlight and of the Blue Color of the Sky* about how the color blue can improve the growth of crops and livestock and can help heal diseases in humans. We can recognize in this what has been called the "Florence Nightingale effect", referred to in the previous chapter.

Blue light seems to be the big one but other colors which have a known effect on pain include dark yellow and violet/deep purple. Avicenna (980-1037), no less, wrote that yellow light cools and soothes inflammation, and reduces muscular pain.

Chromatherapy is administered with the use of special color filters. The benchmark has always been Dinshah Ghadiali filters, using his original 5 matched colored glass plates to produce 12 Spectro-Chrome colors, as described in the book, *Let There Be Light*.

However color gels seem to be virtually as good. You can buy inexpensive kits of 4 x 4 or 6 x 6 Eleven Roscolene Color Filters of a very specific and closely matched hue (color frequency), which have been found to achieve the same therapeutic results obtained by the Ghadiali set.

Ken Adachi has assembled the filters you need and is offering them as a set on this page: http://educate-yourself.org/products/index.shtml scroll down to the heading: Spectro-Chrome Light Therapy

You might also like to get a copy of William Campbell Douglas MD's book *Color Me Healthy with 6.5' x 6.5' Roscolene Color Filters*, which can be found on Amazon.

CAUTION

Just remember blue isn't always good; at the wrong time of day it has adverse effects by disjointing our circadian rhythms.

Here's what Nature does: in the mornings, we awake to yellow light (that delicious golden glow of sunrise!); at midday, when we are at our most active, blue light is dominant; in the evening, mellowed reddish colors calm us and prepare us for sleep.

Red light encourages the release of melatonin, our "sleep hormone" (blue light suppresses this vital, healthy rest hormone).

The answer is to have a variety of colored lamps, bulbs and shades. Use photographic gels, if you can't do it any other way.

- Put on yellow light in the morning.

- Switch to blue during the working day

- Go orange in the late afternoon and warm red for the evenings.

The ultimate smart lighting system is coming: you walk into your house, the sensor system detects who you are and what you need, and adjusts the lights accordingly. Your alarm clock could turn on your bedroom light in yellow wakeup mode in the morning.

CEREBRAL PATHWAYS

Most of today's light therapy work, color therapies included, is concerned with light delivered directly to the eyes. It travels the optic pathways and stimulates, among other regions, the hypothalamus, which is part of the endocrine system and thus influences almost all bodily functions. It seems likely, in the light of modern research, that the pineal gland is far from the vestigial organ it was once thought to be but is actually a master gland which regulates the body's circadian rhythms.

As befits the 'Third Eye', it is truly light-sensitive and once again the quality of light received is the crucial factor in maintaining the delicate impulses that regulate the fundamental balance of functions and maintain health.

But I'm able to report revolutionary healing work with light energy radiation shone directly on the stressed tissues using machines which deliver quantum 'excited' gem substances, such as diamond and sapphire, and which is one of the most fascinating and promising frontiers of medicine.

Probably the most advanced machine of this type is the *Caduceus Lux* (you may also meet it as the *Stellar Delux*), developed by Jon Whale in the 1980s. An electronic engineer by profession, Whale designed electronic transducers using emeralds and blue sapphires and used them to cure a number of cases of psoriasis and chronic cystitis. He now runs a busy practice in Devon, England, and manufactures his equipment for worldwide export[6].

The essence of this approach is that light can be 'stressed' with the characteristics of the gems. The changes to the light are probably at the quantum level and we are unable to perceive them. But the body tissues can detect the changes and react differently to each type of light, in a most remarkable and consistent fashion.

The important point to grasp is that light travels very far into the tissues. The experience of shining a torch through your hand on a dark night will tell you this; even the small wattage of a 3 volt battery torch will make the back of the hand glow red as the blood vessels and deep tissue are illuminated.

The Caduceus Lux lamps use high-intensity bulbs. The powerful beam is filtered and focused through lenses and consequently has far more penetration. Whale has developed lamps which house the gems in the path of the light and concentrate it in a useful beam. The whole apparatus is simple to use and, indeed, a number of users are paramedical in status only, yet obtain results that are little short of sensational. Recoveries range from breast lumps to arthritis, eczema to colitis.

AYURVEDIC GEM ELIXIR THERAPY

This whole new science is really an extension of existing Ayurvedic gem elixir therapy, which has a long and distinguished tradition in the Indian subcontinent and can be traced back to Egyptian times. Gems are placed into the tincture liquid and the whole exposed to sunlight until the elixir takes on the characteristics of that gem substance. Theory views disease and disharmony as basically color starvation; the 'excited' liquid of the elixir rectifies the energy deficit[7].

As Whale explains, the huge bejeweled rings once worn by Indian princes, nabobs and potentates were not always merely for the display of wealth and self-aggrandizement. Some rings were intended for therapeutic purposes. Such a ring had no back, so that sunlight could shine straight through the precious stone and so irradiate the skin and tissues beneath with beneficial rays.

The other major traditional route of administration was using ground-up gem powders. I consider this a very dangerous practice and it is not to be recommended. It is wrong and over-simplifies the case to feel that gems are safe just because they are manifestly not chemically toxic or come from an esoteric oriental tradition. These substances can be very powerful emanators and modulators of quantum electromagnetic force, as we shall see below, and should be regarded seriously as such. Introducing solid substances which perhaps may never be removed or excreted fully from the body if they are the wrong choice, may prove disastrous. Even when we understand these things much better than we do now, it still lacks sensible rationale, because these gem powders may preempt any possibility of changing modalities as the body's state or disease process alters.

Readers who wish to experiment with gem elixirs should make them up as described above and not take the solid form—even if cost is no object!

GEM SCIENCE

Unfortunately, this fascinating yet cogent discipline has too long languished and is still little known outside its country of origin. Modern light therapists and researchers such as Jacob Liberman and John Ott seem to ignore it. But with the advancement of science and the ability to translate older methods from a stultifying background into a modern framework and quantifiable results, we may say 'gem therapy' has indeed come of age and will grow steadily in applications in the West.

Speaking of gem therapy in the West, Jon Whale has a remarkable book, kept under lock and key, but which I have been privileged to see: a 12th century gem stone medical manual by the Spanish king Alphonso el Sabio (Alphonse the Learned). The original, in lapidary form, is held in a museum, on a hill, just outside Madrid. Only three known 19th century lithographic copies exist in the world today and Jon Whale has one.

Alfonso translated details of at least three hundred and sixty different stones and gems. The original sources were in Arabic. Undoubtedly this knowledge had come west along the old Silk Route, together with the gem medicines and stones themselves. The illustrations are gorgeously painted, with depictions of the twelve signs of the zodiac and illustrations of medieval life surrounding the mining and preparations of gems and minerals.

Possession of this important source reference alone positions Jon Whale as the undoubted leader in this field[8].

THIS IS NOT CRYSTAL THERAPY

Despite superficial similarities, the Caduceus equipment is not crystal therapy. Quartz, amethyst, tourmaline, moonstone and many other commonly used therapeutic crystals the reader may have heard about seem to have little or no value in this 'quantum light-stressing' context.

Nor is it exactly color therapy. Tests show that the color of the light is irrelevant. In other words, it is the gem properties which dictate the resulting effect and not its color as perceived by the patient. This is odd, since the Indian tradition regards the need for gems and their effectiveness as being evidence of color starvation.

Notwithstanding, Whale adds the colors traditionally associated with each gem (see list below). But he emphasizes that these color filters could be dispensed with. The gem carries the energy signal.

What you feel when you put your hand in the beam is a distinct and palpable pressure from the radiation. It is an astonishing thing to experience. Light from the Caduceus Lux has the power to shine right through the skull or chest and will thus reach all tissues, even bone, though in varying intensity according to its density.

The applications are remarkably diverse. Thus emerald and sapphire, when excited, emit cooling soothing energies which can stop eczema or inflammation dead in their tracks. Focused on the bowel, this represents a totally new method of calming the gut in, say, colitis or diverticulitis. Ruby will energize cells and glands, and Whale asserts it is excellent for rejuvenating tired male potency. Diamond, on the other hand, is stimulating and, mixed with yellow citrine, peps up lethargy and fatigue states such as those which characterize ME, Candida and complex allergy conditions. But too much diamond can cause a patient to lose sleep for several days.

The principal effect of the main gems and their associated colors are shown here:

Gem	Color	Energy Output and Properties
Carnelian	Orange	Cooling, moist and harmonizing, anti-allergic
Chrysoberyl	Infrared	Hot, penetrating, cleansing, deep heating
Citrine	Yellow	Warm, enlivening, cleansing
Diamond	Indigo	Stimulating, invigorating, clarifying, antidepressant
Emerald	Green	Cold, unifying and solidifying, analgesic
Ruby	Red	Heating, drying, energizing, expanding
Sapphire	Violet	Tranquillizing, soothing, analgesic, antispasmodic
Topaz	Blue	Cool, soft, satisfying, antiseptic

COMBINATIONS

Traditional Ayurvedic gem therapy includes the use of certain combinations of gems. Sure enough, these too are effective when supplied electronically. Thus emerald and sapphire make an excellent combination which is cooling, soothing and analgesic. Carnelian and diamond through the chest is a good combination for asthma, to allergically cleanse and energize the struggling lungs. Obesity might be benefited by ruby and diamond, to increase heat and stimulate blood flow, especially if directed to the thyroid to increase metabolism.

Two classical compound mixtures frequently used are IBGO (Indigo-Blue-Green-Orange) or, in other words, diamond-topaz-emerald-carnelian, and the so-called 'Seven Gems' mix, which combines all the principal stones except Chrysoberyl. These can be used when the picture is complicated, uncertain or simply in cases where generalized light and energy support therapy is needed.

Some conditions, and their suggested gem treatments, are given here and should make the overall principles clear:

Acne	Citrine/Topaz
Alopecia	Sapphire
Anemia	Ruby
Arthritis	Sapphire/Emerald
Asthma	Carnelian/Diamond
Bronchitis	Citrine/Diamond
Burns	Emerald
Cystitis	Emerald
Conjunctivitis	Carnelian
Constipation	Citrine
Depression	Diamond
Debility	Ruby/Diamond
Diabetes	Diamond/Citrine
Diarrhea	Emerald

Eczema	Emerald/Sapphire
Epilepsy	Diamond
Gastritis	Emerald
Headache	Sapphire
Insomnia	Sapphire
Irritable bowel	Emerald/Sapphire
Menopause	Carnelian
Migraine	Sapphire
Pain	Sapphire/Emerald
Pleurisy	Topaz
Psoriasis	Sapphire
Rheumatism	Ruby/Sapphire
Sciatica	Sapphire
Shingles	Sapphire/Emerald
Sterility	Diamond
Stomach ulcer	Emerald/Sapphire
Tonsillitis	Topaz
Varicose ulcer	Ruby/Diamond

ELECTRONIC FREQUENCY

But—and here's the beauty of the Caduceus device—it isn't merely the "gem quality" of the light which creates the therapeutic effect. Whale's innovative idea was to develop a machine which allowed programming of the incident light with brain wave frequencies (delta, theta, etc.)

This can enormously influence the power and range of effects. For example, a frequency of 3.3 Hertz (Hz) is identical to the brainwave pattern known as theta, which is associated with trance and dreamlike states (see list of brainwave frequencies, below). If we take emerald and sapphire light and beam it into the skull at 3.3 Hz, the results are quite dramatic. The subject will rapidly descend into a beautiful dreamlike trance, which is very potent at countering stress. We call this *Samadhi*, an Indian word meaning 'bliss', which gives a fair description of its subjective result. I used it before all other treatments on my own Caduceus. I argue that all patients are stressed and miserable by virtue of being ill, and this wonderful eased state of mind is a very sound concomitant treatment. The effect lasts up to 24 hours, sometimes longer.

Other useful frequencies are 8 Hz, the Earth's own 'Gaia' resonant frequency, and around 1.5 – 2.5 Hz, which is the lowest band, delta brainwaves. The latter frequency accords with deep unconsciousness and therefore has analgesic potential, rather like an anesthetic. Combined with soothing emerald it can work wonders for bruised tissue or painful joints.

Logically, diamond would be coupled with 15 – 20 Hz, which is low beta, to energize someone. We never use high beta (above 25 Hz), which is excessively stimulating, since all healing requires calm and ease.

Rhythm	Frequency	State of Consciousness
High beta	above 25 Hz	Anxiety, panic, anger, psychosis
Beta	14 – 25 Hz	External focus, 'normal waking'
Alpha	7.8 – 14 Hz	Relaxed, attention part internalized
Theta	3.2 – 7.8 Hz	Dreaming, trance, hypnosis, internalized
Delta	01. – 3.2	Deep sleep, unconsciousness, coma

As with all advanced technology, the degree of success with the equipment depends considerably on the knowledge and competence of the practitioner. Whereas anyone can get basic results of value, if the use of electronic gem therapy is combined with a good working knowledge of the alternative models, many possibilities open up. For example, eczema is often a symptom of gut overload, especially liver toxicity ('liver anger'). Therefore supporting energies at, say, Gaia frequency to the liver can be an excellent complement to the direct use of soothing emerald light onto the skin.

Carnelian and diamond is an ideal mixture for the circulation and lymph system (8 Hz) and can be used in many ways, for example in the treatment of varicose ulcer or dependent edema—the latter can be viewed by the layman as an inefficient heart pumping action. But this mixture can create healing pathways at many deeper levels. Thus diamond and carnelian to the spleen area can produce a dramatic benefit for the immune system, resulting in improvement or elimination of many complex allergies. Whale even reports the resolution of two lymphoma cases (malignant condition of lymphoid tissue).

I myself use the mixtures known as VIBGYOR or 'Seven Gems' to the thymus, since this gland is associated with white cell education and maturity and I am deeply involved with the immune system, being known primarily as an allergist. In addition to detox and homeopathic cleansing of the intercellular tissues, this is of great benefit to the chronically ill patient.

MULTIPLE CHANNELS

Whale's Caduceus has the further refinement of multiple channels. More than one lamp can be rigged and used simultaneously, each with different programming. Thus, for example, the deeply relaxing Samadhi can be administered at the same time as other specific organ therapy. Or a stimulating mixture at energizing frequencies can be shone into the thymus gland at the same time that soothing emerald and carnelian at theta are used on allergic eczema of the lower leg.

Electronic gem therapy also lends itself very well to being combined with other healing models. Instead of organ or tissue support therapy, excited light can be used to enhance or 'open' chakras.

This is the basis of Whale's claim for enhancing male potency. He has discovered that a series of treatments using ruby light to the base chakra has a powerful stimulating effect and is certainly safer and preferable to modern drug and psychotherapy prescriptions for this commoner-than-supposed condition.

Diamond and topaz to the throat chakra will sometimes produce an immediate change in voice and expression, and 'Seven Gems' to the heart chakra is the nearest thing we have to a treatment for lost love and the pain of separation.

Naturally, this is further support for the validity and existence of chakras since they can be positively influenced in this way, the results becoming unarguably manifest in this reality.

Casebook: Female, 45 Years

A woman therapist had torn a muscle in an amateur stage production. The noise of the muscle rupture was so loud it was heard in the second row. She was promptly incapacitated and in great pain.

She came to see me a few days later, limping badly, all other attempts at therapy having failed. I gave her first a routine 20 minutes of Samadhi, with emerald-sapphire stones at 3.3 Hz. This very aware patient was able to tell me that her pelvis underwent a shift back into the normal energetic position during this stage.

I followed through with about 30 minutes to the injured calf. All pain had now vanished from the affected leg, but now a new pain had appeared in the opposite knee. This was probably due to the stress of limping and bearing all her weight on that side, but the pain had, of necessity, been suppressed.

A further 15 minutes on the uninjured side removed that discomfort too, and the patient walked to her car with no discernible limp. Next day she phoned to say there was only mild discomfort, she was back at work and she was content with just one treatment.

Casebook: Male, 6 Years

This boy had been diagnosed as having disintegrative psychosis, a variety of autism which I have long suspected comes on after vaccination, particularly for measles. My reasoning was as follows: an autistic youngster seems to be very 'out of contact' and 'dreamy'; he (they are usually males) is very introverted into the right brain hemisphere. If we can use the gem therapy to accelerate the left brain and inhibit right-brain activity, we may be able to wake up his logical and reasoning faculties.

Accordingly, I put him on a one-week program of diamond, citrine and ruby to the left cranial hemisphere and emerald-sapphire to the right brain. I further refined this strategy by using beta (high brain activity) of around 15 Hz to the left side and a retarding and soothing 3.3 Hz to the right hemisphere. I lowered the penetration

398

to minimal wattage in order not to 'cross-over' and inadvertently stimulate the opposite side, or vice versa.

Within days he began vocalizing well and within a month was forming intelligible sentences. For a number of reasons he was unable to continue any further treatments with the Caduceus Lux, but despite this he continued to make rapid progress. He has learned to use a computer keyboard and happily spends hours amusing himself with electronic games, which of course require considerable left-brain dexterity. His mother reports he has learned to integrate well with his peers. One year later he was able to join a more advanced learning stream at school.

One of my major plans for the future is to explore this healing route for autism.

WATCH OUT FOR CHEAP (AND DANGEROUS) KNOCK OFFS

The Lux IV and Stellar Delux Electronic Gem Therapy® instrumentation is housed in a double-cased steel enclosure, the gem therapy lamps are machined from solid metal. One of the reasons for this substantial engineering construction is to eliminate electromagnetic radiation from affecting the practitioner, patient or the local environment.

The solid metal gem lamps prevent sideways and backwards radiation of the gem energy emitted by the lamps from affecting the practitioner, it also eliminates undesirable electromagnetic radiation exposure to patient and practitioner.

In 2002, Jon Whale researched the possibility of using Light Emitting Diodes (LED's) to reduce the manufacturing costs of his Lux IV Electronic Gem Therapy lamps.

After conducting a series of tests and measurements, Light Emitting Diodes (LEDs) were discounted for use in Electronic Gem Therapy lamps for treating injury or disease. The light output from LED based "gem therapy" lamps, such as the Theragem, could not penetrate much deeper than the skin. They were not be able to penetrate to deep organs, glands, joints and cartilage levels.

Below is the scientific explanation which can be confirmed by using any standard calibrated light measuring meter. Note that: 1.0 Watt of light is equivalent to 683 Lux (close up to the light source).

Each of the Lux IV & Stellar Delux Electronic Gem Therapy transducer lamps emit 62.5 Watts of light, this is equivalent to 42,687 Lux close up. These gem lamps provide greater than 20,000 Lux at a distance of 10 centimetres.

By contrast a single 1 Watt Luxeon LED lamp emits 70 Lux at a distance of 10 centimetres and provides only 0.35% of the light output when compared to the Lux IV or Stellar Delux Electronic Gem Therapy Transducer Lamps. This amounts to a little bit more than the light output of a common hand held battery powered torch.

Also the light emitted by white LED based lamps contained too much blue light and insufficient light in the red part of the spectrum.

The electromagnetic radiation of LED gem lamps made of molded plastic was considered to be far too high for clinical use, such as the Theragem, producing 500 milligauss, compared to the machined metal lamps which produce only 1.5 millgauss. In other words, the underperforming Theragem lamps spill toxic radiation while supposedly healing.

BIOLUMANETICS

Let me finish now with something very "beyond"! Nature has the endless capacity to surprise and fascinate us. Biolumanetics, a new science of healing, is just about the most unusual medical application of light in therapy I have heard of. The system was developed by a 62-year-old American engineer called Patrick Richards. In 1983 he designed an instrument called a Luminator™ which balances air temperatures for efficient office energy management. In fact his invention turned out to have a far more important and totally novel application than the one for which it was made.

While testing the unit in an open plan office, Richards found that many people reported unexpected health gains, from reduction of stress and migraine levels to disappearance of low back pain. The big question was: Why?

The Luminator™ alters the local environment in three main ways:

1. Temperatures are balanced uniformly throughout (wall-to-wall, floor-to-ceiling).
2. An altered magnetic field is created.

400

3. The available light in the room is altered from incoherent (light going in many directions) to coherent (polarized into one plane only).

In 1985 Richards discovered by serendipity that light from living cell forms could be imaged in the field of the Luminator™. Late 1985 found him photographing people holding their medications and noting how, as Abrams and Voll had discovered before, that the patient's energy status alters for the better dramatically. In the case of Richards' equipment, a sick person may have a very blurred, indistinct image, but simply by holding an effective medication the person's special photographic image becomes immediately sharp and clear. Logically, if the medication is not suitable, the image remains blurred or becomes even foggier.

Subsequently, Richards went on to develop a unique and sophisticated method of assessing patients and establishing suitable remedies. He calls his system VRIC (visual reference of image coherence) and it basically entails the use of enhanced photography to measure the vitality and coherence of any life form—human, plant or animal. To make a VRIC assessment image requires a fixed focus Polaroid camera and the Luminator™ as a source. The brightness, intensity and coherence of the light reflected by the patient and captured on the photograph are a precise indication of his or her health and energy status[9]. Therapy would then consist of taking a base image and endeavoring to find a remedy, or more than one remedy, which will make it sharper and brighter, much as the EAV practitioner does by eliminating the ID drop.

Arguably this is a milestone development for practitioners in the field of energetic healing, indeed all therapeutic practice. We can now see objective changes after Reiki, homeopathy, flower essences, shiatsu and color therapy, to name just a few.

Again, the vital side of the body energy information field is made abundantly clear: the medication need only be put on the floor close to the subject to transmit its signal. No contact is required, but provided it is within the energetic aura the light coherence may change markedly. No smoke, no mirrors! That's about as much 'proof' as we have for you at present of the tenets of energy healing expounded in these pages.

A patient can of course bring his or her own medication for assessment, but VRIC specialists have their own repertoire of preferences and a range of special frequencies called 'Lumanetics' which Richards claims are not affected by Gaia fields. When a suitable therapeutic match is made, the 'vibrational signature' is transferred to an anionic chelate fluid, which is a negatively-charged fluid made in a special field. It is said not only to hold the required therapeutic energy but actually to bind magnetically with toxins and impurities in order to help them be eliminated[10], though I find statements like this hard to take without some experimental support.

Probably the most exciting potential of all with the VRIC system is in assessing the energy dynamics of interpersonal relationships. The photograph can tell a person if the partner he or she is with is 'right' for them or not. The common complaint 'I feel really drained with that person' can now be expressed in an objective and impersonal way. With a stressful individual standing in close proximity to the subject, the assessment image is blurred, whereas with other neutral companions it remains relatively sharp. It is remarkable to reflect just how radical a change it could bring to our turbulent over-emotional society to be able to assess family, love relationships, professional and personal relationships (in fact any relationship at all) in a clear, precise and non-judgmental manner.

On a recent visit to the practice facility of Thrity Engineer, a London-based practitioner of Biolumanetics, I was shown several fascinating examples of family group dynamics. In one instance, a child taking Ritalin for ADD (attention deficit disorder) was quite coherent without the medicine. When his sibling and father stood next to him, he remained fully coherent. But as soon as his mother joined the group, the child's image went incoherent. The surprising course of action was therefore to give the mother a remedy, which restored the boy to coherence when she held it.

The mother was subsequently treated and the boy recovered completely, without any further need of medication.

Thrity also showed me what Richards calls right and left brain coherence. This is accessed by photographing the patient with the left eye open, right eye closed and then vice versa. An individual will sometimes be incoherent in one modality but not the other.

Casebook: Female, 43 Years

A woman was distressed by the loss of her son some years before. When she held a photograph of the deceased in her right hand (left brain), she remained coherent. But when the photograph was put in her left hand (right brain) her Luminator™ image became quite visually incoherent. It is easy to see that she could rationalize her loss (left brain logic) but could not come to terms with the emotions (right brain).

A suitable remedy was chosen photographically and her emotional patterns changed at once to a better and healthier regard for her lost son.

Incidentally, I was fascinated to see that even the house-plants which appear in Thrity's photographs would become incoherent when there was an incoherent human source nearby. But recovered fully next to a healthy individual!

Biolumanetics claims not to address directly the symptoms of illness. There is nothing to tell the practitioner at what level the bio-energetic disturbance lies, whether energetic, emotional or physical. Thus question being approached is not 'What is causing this incoherence?' but 'What will make this system vital or coherent?'

CHAPTER 23

In Tune with Yourself

Nonsense is that which does not fit into the pre-arranged patterns which we have superimposed on reality...Nonsense is nonsense only when we have not yet found that point of view from which it makes sense.

— Gary Zukav

Are you with me so far? Good. Now, let's throw everything you've read so far into the trash (well, almost). We are going beyond *Medicine Beyond!*

As I have been repeating over and over, the new reality is based on information and I believe information *implies* consciousness. The cosmos is alive and aware, basically. The old, dead machine model of mainstream science is what's dead, not the universe we live in.

Matter and energy are now somewhat out of date concepts; 20th century ideas, as opposed to 21st century innovations. Information leads in creating reality, as I explained in Chapter 4; energy is just the carrier; "stuff" is the result. Healers who are peddling "spiritual energy" have not grasped the fact that energy is something physical; it's not spiritual but totally in the material domain. Energy, as Einstein taught us, is just matter in a different form.

The highest level of healing must take place in the dimension of consciousness, not here in the material place.

THE CONSCIOUSNESS INTERFACE

Let me rock your beliefs by stating that most of today's diagnostic and bioresonance devices work just as well if they are not plugged in and switched on!

This weird "discovery" is from the dubious Mr. Bill Nelson, manufacturer of the EPFX/SCIO humbug. I do not pretend to like Mr. Nelson (he calls himself "Doctor" Nelson but he is not medically qualified), nor do I appreciate his marketing methods, or the fact that he seeks to emulate the fairer sex by walking around in dresses.

But credit where credit is due: Nelson's slick scam is in fact a rather special breakthrough in this field! As the US representative for the BICOM device, he discovered by chance that people were getting well, even if the device was disconnected. So he decided to manufacture his own empty shell, pretend it was a diagnostic device and market it for $10,000, using impressive sounding pseudo-scientific babble. Nice work, if you can get it.

What the majority of fans of the EPFX/SCIO don't know is that Nelson built his system around a random number generator, to create what the scientists call noise, and then processed that in various ways to make it look like a diagnostic and healing procedure was taking place. The effrontery to do this is the measure of the man.

But the curious irony is that his system actually works; people do get well... on an entirely different principle to the one he markets. It's processing information, not energies. I had better explain...

OPERATOR INVOLVEMENT

There is nothing wrong with using a random number generator... if you know what you are doing and if you are open and honest about its use. What I believe happens, as a result of in depth conversations with Kiran Schmidt of Inergetix Inc., is that the stream of random numbers will contain real data and this will be influenced by present consciousness. In this case, I am talking about the consciousness of the operator.

405

Since the first publication of *Virtual Medicine* 15 years ago, I have been at pains to make it clear that all these electronic devices don't really detect anything; it's the operator who is a sensitive detector and he or she gets results, based on their deep knowingness. I introduced the term "electronic dowsing" to describe this process. Using a Vega, a BICOM or a MORA is no different to using a pendulum to gain insight; it just looks fancy and electronically-engineered. The shiny knobs and electrodes add credibility.

But right away, we have a problem: some people are good sensitives and dowsing works well, others are poor at it and cannot get the same results. Ask around and that's what you'll find: some EPFX operators, for example, will find accurate dates, when something truly significant happened to the case, something that maybe even the patient could not have remembered, without first checking it out.

Other people won't be able to get any sense out of the device at all. Call up somebody with a used EPFX for sale and see if I am right! You'll probably hear some pretty stern criticisms of its performance.

On one occasion, while taking EAV readings, I got an awful indicator drop on the adrenal point with my EDS machine. It went down and down and down, till it was almost off the bottom. That patient had a history of Addison's disease (adrenal failure), which I didn't know at the time… well, I didn't know at the ordinary conscious level.

Do I believe Voll's idea, that energy in the endocrine meridian was low? No, I don't. The patient would be dead at that abysmal reading. I believe that the patient's consciousness merged with mine and produced an information package that I unknowingly unwrapped.

I am very good at EAV and I can do that. But, as I said, most people can't. That means we are not really talking science; this is a black art! Or at least I should say, to save the Christians their blushes, that it works below the obvious level of reality that I call Simple-IS.

A LITTLE "BIT" OF INFORMATION THEORY

Information may be quantified by the count of characters, as when describing the length of an email message or in digits (as in the length of a phone number). In conventional information theory, information is measured in bits.

There are 8 "bits" to a "byte" remember. A "bit" (the term is a contraction of binary digit) is either a zero or a one: so with a random number generator, there is a chip designed to produce a stream of random zeroes and ones (0 or 1).

Obviously, from time to time, a whole word or concept is spelled out, rather like the monkeys with typewriters will—sooner or later—type up the whole of Shakespeare. But small patterns, or what Kiran calls "coincidences", will come up much more often. How does this work?

Suppose you flip a coin ten thousand times and write down the sequence of results. If you want to communicate this sequence to another person, how many bits will it take? If it's a fair coin, the two possible outcomes, heads and tails, occur with equal probability. Therefore each flip requires 1 bit of information to transmit. To send the entire sequence will require 10,000 bits.

But suppose the coin is biased so that heads occur much more often than tails. Then you can use your knowledge of the distribution to select a more efficient code. You are then transmitting a pattern or formula, so it should take fewer bits to transmit.

Let's look at an example. Suppose the coin is heavily biased, so that the probability of getting heads is 99% and tails show up only 1% of the time. That's excessive, of course, even for a bent Las Vegas casino!

In 10,000 tosses of this coin we would expect to see about 9,900 heads. Rather than transmitting the results of each toss, we could just transmit the number that came down tails and assume the rest of the tosses came down heads.

So that would require just 100 bits.

But supposing we wanted to encode the actual sequence, not just the totals? Then we would need an algorithm, based on the position of each tails toss in the sequence. Any position in a sequence of 10,000 can be encoded using just 5 bits. So, if we transmit one hundred 5-bit numbers, we will have transmitted all the information content of the original 10,000 toss sequence, using only around 500 bits, instead of the 10,000 required for an unbiased coin.

Now do you begin to understand information theory enough to know that random numbers, so-called, can contain very large quantities of hidden information, patterns, formulas or "coincidences"?

Here's the real point: an illiterate person reading a "message" would require more bits of information in processing the letters on the page than a literate person reading the same message. The illiterate person would take in all the characters (and still be none the wiser); the literate person has more efficient coding and is able to see the patterns we call *words* quite easily.

For example, the previous paragraph is 380 characters (with spaces) but it's only 65 words. If you can spot the words that saves you 315 computations! And in fact half the sentences you could complete in your mind, before you finish reading them, by anticipating what I was going to say; that brings it down to 40 computations or less.

COINCIDENCE RECOGNITION

We do this processing of randomness, looking for data among "noise", all the time. It's how we view our world. We take in huge amounts of information every second. The eyes alone process anything up to 50 billion bits per second[1].

We cannot fully comprehend all this data; we are just looking for patterns, repeats and coincidences. So, for example, we see the same pretty girl several times over the course of a few weeks: that's a pattern. We decide that we should maybe ask her for a date.

When we are born, we see the same face over and over, we associate it with milk and feeding, so we become attached to this "pattern". It's mother.

All learning is establishing patterns: mealtimes, the highway code, study for exams, how to please another person sexually, how to make a million dollars, are all learning processes based on selecting coincidences (patterns) from random noise.

You could call these synchronicities, a word that many people use, without understanding the significance of it.

The trouble is, there are too few synchronicities in life, because our limited consciousness cannot see them. So they appear to be somewhat mystical in nature. Now, for the first time in history, we have computers that can process vast quantities of data, looking for patterns. That's how Alan Turing and the team at Bletchley Park broke the German Enigma code—developing a machine that could detect repetition or patterns in vast amounts of data.

That's all a computer is: speeded up processing, allowing fast, in depth analysis. Before that we had only inspired insights and lucky guesses. Now we can search in earnest. It's remarkable to think that a man like Bill Nelson led Kiran Schmidt to this insight.

Consider a real world example of a tarot reader: he or she lays down several cards and makes an interpretation by processing, looking for significant patterns. That's a "reading". But if you try and get a tarot reader to repeat the process in the same sitting, it won't happen! He or she will make excuses; it's offending Lady Luck or the gods, or whatever excuse… He or she knows it won't come out the same.

I think we all know that.

The reason is simple: the tarot reader would have to lay (as it's called) millions of times, to start seeing really significant coincidences. It becomes an exercise in statistical analysis.

And that is why the EPFX and all the rest are a fraud: there is no statistical analysis, just a radionics "black box" in disguise. I know a number of very good radionics dowsers; but they are not charging $10,000s for their device!

THE CoRe DEVICE

The renowned Brazilian spiritual healer John of God gave Kiran Schmidt the title of "Son of his House". Kiran has developed a new generation of machine, the Inergetix CoRe system, utilizing the coincidence recognition principle, to balance energetic frequency, based on an informational analysis of the clients' resonant frequencies (CoRe for coincidence recognition).

This information can be turned into a healing code. It is an electronic device but is "controlled" ultimately, by the operator's consciousness interface.

I asked how they tune it to the patient, who may not be present (see Albert Abrams original development on remote healing, chapter 8). There is a Babel of human noise here on the planet, over 7 billion and counting. How can such a device be "tuned" to one specific individual out there?

The answer is they use a "seed", equivalent to the radionics "witness"; some object to make the target more substantial or more real. Something that belongs to the patient will work fine; just a photograph is sufficient. All that matters is that the operator has the patient clearly in mind and is tuned to certain basic questions, like what is wrong with him or her? What would be the best approach to healing? And so on. Really skilled operators can probably even dispense with the seed.

The Inergetix CoRe system analyses the clients' specific frequencies and balances the body with frequencies that have the greatest resonance in context with the symptoms entered during analysis. The practitioner can also use designated frequencies from a disease list containing 1100 conditions.

Informational broadcasting of frequencies by the Inergetix CoRe system is NOT fooling people with a supposed energetic "output". It affects the body on a purely informational level, for example by reestablishing control functions or mental-emotional issues. This activity will indirectly affect the energetic, biochemical and structural levels, helping to return the client to health.

The CoRe frequency database contains 25,000 remedies divided into 400 groups to help focus analysis, and additional items and remedies can be added to the database by the practitioner as required. The CoRe system also contains a catalogue of emotional concepts, which reveal psychological connections.

The CoRe interface unit has an audio connection to external speakers for broadcast of audible frequencies; a connection to the gold-plated imprint tray for imprinting of potentized remedy information; a connection with hand and foot electrodes; optional Electric Frequency Therapy Unit; and optional "Plasma Generator".

More information here: http://energetic-medicine.com/

Kiran is not tricky with his explanations. He admits the main Inergetix CoRe interface unit acts as both the symbolic connection to the client, enabling radionic interaction, and the physical connection for energetic interaction.

It's really about connecting the person with self, utilizing and enhancing the individual's own Eigen-resonance. What does that mean?

EIGEN RESONANCE

Here's some really good stuff for your understanding!

Kiran introduced me to the German word *Eigen*. "Eigen" means *self* or something that is "specific for the individual" and it is a common term in physics and mathematics as in Eigen-frequency, Eigen-vector, and Eigen-value and so on.

However, as always in our outward oriented culture, scientists accept this basic concept, but fight like tigers to resist the idea it has any application in sociology, biology and healing.

Health really means to be in a more constant state of "Eigen-resonance", or integration with self, in all key respects: sensually, emotionally, mentally and spiritually. If this Eigen-resonance is inhibited, disease starts to enter and vice versa.

As children we have many forms of Eigen-resonance still working properly. We examine our bodies in detail, we test things by putting them in our mouth, chew on our nails, we suck on our fingers, we spend hours under a blanket and breathe our own breath and smell our own body-odor. We "learn self".

Then all our cultural taboos and non-sensual education enters and is established and all this becomes objectionable. From then on, we develop all kinds of replacements for interaction with self: instead of putting our own thumb in our mouth, we put in a cigarette; instead of smelling our own body-odor, we cover it with the latest perfume; and instead of being in love with our own body, we cover it with fashion clothing that has nothing to do with us.

Instead of resonating with our own "Eigen field", we engage in absurd substitute behaviors, like addictions to shopping, status-symbol cars, drugs, sex, eating, work and possessions, all in pursuit of admiration from others. Gradually, we sever contact with our dynamic life equilibrium and, once lost, it becomes difficult to regain it, without special insight as to its nature.

FINDING YOURSELF

Many spiritual traditions talk about the "the need for self", "I am-ness", "know thyself" but usually stay on a mental level or abstract metaphysical level in explaining what this would practically mean. Gurus and "adepts", I have noticed, are peculiarly inept at revealing the truth of these matters. It makes one suspect they don't really know what they are talking about. Sometimes explanations descend into complex pseudo-psychology jargon, using artificial constructs, like ego, id and identity.

But in order to know yourself, as Kiran Schmidt points out, you first have to *sense* yourself, a very simple prerequisite with the most revolutionary implications.

Many healing modalities can easily be understood from this point of view, e.g. Eigen-blood therapy (electrophoresis) or Eigen-Urine therapy (auto-immune urine therapy), or the practice of extracting other body fluids or tissues and feeding back certain parts of it, as in stem-cell therapy. In Homeopathy we have the little-understood practice of sarcode remedies (page 158), which would certainly much improve if the sarcodes were produced from the clients very own tissues.

As children we were constantly humming to ourselves or even talking to ourselves. Yet as adults all this is considered childish or even a sign of insanity—but we do not object to bombarding ourselves constantly with sounds that are not our own. Some sounds, we know, like heavy metal rock, are definitely unhealthy.

But I believe, and have written elsewhere, that we all have a unique "shamanic song" within; it is our own personal tune, with harmony. If we can find it and sing it, often, we can be healthier, more loving and more in tune with ourselves and the environment. This means we are resonating strongly with our Eigen-field.

CLASSIC BIORESONANCE IS ALLOPATHIC MENTALITY

According to Kiran Schmidt, the typical bioresonance explanation of inverting and cancelling out unhealthy frequencies or "bad energies" is no different in mentality to that of killing microbes with antibiotics, poisoning the nervous system with pain killers or cutting out malfunctioning parts of the organism.

He even rejects Rife's work and that same model of zapping pathogens or cancer cells, further encouraged by the misguided writings of Hulda Reger Clark and others.

I am inclined to agree, for a very good reason: it is not possible to penetrate far into the body with "healing frequencies", simply because the body will modify everything thrown at it. It's back to the "war of frequencies", first postulated by Lakhovsky—every atom, molecule, cell and organ has its own resonating frequencies. Sooner or later, the external frequencies are modified by those in the body.

A better plan is to enhance healing energies and get the person into healthy resonance with the self.

But the MORA and BICOM work and work often, especially in skilled hands, I pointed out to Kiran. That's using classic physics and inversion technology, isn't it? No, he says. Remember, there is no real output from these machines; or at least no energetic output. Take a $10 electrical multimeter and check that for yourself.

Inversion is a myth and just sales talk. It does not happen. There is a totally different reason why these machines work—and they do work, make no mistake. I'm not knocking bioresonance practitioners, I'm merely re-writing the musical harmonies to it!

CONNECTED TO SELF

The answer lies in this phenomenon of Eigen-resonance. The person is simply being wired up to their own self. This is why electronic resonance devices work: the person is *wired to self* and collects information about the self, with the remedy or pathogen in the "diagnostic" cup or plate.

This reminds me of polarity therapy, developed by Randolph Stone (1890-1981). In it, the patient is wired up to his or her own self, typically in a 5-point star formation. A lot is claimed for it but, according to Kiran, the key point is the person is connected to their own sense of self.

Like other systems, we are using the endogenous energy field for healing. That's back to the flow of *Ch'i, prana* and so on. The energy can flow through a practitioner, as surely as through wiring. So hands-on healing methods also have a slice of this delicious pie! My wife Vivien pointed out the connection with Tai-Ch'i, in which the technique of causing the personal energy field to flow freely is what is being learned; connection or reconnection to self. It's very healing.

The same could be said of yoga; it is enhancing the Eigen-resonance with the field of self.

Maybe acupuncture, which is about unblocking meridians, is also in a very real sense about opening up the channels through which "self" flows. Vivien suggested this too and I like her idea; it connects Western thinking with the ancient Chinese model.

I notice that Alex Lloyd's "Healing Codes" method uses—or re-cycles—energies from our own body, to re-direct them back inwards from the finger tips, while adding healing love messages from God, such that the self-energies already present are enhanced.

As we embrace the energy healing model more and more, it becomes clear that our own natural energies, filled with information of self (the self-field), is really what does the good. In that sense, all modalities which work, work to some degree on this principle. We left behind conventional explanations of healing, remember, along with objective science, in Chapter 18. This is better.

THE HEALING BLANKET

You may come across the concept of healing blankets. Disregard gobble-dygook marketing words and pseudo-science. Just focus simply on the fact that these blankets are reflectors. There is a metalized layer inside the fabric, designed to bounce off hostile radiations (the original concept).

They are also intended to reflect radiations back inside the patient's own body (same principle as a Thermos vacuum flask). That means far infrared and extreme high frequencies (EHFs) are returned to the patient. The person will literally warm up, like sitting in a sauna.

There are a number of pseudoscientific claims for this therapeutic adjunct. Wilhelm Reich and his unsubstantiated orgone theory are often invoked. This I feel is nonsense and misleading. What seems clear to me is that the blankets sustain and enhance the Eigen-resonance field, specifically:

• reflect back the body's own far infrared healing radiations and so bathe the body in additional supportive energies

414

- reflect back biological extreme high frequency (EHF) Eigen radiations generated by the cells and organs in the range of 30 to 300 GHz

- reflect away exogenous man-made EMF fields which we know can be harmful

All this relates far more closely to the work of Georges Lakhovsky and cellular radiations, visited in Chapter 7, than it does to the tenuous theories of Reich. Remember, Lakhovsky taught that whichever radiation wins, that is what will happen to the tissues. So shielding the body from unwanted radiation while intensifying what is good and natural can only be nurturing and healthy.

The ridiculous prices are hard to justify. But the benefits are real enough.

EMBODIMENT LEARNING

The Eigen-field looms large in education (or should).

My own philosophic system of "transformational psychology" that I call Supernoetics ™ lays great emphasis on the matter of embodiment learning. I have developed a science of Being and knowledge. One of its core principles is that *we are what we know*.

A simple example would be a plumber: he knows how to fix leaks, solder joints and lay pipes. He "is" a plumber because of what he knows.

Embodiment learning is crucial to us and it means to take data and understanding into the fabric of our self; we make it part of us. Put into this context, it means knowledge is only valuable for an individual after it becomes part of his or her Eigen-resonance field. You have not truly learned (absorbed) something that is not integrated with your Eigen-field.

Data, as such, is not knowledge or learning. It is not about being; data is alien. Understanding is what creates true knowledge. Information today has become simply overwhelming and it is hard for the individual to relate to anything more than the tiniest fraction of it (typically, the snippets we learn early in life).

The kind of education forced on children by society today is a totally opposite precept to this kindly view of learning. To learn more about Supernoetics ™ go here: http://www.supernoetics.com

PEOPLE ARE ISOLATED FROM SELF

Largely as a result of mis-education, people on the whole today are deeply disturbed by disconnection from the self. It's a massive health problem. Look where mis-education leads us...

We learn to reject others or despise certain religious or ethnic groups, because others say we should (or we'll be killed if we don't).

The media creates a nightmare artificial world that is basically a kind of brainwashing or mind-control imposing a reality that is chosen by the powers in charge, with their own devious agenda.

Instead of loving our bodies, we are taught to hate them (too fat, too thin, too short, wrong hair, wrong color, etc.) So we work out at the gym, go on slimming diets, choose layers of cosmetics and have surgery, to alter how we look. We are no longer familiar with our own smell, but smother our bodies in oils, perfumes, aftershave and scented soaps.

Then we clothe the body in synthetic fabrics, with shapes and designs we imagine to be important but which do not suit us, just because commercial magazines say we should. We walk on synthetic floors and concrete, isolated from Mother Earth and hence ungrounded.

The majority in the Western world eats food that is not recognizable for its origin and yet expects this mélange of synthetic garbage to nourish us. It is not even sustainable; how can it be healthy in any sense?

In some countries in the "developed" world, the admired human is created by unnatural workouts, with bizarre machines that outdo each other in weirdness (in order to outsell the competition), resulting in bodies that are anything but natural. Witness the example of the Crossfit cult, where bodies are abnormally distorted and serious injuries are common, due to pushing the physical frame beyond its inherent design parameters.

How different in the less developed (some would say less off-centered) cultures, where sensual feedback through natural pathways and what we are pleased to call engagement with nature and the real world renders an abundant sense of self, with appropriate satisfaction and harmony with the world.

AN ATTACK ON SELF

All this unnaturalness amounts to a serious disintegration of self: the immune system, which most closely reflects our own inner harmony, is so out of tune that allergies, environmental chemical sensitivity, parasites and stealth pathogens are now virtually the "norm".

This leads to plague conditions, like AIDS, autism, lupus, and a host of autoimmune diseases that have now reached epidemic proportions. Estimates by the American Autoimmune Related Diseases website place the incidence at up to 50 million affected individuals[2]. Autoimmune disease is now one of the top 10 leading causes of death in female children and women in all age groups up to 64 years of age. Researchers have identified 80-100 different autoimmune diseases and suspect at least 40 additional diseases of having a strong autoimmune component.

Isn't the condition of anti-self I am describing the very basis of auto-immune disease? The body is so alienated from its own identity that it begins to attack its own tissues?

It is a classic case of a person not in resonance with his or her own "Field Of Self". Instead the modern individual is in another place: in Facebook, stuck in the day's news, in a book, on their smart phone, tablet, in the latest fashion or scandal—anywhere but "at home".

Good health is often just a case of coming back to our true self, as many people have found to their delight. As Kiran Schmidt remarks, there is really nowhere else to go!

GETTING A RESET

There is so much more to this model. For example, getting a "reset". This is a concept that goes back thousands of years. A shaman or traditional healing figure will cause a sudden, sharp shock to the system. This may take the form of a sudden slap on the back (as in Carlos Castenesa's shifting the Assemblage Point, page 208), any sudden pain, running over hot coals or wearing a mask that scares the patient half to death, are all versions of sudden shocks. Sticking sharp needles into the body, as in acupuncture, could even be conceived under this model.

What happens is a sort of generalized reset; the body's own energies kick in, to restore balance and harmony, which results in a healing process.

It's not as crude as you think. Nobel Laureate Ilya Prigogine, who gave us the concept of dissipative structures (isolated portions of the universe moving against the trend of entropy), also wrote about the phenomenon of *perturbation*. This means a displacement from what is current, a sort of shake up, which then allows a step towards a higher level of organization.

Evolution, if it happens at all, could be seen to reflect this idea. Some stress is placed upon the animal or species, it reacts with a perturbation and evolves a higher level or organization (new form or new behavior), which equips it better in the future to meet with stress or environmental resistance. When this perturbation continues for a long time, a whole new species may emerge, at a higher level of organization.

So you see the sudden, sharp shock approach to a health problem is rooted in advanced science principles.

HERE'S A NEAT EIGEN RESONANCE TRICK

Once we were a hard-working, far-from-sedentary species, fully engaged in the physical exercise that was naturally part of a life of farming or journeyman crafts; that is, before the advent of machines. We have been taken over by labor-saving devices and equipment—what a smart phone can do today is truly astonishing. They say a smart phone today is more powerful than the first computers that put a man in space. But this technological power may be undermining our very Being.

These days, the sensual feedback contact with our own body is usually limited to washing hands, shaving or (for women) mussing one's hair. I heard British educator Sir Kenneth Robinson quip that some people regard their bodies as no more than a tool to get their heads to a meeting: very humorous but also apt.

There is very little cultivation of our sensual body self-awareness, as for example touch, texture, movement, grace, feel, heartbeat and breath rhythms.

That's why the first thing you learn in an Ashram is breath awareness. There is no magic to it; often it's nothing more than hyperventilation, producing supposed spiritual experiences. But being more in touch with yourself and your own energies is soothing, reassuring and balancing. I'm OK with that as a healing concept.

418

ADD, ADHD and any cause of hyperactivity and restlessness is probably nature's attempt to force the self-awareness on us, by providing a rudimentary amount of self-feedback. Go to places where people are supposed to sit still and quiet, like libraries, classrooms and offices, and just watch. You can observe legs incessantly moving to create this minimal feedback. In children this has already become an epidemic called attention deficit hyperactivity disorder (ADHD) or even worse... self-cutting or self-mutilation, bulimia or other masochistic behaviors, which are desperate attempts to hide the pain of disconnection and to create any kind of sensual awareness of self, no matter how bizarre.

Here's a simple Eigen-resonance exercise that Kiran Schmidt suggested to me. If you get a stethoscope (cost about $50 or less) and listen to your heart sounds for 15 minutes you will understand the profound calming and meditative power of this simple practice. We never were taught to do that or, if at all, only as a curious biology experiment in school. However the future will show that this sort of engagement is a key to recreating a sense of self that will provide the power to recover from disease and addiction as nothing else can.

Biofeedback, I need hardly say, is based entirely on this concept of Eigen resonance. Patients are taught to listen to their own body and begin to dialogue with it, feeling its responses and gently modifying them with the power of thought and suggestion.

Perfect!

SELFIES AND FACEBOOK

Based on something Kiran Schmidt said to me, I wonder if the current obsession with "selfies" (pictures of yourself, taken by yourself, using a smart phone etc.) is not about hunger for strengthening the Eigen field? I have already remarked how very disconnected people are, partly due to technology.

But everyone likes to see a photo of self, to smile at self and, let's face it, *be more self!*

Maybe FaceBook and similar social media sites also fulfill this longing. We can see ourselves online, paint our identity as we would like it, rejoice in being "me" and also get approval or "likes" from others.

This may be more powerful psychology than anyone realizes.

CHAPTER 24

Weird or What?

It is often stated that of all the theories proposed in this [20th] century, the silliest is quantum theory. In fact, some say that the only thing that quantum theory has going for it is that it is unquestionably correct.

— Michio Kaku,
Hyperspace: A Scientific Odyssey through Parallel Universes, Time Warps, and the Tenth Dimension

I include this chapter, updated of course, from the original *Virtual Medicine*, because it has some very important healing lessons for us. Teeth and jaws are much more significant to health and disease than you could possibly imagine.

Right at the start of the 20th century, the biggest single risk factor for death due to heart disease was tooth and jaw infections. Numerous pathology specimens in medical school museums, showing sub-acute bacterial endocarditis, cavernous sinus thrombosis and brain abscesses, testify to just how precarious life could be in the age before antibiotics (and also what we may be facing again if we go on abusing them foolishly). A single unhealthy tooth could lead to an early grave.

Now, at the very end of the century, what do you suppose is among the biggest predictors of death due to heart disease?

Teeth: Well, more exactly, gum disease. This one risk factor has been shown to be just as important as smoking, obesity, blood pressure or an unfortunate family history in determining whether you or I will die before we should[1]. This seems very new and startling. Yet it has been talked about by EAV practitioners for decades and by switched-on dentists like Weston Price for even longer than that.

Periodontal disease, so called, comprises a group of infections involving the supporting tissues of the teeth. These range in severity from mild and reversible inflammation of the gingiva (gum) to chronic destruction of periodontal tissues (gingiva, periodontal ligament, and alveolar bone) with eventual loss of teeth.

Other organ systems can be damaged in the process, due to the continuous release of pathogens into the bloodstream, a phenomenon called bacteremia.

Did you know that the risk of heart disease or stroke is reduced by around 40% if you clean your teeth several times a day? Probably you didn't. A good tip is to brush your teeth with coconut oil, instead of toothpaste. Tip your brush more vertically and get the softened oil down the crevices between your teeth and gums. It will help pull out toxins.

But you must spit out the oil afterwards, *do not swallow it*; it's loaded with toxins.

THE DANGERS IN YOUR MOUTH

Why is what goes on in your mouth so dangerous?

My holistic dentist friend John Roberts, secretary of the British chapter of the International Academy of Oral Medicine and Toxicology points out, teeth sockets are a royal highway for disease pathogens leading straight into your bones. If we were to piece together all the patches of infection that a dentist sees in a typical mouth, he tells me it would be the equivalent of an ulcer eating away at half the back of your hand. Would you stand for that? Of course not, you say. But that's exactly what most of us are doing—we just don't see it, because it is in our jaw bones.

A tooth abscess is really just another kind of osteomyelitis, that is: a bacterial bone infection. We take the condition of our teeth far too lightly. No-one in his or her right mind would allow a hole to be drilled into a femur or other bone and have it left draining to the outside world; serious infectious complications would be bound to ensue. Yet that is what we do with our teeth. Some people live with what is virtually an open untreated wound.

Streptococcus mutans is the usual cause of tooth decay (dental caries).

A particularly nasty bug called *Porphyromonas gingivalis* is a major causative agent in the initiation and progression of severe forms of periodontal disease. It can become what we call a stealth pathogen and cause widespread loss of immune competency.

COSMETIC WORK IS A BAD IDEA

The position is not helped by techniques such as veneers or the crowning of teeth. It may make them appear cosmetically attractive on the outside. But often these veneers or caps do nothing more than cover and hide a seat of purulent infection, waiting to explode at some time in the future when the body's defenses are compromised.

In an address on 'The Role of Sepsis and Antisepsis in Medicine' to the Faculty of Medicine at McGill University, Montreal, in 1910, Dr. William Hunter baited his colleagues by saying, 'Knowing as we do the pathogenic qualities of staphylococci and streptococci, we have not the slightest excuse for allowing the mouth, so easily accessible to local measures, to remain the chief seat and a veritable hotbed for their development and propagation; on the contrary, it is a severe reflection on our profession if we allow it.'[2]

Elsewhere, in a piece in *The Lancet*, the enlightened Hunter referred to gold fillings, gold caps, gold bridges, gold crowns and fixed dentures built in, on and around diseased teeth as 'a veritable mausoleum of gold'. I feel sure he chose the word advisedly.

The thing is that crowns, bridges, prosthetics and, of course, infamous root canal fillings, are placed in or on teeth which are biologically dead. That means the normal immune protection mechanisms of life are not operative in that particular organ. Really, it's not much different to having a dead gangrenous hand or finger which is left in place, instead of being removed.

Capping it simply hides the process of rot which is going on underneath.

BACK PRESSURE

The late Patrick Stortebecker, Professor of Neurology at the Karolinska Institute in Stockholm, Sweden, carried out a series of experiments in the 1960s which I consider highly illuminating. The results were also rather scary.

Stortebecker injected tooth bone margins under pressure with radio-opaque dyes and then took x-rays of the skull. What he showed was that most head veins do not have valve control and therefore blood could travel backwards into the cranium. His radio-opaque dye appeared all over the head, far away from the tooth into which it was injected. Obviously this effect will take place in life; all it needs is for a change of pressure gradient, which is what happens every time you sneeze or strain at stool.

This was a controlled hygienic experiment, but if the tooth in question should happen to be infected, the results could be very adverse indeed. Bacterial toxic matter could be propelled into the cranium and there set up an unwanted focus of infection right inside the skull[3].

Stortebecker himself mentioned the obvious risk of cavernous sinus thrombosis and suppuration. This was once a killer condition. The cavernous sinus is a large vein reservoir at the base of the brain, and if it should clot and become filled with purulent matter, widespread meningitis and brain abscesses were the almost inevitable result. Many fatal tragedies from nose picking and spot scratching took place in former times. Those of us old enough may remember that parents tended to frown on this behavior and we were slapped for it. Certainly I was.

Now you know there was a scientific reason for the almost universal injunction against spot scratching.

We no longer see this morbid condition in Western medicine, thankfully. But it lurks just beyond view, always a threat from dental infections, averted simply by the use of antibiotics. If we should lose the availability of an effective non-toxic antibiotic, as seems very probable the way they are being overprescribed and pushed by drug companies, then worrying times will return.

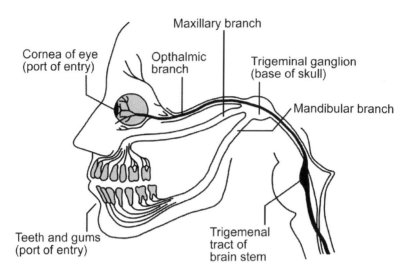

I have already campaigned that "the Golden Age of Antibiotics is over". For over sixty years we have been kept safe, on the whole, from imminent death by suppurating infections that get out of control. But those days of safety are gone. More and more highly resistant microbes are emerging, with some strains resistant to all known antibiotics. Nothing could really be done to save a person who had a brain abscess caused by such a resistant bacterium.

The thing is that teeth and gums are the most likely place for such a serious attack to enter the body. Beware.

MULTIPLE SCLEROSIS

But that's not all. Stortebecker had another disease model which I find very persuasive. He considers that what he found is the principal factor in the pathogenesis of multiple sclerosis[4]. Through extensive research he was able to show that most plaques of nerve demyelination (the unmistakable sign of MS) were located around blood vessels. No one else had noticed this important fact before.

Stortebecker speculated that the back pressure on veins had shunted toxic matter into the brain tissues, where it set up foci of inflammation and myelin loss. What was particularly convincing was that MS cases with optic neuritis (leading to blindness) generally had bad teeth and inflammation plaques in the brain; whereas those who had leg weakness or paralysis, with demyelination plaques in the spinal cord, had pelvic or other lower-body disease foci.

EAV folk find dental foci all the time: but let me tell you that, in my experience the pelvic organs also in particular hide a great deal of smoldering pathology. I myself have started to speak of a woman's 'angry pelvis', it is so common and so much undermines a woman's well-being.

And it's being overlooked, by orthodox and holistic practitioners alike.

Unfortunately, Stortebecker is gone. Apart from a handful of us, his work is ignored and it is very difficult to interest anyone in the medical establishment. Dentists don't even want to think about it. Doctors say it's a dental problem and nothing to do with them. Thus we have here another sad example of how specialization can make medicine ineffective.

THE QUESTION DOCTORS NEVER ASK

When was the last time a doctor asked you if you had any dental work just a few days before your disease problem started? - Never? Of course, it's the one big question doctors never think to ask.

It's been a saying of mine for decades that dentists don't know how many people they kill. There's no feedback; so how could they? And doctors don't realize they may be looking at a dental work complication, because they don't ask the vital question I just shared. So nobody is joining the dots and getting the full picture.

Until now.

It's important to understand the scary fact that any kind of dental work will cause a bacteremia (microbes spilled into the blood) to follow. Even just wiggling an abscessed tooth, can release showers of organisms into the peripheral blood. From there it circulates and can set up infections in the kidneys, adrenals, brain, lungs, bones and any other tissue.

Most notoriously, it can settle on damaged heart valves, a condition called sub-acute bacterial endocarditis (SABE). Clumps of bacteria form and cling to the valves, downstream of the blood flow.

That's not the end of it; from there chunks of bacteria can break off and go to the brain, causing a brain abscess (deadly) or even a stroke, due to blocking a vital blood vessel.

Dentistry can be very bad news! I know plenty of people who had teeth or gum problems, got a septicemia (dangerous form of bacteremia) and died as a result. Antibiotics couldn't save them.

WHAT SHOULD YOU DO?

Unless you have already had all your teeth out, you need to listen up. You need to be aware of this problem.

Never go to a dentist for any reason, even just investigation, who doesn't acknowledge this risk, talk about it and take action.

Always take huge doses of vitamin C (10 – 20 grams) if you can. That's a lot orally but using Thomas Levy's Lipospheric C formation, it's only a couple of sachets [www.livonlabs.com]. Always do this just as you go in for your appointment. In the restroom at the dentist's is even better.

If you are up for major oral work and need an anesthetist, that could be an advantage: you can ask him or her to put up an IV line and run in vitamin C. 20 grams would be about right.

You might consider taking an antibiotic at the same time, as a blanket cover. Yes, there are potential gut flora complications but there are also significant risks in doing nothing, as I have told you. Anyone with known heart valve problems, pre-existing kidney infections, hydrocephalus, known bad tooth abscess, suppurative sinus conditions or immune compromise should insist on antibiotics when visiting a dentist or oral hygienist, as a matter of course.

Clean up the mess afterwards, with good probiotics and prebiotics.

You can also consult my major reference work, *How to Survive in a World without Antibiotics*[5], for suggestions for alternatives to antibiotics. I wouldn't hesitate to set up a peroxide, ozone or UVB appointment as soon as possible after the dental work. And take coconut oil (useful antimicrobial), manuka honey, drink calendula tea and take *Artemisia annua*. Best of all: Quinton marine plasma. These are all in the book!

DENTAL TOXINS

I am not just talking about jaw and teeth infections.

It is not really stretching the human mind too far to suggest that most dentistry is, by its nature, quite toxic. Modern methods rely heavily on materials such as metals, plastics and polymers, ceramics and prosthetic structures of many kinds. Sealants, which are usually applied to back teeth as barriers against decay-causing bacteria, are under fire because they may leach bisphenol-A (BPA), an endocrine disruptor. BPA has been linked to declining sperm counts and increased cancer rates in humans.

Unfortunately, EAV practitioners are discovering that most of this foreign material is stressful to the body. It can be a considerable drain on the immune system and therefore a major contributory cause of fatigue and chronic ill health. In this new context we can only urge people even more emphatically to try to prevent dental problems from starting up. Good diet and adequate teeth hygiene may, even in this day of antibiotics, still be a key life-saver.

I do not exaggerate.

It is possible to reduce the damage by taking sensible anti-tox procedures before, during and after a dental program. EAV tests show that this at least minimizes the impact of high-tech dentistry. Such elementary measures would include taking vitamin C, charcoal by mouth (to absorb toxins), homeopathic support and immune drainage remedies such as HEEL's lymphomyosot or Pascoe's Pascotox (Chapter 18 covers complex homeopathy).

Coenzyme Q10, by the way, has a proven benefit for gum disease of all kinds. This is little known but is of critical importance to those of you with unhealthy mouths.

You can also rinse out the mouth, using chlorine dioxide protocol (again, see my book *How to Survive in a World without Antibiotics* for details). This will lower the pathogen burden.

MERCURY

Then there is the mercury story. Just over a decade ago, most of us were still to be convinced of the problem of biological intoxication with mercury. Official bodies such as the British and American Dental Associations deny it still.

As I said in my last book, gram for gram, mercury is one of the most toxic substances known to humanity, and it is arguably the most serious environmental pollutant we are creating for ourselves. Unfortunately mercury, especially in the methyl or chloride forms which have great biological penetration, has a special affinity for brain tissue. Most people know that the expression 'mad as a hatter' comes from the fact that twitching and dementia were once common among hat manufacturers and were due to poisoning with the mercuric nitrate used for curing felt hat bands.

The first health scare of modern times was the discovery that in the 1950s children who were dying of pink disease were being poisoned by mercury in 'teething powders'. Then, in 1953, the inhabitants of the Japanese fishing port of Minamata began to fall ill with a mysterious illness which caused twitching, mental confusion, difficulty in speaking and eventually paralysis. Autopsy showed considerable brain damage and the agent was discovered to be mercury. A nearby factory was dumping mercuric waste into the bay, which contaminated the fish stocks. It was concentrated in the food chain and reached deadly levels before being eaten by humans.

Despite all this, the dental profession continues to insist mercury is somehow non-toxic when you put it in your mouth! There is considerable hypocrisy about this, however; the instructions to dentists for handling mercury leave no doubt that it is harmful to dentists—even though it is supposed to be safe for patients. Advice to the profession includes storing it under water, not touching it by hand, providing adequate air extraction to eliminate the toxic vapor, and so on. Generally it is illegal for dentists to allow fluids contaminated by mercury to be sent into the sewage system. Filters or extractors are required.

Do all these precautions make sense, for something which is described as safe inside your mouth to suck on 24 hours a day?

The official argument was once that mercury remains firmly in the teeth and cannot spread to other tissues. Then in 1989 a team of doctors in Cal-gary, Canada, under Drs. Hahn and Vimy, proved that the truth was very different. Using radioactive mercury and placing fillings in the teeth of sheep, they were able to show that mercury from fillings spreads all over a mammalian body within hours. The official line then switched to saying that there was no proven connection between mercury poisoning from amalgams and any known disease. This is specious and dishonest. It is not the public's job to prove there is a danger from mercury; it's deadly poison!

What EAV doctors have been finding for years is that heavy metal overloads are a common cause of pathology and, not surprisingly, mercury is the godfather of all. Time and again mercury fillings are at the head of what I described in Chapter 19 as Causal Chains. However, this is not confined to mercury. Poisoning from other metals can occur. Sometimes the question is one of sensitivity, rather than poisoning.

We must accept what Nature tells us, and on testing a male patient with EDS some years ago, I found that the biggest Indicator Drop pointed to danger from a gold-filled tooth and not the more obvious amalgam on the opposing tooth. Scanning the dental nosode list showed that this patient was unusual in reacting to gold. I prescribed a homeopathic detoxification treatment and, next day, the gold filling fell out. Clearly it was rejected by the body, once given a little energetic help. The bemused patient preferred to believe it was 'just a coincidence', even though the filling had remained in place for almost 20 years.

GALVANIC FIELDS AND ENERGETIC DISTURBANCE

Slightly more bizarre is the phenomenon of electrical fields around certain teeth and the effects these produce. I remember well the first time I saw Hal Huggin's slides of teeth cut open to show the scorch marks, where electrical current had been running for many years. Teeth can work like little batteries. This is quite logical: there are two or more metals and a saltwater fluid medium (saliva). This is how Allessandro Volta's original batteries were made; the battery of your motorcar is essentially the same thing.

The trouble starts from the fact that electrical currents actually leach the mercury out of the teeth, because of an effect called electrolysis. This is why patients sometimes complain of a constant metallic taste in the mouth, made worse by hot fluids and salty food (more electrolysis).

If that isn't scary enough, then the reader should know that chewing food and dental work can release deadly mercury vapor. It needs to be said that mercury vapor levels inside the mouth during dental manipulations can reach 10 times the allowed safety levels for mercury vapor in the atmosphere.

Dentists are warned to fit air extractors and take special care not to breathe the mercury vapor cloud that's coming from *your* mouth! It goes straight to the brain tissue where it is highly invasive and toxic. Apparently though, it's OK for you to breathe it.

GALVANIC EFFECT

But the problem is even more complicated than that. The currents generated by amalgams can be quite considerable, and these are being formed very close to brain tissue, which operates at far lower potentials (a few millivolts). I have seen momentary spikes of up to 1 volt when testing teeth for the battery effect. This is enough to light a small torch battery. Remember the brain is really only a few millimeters from the jawbone where the roots of the teeth lie, just the other side of the thin cranial bone and the meninges.

Thus there is potential for mental dysfunction and this is often found in clinical practice, if the appropriate questions are asked.

Casebook: Female, 44 Years

The patient had suffered from Meniere's disease: vertigo and vomiting, with intermittent staggering (sailor's gait). She could not think clearly any more, had trouble with her memory, and could not see clearly: lines appeared not straight. This was accompanied by pain in the nape of the neck.

She was unable to continue working, due to the severity of these symptoms. Her attending physicians could find no clinical explanation and the patient was told it was all in her head (in a way this was true!) Finally, a brain tumor was suspected and tests were required to exclude this grim possibility.

The patient's luck eventually turned and an ENT surgeon referred her to Dr. Helmut Raue, an EAV specialist who understands "biological dentistry", as this new specialty is called. He measured her teeth galvanically and found 215 microamperes of current between a gold filling and a nearby amalgam. One week after having the amalgam removed, all pain had disappeared and the patient's balance had returned to normal. The patient admitted then that she had had suicidal thoughts because of the excruciating pain and baffling dizziness[6].

The reason that not enough of these cases are being diagnosed and the true picture not emerging is that patients do not, usually, consult their dentist with symptoms such as headache, facial neuralgia, dizziness, sleep disorders and digestive disturbance (just to give a few examples).

ENERGETIC FIELDS

Now we come to the main reason that dental hazards are featured in this book. The focus effect (plural foci).

EAV practitioners are regularly finding teeth foci as a common cause of energetic disturbances. The problem is immensely more complicated than it at first might seem. Several key acupuncture meridians cross the line of the teeth as they pass over the face. An abscess or 'transmitting focus' can actually create pathological results anywhere along the line of that meridian. These are further connected with secondary organs and sites. Thus problems with a front incisor tooth may impact on the kidneys, since this meridian passes through the incisors. But the kidneys, in turn, are related to the knee joints. If I see a patient with incisor problems or a bridge in this location I can surprise him or her by asking about the arthritis of the knees.

Sometimes the consequences of these interconnections are very surprising and virtually beggar any explanation but should make us very wary indeed about the effects of dentistry.

Casebook: Female, 33 Years

Here's a case described to me by my old friend Jack Levenson, long deceased.

A dentist had prepared a new crown tooth prosthesis, the type with a post of nickel which fits in a hole drilled down the center of the tooth to give support. As the dentist offered the post to its new location on the right upper jaw, the woman let out a squeal: she'd gone immediately blind in that eye! The dentist removed the tooth and she could see again. He offered it back and she went blind again. This was repeated several times until both were quite sure of what they were observing.

She refused the crown and had the tooth removed instead.

What this striking example of what we might call 'virtual dentistry' tells us is that energetic fields in the mouth are important to brain function. This was an instant reaction; there was no way it could depend on any chemical manifestation, even metal toxicity. Allergies to nickel do occur, though this metal is far less poisonous than mercury. But any such allergy would take a little time to develop. The striking part of the story is the instant loss of vision, which indicates clearly neurological dysfunction along the optical pathways due to a field disturbance, probably at the quantum or information level.

It also makes vividly clear what risks we take when we allow metal into our mouths. The resulting disturbance of the body's energy field can have unpredictable and very serious consequences.

I try to imagine in this case what would have happened if the woman had not lost her vision immediately but had gone blind over the subsequent few weeks. *Almost certainly the correct cause would never have been diagnosed.* She may have ended up with harmful and unnecessary interventions which would fail because they were not aimed at correcting the real problem.

ENERGETIC MERIDIAN RELATIONS WITH TEETH

I have referred already to the energetic connections between teeth and acupuncture meridians.

There are charts published which give a great deal of detail about these biological dental inter-relationships, but I have tried to simplify this down to the general picture for the reader.

Energetic Relationships of Teeth

Upper	relations	
1	incisor	kidney, bladder, pineal, rectum
2	incisor	kidney, bladder, pineal, rectum

3	canine	liver, gallbladder, pituitary, posterior eye
4	pre-molar	lung, colon, posterior pituitary
5	pre-molar	lung, colon, thymus
6	1st molar	spleen/pancreas, stomach, thyroid
7	2nd molar	spleen/pancreas, stomach, parathyroid
8	3rd molar	heart, small intestine, anterior pituitary

Lower	**relations**	
4	pre-molar	spleen/pancreas, stomach, gonads
5	pre-molar	spleen/pancreas, stomach, breast
6	1st molar	lung, colon
7	2nd molar	lung, colon
8	3rd molar	heart, small intestine, ext/middle ear

Note how upper and lower jaw reverse relations on teeth 4 - 7

NICO: WHAT'S IN A NAME?

NICO is an EAV disease. By that I mean only EAV people would usually detect this curious type of pathology. It's a dental problem and has only come to light recently as a result of dentists doing their own EAV testing, though in fairness other good dentists do come across it.

NICO is an abbreviation of neuralgia-inducing cavitational osteo-necrosis. I will explain. First, let me remind you that disease under the roots of teeth is a kind of bone inflammation, hence the term 'osteitis'. Osteonecrosis means the bone has died or lost its viability as a result; it is softened and eaten away, like rot in an apple.

Neuralgia-inducing means that it has been postulated as a potent cause of neuralgia of the face, particularly that vicious kind known as trigeminal neuralgia. The trigeminal nerve (5th cranial nerve, emerging at the ear) is largely sensory and supplies the face, jaws and teeth. A phenomenon known as referred pain means that trouble anywhere within the nerve net can be felt at other places supplied by the same nerves. Thus NICO is a factor to consider in migraine or any kind of atypical headache. It is worth pointing out that the jaws are the only major bony tissue with important sensory nerve endings.

The 'cavitational' part of the name simply means some kind of cyst or space in the jaw bone, not necessarily infected or inflammatory. Quite common is a fatty osteitis, where an old focus of inflammation has finally settled down and turned into a fatty cyst. There may be blood or chocolate matter in the cavity.

But the important point which knowledgeable dentists are making is that this is not really an inflammatory process but tissue destruction caused by insidious loss of blood supply. In this respect it is more like other textbook bone diseases, where destruction comes from impaired blood and nutritional supply, which in 1915 US dentist G. V. Black described as progressive 'death of bone, cell by cell'[7].

NICO is not rare. In one population study it was found in 1 in every 4,900 adults. This makes NICO by far the most common osteonecrotic bone disease. Once again, specialization means that doctors are not talking to dentists as they should. NICO has been seen in people aged 18–94, but typically affects people in the 35– 65 age range. An individual may have more than one focus of this disease process. It is hard to avoid the conclusion that it is the result of poor dental hygiene and maintenance; in other words, the consequence of burnt-out chronic infective foci.

Whatever the primary cause, bone cavities are open to subsequent bacterial invasions. Because the underlying process is caused by lack of oxygen these are likely to be anaerobic bacteria which release dangerous toxins and may in our present view be premalignant. Substances such as mercaptan and thioether, which are found regularly in dental foci by electrodermal screening (EDS), are known carcinogens.

It is unfortunate that NICO is usually not visible on x-ray. Many cases are thus missed even by experienced diagnosticians, since 35–50 per cent of bone loss is necessary before changes become radiographically evident. This is where EAV and "virtual dentistry" come in. I know dentists who are bold enough, and trust good EAV practitioners sufficiently, to drill into bone at the site indicated as a reading focus. It is very satisfying to both parties when the cortex is breached and a cavity filled with toxic sludge makes its presence known.

Once diagnosed, treatment is currently by curettage of the site, sweeping away all the dead and softened bone, and maybe the first millimeter or so of healthy bone, in the hope that new, good bone will form. Coral granules may be used to pack the hole and encourage re-calcification of bone tissue. In about a third of cases this radical treatment fails and may even make the problem worse, but according to one writer only about 10 per cent of patients feel that the process wasn't worthwhile.

Curettage is rather heroic and I have no doubt that in future something a little less aggressive will be the rule. While NICO is chiefly the domain of holistic dentists, such 'commando cures' are rather untypical of holism in general.

ROOT CANAL FILLINGS

Here is a topic where conventional medicine, decades ago, stood right where alternative innovative dentists stand today. The story is a fascinating one and begins in the first decade of the last century with one Dr. Billings. His research, published in 1914, showed that 95 per cent of all focal infections in the body came from the teeth and tonsils. Billing's work, in turn, was found by Weston Price, a leading dentist of his day. Price was an advocate of a healthy natural lifestyle and keynote nutrition; in every way he was a great thinker and a pioneer of values that we cherish today.

Price had a woman patient for whom he had done a root canal filling. She subsequently developed bad arthritis; it was so severe that she had become bedridden most of the time and her hands were so badly swollen she could barely feed herself. Price was honest enough to ask the question that no dentist cares to ask: could he have made her ill? He removed the root-canal-filled tooth, carefully and aseptically, to see what would happen. The woman promptly recovered.

From this case forward Price became very interested in the problem of root canal fillings. He had considerable success in helping patients, and published his results widely. There are copious papers by him in the medical and dental literature, most of it from the early 1920s. It is important to recognize that Price was a leading conventional dentist of the day. His views were listened to and, for a time, it became the fashion among doctors to recommend extracting teeth with root canal fillings as a cure for arthritis.

In fact this progressed to widespread tooth extractions, root canals or not, which was not what Price originally taught. Unfortunately, many cases did not recover as expected. The patient not only continued to suffer the arthritis but was now without any teeth. The approach became unpopular and was eventually discontinued. As a result, Price's views were discredited and lost sight of. It was one of those cases where the pendulum swung too far in a particular direction. Price was right, of course, but there needed to be some way of choosing patients who would benefit from removing root canal fillings.

Voll gave us the means. It is now a common aspect of EAV/EDS diagnosis to consider the safety and viability of root canal fillings. They may not be a problem. If the person is fit and strong, with a good immune system, the situation can continue unchanged for many years. But if at some time in the future he or she undergoes too much stress or suffers from a major illness, resistance may be compromised and the dangers of root canals become manifest and dangerous.

The general consensus among doctors who do what I do—and know what I know—is that it is far safer to get rid of all amalgam root canal fillings in your mouth. If you want the dentist to preserve the tooth anyway, despite the fact that it is dead, you must discuss safer, non-metallic inclusions.

The problem is that, although root canal work looks fine on x-ray and it might appear that there is a perfect occlusion of the former root canal down the heart of the tooth, microscopic examination reveals a different story. Tooth dentine, which is hard and screeches like rock when the dentist attacks it with his drill, is really composed of numerous tiny tubules. It is said there are 3 miles of end-to-end microtubules in every tooth; they are supposed to conduct nutrients to keep the tooth alive and healthy. When a tooth dies bacteria gain access and they lurk in these microtubules. Filling the root canal does not flush the pathogens out of this domain. In fact the bacteria are then trapped in a closed-off space and inevitably this causes trouble.

Pathogens have to go somewhere when they multiply. They can migrate through what are called lateral tubules and escape into the periodontal membrane and subsequently into the bony tissue of the jaw. From there they migrate around the body. As biological dentist and author of Root Canal Cover Up[8] George Meinig puts it:

"These bacteria are kind of like people, if they get to like Seattle or Reno or someplace they decide that's where they are going to have their home. Well, the bacteria travelling round the body, they may get to the liver, the kidneys or the heart or eyes or some other tissue and they set up an infection in that area. This is why the degenerative diseases occur from the teeth."[9]

TRANSMITTING TEETH

Now we come to the part that is definitely weird, hence the title of this chapter. Everything so far is at least logical, if rather unnerving. It makes sense. From here it makes no real sense, except in the insubstantial quantum domain or, at the informational or etheric level. What Weston Price did in the 1920s was to take infected and pathogenic root-canal-filled teeth from humans and surgically stitch them into rabbits for observation. This is an example of one of those experimental situations (like Benjamin Franklin sending his kite up into a thunderstorm) where genius bordering on madness gets a crazy idea and actions it. The results turn out to be an important scientific insight.

What Weston Price found was that the rabbits became ill with the same diseases as the patients, or if not exactly the same diseases, then the same organ was attacked in some way. If the human had nephritis (cured after tooth extraction), then the rabbit got nephritis; if the human had heart disease, cancer or arthritis that was what the rabbit got. Eye problems were particularly striking; if the human had only mild eye trouble, the rabbit would react so severely as to go blind in two or three days.

The only real conclusion is that the tooth carried some message of disease using an unknown code. There was a clear informational transfer, in the subspace realms of Deep-IS. It is definite confirmation of the fact that many, if not all, health issues take place at a level beyond the physical: hence *Medicine Beyond*.

You would think this absolutely fascinating series of experiments would have scientists racing to investigate the significance of what Price found. Instead, his work was promptly forgotten for over 50 years. So much for the progress of scientific thought.

PROFESSIONAL BODY

If all of this scares the hell out of you (it should), then be sure to make contact with the main dentists' representative body taking a responsible line with the hazards of dentistry, the IAOMT. It stands for International Academy for Oral Medicine and Toxicology.

The ideals and goals of the IAOMT are shared by holistic dentists and physicians around the world, who have joined our efforts to promote science-based biological dentistry in their home countries.

Visit their website: http://iaomt.org where you can search for IAOMT members around the world.

Avoid the ADA (American Dental Association). All you'll get is propaganda, dissembling and expedient science.

CHAPTER 25

Earth Radiation And Geopathic Stress Symptoms

A sick bed is a sure way to ruin your health.

—Paracelsus

This is a book about human health and the biological significance of electromagnetism and other energy forces in diagnosis and healing. In an electric universe such as I described in chapter 2, it becomes apparent that we are surrounded by electromagnetic fields of truly astronomical proportions.

It is absurd to suppose that the rich and enormous variable energy field enveloping our planet has no relevance to our well-being. Yet that is what mainstream science continues to believe, against all evidence to the contrary.

We now recognize the phenomenon of "space weather". Massive electromagnetic outbursts on the Sun stream prodigious amounts of energy towards the Earth and these disturb the equilibrium of our atmosphere.

Far from being unimportant, it is now beyond doubt that people are adversely affected by changes in our electric environment. For example, when sunspots are very active, hospital admissions for heart attacks and psychotic episodes rise sharply.

This is hardly surprising: coronal outbursts and other Sun phenomena have been known to fry electrical equipment and produce destructive surges through power lines. Why not dangerous surges throughout the power lines in our bodies: the nervous system? That's without even considering surges through meridians and "chakra storms", all of which have yet to be explored.

THE EARTH'S OWN FIELD

The earth's core is a spinning mass of molten iron. It sets up a huge magnetic field (known variably as the geomagnetic field or magnetosphere), which merges at the poles and spreads out into space for thousands of kilometres. I have likened it to living inside a gigantic dynamo.[1]

The Earth's field in turn is greatly influenced by the even more powerful field of the Sun. We speak today of 'solar wind', which means the outpourings of charged electrical particles streaming into space with incredible energies, pushing matter before it (there is enough force to propel a rocket up to nearly the speed of light, given time). Most of the force is dissipated into empty regions, but where it meets the magnetic field of a planet, such as the Earth, there are considerable interactions.

On the solar side of the Earth, the geomagnetic field is compressed by the pressure of particles and radiation travelling at or near the speed of light. On the far side, the geomagnetic field is thrust far out into space, streaming trails like hair blowing in the wind.

Certain regions on the sunward side are 'sandwich layers' where high-energy particles are trapped, bouncing around endlessly and forming a kind of cushion. These layers are called the Van Allen belts, after their discoverer. If it were not for the presence of the Van Allen belts, absorbing and damping radiation, life on Earth would be totally unsustainable, except far underground.

It comes as a shock to realize that our life-giving Sun's rays are so deadly to life. Astronauts can only survive for short periods in space without being shielded, and rocket missions are carefully timed to avoid maximum solar radiation. Outside the Earth's protective magnetosphere humans would be sizzled if they chanced to be caught in a solar storm. I make this point in the hope that it gives a vivid picture of the intensity of the sun's radiation and what we would potentially face down here on the surface, if our protection should fail.

The sun has great power for health and healing, but it would be absurd to think it was not capable of an adverse influence, even at the radiation levels we experience.

SCHUMANN WAVES

One aspect of Earth's radiation which has only recently attracted attention as a health issue is the Schumann wave effect. The Earth's atmosphere, between the underside of the ionosphere and the surface (especially the salt oceans) forms what scientists call a resonating cavity magnetometer. Due to excitation by the Earth's own magnetism, sunspots and lightning storms, this cavity emits a transverse resonating waveband that we call Schumann waves, after the man who discovered them in the 1940s.

The actual frequency varies according to the height of the ionosphere and large-scale weather patterns, but is generally in the 8 - 10 Hertz range. I feel sure it is no coincidence that this frequency is virtually identical with that of the hippocampus of mammalian species.

What is worrying is that modern cities have very low levels of Schumann waves, as most of these waves are absorbed by the vast masses of concrete and metal buildings. The gradual lowering of the land water table has also added to the deficiency.

This must have severe and unavoidable health consequences for city dwellers. The loss of health-giving Schumann waves could be a contributory factor in 'sick building syndrome'.

TELLURIC CURRENTS

A telluric current (from Latin *tellus*, "earth"), is an electric current which moves through the Earth's crust and mantle, or even through the sea. Telluric currents result from both natural causes and human activity, and the varied individual currents interact in a complex pattern. They are of extremely low frequency (ELF) and travel over large areas at or near the surface of the Earth. You will remember from chapter 8 that ELFs are of great impact and importance biologically.

In September 1862, an experiment to specifically address Earth currents was carried out in the Munich Alps.[2] The idea is thus not new.

The currents are primarily geomagnetically induced by changes in the outer part of the Earth's magnetic field, which are in turn caused by interactions between the solar wind and the magnetosphere or solar radiation effects on the ionosphere.

It has been estimated that telluric currents overall during twelve hours in one hemisphere are in the range of 100 to 1000 amperes. This intensity of telluric currents is sufficient to drive the air movements that create atmospheric electricity, from the global fair weather charge accumulator to thunderstorm bases.

Telluric currents flow in the surface layers of the earth. The electric potential on the Earth's surface can be measured at different points, enabling the calculation of the magnitudes and directions of the telluric currents and hence the Earth's conductance.

Telluric methods can be used for exploring the structure beneath the Earth's surface (such as in industrial prospecting). Uses include geothermal exploration, mining exploration, petroleum exploration, mapping fault zones, ground water exploration and monitoring, investigating magma chambers, and investigating plate tectonic boundaries.

Telluric currents can even be harnessed to produce a useful low voltage current by means of earth batteries. Such devices were used for telegraph systems in the United States as far back as 1859. So don't let anyone tell you that Earth rays are woo-woo and don't exist.

GEOPATHIC STRESS EXPLAINED

The electric universe (EU) model sheds a lot of light on a puzzling health phenomenon we call *geopathic stress*. I first learned of it when I went to Ireland to work with colleagues there; they told me in all seriousness about patients getting well by moving their beds away from "black spots". What are black spots? I wanted to know. And how are they identified?

The answer was so surprising, I was almost shocked. But it takes a lot to really flummox me; so I listened and learned... I was introduced to the ancient art of dowsing (scrying, divination, geomancy). A dowser will undertake to find these danger spots; he or she did not even need to visit the property. It can be done by dowsing a plan of the house, using a pendulum or similar method! Remember, I was talking with qualified and capable doctors; MDs!

And before you tune out, thinking that's nonsense or flim-flam, let me assure you that many major corporations use dowsers to find oil and water; they wouldn't pay for it unless it worked! Moreover, a large proportion of healthcare practitioners in Germany (I am told) are expert health dowsers.

You may also need to know that much of the radiation phenomenon I am writing about is detectable on modern instruments. In the 1980s, before we had good enough devices, there were times when I walked around with a switched on TV set with a long cable, and noticed that the picture would distort in certain spots, suggesting some radiation interference with the actual transmission.

PLACE IS PATHOLOGY

It is a new idea that location can be a factor in disease. There seem to be certain places on the Earth's surface that are unhealthy. People who live in the countryside have known for centuries that there are locations in which cattle and other livestock sicken and die inexplicably.

In 1990 a significant study was carried out by Christopher MacNaney of the People's Research Centre in Cumbria. Assisted by his wife Sheila and five interviewers, he surveyed approximately 750 families of gypsies at the Appleby Horse Fair. It was found that the incidence of cancer among 'travelling' families was a startling 0.6 per cent – lowest in the Western world. Yet the survey also showed their lifestyle – smoking, drinking, etc. – was no healthier than that of the rest of the population. Moreover, of the families with one or more members who had contracted cancer, all had succumbed in the two years after settling down in a static location.[3]

No one knows for sure what the danger factor is but it is very likely to be local disturbances in the Earth's electromagnetic field. Underground water courses seems to be the biggest culprit, but underground caverns, mineral deposits, fault lines and changes in rock strata can have the same effect. Given the fact that I have repeated many times in this book that life is electrical in nature, it hardly seems surprising that this phenomenon would have a potentially negative effect.

But not always: the terms "earth radiation," "e-rays" and "geopathic stress" can be somewhat misleading. Such energies are only harmful when we are exposed to them for too long. In fact, earth rays can affect the energy balance of our bodies positively. When we take a walk in nature, for example, we feel refreshed, less stressed, and more mentally acute. This is, in part, because we cross a wide range of earth radiation lines and our bodies take advantage of these changing impulses.

That's why a walk in nature is always invigorating and relaxing. Brief exposure to different kinds of earth energies tones us up.

OTHER POSSIBLE EXPLANATIONS

Note: the problem is definitely not radon gas, which affects granite areas. In any case, unusual geographical distributions of disease do not necessarily indicate radiation.

In my 1992 book *The Complete Guide to Food Allergy and Environmental Illness*, I reported that areas in Britain where bracken fern (*Pteridium aquilinum*) contaminates water supplies, there is a well-documented high incidence of cancer. In some areas of Wales farmers are advised to wear masks. Professor Jim Taylor of Aberystwyth University is reported as saying 'I regard bracken as a present-day Triffid.'

But geological aspects of terrain could also be an important factor; soil and rock characteristics. I refer to the writings of Georges Lakhovsky and others. Lakhovsky surveyed Paris in the 1930s and discovered interesting geographical variations in the prevalence of cancer. Areas where the incidence was high (Auteuil, Javel, Grenelle and St Lambert) were sited on clay; areas where the incidence was low (Port Dauphine, Champs-Élysées and La Muette) were on sand and sandy limestone.[4]

The disturbance phenomenon may account for 'cold' spots in houses, which as many people are aware do not always relate to draughts. The positive or 'friendly' side of this gives rise to the idea of 'good' places, and dowsing shows that many ancient buildings, such as churches and temples, were built on positively-charged zones, as if the builders were aware of safe, enhancing radiation present in the locality.

LOOKING FOR ANSWERS

The Chinese geomancers knew about this effect 4,000 years ago and so it seems, did ancient man. In a study conducted by Sig Lonegren he did not find one ancient settlement located over negative geopathic stress lines. Part of the problem is that the Catholic Church persecuted dowsers as witches 400 years ago effectively terrifying or killing the practitioners and so the people who understood this phenomenon were either killed or silenced and the knowledge died out.

Modern evaluation of the hazards of Earth radiation began with experiments in 1929 by the German baron, Gustav Freiherr von Pohl. He was an expert dowser and dowsed a town called Vilsbiburg. He used an arbitrary scale of 0 to 16 and reckoned anything at 9 or over was potentially a cancer hazard. He marked all the zones of this dangerous radiation he could find, then went to the town hall to check the records for everyone who had died of cancer in the town, and found, remarkably, that every single one, without exception, had been living and sleeping over one of the radiation lines.

Some doctors were astounded by this discovery; others remained skeptical and asked von Pohl to repeat the experiment in another town. He did and the results were exactly the same.[5]

Dr. Hager, in Stettin, president of the local Medical Scientific Association, tried it the other way around. He took the records of over 5,300 cancer victims and dowsed their homes. He found that in every single case there were dangerous radiation spots. Even more startlingly, some buildings turned out to be extremely dangerous: five houses had resulted in over 120 cancer deaths.

Dr. Manfred Curry, also a dowser, took along impartial witnesses to his experiments and showed that he was able, by dowsing a person's sleeping place, to say with accuracy which part of his or her body was affected. His predictions were right every time, to the astonishment of the onlookers. One bed which he said was 'dangerous in the pelvic area' had seen two successive women die of cancer of the uterus.

Dr. Viktor Rambeau also dowsed; the results of one of his surveys in 1934 are shown in the figure below. Note that he dowsed the danger zones before investigating where the cancer beds lay. Convincing? I think so.

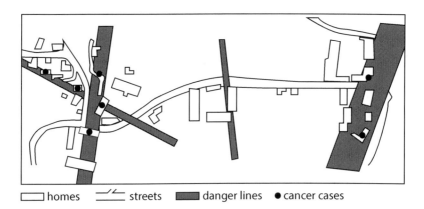

☐ homes ⌒⌣ streets ▰▰ danger lines ● cancer cases

In 1937 Dr. H. Beitzke, a professor at the Institute of Pathological Anatomy at the University of Graz, studied the effect of water veins on cancer in mice. Beitzke placed half the mice over a water vein and the other half in a room free from the influence of water veins. Over a period of thirteen months, thirteen of the mice suffered from cancerous tumors of varying size. Twelve of the thirteen mice suffering from cancer lived over the water vein while only one lived in the uncontaminated room.[6]

MORE UP TO DATE RESEARCH

The modern-day leading exponent of dowsing is Käthe Bachler, an Austrian teacher. She became interested in how Earth radiation might be affecting the health of her pupils and causing behavioral and study problems. She wrote a book called *Earth Radiation: The Startling Discoveries of a Dowser*, which became a bestseller in Austria and Germany and started a health revolution.

I paid out of my own pocket to have 10,000 copies translated and printed in English.

Her work was so respected that she was given a grant by the authorities to carry her studies further. Ultimately Bachler dowsed 11,000 cases in 3,000 homes in 14 different countries, and has made a phenomenal contribution to this field of study. Her files show case after case of earth radiation, particularly affecting the sleeping place, making people ill with such diverse conditions as arthritis, cancer, allergies and mental illness.

Dr. Otto Bergmann, a lung specialist and lecturer at the University of Vienna, conducted a study between 1988 and 1989 funded by the Housing Research Fund of the Austrian Federal Ministry of Economic Affairs. The study included 985 subjects in some 6,943 investigations. It revealed that earth radiation affects our bodily functions, including pulse rate, heartbeat frequency and electrical skin resistance.

Dr. Bergmann published the results in his 1990 book: *Risikofaktor Standort – Rutengängerzone und Mensch (Risk Factor Location – Dowsing Zones and Man)*.

Dr. Rudolf Kessler and Andreas Kopschina (a naturopath and geopathologist) conducted a study of 52 patients in 1992, for which they received a research grant from the Association of German Naturopaths. Both their study and an additional study by Kopschina and Daun (1994) clearly demonstrate that chronic or recurrent diseases have a direct correlation to the presence of geopathic stresses in bedrooms.

The text of the study is available in German on the website of the German Professional Association of Geopathologists and Building Biologists at http://www.geopathologie.de/studien/studie-1/inhalte. (Use Google Translate).

Study of Kopschina and Daun (1994): *"Die krankmachende Wirkung geopathischer Belastung" ("The pathogenic effect of geopathic stress")*.

Andreas Kopschina conducted this additional study of 8,200 patients in collaboration with naturopaths Wolfgang and Ursula Daun, for which the authors received both the 1994 research award from the Foundation of German Naturopaths and the gold medal of merit in 1998.[7]

THE GRIDS

In addition to geophysical influences such as streams and rock strata, there have been defined a number of energy "grids", so far detectable only by dowsers.

The Hartmann Net was discovered by the physician Ernst Hartmann in 1954 and described in detail in his book *Krankheit als Standortproblem* (*Illness as a Location Problem*). It consists of a grid of north-to-south lines, crossed by east-to-west, alternately charged positive and negative. The grid lines are 2-3 m (6-9ft) apart and some 15-20 cm (6-8in) wide. However, these values can vary immensely depending on geographical location The Hartmann grid is often referred to as a global grid, meaning Earth-bound. In his book, Hartmann provides clear evidence for the pathogenic character of the grid.

The Curry Grid, on the other hand, is cosmic in origin. It runs diagonal to the Hartmann Net at approximately 3½ m (7ft) apart and 80cm (2 ½ft) wide, but unlike the Hartmann Net it doesn't vary.

This grid is named after Manfred Curry, an American doctor born in Munich in 1899. Curry spent most of his life in Germany and was an enthusiastic sailor, author and inventor. He invented, among other things, the cam cleat and one of the first velomobiles. Although the grid is named after Curry, who published it in 1952, it was actually discovered by Siegfried Wittmann in 1950.

During the day, the Curry Grid intensity wanes, but at night it can lead to insomnia.

With these grid phenomena, whatever they are, it is held that the intersecting nodes are where the trouble lies. If the nodes from two grids coincide, that is particularly dangerous and when the double-dose also lies over a watercourse, look out!

Finally, the Benker Grid (or Benker Cubical System), named after a master carpenter and avid dowser Anton Benker: this is a 3-D system comprised of rows and columns of cubes with a length and breadth measurement of 10 meters (approx. 32 ft.). Hence it is also sometimes referred to as the 10 Meter System. Each cube is electrically charged and the polarity changes from one cube to the next. A positively charged cube should support and encourage life processes, but it can have the opposite effect if exposure is excessive. Similarly, negatively charged cubes usually have a calming effect but can also extract energy from the body, again if exposure becomes excessive.

Benker conducted experiments on multiple sclerosis and cancer patients, which confirmed their connection with the Benker Cubical System. Researchers have also proposed that, like the Curry grid, the Benker grid is the result of cosmic influences and not of radiation from the Earth's interior.[8]

PLANTS AND ANIMALS

Plants and animals are sensitive to geopathic stress: stunted trees with peculiar growths are often shown to be growing over areas of geopathic stress. It is as if their branches are trying to get out of the way of the harmful 'rays'. Horses, dogs, cows, sheep, pigs and mice would not willingly settle over areas of geopathic stress, so if the dog has a favorite spot in your house, it can be identified as a safe zone.

On the other hand, certain plants seem to like geopathic stress, particularly oak trees, firs, pines, elderberry, peach, and mistletoe. Studies in woodland areas show that lightning is far more likely to strike oak trees than, say, beech, which is known to hate geopathic stress zones. Is this telling us these areas are electrically polarized? Von Pohl is emphatic that lightning only strikes at underground water crossings.

Cats too like disturbance zones; so if the cat likes sleeping with you, better move! Some insects such as ants, wasps and beetles thrive over geopathic stress areas; look for ants' nests along the outer walls of your home. Finally, bacteria and viruses also seem to like affected zones.

The pig avoids irradiated areas. In the past, I learned, farmers used pigs to test the land on where they were planning to build a home. Like horses and dogs, pigs are radiation avoiders who seek out harmonic places, so settling where pigs settled was a smart move; the farmers could build on those sites without worrying about harmful influences.

Here is a summary, according to the Swiss Harmony website, of animals and plants which "like" or "dislike" zones of geopathic disturbance.

Animals which seem to like geopathic zones:

> Cats, bees, wasps, hornets, owls, snakes, mosquitoes, ants, moles, turtles, beavers, and most other insects.

Animals which dislike geopathic zones:

> Badgers, ducks, pheasants, foxes, chickens, dogs, mice, guinea pigs, horses, deer, cattle, sheep, swallows, pigs, storks, pigeons, birds and goats.

Plants which seem to like geopathic zones:

> Ash, willow, oak, firs, pine, apricot, larch, poplar, alder, maple, chestnut, plum, peach, ivy, hazelnut, elderberry, mistletoe, sea buckthorn, holly, belladonna, frankincense, juniper, cypress, verbena, marjoram (oregano), herb of grace, wolf trap, fenugreek, calamus, fever clover, thistle, coltsfoot, mugwort, butterbur, nux vomica, foxglove, hemlock, bracken and nettles.

Plants which dislike geopathic zones:

> Apple, birch, pear, beech, pine, lime, apricot, walnut, sycamore, pine, elm, linden and plum, barberry, blackberry, honeysuckle, lilac, blackcurrant, buckthorn, gooseberry, and hawthorn, aster, azalea, begonia, geranium, cactus, mimosa, carnation, primrose, rose, sunflower, violet and vine.

With the exception of asparagus, all vegetables are radiation avoiders.[9]

CHILDREN

Children are great sensitives when it comes to radiation disturbances. If your child when sleeping insists on curling up in a strange corner of the crib, there is probably a very good reason for that. He or she is trying to avoid geopathic stress which is falling on the rest of the crib or bed.

For the child's sake, you had better move the sleeping place to somewhere safer; another part of the room perhaps.

A child who is geopathically stressed may show up as a case with behavior disorders, mood swings, strange illnesses and an inability to concentrate or study.

Other possible signs include restlessness and crying, being tired a lot, listless and lacking energy, constantly trying to get out of bed, (the child sleeps better in other locations, no problem), bed wetting, nightmares, being "spooked", rapid heart beat while lying still in bed and cramps.

By the time she came to stay with me in 1988, Käthe Bachler had already moved on to the concept of dowsing for a "safe spot". She had spent decades dowsing for trouble and that action had, eventually, taken its toll on her health. To save her health, she stopped looking for trouble and started looking for the harmonious places!

Make sure you find your child a safe place.

Käthe, in her many years of research, estimated that 90% of all children with learning difficulties either slept or had a school desk (or both) over negative geopathic stress lines. This potentially has affected and continues to adversely affect millions of children.

DISEASES

Probably any disease can result when the body is put under any kind of stress. Geopathic disturbance is just another kind of stress. The greatest fear is cancer which, although it has many predisposing factors, may only come to fruition in the presence of geopathic disturbance. In other words, geopathic stress is not just the cause but the proverbial straw that breaks the camel's back.

Probably the most common single finding on a geopathically stressed individual is that he or she is resistant to other forms of treatment. Either there will be partial success followed by a relapse, or treatment will fail completely until the individual is removed from the source of stress.

The sleeping place is particularly important; most of the trouble seems to come when the bed lies on a dangerous spot, and although there are theories about protective devices such as amulets, iron bars outside the house, etc., there is little doubt that Käthe Bachler's advice is best: simply move from the danger zone.

SYMPTOMS

The pathological effects of geopathic stresses are not always immediately obvious. Initial symptoms may arise in the form of disorders of the immune system or in an inconspicuous illness that recurs after a short time despite successful therapy and with no apparent explanation. If medication and complementary therapies follow a pattern of temporary improvement followed by subsequent deterioration in spite of further medical or therapeutic care, then geopathic stress should be considered likely.

Any knowledgeable practitioner would immediately suspect this phenomenon on someone who is resistant to what should be an effective and well-established treatment routine.

You should consider the subtle effect of earth radiation as a possible cause. Often, however, at this point damage is extensive and path to recovery may prove long and tedious.

We assume that geopathic stress symptoms only have an effect when we expose ourselves to them for prolonged periods on a daily basis. This applies primarily and especially to exposure in the bedroom. When we sleep we usually relax completely, reducing our body functions to a minimum. This gives the negative effects of earth rays a better chance to influence us. In most cases, these influences manifest as sleep disorders (e.g. restless sleep, insomnia, and frequent waking). Children are particularly susceptible: when they toss and turn in bed, it may be an unconscious effort to find a stress-free place to sleep.

Anyone who wakes up feeling exhausted should investigate his or her sleeping quarters.

If you sleep over a source of geopathic stress, more often than not, you will feel exhausted in the morning and may experience back or neck pain. The effects, of phenomena such as geopathic stresses, are subtle and not everyone notices them readily. Even if we cannot observe them, however, they can still affect our health negatively. Long exposures can lead to serious symptoms and diseases.

Scientists have observed that it can take up to five years for diseases, such as cancer, to become symptomatic. In this context, we can also assume that symptom-free people, who have slept in the same place for seven years or more without having moved their bed, can be assured that they have no unhealthy earth radiation or water veins affecting their bedroom.

Anyone who has a desk job and sits in the same place for eight or more hours a day should explore the possibility of harmful earth radiation. This is especially true if he or she feels tired, drained, or exhausted after work, or frequently suffers from headaches or back pain at the end of the day.

THE ARCHITECTURAL MOVEMENT

I remember an architect making his point by boasting that he could design a house that would result in the divorce of any couple living there. He wasn't talking about geopathic stress, as such, but he was certainly talking about house harmony.

Safe siting of houses and buildings is now no longer the province of the Chinese 'dragon men', as traditional dowsers were called ('dragon's breath' being a Chinese name for good influences). Western architects have begun to take the matter very seriously.

Building biologists, as we might call them, are conventionally trained and understand structure, math and design stresses as well as the next architect. But such experts also acknowledge the existence of geopathic stress and the effect of disturbances within the home and office.

They consider these phenomena self-evident and include their locations in analyses of indoor living and working environments. Additionally, they provide information about how to protect oneself from such effects

This isn't the time to discuss geomancy at length, or the principles of *Feng Shui*, but let us say that other cultures have had a grasp on the importance of this issue is siting buildings, whereas it has been almost entirely ignored in the West.

Farmers have known for centuries that there are certain patches of land, or "badlands", where cattle and other livestock sicken and die. So what happens? Farmers sell the land, developers move in and build houses... and then the humans start to sicken and die too.

Another example of my oft-quoted saying: the commonest cause of death is ignorance!

HOW TO DEAL WITH IT

First, if you are seriously sick, chronically sick or keep relapsing, assume geopathic stress is a possibility. You can try to find an expert dowser. Meantime, move your bed. There is a small chance you will move it into a worse location but that's a better risk than doing nothing, which is *already* making you ill.

You will find two sorts of recommendation from experts, or those who want to sell you something:

1. The first is the idea of changing location. You can move your bed to a safer location, or change bedrooms, or change buildings! If your home is in any other way a "sick building", you may want to consider seriously that last.

2. The second strategy suggested is that of neutralizing the rays in some way. There are lots of devices on the market which you switch on and are claimed to absorb, deflect or modulate unhealthy rays. I wouldn't trust any of them. The person who tells you that you are now "safe" is usually the same person that just sold you a gizmo for several hundred dollars. I don't go for it.

You could go to the trouble of setting up a second dowser, to check that recommendation from your first dowser is working, after all.

Better to take the change of location option, if you can possibly manage it.

CRYSTALS

I don't want to go on record as a fluff, a flake or a woo-woo. But crystals may have something to offer, maybe on a temporary basis. Let me share a few thoughts with you about the use of crystals and their ability to absorb or modify radiation.

There is a large and flourishing healing movement using the properties of crystals to improve body energy.[9] The idea is not as unscientific as you might think.

The ordered structure of crystals has a constant, coherent and reproducible energy vibration. Crystals can be used to transmit, receive, amplify, modulate (transform) or ground (earth) energies. In fact, society as we know it could not exist without these properties of crystals; they are used in radio, television, computers and other electronic devices. The laser relies absolutely on the coherent intense light propagated by ruby crystal.

Crystals can also store energy. If you hit a crystal with a mallet it will give off a brief flash of visible light; the so-called piezo-electric effect of rock crystal. Earth crust pressures do this on natural rock and this may be the source of many strange 'UFO' effects, especially in mountain zones, such as the Andes, where many strange lights are to be seen.[10]

If you consider that you are no more than flesh and blood, then you might reject the idea that crystals can affect you in any way. But if you have been following the main thread of this book and accept that we are a composite 'energy being' then you will readily understand it is quite obvious that crystals can influence our 'aura'. If you put a coherent crystalline structure in your body's energetic field, it is bound to change it in some way; and if you are very sensitive you may even feel this.

Amethyst is known as a receiver. There is no argument. It was used in crystal radio sets. Popes and Bishops have traditionally worn amethyst rings to receive messages 'from above'. Rose quartz was also used in the days of crystal radio, but as a transmitter. Tourmaline is an amplifier, aquamarine a tuner and carnelian a grounder. Amazonite is said to open the higher psychic centers. I didn't know of this property when I once carried some in my pocket and had the strangest other-worldly sensations, until I realized what it was and removed it.

If you suspect geopathic stress (or if you use a computer a great deal), you might like to keep a large crystal close by, to it to absorb some of the radiation. Smoky quartz is said to be best. I sleep with a large chunk of rose quartz next to my bed.

CHAPTER 26

Biology Beyond Death

> *There is nothing in biology yet found that indicates the inevitability of death.*
>
> — Richard P. Feynman

Harking back to the original 1999 theme of "virtual" life and biology, let me introduce some remarkable evidence for living forms in other dimensions than the real (using the word forms perhaps closer to Plato's original definition).

Puzzled? Hang on tight again!

In Chapter 11 the reader will recall I spoke of "biology beyond the skin", meaning that life phenomena are not limited to events taking place inside the body. The whole tenet of this book is that we, as life forms, are not really material in nature but immaterial consciousness, working with information and energy. All matter forms, including our physical bodies, are really just an expression of the energy field that is manifested by a yet higher field of information. The correct path to healing therefore is by energetic readjustment or, even better, by changing the information field (such as with thought power or psychically derived energy).

456

The implications are huge: if we are in part or whole information and energy, we cannot die! That's basic physics. Information and energy cannot be destroyed, not even at the edge of a black hole, if there is such a thing (the so-called event horizon is a place where information is lost and the physical turns into the virtual).

Something must survive beyond death. I'll deal with that in the major part of this chapter. But look: think in the other direction as well. We can exist as information before we are even born. That's what DNA is for. DNA is a pure information carrier; we are born of information!

Today we can make this pre-birth information-self even more real; we can exist in a computer software program before we are even conceived, never mind being born. Patent technology now exists which can predict traits such as eye and skin pigmentation, height and waist size, eye and hair color and, of course, gender.

You don't have to wait for actual conception any more, when amniocentesis will give some clues as to what is coming. You can meet your "virtual" baby! The software has the potential to change the experience of what it means to be a parent.

Of course there are important medical issues here too; otherwise I wouldn't be introducing it in this text. In the future it will be possible to shuffle genes, lay them out and predict—at least approximately—what health issues a child may have when born.

The company with the patent—GenePeeks—intends the screening primarily for unfortunate genetic afflictions, such as Tay-Sachs disease and cystic fibrosis. It will also be possible to screen for more complex inheritance malfunctions, such as schizophrenia (an essentially metabolic and nutritional disorder, not madness). But who knows where it will lead? Perhaps parents will be tempted to screen their virtual offspring for behavioral, social and cosmetology traits; a very bad thing in my view.

And although I am introducing it in a slightly whimsical way, nevertheless, it has a serious side. We can "exist" in a virtual reality before we are born[1]!

Which nicely sets the stage for what follows about death...

VOICES BEYOND THE GRAVE

OK, the book has been novel and interesting so far; maybe a little challenging in places. We have revised our understanding of life upwards and recognize that it has at least some electrical characteristics. Now we come to something truly mind stretching.

Consider the words, "I think the problem is an impedance mismatch into that third transistor in the pre-amp unit... It can be corrected by using a 150 ohm 100 watt resistor in parallel with a 0.0047 micro-farad ceramic capacitor..."

Nothing extraordinary about these words: However they were spoken by a man called Dr. George J. Mueller, an electrical engineer *who had been dead for 14 years*! His speech was captured on an audio tape with a device called a Spiricom by William J. O'Neil, an inventor and electronic technician.

No, I have not lost my mind; I have heard recordings of conversations between O'Neil and Mueller. Dr. Mueller authenticated himself, some-what, by telling researchers in these post-mortem conversations where to find his birth and death certificate records. He even provided his so-cial security number[2]!

If you want to do some authentication yourself, check this pdf file: http://dspace.library.cornell.edu/bitstream/813/3586/17/045_14.pdf [3]

Mueller also explained intimate details of his life and career at the University of Wisconsin and Cornell University, which were later verified.

In the conversation just referred to, Mueller was helping O'Neill im-prove his device for talking with entities from the world of the dead. It's the weirdest imaginable scenario of a ghost helping someone Earthside develop their technique for recording the presence of non-material specters!

If you miss the point then, truly, the world of wonders we have is lost on you and I'm sorry.

Well, more of Mueller later. Meanwhile, let's get directly to grips with the meat of this chapter: electronic communication with "dead" former life entities. Remember, as we go, that physics tells us that energy cannot be created or destroyed, only transformed. If our living self is indeed an energetic entity, it cannot go away but only be transformed.

Communication with the dead is not crazy or impossible if you have a model which makes it realistic. My Virtual Medicine paradigm not only allows for information and energetic entities but makes it quite clear they MUST be out there, by the laws of physics. In this exciting new chapter it is my intention to share abundant evidence that information and energy are superordinate to matter and that it is our TRUE nature; we are not biochemical "stuff".

Those who loudly proclaim it is all nonsense or flim flam (James Randi, for instance), are likely to go down in history along with the pigmy wit of a French scientist, who told his colleagues, "I have investigated Thomas Edison's phonograph and can assure you it is nothing more than clever ventriloquism" (a popular view of the day).

ELECTRONIC VOICE PHENOMENA (EVP)

Face it! "Communicating with the dead" has an automatic disqualifier built in! Those who have engaged deeply in research into voices captured on electronic devices have preferred the more evasive and less dramatic expression "electronic voice phenomena" or EVP for short. It has a surprising history, unknown to most people.

One of the earliest proponents was none other than Thomas Edison, inventor of the electric light. His last major project before his death was building a machine to achieve spirit communication with the dead. His assistant, Dr. Miller Hutchinson, wrote, "Edison and I are convinced that in the fields of psychic research will yet be discovered facts that will prove of greater significance to the thinking of the human race than all the inventions we have ever made in the field of electricity."

As we come around to the understanding that life is essentially electrical and not biochemical, we see how profound his thoughts were.

Edison himself was quoted as saying, "If our personality survives, then it is strictly logical or scientific to assume that it retains memory, intellect, other faculties, and knowledge that we acquire on this Earth. Therefore ... if we can evolve an instrument so delicate as to be affected by our personality as it survives in the next life, such an instrument, when made available, ought to record something."[4]

No matter. We don't need Edison in this story.

In the 1940s, American photographer Attila von Szalay began experimenting with a record cutter and had moderate success capturing spirit voices on phonograph records. In the 1950s he had better success with the newer but still primitive wire recorder. Von Szalay was a psychic and reported hearing voices in the air around him, which may be significant in some way not yet understood.

Working with Raymond Bayless, von Szalay conducted a number of recording sessions with a custom-made apparatus, consisting of a microphone in an insulated cabinet connected to an external recording device and speaker. Szalay reported finding many sounds on the tape that could not be heard on the speaker at the time of recording, some of which were recorded when there was no one in the cabinet[5].

In 1949, Marcello Bacci of Grosseto, Italy, began experimenting in the paranormal. Soon he began recording voices using an old Nordmende vacuum tube radio. A team of spirits developed around his work, and they spoke to him through the radio sounds. People would visit him in his lab at home, and very often their departed loved ones would talk to them through Mr. Bacci's radio.

It is important to observe that Bacci never asked for money or other kinds of financial incentive, which effectively precludes a fraud motive. You could argue he was sincere but an old fool, but I don't think so.

In his experiments, Bacci tuned his radio to the short-wave band, in a frequency ranging between 7 and 9 MHz, in a zone clear from normal radio transmissions. After a few minutes the existing background noise disappears and a typical acoustic signal comes out of the loudspeaker, similar to an approaching wind vortex, repeated three or four times at short intervals. Silence then follows, at the end of which an invisible speaker starts to communicate by establishing with Bacci, or with the people attending the experiment, something like a dialogue. Today, Marcello Bacci still uses the vacuum tube radio[6].

THE HOLY FATHER TUNES IN!

In the early 1950s in Italy, two Catholic priests, Father Ernetti and Father Gemelli, were collaborating on music research. Ernetti was an internationally respected scientist, a physicist and philosopher, and also a music lover. Gemelli was President of the Papal Academy. In other words, neither of these guys were flakes.

On September 15, 1952, while Gemelli and Ernetti were recording a Gregorian chant, a wire on their magnetophone kept breaking. Exasperated, Father Gemelli looked up and asked his (deceased) father for help, as was his habit, though until that day he had never received a direct re-

460

ply. To the two men's amazement, this time, his father's voice, recorded on the magnetophone, answered, "Of course I shall help you. I'm always with you."

The voice addressed Gemelli as Zucchini. It was a nickname his father had teased him with when he was a boy and no one else could have known this.

Surprisingly, His Holiness Pope Pius XII in Rome was very accepting and told Gemelli "You really need not worry about this. The existence of this voice is strictly a scientific fact and has nothing whatsoever to do with spiritism. The recorder is totally objective. It receives and records only sound waves from wherever they come. This experiment may perhaps become the cornerstone for a building for scientific studies which will strengthen people's faith in a hereafter."

Gemelli made certain that the experiment did not go public until the last years of his life, so this story wasn't released until 1990[7].

TAPE RECORDINGS

Things started to hot up in 1959, with the work of Swedish opera singer, artist and film producer Friedrich Jürgensen. He first captured voices on audio-tape while taping bird songs. He was startled when he played the tape back and heard a male voice say something about "bird voices in the night." Listening more intently to his tapes, he heard his mother's voice say in German, "Friedrich, you are being watched. Friedel, my little Friedel, can you hear me?"[8]

Jürgensen said that when he heard his mother's voice, he was convinced he had made "an important discovery." During the next four years, Jürgensen continued to tape hundreds of paranormal voices. He played the tapes at an international press conference and in 1964 published a book in Swedish: *Voices from the Universe* and then another entitled *Radio Contact with the Dead*.

In 1967, Jürgensen's *Radio Contact with the Dead* was translated into German, and Latvian psychologist Dr. Konstantīns Raudive read it skeptically. He visited Jürgensen to learn his methodology, decided to experiment on his own, and soon began developing his own experimental techniques[9].

Like Jürgensen, Raudive too heard the voice of his own deceased mother, who called him by his boyhood name: "Kostulit, this is your mother." Eventually he catalogued tens of thousands of voices, many under strict laboratory conditions.

In 1971, the chief engineers of Pye Records Ltd. decided to do a controlled experiment with Konstantīns Raudive. They invited him to their sound lab and installed special equipment to block out any radio and television signals. They would not allow Raudive to touch any of the equipment.

Raudive used one tape recorder which was monitored by a control tape recorder. All he could do was speak into a microphone. They taped Raudive's voice for eighteen minutes and none of the experimenters heard any other sounds. But when the scientists played back the tape, to their amazement, they heard over two hundred voices on it.

THE SPIRICOM

The next wave of serious investigators in the US were Paul Jones, George W. Meek and Hans Heckman, who together founded the Metascience Foundation. Their intention from the first was to create a system which would allow two-way voice communication with "The Other Side".

Despite stellar exceptions, as described above, the results from various arrangements of tape recorders, microphones, diodes and radios up to this point had been dogged with several problems. The "voices" were very faint, so that only a person with very acute hearing could detect anything at all. Most of the sounds involved very few words, which raises the likelihood of just coincidental sounds, not true speech. The voices spoke very rapidly (about twice as fast as a typical human being speaks) and often it was difficult to distinguish one word from the next.

Excessive background sound, such as tape hiss, static, white noise, cross talk and equipment hum, added to the difficulty of hearing. To make matters even worse, the shortest phrases would often contain words from two or even three languages (Konstantīns Raudive was exceptional in being a multilinguist).

The results of these problems meant that the messages or phrases were so difficult to understand that, if five people were listening, they might have five different opinions as to what was being said.

Not surprisingly, the few parapsychologists who bothered to investigate EVP quickly lost all interest in the subject.

The real breakthrough came when the Metascience Foundation team was joined by a psychically gifted man, William O'Neil, who could not only see and hear spirits, but also knew in-depth electronics. O'Neil recruited several of his spirit friends into the project. One of his invisible colleagues was the spirit of Dr. George Jeffries Mueller, already referred to, who simply appeared in O'Neil's living room one day as a semi-materialized spirit, and announced that he was there to assist in the project of Meek and O'Neil.

It became a rather astonishing collaboration with the "dead" Doc Mueller helping Bill O'Neil on Earth design a new piece of electromagnetic equipment that would convert spirit voices into audible voices. Appropriately christened Spiricom, the new device was a set of tone generators and frequency generators that emitted 13 tones spanning the range of the adult male voice[10].

If you think I have now completely lost contact with reality and reason let me assure you I have heard a recording of Mueller and O'Neil in dialogue myself and am convinced that we have another breakthrough in our understanding of reality. This is totally consistent with my model of *Medicine Beyond* and to me only serves to further underline my view that the Universe is a playground of delights and discoveries. There is so much we don't know and so much yet to discover.

One thing is clear: we survive as energetic and information entities and to repeat my oft-quoted aphorism, advanced physics not only says that it could happen but that it *must* happen.

THE SPIRIT OF SHARING

One big difference between the attitude of these researchers and the craven self-seeking approach of regular scientists is that they view knowledge as a universal property. Meek and the others have gone out of their way to make all their discoveries public property.

In 1982, G. W. Meek made a trip around the world to distribute tape recordings of 16 excerpts of communications between O'Neil and Mueller. He also distributed a 100-page technical report giving wiring diagrams, photos, technical data and guidelines for research by others.

In the notable words of George Meek, "All researchers affiliated with Metascience Foundation during the ten years of world-wide study of problems and potentials of electronic communication with the so-called "dead" have shared a common goal. They want the fruit of their labors and financial contributions to be made freely available to people of all races all over the world.

"But please note! Everything in the cosmos is energy of one sort or another, and although all energies can be used for good or for evil, it is our hope that the hundreds of individuals and organizations which will carry these developments forward in the decades ahead will use them only for the good of all mankind"[11].

The Foundation did not file any patents in any countries on their many inventions. The name *Spiricom* was never trademarked.

Nevertheless, Meek issues a solemn warning: "If any individuals acting alone or as part of a corporate entity endeavor to use these inventions solely for money-making purposes, or to the detriment of any person, they are herewith forewarned: They should know that the first stop for them, after they sooner or later shed their physical bodies, will be at the bottom of the Lowest Astral Plane".

Ouch!

PHONE CALLS FROM THE OTHER SIDE

If somebody had suggested, decades ago, that I freely accept the idea of dead people contacting the living via telephone, I would have been resistant, I admit.

But in the context of this other irrefutable work in EVP, it's not so hard to believe. In 1979 D. Scott Rogo catalogued them in his book, "Telephone Calls from the Dead"[12].

Possibly the most vivid series of calls were those received from Konstantīns Raudive himself. Raudive told several Earthside colleagues that since his death it has been his calling to continue the development of EVP systems from the other side of the veil. He called researcher Mark Macy by phone seven times after his death, and on one occasion the two chatted for nearly 15 minutes before the contact ended.

On another occasion Raudive spoke to Sarah Estep, who had founded the American Association of EVP in 1982. In her shocked surprise, Sarah lapsed to social protocols and said "How are you?" Raudive replied "As well as can be expected for a dead man!"

Is this stretching things too far? Well, why not information systems over the phone (non-local)? Albert Abrams stumbled across it in 1922, remember (page 132). Time and again it comes back to this man of genius and vision.

COMPUTER ENTITIES

How many of us have been convinced at times that our computer was infected with some kind of demonic life energy that keeps losing files and corrupting data? Well, maybe it was literally true.

Take the case of English school teacher Ken Webster and his haunted computer. Beginning in the autumn of 1984, a series of poltergeist events took place, focused on the kitchen area, including the stacking of objects, noises, marks on the walls and 'thrown' objects. What made this visitation different was the appearance of messages on a word processor.

Personal computers were only just appearing in 1984 and, as a school teacher Webster had borrowed a primitive BBC `B' computer from school. These machines had around 32k of memory, a word processor on an installed chip and the only means of saving files was to a floppy disk on an external drive. No networking, no modem, definitely no Internet.

One evening, the computer was accidentally left on and when Webster and his girlfriend Debbie returned there was a 'message', a poem of sorts. It was treated as a joke of course, but saved to disk anyway.

A different machine was borrowed on another occasion and another inexplicable communication was received.

This time the language had an archaic flavor, seemingly of Elizabethan English. The tone of this second message was threatening and Webster felt the joke was now in bad taste.

In an attempt to catch the obvious hoaxer, yet another computer was brought home. Its disk was examined for preloaded material (there was little software in those days, in any case; hackers and other geeks were a long way into the future). Webster and his girlfriend checked the locks on the house and left the computer running in the kitchen. Another message appeared in the same quirky 'mock Tudor' style.

Webster decided to type in a reply and, astonishingly, this was met with a further response. Two-way communications began in earnest with a male entity who declared himself to be one Tomas Harden, which lasted over a period of sixteen months.

Various investigators have offered no reasonable explanation (beyond a true electronic incarnation). But Debbie Oakes, Webster's girlfriend, seems pivotal: neither the mysterious moving objects nor cyber messages from "beyond" occurred unless she was in the vicinity.

Time and again I have learned that discarnate entities need the energies of others in order to "perform" their tricks. Poltergeist activity is known to be a telekinetic effect that surrounds one particular person (usually undergoing some kind of emotional turmoil). Maybe she was the fuel tank of this computer ghost?

Given the primitive standard of the hardware, it is not possible to offer as an explanation that these computers were capable of developing AI. So maybe the presence in the machine was none other than Mr. Tomas Harden, deceased. Was he angry at the couple for occupying his house? Or lasciviously inclined towards Ms. Debbie Oakes?

The whole story is told in Webster's book, now out of print and selling for black market prices: The Vertical Plane, Grafton, London, 1989[13].

The manifestation of an apparently ancient spirit in modern guise seems remarkably similar to another computer possession story. Reverend Jim Peasboro, from Savannah, GA not only believes in computers being possessed by evil energies, he has written a book about it entitled *The Devil in the Machine*. According to him, today's thinking machines have enough space on their hard drives to accommodate Satan or one of his cronies. "Any PC built after 1985 has the storage capacity to house an evil spirit," the minister confirmed.

Don't laugh.

Whereas I respectfully submit that Peasboro's obsession with Lucifer has more to do with his own world view, I see no reason, in the light of many other examples of contact we are sharing here, to doubt that some kind of malicious energy was seeking a confrontation with this man of the Church.

On the day in question Peasboro was sitting at the keyboard of one of his parishioners, investigating the possibility of a possession, when to his surprise, an artificial-intelligence program fired up—without him clicking it on. Then according to the reverend's testimony, the machine began mocking him by typing out the words 'Preacher, you are a weakling and your God is a damn liar.' (It happens often that voices from the other side are vicious, mean, cruel or threatening).

After that the device went haywire and started printing out what appeared to be gobbledygook.

"I later had an expert in dead languages examine the text," the minister said. "It turned out to be a stream of obscenities written in a 2,800-year-old Mesopotamian dialect!"[14]

Peasboro estimates that one in ten computers in America are host to evil spirits, and advises anyone suspecting that their computer is possessed to consult a clergyman, or, if the computer is still under warranty, to have the hard drive replaced. Nice to know our immortal souls are being protected from satanic viruses by this cybercop!

Stop laughing at the back there!

VOICES ON RADIO

There have been well-documented instances of strange apparitional voices coming over on radio and TV. I remember one startling occasion back in the 1960s, this happened while I was watching TV. The BBC, I remember, apologized for the "technical hitch", so it was not my imagination at work. The fact is that it would take some massive energetic source to take over the BBC channel, even for a few seconds. Who, what, or from where, could such a hijack take place?

These events are naturally dismissed as quirks of the ionosphere that somehow result in distant channels breaking into the local broadcast (the UFO people, predictably, think it's aliens trying to make contact from craft hovering near the Earth).

Probably intrusive transmissions do happen. But I believe that many instances of genuine communication are being lost because nobody is thinking along EVP lines. It's almost automatic to dismiss such events as a technical anomaly and not even consider other possibilities.

However, there is good reason not to dismiss all events so lightly.

Let me share a historical and well-documented contact which defies science. The Dawkins and other rigid conventional scientists can only fall back on trite explanations like "mass hysteria" and "technical hitch" (since their world will not admit the obvious simple explanation: that these events actually occurred in the terms described).

In 1983 Hans Otto Koenig appeared on a popular radio program on Europe's largest radio station, Radio Luxembourg, featuring his extremely low frequency oscillators, with lights in the ultraviolet and infrared range. The program host, Rainer Holbe, had Koenig set up his equipment under close supervision of the station engineers. One of the engineers asked if a voice could come through in direct reply to a question, and a discarnate voice quickly replied over the system, "We hear your voice. Otto Koenig makes wireless contact with the dead."

Stunned, Rainer Holbe addressed the millions of listeners across Europe, "I tell you, dear listeners of Radio Luxembourg, and I swear by the life of my children, that nothing has been manipulated. There are no tricks. It is a voice, and we do not know from where it comes." The station issued an official statement afterwards. Every step of the program was carefully supervised. Staff and engineers were convinced that the voices were paranormal.

Numerous other experiments with radio have had similar success, inexplicable in any other simple terms than contact from other planes of consciousness.

VIDEO FROM "THE OTHER SIDE"!

Well, why not? Given that discarnate beings can leave audio traces on a magnetic tape, why not images on a VCR?

Klaus Schreiber began to receive spirit images on his TV set in 1985, including likenesses of Albert Einstein, Austrian actress Romy Schneider, and various departed family members, especially his two deceased wives and daughter Karin, with whom he was particularly close. I have seen these recordings and can assure readers they are not artefactual or just "interpretations". I wasn't sure about the Einstein likeness; all I will admit is it looked very like him. The Romy Schneider image was very convincing.

The technique here is rather special. It involves pointing a video camera at a television monitor, which is playing the image captured by the camera. So the camera records its own output; a kind of feedback loop. This

468

is so like the foundation of fractals and Ludwig van Bertalanffy's natural living "systems" that I concede its plausibility right away.

What happens is that the swirling cloud of energies captured on screen gradually resolves into a recognizable image. Sometimes these move; sometimes the eyes or mouth of the "ghost" image will open or close. It's very eerie to watch.

Maggy Harsch-Fischbach and her husband Jules Harsch of Luxembourg began to get spectacular voice contacts through radio systems early in their experiments in 1985. A high-pitched, computer-like voice came through their radios with growing frequency to share amazing insights with the couple.

The voice identified itself as a conscious entity, that was never human, never animal, and never in a physical body. "I am not energy and I am not a light being. You are familiar with the picture of two children walking across a bridge, and behind them is a being who protects them. That's what I am to you, but without the wings. You can call me Technician, since that is my role in opening up this communication bridge. I am assigned to Planet Earth."

He lived up to his promise.

The small apartment inhabited by the Harsch-Fischbachs became a place of astounding manifestations, as visiting scientists and reporters from all over the world saw spirit images flash across the TV screen and heard long discourses by various deceased personalities through radio sounds. The supposed spirit of Nelson D. Rockefeller told German physicist Ernst Senkowski, "The Mahatmas are a reality."

Nineteenth-Century chemist Henri Ste. Claire de Ville appeared and told American and German researchers, "It is our job as well as your job to set fire to minds—to set fire to minds in your world, and in that moment to try to master time."

Fritz Malkhoff and Adolf Homes began EVP experiments independently in 1987, and each began to get spirit voices on tape rather quickly. In a few months, they learned of each other's work, and they became colleagues and friends. During their experiments, small voices on radio quickly developed persistent, clear voices.

Then they began to receive phone calls from spirits, and in 1988 they set up Malkhoff's computer in the house of Adolf Homes, where they did most of their experiments. They posed a short question, and two days later a short answer appeared miraculously on their computer screen.

THE OLD TIMERS COME AROUND AGAIN!

Homes received spirit images on his television and messages on his computer screen rather routinely. One morning in 1994, Homes climbed out of bed in a trance, aimed a video camera at his television, and received the first color picture from the spirit worlds. It was a picture of deceased EVP pioneer Friedrich Jürgensen.

At the same time, a message from Jürgensen printed itself out on Homes' computer, stating, "This is Friedel from Sweden. I am sending you a self-portrait... The projection since January 17, 1991, has been in the quantum of spacelessness and timelessness. All your and our thoughts have their own electromagnetic reality which does not get lost outside the space-time structure... Consciousness creates all form...."

In other words, Jürgensen seems to be reassuring us that we do, as physics predicts, survive as an electromagnetic reality.

This of course says nothing about the true nature of the soul and I have no wish here to intrude on the religious beliefs of any reader or group.

Where is all this leading? Well, one of the fascinating developments is that the first generation of pioneers, as they aged and died, have started to come back through EVP systems and continue their work from the "other" perspective!

INSTRUMENTAL TRANSCOMMUNICATION

In 1995, Macy went on to join with other researchers and found INIT, the International Network for Instrumental Transcommunication. At the same time EVP took on a new label: ITC or "instrumental transcommunication".

INIT members report regular and helpful contact from spirit friends. The most inspiring and helpful information came from a group of timeless beings who said they had never been in physical bodies, but had observed human development over many thousands of years.

This group of entities told INIT on more than one occasion that simply opening the door to the spirit worlds can be dangerous, but researchers who work together and dedicate their efforts to higher human principles will receive ethereal guidance and protection.

As years passed, the entity Technician and his six ethereal friends, along with a team of more than 1,000 spirit beings who had once lived on Earth, shared vast and astonishing information with INIT members through computers, telephones, radios, and other technical media. The ethereal beings said they had accompanied our world for many thousands of years and had come close six times when the Earth had reached a crossroads leading either to a dark age or to a period of enlightenment.

This, they said, was the seventh time, and they wished to establish a lasting bridge between Earth and their formless realm of wise, loving consciousness. ITC research would be the means by which to establish that bridge.

That being so, I would suggest that this chapter covers matters of grave importance to us all.

ON A DARKER NOTE

INIT was told that contact with spirits are made possible by a "contact field", which is a pool of thoughts and attitudes of all researchers collaborating on an ITC project (to me, this sounds like a Sheldrake morphic field). When the thoughts and attitudes of all those entities on both sides of the veil are in harmony, these entities claimed, the contact field was clear. The discarnate entities could then see into our world and work with our equipment.

When doubts, fears, envy, resentment, and other troubled feelings created dissonance, the contact field becomes cloudy.

Unfortunately, that's what happened to INIT. After several years, troubles developed. Some members began working with scientists in their home country, who predictably dismissed the validity of this research. The "scientists" told the INIT members they should be more skeptical of the contacts their colleagues were reporting. So some members began to express doubts publicly about the legitimacy of other members' contacts. There were shocks and betrayals, leading to breakdown of camaraderie.

As a result of the dissent, the contact field became cloudy, and the miracles of ITC virtually dried up. Mark Macy reports that messages of great depth and import have not been reported from any researchers since the year 2000, to the best of his knowledge. Perhaps those on the other side are annoyed with us? (My humor, not Macy's).

Nowadays the American Association of Electronic Voice Phenomena has taken over center stage (http://www.aaevp.com). I notice that the website has been taken over by Association TransCommunication, without any announcement as to their connection with AAEVP (retrieved 4-3-15 at 11.55 am PST).

DO YOU WANT TO TRY?

Anybody can do this. It could be your first real reach into dimensions beyond this one. It's certainly a novel way to surf reality! I've extracted the following beginner's advice from Mark Macy's website at www.worlditc.org

First, says Macy, when conducting EVP experiments take a sober, serious approach and focus on the positive. Experiment only when you're in a happy, enthusiastic, unfettered frame of mind.

Use an audiocassette recorder with an external microphone and a source of mild white noise (such as a radio tuned to the hiss between stations). Place the microphone a few feet from the radio. Turn on the tape recorder and introduce the session.

Name the date and time and ask a few short questions, then replay the sequence and listen closely. A set of earphones can help make the short, faint voices more audible.

Some people get voices on their very first try; others work for months before getting their first voice. Konstantīns Raudive, remember, experimented diligently for three months before getting his first voice. Yet he went on to record, analyze and collect more than 70,000 voices, many under strict laboratory conditions.

EVP researchers all agree you must conduct voice experiments on a regular basis. In that way you grow your "contact field" and the voices will become louder and clearer (again, this is consistent with Sheldrake's teaching about habits and usage "building" morphic fields). I see nothing in Sheldrake's theory that precludes the idea of contributions from beings from other dimensions.

Always remember, as I said about the EAV machines (Chapter 15, the psychokinetic effect), you are part of the equipment. This isn't a matter of building self-delusion. Other people can hear the voices quite clearly too, when the recordings are good.

Be warned: Entities may occasionally menace researchers and perhaps announce that the experimenter will have bad experiences very soon. Troubled voices sometimes predict illness for the experimenter, relatives or friends, and even death. Words of hate and pessimism, destruction and violence can sometimes be heard.

My own belief is that screwed up and out of balance entities are no more powerful than everyday inept and dysfunctional humans. They can accomplish nothing, unless you react with a negative state of mind and concede your own power to them.

The only possible danger arises if you yourself take it on board, like a suggestible hypnotic subject. Therefore do not enter this communication domain if you do not have a point of balance. You need to be strongly centered within your own energetic being.

BETTER EQUIPMENT

As you get more experienced, you can consider technical improvements.

Germanium Diodes

Konstantīns Raudive himself devised a way to improve EVP voices with a germanium diode instead of a microphone connected to the audio input of a standard tape recorder. Solder a 1N914 germanium diode (available from Radio Shack) to a jack, or male plug that will fit the microphone input of your tape recorder. Plug this modified jack into the recorder, turn the volume up all the way, and start recording. With this setup, the recorder will be unable to record human voices or other Earthside sounds in the room; only "spirit voices".

Radios

Discarnate voices have intellect and information but lack energy. They have to parasitize existing energy. You can provide that, using white noise ("static") between channels on a radio tuner. In fact I have been told (by humans, not voices!) that at a pinch you can use the sound of running water. Since learning that, many transcendental poetic experiences near flowing streams and the sea have suddenly made sense to me!

Spirit voices apparently find it easier to create their voice from existing voice fragments than to fashion one out of blank white noise. So tuning in to foreign language broadcasts is a good idea, it makes it easier to distinguish between the radio noises and possible spirit voices you receive in your language.

Again, at a pinch, operators can simply talk inconsequentially to each other and then play back the recording, listening for superimposed voices.

Reel-to-Reel Tape recorders

Some people claim to get better results with a reel-to-reel tape recorder than with the more common cassette recorder. On cassette recorders it's good to have a "cue" or "review" function so that while the recorder is in "play" mode you can press down a bit on the "reverse" or "fast forward" button to move quickly a few inches backward or forward on the tape, then resume playing simply by releasing the "reverse" or "fast forward" button. Make sure it has a rev counter, so that you can quickly get back to any significant sections.

Computers

Some voice experimenters today are using computers with attached microphones instead of tape recorders. Advantages of the computer, says Macy, include clarity of the voices, immediate playback, reproduction without loss of quality, and easy transportability of sound files to the internet. The drawback of computers is the fact that voice files take up a lot of memory.

Digital Pocket Recorders

That last word in EVP technology, apparently, is the Sony ICD B7 digital pocket recorder. I got mine for only $50, so the cost of getting involved is not high!

YouTube

Finally, if you don't want to go to all this trouble, check out what other people have been doing in this field. If you go to YouTube and type in EVP, you will get numerous videos of people who are claiming to have recorded both auditory and visual contact with discarnate entities. You will have to make up your own mind which of these you want to accept as genuine and which seem to be hoaxes.

IS THERE ANY EXPLANATION?

I know my readers will be expecting an explanation of some sort: so what do I think is going on?

You will realize that what follows is mere opinion. But it is based on decades of research, the opinions of other good people, direct experience and a long but secret history.

There are discarnate beings out there, for sure. But I think the vast majority of EVP is created by what I call *psychic debris*. My colleague Dr. Samuel Sagan MD calls them *astral fragments*. In a nutshell, an astral fragment or debris is a piece of the discarded energy body that the soul left behind upon death. It keeps replaying some of its former efforts and emotions, which can have a really strong effect on sensitive people. Mostly, of course, it's not a good residual effect.

These psychic fragments are imprinted on the physical and, since they are immaterial (no time), they potentially last forever. Or at least until discovered and erased by a secret technique we use in Supernoetics™.

Their fragmented and incomplete nature would explain the very limited life and consciousness aspects of these residual entities. Mostly we get sound bites, not conversations. Long discourses, like George J. Mueller's discussions with William J. O'Neil, are the exception, in every sense. Mostly EVP contacts are a few words or phrases at most. They are repetitive and limited. I think of them more like someone leaving a long-playing record running and it's stuck in a groove (no idea what the modern electronic music version of that would be!)

There's energy to turn the record player, there are a few key phrases that remain. These are played over and over.

It's the same with visuals. If you have properly followed what I have been teaching in this book, you will now understand that our body *in life* is only a projection from consciousness. It's real enough in this universe of course but, like everything around us, it's only there because we put it there. Hardly surprising then that this "projection" can be left running on automatic and the being still projects its form into our reality, even when departed.

The important thing to grasp is that these fragments of identities are no longer animated by a live spiritual being. As I said, the soul has departed; but the machinery and circuits it left behind are still running on automatic. A "ghost" is no more than energized psychic debris, left behind by a former departed soul.

Now don't think that Prof. has finally "lost it" in these last few pages. Trust me, this is real. To quote Hamlet (Act 1 scene 5): "There are more things in heaven and earth, Horatio, than are dreamt of in your philosophy." But if you'd told me, forty years ago, I would be writing this kind of stuff in a medical textbook, I would have thought you were crazy!

WHAT HAS ALL THIS TO DO WITH MEDICINE BEYOND?

You may think I have spent too long on a curious byway in knowledge. Ghosts and discarnate beings tell us more about the nature of life itself but nothing about healing.

I disagree. This is confirmation, if confirmation were needed, of the non-material aspect of our biology and being. It's not possible to demonstrate something non-physical, using physical means, which is where science falls down; it's interested *only* in the physical: whereas we need the psychic to investigate the psychic and non-material reality.

Moreover, psychic healing is no longer troubling or weird in the *Medicine Beyond* model. In fact it's a given; it can be predicted.

One of the common themes I meet in my contact with many peoples and races in connection with my profession is that of "spirit helpers". Remarkable psychic healings have been achieved, that defy all scientific rationale. Often the gifted individuals who are capable of these miracles of recovery speak of other presences, perhaps with more power than they have alone, and which aided the recovery (I almost wrote recovery process but these events seem to me more like transformations than mere recovery through process).

Those who have been healed sometimes report the sensation of several pairs of hands working on their body. Healers too often describe the feeling of extra hands working alongside their own.

476

I have not introduced this dimension before but on reviewing the work for this edition I think it is only right that this element is now considered, because of the technological nature of these apparitions. They are "virtual beings" which come to us in an electromagnetic energy format. Their role in healing may soon become apparent and I for one would like to help birth it.

We have seen from their comments that deceased entities are willing to work with us in evolving better functioning communications equipment. Well, why not better healing devices and procedures? It's probably already happening but largely unrecognized.

Who knows: Royal Raymond Rife may show up and tell us more about his amazing technical system for healing. I hope so!

In keeping with the forward-looking theme of these final chapters, I would like to suggest that it may be the next big direction we go to in health sciences and healing devices.

In fact conscious discarnate entities may already be controlling the information output of devices like the MORA machine and so-called "conscious interface" devices (EPFX, SCIO and similar). For all we know, this could be a primary mode of mechanism. Compare that idea with what I was saying about Eigen-field in Chapter 23.

SKEPTICS

Of course there are skeptics, to whom everything outside (their) consensus reality is anathema.

Brian Regal in *Pseudoscience: A Critical Encyclopedia* has written, "A case can be made for the idea that many EVPs are artifacts of the recording process itself with which the operators are unfamiliar. The majority of EVPs have alternative, nonspiritual sources; anomalous ones have no clear proof they are of spiritual origin."[15]

Regal, incidentally, provides no evidence for his claim. It is an opinion, nothing more, disguised as scientific objectivity.

According to the dissenters, says Wikipedia, there are a number of simple scientific explanations that can account for why some listeners to the static on audio devices may believe they hear voices, including radio interference and the tendency of the human brain to recognize patterns in random stimuli[16].

Some recordings, it is claimed, though again without any evidence whatever, may be hoaxes created by frauds or pranksters[17].

Such opinions clearly come from individuals who have never actually listened to key recordings. The words are as clear as day on many such and could not possibly be described as random sounds.

My position remains the logical one: if even one instance of EVP is authentic, all criticisms are off and a proper explanation of electronic contact with entities beyond this realm is required: Because even one transmission from the dead changes all of accepted reality.

Not that it is so strange, when you embrace the new electric universe model I have outlined in detail, in which consciousness, life energies and electromagnetic forces combine to create our sensate world.

SPECIAL NOTE

A correspondent of mine alerted me to an interesting story and I would like to share it before closing.

The Rubinoos pop group were recording at Ramport Studios, Battersea (London). They had recorded much of their second album, *Back To The Drawing Board* and were cutting basic tracks for later use. But when listening to playbacks in the headphones, there came an eerie kind of moaning and screaming, which made the tracks quite unusable.

It turned out that the building had been used for executions (hangings) and perhaps other unpleasant goings on.

I got this story from group founder Tommy Dunbar (personal communication).[18]

LAST WORD, IN EVERY SENSE

Let me leave the closing words of this chapter to long-dead Swedish film producer Friedrich Jürgensen. He told eager experimenters in Germany, watching through the television of Adolf Homes, "Every being is a unity of spirit and body that cannot be separated on Earth or in spirit. The only difference is the fact that the physical body disintegrates and in its place comes the astral body.

"Our message (from this side) is to tell you that your life goes on. Any speculations on how an individual will experience it are bound to be limited in accuracy. All your scientific, medical or biological speculations miss the mark of these realities. What serves as 'real' to science is not close to reality in the broad picture. It is no more than a word in a book."

I couldn't agree more. That's what I have been telling you for the last 26 chapters!

CHAPTER 27

Electronic Kundalini

*For the last four hundred years, an unstated
assumption of science is that human intention
cannot affect what we call "physical reality." Our
experimental research of the past decade shows
that, for today's world and under the right conditions, this assumption is no longer correct. We
humans are much more than we think we are
and psychoenergetic science continues to expand
the proof of it.*

- William A. Tiller

In the original closing chapter of *Virtual Medicine*, which I also entitled
Electronic Kundalini, I allowed myself a number of wild speculations.
It's amazing how much of my new medical paradigm has already come
true.

One of my original subtitles for the book was "Chinese medicine
meets Dr. Kildare in cyberspace..." meaning that traditional energy

models of healing were now being joined with conventional medicine, using computer or "virtual" devices.

What was then just a joke phrase has actually become real. Health and diagnosis has moved into computers; medical imaging and testing has moved into computers; even aspects of human psyche have moved into computers and, no, I don't just mean the Turing Test has fallen. I mean people are interacting with machines to the point where they are fast becoming machines, to the delight of the strong AI lobby.

Humankind seems to be being drawn into cyberspace, in the way that a bug is drawn into a UV zapper, totally unable to prevent itself from committing suicide. We could no more pull back now than fly to the moon by flapping our arms!

One can ask penetrating questions, like: is our cellphone now actually a part of our mind? Is it just an extension of our psyche, or forever a device beyond the brain and skin, that does not really hold our thoughts and communications? It all seems so inevitable today that people have begun to assume that we are, after all, just a complex set of electronic relays in that squidgy organ inside our skulls called a brain. Some people not only think that but would attack or ridicule anyone who says it may not be true!

Yet repeatedly in this text, as in the earlier book, I have shared valuable research and insights, pointing to the fact that we are more than just "meat", with electrical impulses running through the brain, that fool us into the illusion of a self and soul. There is a far bigger picture, where science becomes almost scriptural, in which consciousness flourishes its amazing powers beyond the physical matrix and can adopt any viewpoint; I have likened this to being on the "outside", peeping into reality from a distance.

We exist outside the skull and we are not limited by our skin! We are the bringers of our own reality. The only reason we continue with the insupportable belief that everything is physical "stuff", is that's what is hammered into us from birth. As kids we knew better but we are "taught" what's real, instead of simply experiencing what's real. They knock it out of us and we have to give up playing powerful creators, who can invent worlds, beings and games.

So we begin the rest of our lives in the confines of a material reality, which we have learned not to question. Scientists, who in truth ought to know better, spend uncountable hours and waste billions of dollars studying how the brain creates our identity and experience. I call this brain-base being (the B3 model).

Nothing could be further from the truth of things than the adoption of a cold, mechanistic world which our education demands. The paradox has become that *we are the reality and the old mechanical universe is a scientific delusion*, which is rapidly collapsing under closer scrutiny. Once we were called "the ghost in the machine"; the universe was the machine, we had no impact on it whatever. In the 1930s Oxford don Gilbert Ryle coined this phrase but he meant it with derision (in much the same way that Fred Hoyle coined the term "Big Bang" because he thought it was total nonsense).

Today, as Professor of Mathematical Physics, Paul Davies jokes, "We can see that Ryle was right to dismiss the notion of the ghost in the machine—not because there is no ghost, but because there is no machine"[1].

There is only us and our conscious perceptions. Objectivity has been found not to exist in the way that science once dreamed it did. We are left with only an experiential universe, in which we are the prime participants.

DOCTORS MUST FOLLOW

To me these new horizons are significant, since it is a doctor's role to be knowledgeable in these important matters. One could not presume to be an expert in health and yet cling to the view that we are merely physical entities, with thoughts and feelings solely attributable to a 3-pound jelly organ in the skull. A doctor must know and practice according to precepts that are current, not just the fashion. He or she cannot ignore the role that the new physics plays in our lives.

The word "revolution" is perhaps overworked. But there is no question that physics is in turmoil and upheaval, with exciting new finds sweeping away comfortable and established paradigms. A better word would be a *transformation* and it is affecting our entire mental, spiritual and scientific landscape.

In that sense, *Medicine Beyond* is a small light in the new dawn. It was written in the hope that, by sticking fairly close to the scientific model, it would partly persuade those who think otherwise that there are many strange and vital manifestations of life which are not merely illusions.

In fact, using the equipment I have described in this book, one cannot fail to be impressed by the obviousness of mysterious forces, beyond the bounds of ordinary physics that interplay with our lives and give it far more meaning than just the foraging and procreation of a carbon dioxide engine.

I have found the kind of devices I have described to be not merely diagnostic tools but they are in a sense learning systems. If only medical students were shown some of the properties of tissue and pathogens that are seen clearly when using interactive diagnostic devices of the type outlined in these pages, it would give them a totally different orientation in their chosen profession. They would gain respect for the divine, the supernormal and the simply awesome characteristics of nature and life. To see how the human energies kick over when a pathogen is merely brought close to the body (but not touching it) I always feel is to teach us something about ourselves and our true nature, not just the mechanism of disease.

Most of these devices are not absolute detectors, in the precise sense that a blood test or an x-ray radiograph is. I make this point repeatedly: The individual practitioner influences the results considerably by his or her understanding and knowledge system.

Far from making *Medicine Beyond* unscientific, it means that we share some of the interpretation difficulties of modern physics. Indeed Niels Bohr's extreme view of quantum mechanics, the so-called 'Copenhagen Interpretation' (Bohr was Danish), is that one cannot detach objectivity from the measurer. There simply is no means of contacting the objective, even if such a thing were to actually exist; if we touched it, even for a moment, then it would no longer be objective, but would have become subjective. So we may as well forget about it.

Add to that my friend Bill Tiller's shocking revelation, that one cannot devise any scientific experiment in which the investigator's intentions can be excluded from the discovery process, and you will readily see the difficulty faced by scientists who insist that consciousness is an irrelevant distraction[2].

They are trying to test something which does not exist and, by all appearances, can never exist: a world without human minds.

Instead of the imagined world of "stuff", we have a deeper process reality, in which objects, phenomena, forces and energies are represented by reproduction copies (like faxes) we call "information fields". The real "nature" of nature is at a hidden level, which will not be accessed unless we look for it. There is an "otherness" to our world that is magical and inspiring if we enter it. Instead of the Simple-IS of high school physics, I call this newer, greater awareness Deep-IS, meaning deeper than materiality. Let me repeat again the insight of Nobel laureate Carlo Rubbia quoted in Chapter 4: *our universe is only one billionth matter; the rest is energy and information.*

The well-trained doctor of the future may begin to talk a little bit like the shamans or magicians of old. I don't think that means we will never use antibiotics, anesthetics, lasers, MRI scanners or the other paraphernalia of modern high-tech medicine. But I hope that, through time, the adoption of the techniques and (even more importantly) the principles outlined in this book will become the mainstay of medical practice.

It has been the purpose of this text all through to avoid everything that is New Age sugar cake and concentrate on verifiable facts and objective experience, albeit novel ones. This is for a very good reason; it is necessary to demystify these life phenomena and get rid of the silliness and supposition that science is somehow 'wicked' and that everything that matters and is nourishing in healing is somehow superior, other worldly (even 'divine') and forever beyond Man's ken. This mystical and fairy story rhetoric is proving a serious barrier to wider acceptance of this knowledge by the scientific and medical community.

In fact in the original book, I posed a very pertinent set of questions:

1. Is there any separation between the supernatural or divine and our reality?

2. If there is a boundary, is it sharp (in other words one can never mix with the other) or blurry?

3. And finally: can the boundary be moved or is it cemented in place?

I can finally come down heavily with one answer for all three questions, which is that the division is entirely artificial. There is no such thing as supernatural or divine—just that which is beyond present knowing. As we learn more and more, we are overrunning what was supposed to be God's territory. The fact is that *everything is spiritual or divine*, from our own origins, to the structure and make up of the so-called material universe.

CHILDHOOD'S END

It is not conceited to aver that perhaps Mankind has at last begun to expand our awareness to the point where we can begin to move out into the bigger cosmos. It may be that what we have clung to as religion thus far is nothing more than childish metaphors for a nascent reality that has been dimly perceived and yet just beyond our grasp.

We need to think again about consciousness and use it to reframe science. I would like to see a gentler, more intelligent science, which recognizes that the properties of the physical universe (physics) are the same as those of the mind. Indeed, as long ago as 1911 the now beloved 11th edition of *Encyclopedia Britannica*[3] stated plainly that space and time have no meaning outside the mind and that these two elements of reality would only be understood when the mind's role in manifesting them became known.

If this comes about then we can stop thinking of ourselves as lowly admirers of a vast and almost incomprehensible cosmos but take our place as part of the very process of creation. Far from being overwhelmingly large, it becomes a testimony, a statement of the power of our consciousness and the immanent, ineffable qualities of our Being.

This blurring of the boundary between the properties mind and theoretical physics was the theme of a general public wake up in the late 1970s, occasioned by popular texts such as *The Dancing Wu Li Masters* by Gary Zukav and *The Tao of Physics* by Fritjof Capra. Both authors brought together the existing knowledge in the mysterious world of quantum physics and showed how closely our present understanding of the supposedly objective and 'real' world paralleled the postulated creation of existence described long ago in the Sanskrit Vedas and the Pali canon. One was indeed impressed by the striking convergence of two (apparently) alien intellectual streams.

It was, as I said earlier, a matter of science catching up with esoteric wisdom, rather than the other way round. I think Einstein's metaphor is even more apposite:

'...creating a new theory is not like destroying an old barn and erecting a skyscraper in its place. It is rather like climbing a mountain, gaining new and wider views, discovering unexpected connections between our starting point and its rich environment. But the point from which we started out still exists and can be seen, although it appears smaller and forms a tiny part of our broad view gained by the mastery of the obstacles on our adventurous way up.'

The truth is we have climbed a long way up the mountain; it's just that the diehards won't admit to anything that disturbs their comfortable mindset. *Medicine Beyond* is about the view from on high and I sincerely hope it makes many old stagers uncomfortable. They give others a hard time for what they arrogantly call "voodoo science"; it's time to rattle their cage!

THOUGHT MACHINES

One of science's fashions is to chase the grail of computers which can think like humans. The so-called Turing Test, named after British mathematician Alan Turing, is supposed to define the moment at which a machine can actually 'think' or at least appear to think by fooling the observers[4].

He called his famous paper "The Imitation Game", made over as the title of a very fine movie of his life and achievements, starring Benedict Cumberbatch, in an Oscar-nominated lead performance.

And by a coincidence, the same week I type this close, my latest MENSA Bulletin (Feb 2015, pp. 20 - 23) carries a startling claim that a chatbot nicknamed Eugene Goostman, created by a team under John Denning, a health care quant from San Francisco, has actually passed the Turing Test!

Reading the article carefully, I don't fully buy into it, though it's clearly a worthy effort. It fooled only 30% of the judges. More to the point, the Archangel of AI, Ray Kurzweil was not impressed. He has a $20,000 wager running, with software magnate Mitch Kapor (founder of Lotus Development Corporation), that a machine will pass the Turing Test before 2029.

Kurzweil could try to call in that bet but hasn't. According to Kurzweil, Eugene does not keep track of the conversation, repeats itself word for word and often replies with typical chatbot non-sequiturs.

It seems like we'll have to wait a while for a definitive win.

ELECTRONIC HOLISM

Another more important search is under way, a kind of electronic holism, in which we may soon have machines which embody real (fully cognitive), human thought. In other words machines which are a composite of physical matter and human mind; meaning thought and identity sucked into the computer.

The fact is, as I have explained throughout this text, the horizon between consciousness and physical reality is fast becoming so blurred that I predicted that within the first twenty years of this millennium we will have computers which can interact directly with thought. We think a thought and brain activity readers translate that into digital electronics. That has already come true.

What I am excited to write about in *Medicine Beyond* is not machines that can be human but humans that can occupy and "be" machines! It has been postulated that man may one day abandon his flesh body and become so integrated with computers that our personality resides entirely within software in the cyber domain. This would be *virtual living*, rather than the virtual reality being debated today; consciousness would be in the computer world looking out into what we assume to be reality, instead of the other way round.

Celebrated writer Arthur C. Clarke first put forward this idea in a 1956 book *The City and The Stars*, though how the fictional civilization managed this trick he does not reveal in the story.

But writer Bob Ettinger takes it very seriously and his book *Man into Superman* is definitely non-fiction. He foresees the day when it will be possible to transfer our human personalities into a software package that thinks, feels and communicates as "me".

We would then dispense with the inconvenient restrictions of the body and its incessant demands for foraging and procreation. Should such a scenario ever come to pass, we would of course be 'immortal', though there would need to be back-up copies for safety. These back-up personalities would have to be updated regularly; otherwise they would become invalid because they were missing too many experiences.

Ed Regis, author of *Great Chicken Mambo and the Transhuman Condition* (which for both our sake's I had better state is subtitled: *Science Slightly over the Edge!*) calls this state post-biological man. You might worry that, even if you felt you were now inside a computer—that you were really there—you would no longer be able to experience anything real. Any input sensations would be mere simulation; an apparent reality.

Well, according to David Hume (1711-1776), greatest of the British Empiricist philosophers, that's all you ever get in life anyway! All of living is only a *mind simulation* of whatever is 'out there' (if anything). We've no idea if it's "true" or what true really means.

It may come as a shock to readers to realize that these ideas are being seriously debated. Do not be tempted to scoff at this possibility of cyber-life. It may be closer than you think. 'What Nature can do,' the late Arthur C. Clarke wrote, 'Man can also do in his own way'.

Or as Frederik Pohl, also a sci-fi writer, stated in a 1964 Playboy article "Intimations of Immortality": 'The essential 'you' isn't your body. It is what we call your personality, your memory, your mind. This essential 'you' could be preserved inside a computer; a collection of magnetic impulses in an IBM machine'.

What then will be the state of *Medicine Beyond*?

Presumably physicians like me would have to be computer geeks and know how to handle floppy disks, save, copy, backup, upload, download, restore and edit files. Illness might then be a question of corrupted memory or glitches and we would have to put this right. A major operation would be to shut down the computer system and re-install you from a backup. By then evolution would be reduced to thinking up newer and better software packages to broadcast ourselves from.

This prospect makes Aldous Huxley's *Brave New World* seem like a vicarage tea party. But if in the far distant future it came about, and there just happened to be a moldering centuries-old copy of my book found on a forgotten shelf somewhere, no one will be able to read those foolish words: it could never happen!

COULD YOU BE A ROBOT?

It seems appropriate to end this startling overview of a coming world, beyond the bounds of ordinary physics, with a description of an experiment in which a human psyche was projected into an electrically-powered robot body. It's the immediate future. In fact it is now. Maybe it's teaching us something important.

In this experiment, a human subject in a laboratory was wired to a functional MRI (fMRI) scanner, which read his movement intentions according to which parts of the brain cortex were lit up (as I said, we have reached that stage already). This notional action was then relayed as instructions to a robot, thousands of kilometres away that made the movement which the lab experimenter was thinking about. He would think "left arm" and the left arm of the robot would respond.

Shades of the Avatar movie! It's closer than you think. We may soon reach a time when we can use a computer-controlled surrogate body to trek across the Sahara, shoot the rapids in the Grand Canyon, have dinner in Paris with a friend and even go to the moon, while we are lying on the sofa back home!

TRUE EMBODIMENT

Tele-operated robots, those that can be remotely controlled by a human, have been around for decades.

But this new approach goes way beyond that. What was truly remarkable about this experiment was that *the human subject began to feel he actually was the robot.* He felt it was part of himself. We call that embodiment.

Researchers from the Advanced Virtuality Lab at the Interdisciplinary Center in Herzliya, Israel, and colleagues took student, Tirosh Shapira, through several training stages in which he attempted to direct a virtual avatar by thinking of moving his left or right hand or his legs. The fMRI scanner tracked Shapira's brain activity and, using this, the team was able to translate his intentions into computer signals.

The commands were then sent via an internet connection to a small robot at the Béziers Technology Institute in France, over 3,000 kilometres away. When Shapira thought of raising his right arm, the robot would raise its right arm. Imagining moving his legs made the robot walk forward.

The set-up allowed Shapira to control the robot in near real time with his thoughts, while a camera on the robot's head allowed him to see from the robot's perspective.

Shapira soon learned to move the robot around freely. He could navigate a room, follow a person and even search for objects placed somewhere in the room.

BEING AN AVATAR

It's amazingly engaging, Shapira tells us. He really felt he was there, moving around. There was a need to concentrate, obviously, and he had to calculate a few steps in advance because there's a small delay between thinking of a movement and it actually happening. But once you master that, it feels like being a puppet master.

To create a left turn, right turn or leg movements, Shapira found it helpful to think about very specific actions. This enabled the computer to more easily recognize the activated areas of his brain. "I imagined turning the knob of a faucet with my right hand and a gear with my left hand," he reported. "It worked best when I thought about everything in really vivid detail, like what the faucet felt like to touch."

To test the extent of Shapira's feelings of embodiment, the researchers surprised him with a mirror. "I turned around and they'd put a mirror in front of me," he says. He caught the first glance of his reflection. "I thought, 'oh I'm so cute, I have blue eyes'; not 'that robot is cute'. It was amazing."

At one point the connection failed and one of the researchers picked the robot up to see what the problem was; Shapira had the feeling of being grabbed in person and wanted to shout, "Hey, put me down!"

By this stage he was "being" the robot. That's what we mean by embodiment[5].

THE MATRIX

I doubt the reader would be satisfied without some reference, in this context, to the idea of life in a simulated matrix, as portrayed in the Hollywood movie of that name.

The fact is that this idea is being seriously debated by philosophers, including (but not confined to) Dr. David Chalmers, professor of philosophy at the University of Tucson, Arizona. Chalmers wrote a paper entitled *The Matrix as Metaphysics* and he was deadly serious. You can access his paper online. I found it fascinating[6].

Not that I am suggesting that academics like Chalmers actually believe we are living in such an illusory reality, merely that they are left struggling to find ways to reason around it and prove that we are not.

Put another way, we *could be* living in the Matrix, without knowing it.

As Chalmers tells us, *The Matrix* movie presents a version of an old philosophical fable: the brain in a vat. A disembodied brain is floating in a vat, inside a scientist's laboratory. The scientist has arranged that the brain will be stimulated with the same sort of inputs that a normal embodied brain receives. To do this, the brain is connected to a giant computer simulation of a world. The simulation determines which inputs the brain receives. When the brain produces outputs, these are fed back into the simulation. The internal state of the brain is just like that of a normal brain, despite the fact that it lacks a body. From the brain's point of view, things seem very much as they seem to you and me.

Neo's situation at the beginning of *The Matrix* is something like this. He thinks that he lives in a city; he thinks that he has hair; he thinks it is 1999; and he thinks that it is sunny outside. In reality, he is floating in space, he has no hair, the year is around 2199, and the world has been darkened by war.

Of course we need to point out one or two minor differences from the brain in a vat set up: Neo's brain is located in his body, where it should be, and the computer simulation is controlled by machines rather than by a scientist. But the essential details are much the same. In effect, Neo is a brain in a vat (*envatted* is Chalmers' delicious word for this).

My question to you, dear reader, is figure out in what way, if any, this Matrix scenario is different to what we experience in our lives and—more to the point—couldn't all of the supposed physical reality that scientists keep throwing at us be no more than a brain-based response to external stimuli which are fooling us? - A Matrix illusion?

Bishop George Berkeley, another of the British Empiricists, made this point very strongly in the 18th century. We don't *really know* what's out there and can never know. All we have to go on is what our sensory input is telling us.

Move over Neo!

FOOLING YOUR SENSES

Apparently, the mind is very easily fooled into incorporating an external entity as its own. Over a decade ago, psychologists discovered that they could convince people that a rubber hand was their own just by putting it on a table in front of them and stroking it in the same way as their real hand.

It's only a matter of time before scientists figure out clever add-ons, like stimulating muscles to create the sensation of movement. Smell, sight, sound and the sensation of moving one's muscles will all add to the illusion. Indeed, one may be wrong to call it an illusion.

In 2011, scientists in America said they had "immersed" volunteers into the body of an avatar—a computer generated version of themselves.

Volunteers were asked to wear virtual reality goggles and then stand in front of a camera. The subjects saw the camera's view of their back on screens in the goggles, computer enhanced to create a 3D virtual version or avatar.

When their back was stroked with a pen so was the virtual avatar in front of them, making them think that the virtual body was in fact their own. They felt the stroking and that 'thing' in front was getting the stroking, so that 'thing' must be me. In this way people became confused about their real and the virtual self, even though they were effectively two meters apart from each other.

In another experiment, researchers at Anglia Ruskin University in Cambridge fitted volunteers with head cameras and showed them a live video of themselves from behind. Some of the volunteers were shown images which flashed in time with their own heartbeat. The scientists found that those who were in effect watching their own heartbeat began to identify with their "virtual self" more than their own body. It's a novel kind of out-of-body experience[7].

I am already asking myself are we merely embodied in our current flesh, through much the same delusion of "being there" as these tests are showing?

I think so. I am not a body; I am a conscious entity. Experiences such as OBEs convince us that consciousness itself is independent of the physical body. These new discoveries go one step beyond that.

I put it to you that consciousness is wherever it considers itself to be and that even an avatar body makes a convenient peg on which to hang our awareness. This experiment further reinforces my point, that we don't need sense organs to sense things (non-sensory per-ception, page 102). The reality we experience is reality, because it's what we experience. It's a kind of sensory tautology.

As the robot avatars get more sophisticated, the sense of embod-iment will grow until it is spookily real. Once fully life-sized robots are available, the illusion of being an electronic self will grow more convincing.

LOCKED IN SYNDROME

One of the outstanding possibilities of this technology could be solving the problem of patients who are locked in. These unfortunate individ-uals are almost totally paralyzed and helpless, yet perfectly aware and wide-awake conscious. They are a living identity which is physically trapped or, literally, "locked in" to a worthless body, which will never recover its function.

Now there is the possibility of rejoining life in a mechanical surrogate body, which is not paralyzed but quite functional. And early results sug-gest it won't be too bad an experience—at least nothing like the misery so aptly and movingly described by Jean-Dominic Bauby, the celebrated former editor of Elle magazine, who was himself "locked in", after a di-sastrous cerebral accident. He wrote a remarkable book, dictated one letter at a time (by blinking his left eye), about how it felt, called *The Butterfly and The Diving Bell*. The book was later made into a movie of the same title.

Researchers, along with Rafael Malach's group at the Weizmann Insti-tute of Science, in Rehovot, Israel, hope to collaborate with groups such as Adrian Owen's at the University of Western Ontario in Canada, to test their surrogate on people who are paralyzed or locked in.

This will be a very special version of the "virtual medicine" that I pre-dicted so many years ago and now ranks high as *Medicine Beyond*.

GOD-LIKE INVOLVEMENT

It comes down to this: the so-called objective universe has no meaning, no reality, without us. This is far beyond the observer effect, which trou-bles scientists enough as it is. We ARE the reality, not just looking at it.

You have seen all through this book that conventional science and its wispy "explanations" of our world is on the retreat; that nothing they say adds up; that getting closer to understanding the nature of things is marketing and sales talk only. Everything is propped up by frenzied and obsessive beliefs, defended against all reason and by impugning anyone who wants a better story. It's like they fear a more open dialogue with the cosmos!

The truth is, the deeper we dig into the nature of reality, the less we find. It is tending towards a non-material universe or, as Sir James Jeans famously said: "The stream of knowledge is heading towards a non-mechanical reality; the universe begins to look more like a great thought than a great machine. Mind no longer appears to be an accidental intruder into the realm of matter. We are beginning to suspect that we ought rather to hail it as the creator and governor of this realm."[8]

The mind—hence thought and awareness—is non-material by almost any definition. This is the main reason science is stumbling in the study of these key phenomena. By refuting the idea of non-materiality and insisting that all mental processes are a function of the brain, science has no way of accessing the real nature of mind and Being.

So it derides the idea and scoffs at those who have better suggestions to offer.

SUPERNOETICS™ TO THE RESCUE

My own model of Being and consciousness I have called Supernoetics™. It answers all these confusing questions about reality by adopting one simple, almost indisputable viewpoint: *we are a non-material consciousness that is external to the space-time continuum and looking in on it.*

The robot embodiment experiment makes it clear to me that we can quickly make the shift to think our "being" is somewhere else, anywhere we choose, even thousands of miles away from our immediate flesh and bone. I don't think enough people are thinking through the implications of that.

The sole reason we tend to see things through our eyes is not that we are truly "inside the skull" but that we choose to adopt a viewpoint which says we are using only our eyes. The moment you throw away that choice, all bets are off. You will be able to travel out of the body, with full perception (non-sensory perception, as I call it); telepathy and remote viewing will be a fact of life; levitation and bilocality shouldn't be so weird!

Moreover the fact that you are an immaterial and therefore indestructible presence will soon lead you to the question of past lives. Where have you been all this time, if you are not a body and so don't die? Certainly not just on planet Earth!

In fact explorers in my "Tunnels Of Time" recall project very quickly realize they have lived before, many, many times, on many, many worlds; in many other dimensions even (as I said, once you dump the fixation that you are bound inside your skull, all bets are off).

Through this research I have formulated many bold propositions, which seem now obvious to me, though they may be somewhat shocking to you. For instance, that Atlantis did exist, but not here on Earth. Our geography simply isn't big enough to hide a sinking continent. But what if it were another planet? - Still there? The idea of an advanced society, filled with wisdom, love, magic, science and medicine suddenly becomes more believable.

What if Tolkien's *Middle Earth* were such a powerful experience for us all because it actually existed, in another time and place? If that were true, then Tolkien was just remembering the past, not creating fiction. There really were dwarves, dragons, wizards, orcs and (sigh)... elves!

Once you let go of formal concepts of time and space, anything can happen. We can go back to childlike values of amazement, fantasy, mystery and magic. There's a beautiful world out there.

Care to join me?

What Is Supernoetics™?

You have seen mention of Supernoetics™ at several points in this text. You might be wondering, "What is it, exactly?"

Supernoetics™ could be described as a revolutionary and profound spiritual grammar. It realigns our view of consciousness with the world and teaches us many novel ways to change our experience of life.

We have a large library of tested transformational and self-growth techniques. These are easy to learn and easy to apply, once you understand the underlying mechanisms of mind and reality.

Supernoetics™ is not a religion or religious philosophy. It is definitely not psychology or psychotherapy.

> *Super-* as you know, means biggest, best, most worthy, above, beyond, excellent; it occurs as part of the words superb, superlative and superior; it means the finest of importance, quality, or grade (from the Latin).

> *Noetics* (from the Greek) is the study of mind and spirit, in context, and how we know what we know and why we experience what we think we experience.

There are a number of key components of the system:

- Educational Techniques and Reform
- Success and Prosperity
- Self-Growth

- Advancement into previously unknown territory of the mind*

  *The latter has strong spiritual overtones but is non-denominational and does not conflict with any religion or culture which allows freedom of thought and rational activity.

If you want to know more, please visit the website: www.SuperNoetics.com (or www.supernoetics.com.au). There you can sign up for a series of free instructional emails.

Supernoetics™ is intensely practical, laying out advanced stratagems, and releasing past patterns stuck in place, so leading to better decisions and more desirable outcomes.

It is supremely rational and does not sit astride emotions or dogma. It has methods for evaluating knowledge for context, value and function.

Every aspect of Supernoetics™ teaching has been tested and found to work. It is the outcome of several decades of (ongoing) research.

One of our core activities is personal advancement, through a system of mind explorations and adventures called *Transformational Mind Dynamics*™. If your life is less than 100% satisfactory, you can experience the amazing results of this in-depth inner journey, by sending an email to: introductorysession@supernoetics.com and booking a free trial session dellivered over the phone.

It could change your whole life here on Earth!

www.supernoetics.com

RESOURCES

INTRODUCTION

1. Annals of Internal Medicine, vol 136, P. 888
2. The Lancet, vol. 350, p. 1752

CHAPTER 1

1. J. Silk, "Cosmic Conundrums," New Scientist, 8 Mar 2014, p. 26
2. Meeting of the Royal Astronomical Society, 11 Jan 1935, The Observatory 58 (February 1935), pp. 33-41
3. Russell Stannard, "No Faith in the Grand Theory," The Times (London), 13 November 1989
4. "Firefight at the Black Hole Corral," New Scientist 21, 2955, p. 8.
5. Swanson C., Life Force, The Scientific Basis, Poseidia Press, Tucson, 2009. p. 10
6. Grant J, Discarded Science, Ideas That Seemed Good at the Time, Facts, Figures and Fun, Wisley, Surrey, UK, 2006, p. 14
7. Haldane, J.B.S., Possible Worlds: and Other Essays (1927), Chatto and Windus: London, 1932, reprint, p.286 - Emphasis in the original
8. Feb 2003, the findings of WMAP (Wilkinson Microwave Anisotropy Probe)
9. http://map.gsfc.nasa.gov/universe/uni_shape.html
10. Young, Kelly, "Satellites Solve Mystery of Low Gravity over Canada," NewScientist.com, May 10, 2007.
11. New Scientist, vol 223, No. 2978, July 19th- 25th, 2014, p. 12
12. http://www.dailygalaxy.com/my_weblog/2008/03/is-time-disappe.html retrieved 21 Feb 2014, 7.29 pm PST

13. New Scientist, Vol. 222, No. 2966, p.33

14. New Scientist, Vol. 222, No. 2966, p. 33.

15. http://biomatics.org/index.php/Mandelbrot

16. Hoyle F. Home is Where the Wind Blows. Calif: Univ Sci Books, 1994; p. 413

CHAPTER 2

1. Weber R., Dialogues with Scientists and Sages: The Search for Unity, Routledge and Kegan Paul, London, 1986, p. 44

2. National Earth Science Teachers Association website: http://www.windows2universe.org/glossary/plasmasphere.html

3. National Oceanographic and Atmospheric Administration website, USA: NOAA.gov

4. New Scientist, Vol 223, No. 2978, 19 July 2014, p. 8

5. Nature Proceedings: hdl:10101/npre.2007.1312.1; Posted 12 Nov 2007

6. Geoffrey Goodman, Dani Bercovich, "Melanin Directly Converts Light for Vertebrate Metabolic Use: Heuristic Thoughts on Birds, Icarus and Dark Human Skin," J Altern Complement Med. (2008 Jan-Feb), 14(1), pp. 17-25. PMID: 18479839

7. Nature Proceedings: hdl:10101/npre.2007.1312.1; Posted 12 Nov 2007

8. http://firstlook.pnas.org/naturally-occurring-mela-nin-could-be-the-future-of-edible-electronics/

9. E. Dadachova, R.A. Bryan, X. Huang X, T. Moadel, A.D. Sch-weitzer, et al. (2007), "Ionizing Radiation Changes the Electronic Properties of Melanin and Enhances the Growth of Melanized Fungi," PLoS ONE 2(5): e457. oi:10.1371/journal.pone.0000457

10. P. Meredith and J. Riesz, Photochem. Photobiol (2004), 79(2), pp. 211-216

11. Biochemistry, 82 (2011), pp. 69–73

12. https://sora.unm.edu/sites/default/files/journals/condor/v079n03/p0321-p0327.pdf [THE FUNCTIONAL SIGNIFICANCE OF THE AVIAN PECTEN: A REVIEW]

13. E. Dadachova, R.A. Bryan, X. Huang, T. Moadel, A.D. Schweitzer, et al. (2007), "Ionizing Radiation Changes the Electronic

Properties of Melanin and Enhances the Growth of Melanized Fungi," PLoS ONE 2(5): e457. oi:10.1371/journal.pone.0000457

14. "Biologically Derived Melanin Electrodes in Aqueous Sodium-Ion Energy Storage Devices," PNAS - Published online before print December 9, 2013, DOI: 10.1073/pnas.1314345110

15. Lyall Watson, Supernature, Hodder and Stoughton, London, 1973, p. 5

16. Nature 390, pp. 237-238 (20 November 1997). doi: 10.1038/36747.

17. http://www.dailygrail.com/Essays/2014/7/Our-Alien-DNA

Press release, Cornell University, September 26, 2014

CHAPTER 3

1. Constable and Robinson, 2012

2. Prof. Cyril Smith, personal communication, April 2014

3. The Lancet, Vol. 224, Issue 5808, pp 1403 - 1404 (22 December 1934). doi: 10.1016/S0140-6736(00)43351-9

4. Pethig R, (1973), "Electronic Conduction in Biological Systems", Electronics & Power, 19,445-9

5. S. Best, C.W. Smith, Electromagnetic Man, Dent, London, 1989, p262

6. Personal communication, 6 September 2000

7. Best S and Smith C W, Electromagnetic Man, Dent, London, 1989, p. 56

8. Personal Communication, 15 Apr 2014

9. House of Commons Science and Technology Committee, "Evidence Check 2: Homeopathy. Fourth Report of Session 2009-2010", London: Stationery Office, HC 45 pp.103-110, 22 February 2010

10. Pat Delgado and Colin Andrews – 1989, Circular Evidence - Grand Rapids, Mich.: Phanes Press

[...]aden, The Circles Effect and its Mystery – [...] Wiltshire: Artetech, 1989

[...]rg/si/show/circular_reasoning_the_mys-[...]_and_their_orbs_of_light/

13. W.C. Levengood and Nancy P. Talbott (1999), "Dispersion of Energies in Worldwide Crop Formations" – Physiologia Plantarum 105: pp.615-624

14. E.H. Haselhoff, "Natura Complessa dei Cerchi nel Grano, Reggio Emilia": Natrix Edition, 2002. In English:

15. http://www.openminds.tv/light-balls-bizarre-events-2013-dutch-crop-circles/25345

CHAPTER 4

1. Mindful Universe: Quantum Mechanics and the Participating Observer (The Frontiers Collection) 2007

2. Michael Bellomo, The Stem Cell Divide: the Facts, the Fiction, and the Fear Driving the Greatest Scientific, Political, and Religious Debate of Our Time, Amacom, 2006, p. 134. ISBN 978-0-8144-0881-0

3. E. Dayenas, F. Beauvais, J. Amara , M. Oberbaum, B. Robinzon, A. Miadonna, A. Tedeschit, B. Pomeranz, P. Fortner, P. Belon, J. Sainte-Laudy, B. Poitevin, and J. Benveniste (30 June 1988), "Human Basophil Degranulation Triggered by Very Dilute Antiserum Against IgE," Nature 333 (6176), pp. 816–818

4. http://www.sheldrake.org/research/morphic-resonance

5. Vlail P. Kaznacheyev et al., "Distant Intercellular Interactions in a System of Two Tissue Cultures," Psychoenergenetic Systems, March 1976, pp. 141–142

6. Interdisciplinary Sciences: Computational Life Sciences, DOI: 10.1007/s12539-009-0036-7

7. http://www.keelynet.com/news/041914f.html

8. arxiv.org/abs/1012.5166

9. J. Phys. Chem. B (2008), 112 (4), pp. 1060–1064. DOI: 10.1021/jp7112297.

10. New J. Phys. 9 (2007) 263. doi:10.1088/1367-2630/9/8/263

CHAPTER 5

1. "'It Might Be Life, Jim...' Physicists Discover Inorganic Dust with Life-Like Qualities," New Journal of Physics, Aug 09, 2007. http://phys.org/news105869123.html. Retrieved on 2007-08-16

2. http://en.wikipedia.org/wiki/Futility_(poem)

3. The Bridging Tree, Vol. 1, No. 1 (Winter, 1997 – 1998)

4. Tractatus Logico-Philosophicus, 1921, 6.4312

5. Robert Lanza MD, Biocentrism. How Life and Consciousness Are the Keys to Understanding the True Nature of the Universe, Benbella Books, Dallas, TX, 2009

6. New Scientist, Vol. 222, No. 2964 (12 Apr 2014), p.29

7. Harner M., The Way Of The Shaman, Harper, San Francisco, 1990, pp. 2-8

CHAPTER 6

1. See Paul Davies, "That Mysterious Flow," Scientific American, September 2002

2. SFGate website: http://www.sfgate.com/science/article/Science-hopes-to-change-events-that-have-already-2655518.php

3. Anita Moorjani, Dying to Be Me, Hay House, 2012.

4. http://www.sfgate.com/science/article/Science-hopes-to-change-events-that-have-already-2655518.php

5. Henderson, Mark. "Theories of telepathy and afterlife cause uproar at top science forum." The Sunday Times, 6 Sep 2006. http://www.thetimes.co.uk/tto/news/uk/article1942668.ece (accessed 7 Mar 2015)

6. The Source Field, Dutton (Penguin Group, USA), New York, 2011, p. 37

7. J.B. Rhine, Extra-Sensory Perception. Boston, MA, US: Bruce Humphries, 1934

8. Radin D. The Conscious Universe. The Scientific Truth of Psychic Phenomena. HarperCollins, New York, 1997, pp. 96-97

9. Eysenck, HJ. 1957. Sense and Nonsense in Psychology. New York: Penguin

10. http://www.geoffreylandis.com/heim_theory.html

CHAPTER 7

1. http://en.wikipedia.org/wiki/Jan_Smuts

2. Bulletin of Experimental Biology and Medicine (February 1971), Vol. 71, Issue 2, pp 192-193

3. R.O. Becker, and Gary Seldon, The Body Electric, William Morrow, New York, 1985, p. 296

4. H.S. Burr, Blueprint for Immortality: The Electric Patterns of Life, London: N. Spearman, 1972

5. H. S. Burr, Blueprint for Immortality (Saffron Walden: C W Daniel and Co, 1972)

6. G. Lakhovsky, The Secret of Life (True Health Publishing Co, 1951 [English translation copyright 1970 by Mark Clement]): 3.

7. Ibid.

8. K. Mumby, The Complete Guide to Allergy and Environmental Illness, Thorsons, London, 1993, p. 90

9. A. Nodon, 'Les nouvelles radiations ultra-pénétrantes et à cellule vivante', Revue Scientifique 22nd October 1927: 609

10. Lakhovsky, op cit. p. 111

11. [http://en.wikipedia.org/wiki/Antoine_Prioré]

12. R. O. Becker, The Body Electric, Quill (William Morrow), New York, 1985

13. R.O. Becker, Cross Currents. The Promise of Electromedicine, the Perils of Electropollution, Los Angeles: Jeremy P. Tarcher, Inc., 1990

14. Becker RO, The Body Electric, Quill (William Morrow), New York, 1985, p.99

15. J. L. Oschman, 'What Is Healing Energy? Part 2: Measuring the Fields of Life', Journal of Bodywork and Movement Therapies January 1997: 117–22.

16. T.H. Sander, J. Preusser, R. Mhaskar, J. Kitching, L. Trahms and S. Knappe. Magnetoencephalography with a chip-scale atomic magnetometer. Biomedical Optics Express. Vol. 3, Issue 5, pp. 981–990. Published online April 17

17. Am J Chin Med. (1998), 26(3-4), pp. 251-63

18. H.S. Burr, H.S., and F.S.C. Northrup, "The Electro-Dynamic Theory of Life," Quart. Rev. Biol. 10, pp. 322-333, 1935

19. Ho, M.W.: Quantum Coherence and Conscious Experience. Kybernetes, 26: 265-276, 1997

20. Knight, D. and D. Feng, Collagens as liquid crystals. Paper presented in British Association for the Advancement of Science, Chemistry Session, Molecular Self-Assembly in Science and Life, Keele, 1993

21. Leikin, S., V.A. Parsegian, D.C. Rau and R.P. Rand. Hydration forces. Ann. Rev. Phys. Chem. 44: 369-395, 1993

22. S. Peto, and P. Gillis, "Fiber-to-Field Angle Dependence of Proton Nuclear Magnetic Relaxation in Collagen", Magnetic Resonance Imaging 8 (1990), pp. 703-712

23. N. Sasaki, "Dielectric Properties of Slightly Hydrated Collagen. Time-Water Content Superposition Analysis", Biopolymers (1984) 23, pp. 1725-1734

24. Ho, M.W. The Rainbow and the Worm, The Physics of Organisms, 2nd ed., World Scientific, Singapore, 1998

25. Roger Lewin (December 12, 1980). "Is Your Brain Really Necessary?" SCIENCE 210 (4475): 1232–1234. doi:10.1126/science.7434023. PMID 7434023

26. Tsukamoto, I. and K. Ogli. Effects of anesthetics on the interfacial polarity of membranes - evaluated by Taft's polarity parameters. Prog. Anesth. Mech. 3: 368-373, 1995.

27. Ho, M-W: Quantum Coherence and Conscious Experience. Kybernetes, 26: 265-276, 1997

28. Becker, R.O. Cross Currents. The Promise of Electromedicine, the Perils of Electropollution. Jeremy P. Tarcher, Inc., Los Angeles, 1990

29. Libet, B., E.W. Wright, Jr., B. Feinstein and D.K. Pearl, Subjective referral of the timing for a conscious sensory experience. Brain 102: 193-224, 1979

CHAPTER 8

1. Abrams, New Concepts in Diagnosis and Treatment (San Francisco: Philopolis Press, 1916).

2. H. Gaier (ed), Thorsons Encyclopaedic Dictionary of Homeopathy (Thorsons, 1991).

3. R. O. Becker, Cross Currents: The Perils of Electropollution, The Promise of Electromedicine (NY: Tarcher/Putnam, 1990): 239.

4. J. R. Thomas, J. Schrot and A. Liboff, 'Production of passive behavior in mice by means of lithium cyclotron resonance', Biomagnetics 7 (1986): 349.

5. Robert O. Becker, The Body Electric. New York: Morrow, 1985, p.297

6. Electromagnetic Biology and Medicine (Impact Factor: 0.77). 02/2008; 27(2):127-33. DOI: 10.1080/15368370802072117

7. Electromagn Biol Med. 2007; 26(4):283-8

8. Magn Reson Med. 2004 Mar; 51(3):452-7

9. Corbellini E, Corbellini M, Licciardello O, Marotta F, Paper presented at SENS6 Conference Reimagine Aging, Queen's College, Cambridge, UK, Sept 2013. See also: Lisi A et al. S. Ion cyclotron resonance as a tool in regenerative medicine. Biol Med. 2008; 27:127-133

10. Capra F, "The Dance of Shiva: The Hindu View of Matter in the light of Modern Physics," Main Currents in Modern Thought (Sept-Oct 1972).

11. AK Coomaraswamy, The Dance Of Siva, Essays on Indian Art and Culture, Dover, 1985, p. 56

CHAPTER 9

1. Homeopathy. 2010 Oct;99(4):231-42.

2. Davenas E, Benveniste J et al. 'Human basophil degranulation triggered by very dilute antiserum against IgE, Nature 333 (1988):816; 1988.

3. Davenas E, Benveniste J et al. 'Human basophil degranulation triggered by very dilute antiserum against IgE, Nature 333 (1988):816; 1988

4. Physica A: Statistical Mechanics and its Applications, Volume 323, 15 May 2003, Pages 67-74

5. Lionel Milgrom , Icy claim that water has memory, New Scientist, 11 June 2003: http://www.newscientist.com/article/dn3817-icy-claim-that-water-has-memory.html#.VRNKXrr5pro

6. Lancet (1994), 344, pp. 1601- 06.

7. Editorial, The Lancet (Dec 10, 1994), 344, p 1585.

8. M. Frenkel et al., "Cytotoxic Effects of Ultra-Diluted Remedies on Breast Cancer Cells," Int J Oncol, (2010), 36, pp. 395-403

9. Int J Oncol. (2003 Oct), 23(4), pp. 975-82. http://www.ncbi.nlm.nih.gov/pubmed/12963976 accessed May 10, 2014 1.02 pm PST

10. The Lancet, Vol. 351, Issue 9099, p. 366 (31 January 1998). doi: 10.1016/S0140-6736(05)78311-2.

11. M. Lukas "The World According to Ilya Prigogine", Quest/80 (December 1980), p. 88

12. Paolo V. Castro, Shilpi Khare, Brian D. Young, and Steven G. Clarke, (2012), "Caenorhabditis elegans Battling Starvation

Stress: Low Levels of Ethanol Prolong Lifespan in L1 Larvae." In Shree Ram Singh, PLoS ONE 7 (1): e29984. Bib code: 2012PLoSO...7E9984C. doi:10.1371/journal.pone.0029984. PMC: 3261173. PMID: 22279556

13. David Gems and Linda Partridge (2008), "Stress-Response Hormesis and Aging: 'That which Does Not Kill Us Makes Us Stronger'", Cell Metabolism 7 (3), pp. 200–3. doi:10.1016/j.cmet.2008.01.001. PMID: 18316025

14. E.J. Calabrese, and L.A. Baldwin, "Hormesis as a Biological Hypothesis , Toxicological Defense Mechanisms and the Shape of Dose-Response Relationships," Environmental Health Perspectives 106, Supplement 1, February 1998

15. Hum Exp Toxicol (1998 May) 17(5), pp. 263-5

16. S. Bawin and W. R. Adey, "First Report of ELF Fields Producing Calcium Efflux from Nerve Cells," Proceedings of the National Academy of Sciences 73 (1976), p. 1999

17. Hahnemann, S. The Lesser Writings of Samuel Hahnemann. (Dudgeon Edition), Cure and Prevention of Asiatic Cholera, p., 755. http://homeoint.org/morrell/londonhh/outbreak.htm

CHAPTER 10

1. 1996 Modulation of human neutrophil activation by "electronic" phorbol myristate acetate (PMA) Federation of American Societies for Experimental Biology Journal (10:A1479(abs)) Y Thomas, H Litime, J Benveniste

2. 1997 Transatlantic transfer of digitized antigen signal by telephone link. Journal of Allergy and Clinical Immunology (99:S175 (abs.) J. Benveniste, P. Jurgens, W. Hsueh, J. Aïssa.

3. From his website www.digibio.com "Understanding Digital Biology; accessed 4/15/2008 at 2.18 PDT

4. L. Watson, Supernature (Hodder and Stoughton, 1973)

5. Davenas E, Benveniste J et al. 'Human basophil degranulation triggered by very dilute antiserum against IgE, Nature 333 (1988):816; 1988

6. FASEB Journal, 1999, vol. 13, p. A852

7. Journal of Experimental & Clinical Cancer Research 2009, 28:51doi:10.1186/1756-9966-28-51

8. Suleyman Seckiner Gorgun, Collegno, Italy. Frontier Perspectives, ISSN: 1062-4767, Volume: 7, Number: 2, Fall, 1998.

CHAPTER 11

1. Backster C, Primary Perception, White Rose Millennium Press, Anza, California, 2003, pp.

2. Peter Tomkins and Christopher Bird, The Secret Life of Plants, Book Club Associates, 1975, p. 31

3. www.alternative-doctor.com/specials/SLacupuncture.htm

4. Berkeley, CA: University of California Press, 1993

5. Chang Tsai, quoted in Fung Yu-lan, A Short History of Chinese Philosophy (NY: Macmillan, 1958): 279

6. Sir T. Lewis, 'The Nocifensor System of Nerves and its Reactions', British Medical Journal 27th February 1937: 431.

7. Cheng K, Zou C. Biomedical Infophysics Models of Meridian Channel System. WebmedCentral BIOPHYSICS 201; 2(12):WMC002555 doi: 10.9754/journal.wmc.2011.002555

8. P. de Vernejoul et al., 'Etude Des Méridiens D'Acupuncture par les Traceurs Radioactifs', Bull. Acad. Natle. Med. vol. 169 (22nd October, 1985): 1071-5.

9. Nuclear Medicine and Acupuncture Message Transmission J Nucl Med 1992 33:409-412

10. Nebrat V., The physical model of the low energy electromagnetic field influence on the human body through acupuncture points. Saint-Petersburg; 2nd European Congress "Acupuncture White Nights-97". Poster

11. Taiwan J Obstet Gynecol. 2012 Dec; 51(4):506-14. doi: 10.1016/j.tjog.2012.09.004

12. Becker, R.O. Cross Currents. The Promise of Electromedicine, the Perils of Electropollution. Jeremy P. Tarcher, Inc., Los Angeles, 1990

13. Tiller, 1973; Reichmannis et al, 1976; Becker, 1990

14. Tiller, W.A, What do electrodermal diagnostic acupuncture instruments really measure. American Journal of Acupuncture 15(1), 18-23, 1987

15. M. Wexu, The Ear, Gateway to Balancing the Body: A Modern Guide to Acupuncture (NY: ASI Publishers, 1975)

16. http://www.dailymail.co.uk/news/article-2601281/Why-lucky-7-really-magic-number.html accessed 26 mar 2015, 8.58 am PDT

17. H. Motoyama, Theories of the Chakras (IL: Theosophical Publishing House, 1981)

CHAPTER 12

1. A. Linde, 'The Self-Reproducing Inflationary Universe', Scientific American vol 9, no. 1, 1998

2. http://en.wikipedia.org/wiki/Paracelsus

3. J. R. Wosley, Everyone's Guide to Acupuncture (Cassell, 1973): 43

4. Ibid: 44

5. Bell IR1, Lewis DA 2nd, Brooks AJ, Lewis SE, Schwartz GE: Gas discharge visualization evaluation of ultramolecular doses of homeopathic medicines under blinded, controlled conditions. J Altern Complement Med. 2003 Feb; 9(1):25-38

6. Homeopathy. 2008 Jul; 97(3):129-33. doi: 10.1016/j.homp.2008.06.003

7. http://www.positivehealth.com/article/energy-medicine/core-energy-surgery-for-the-electromagnetic-body and http://www.positivehealth.com/author/jon-whale-phd

8. THE AGE - News Special - Saturday 7 November 1998

9. Whale J, Naked Spirit. The Supernatural Odyssey, Dragon Rising Publishing, Eastbourne, UK. 2006 pp. 47-56] http://dragonrising.com/store/naked_spirit/

10. Whale J, Naked Spirit. The Supernatural Odyssey, Dragon Rising Publishing, Eastbourne, UK. 2006 pp. 128] http://dragonrising.com/store/naked_spirit

11. Whale J, The Catalyst Of Power. The Assemblage Point of Man, Dragon Rising Publishing, Eastbourne, UK. 3rd Edition 2006] http://dragonrising.com/store/catalyst_of_power/

CHAPTER 13

Electrical signals control wound healing through phosphatidylinositol-3-OH kinase-bold gamma and PTEN, Nature, vol 442, p 457

Proceedings of the National Academy of Sciences (DOI: 10.1073/pnas202235299)

1. Robert O. Becker, The Body Electric, Morrow, New York, 1985, pp. 994-102

2. IEE Review, Volume 47, Issue 3, May 2001, p. 23 – 28. DOI: 10.1049/ir:20010304

3. Potter and Funk, quoted in: Odell, Robert H., MD, PhD, and Sorgnard, Richard E. PhD (2008) Pain Physician, 11:891-907 Las Vegas

4. http://inventors.about.com/od/tstartinventions/a/Nikola_Tesla.htm accessed Feb 28, 2014, 11.50 PST

5. 1893 work The Inventions, Researches and Writings of Nikola Tesla

6. "Corona Discharge Electrographic Imaging Technology" Kirlianlab.com

7. Tesla, N (1898) "High Frequency Oscillators for Electro-Therapeutic and Other Purposes," The Electrical Engineer, Vol. XXVI, No. 550, Nov. 17, p.477

8. http://en.wikipedia.org/wiki/Tesla_coil#cite_ref-49

9. Radio News (February 1925, pp. 1382-1283)

10. Sir T. Lewis, 'The Nocifensor System of Nerves and its Reactions', British Medical Journal 27th February 1937: 431

11. Diabetes, vol 62, p 2905

12. K. Famm et al. Nature 496, 159–161; 2013

13. Nature 511, 18 (03 July 2014) doi:10.1038/511018a

14. http://en.wikipedia.org/wiki/Microcurrent_electrical_neuro-muscular_stimulator

CHAPTER 14

1. C. R. des séances et mémoires de la Soc. De Biolog., 1888, p. 217

2. Sticker, G, Uber Versuche einer objektiven Darstellung von Sensibilitatsstorungen, Wiener klinische Rundschau, 1897, 11, 97-501, 514-518

3. F. Peterson and CG Jung, Psycho-Physical Investigations With The Galvanometer And Pneumograph In Normal And Insane Individuals. Brain, 30, 1907, pp. 153-218

4. Corydon, Bent (1992). L. Ron Hubbard, Messiah or Madman?. Barricade Books. pp. 332–333. ISBN 0-942637-57-7. See also: http://en.wikipedia.org/wiki/Volney_Mathison

5. Singh, Simon; Edzard Ernst (2008). Trick or Treatment: The Undeniable Facts about Alternative Medicine. W. W. Norton & Company. pp. 163–165. ISBN 0-393-06661-4

6. Müller, Tilo (2010). Dianetik und Scientology in ihrem Anspruch als Wissenschaft. GRIN Verlag. p. 32. ISBN 978-3-640-58010-1

7. Personal communication, Hank Levin, San Rafael, CA, Dec 21st, 2014

8. Tompkins P. and Bird C., The Secret Life Of Plants, Book Club Associates, London, 1975, pp. 17 – 20

9. Root intelligence: Plants can think, feel and learn, from issue 2998 of New Scientist magazine, Magazine, page 34-37

10. http://www.digitaljournal.com/article/322993

11. Personal communication, Hank Levin, Jan 3rd, 2015

CHAPTER 15

1. Chinese Academy of Traditional Chinese Medicine, An Outline of Chinese Acupuncture, Foreign Languages Press, 1975, Beijing

2. Stortebecker P., Dental Caries as a Cause of Nervous Disorders, Bio-Probe Inc, Orlando, USA, 1986. P. 39

CHAPTER 16

1. Mumby K, The Complete Guide To Food Allergies and Environmental Illness, Thorson's, London 1993, p. 162

2. Clark H R, The Cure for All Cancers, Promotion Publishing, San Diego, 1993

3. Per-Henrik Zahl, MD, PhD, Jan Maehlen, MD, PhD, H. Gilbert Welch, MD, MPH (2008). The Natural History of Invasive Breast Cancers Detected by Screening Mammography Archives of Internal Medicine, 168 (21), 2311-2316

4. J. Kenyon, 21st Century Medicine (Thorsons, 1986).

5. R. Van Wijk and F. A. C. Wilegart, 'Homeopathic Remedies and Pressure-induced Changes in Galvanic Resistance of the Skin', Dept. of Molecular Biology, State University of Utrecht, Research Unit for Complementary Medicine, Padualaan 8, 3584 CH Utrecht, 1989.

6. R. Van Wijk, 'Homeopathic Medicines in Closed Phials Tested by Changes in the Conductivity of the Skin: A Critical Evaluation. Blind Testing and Partial Elucidation of the Mechanisms', Dept. of Molecular Biology, State University of Utrecht, Research Unit for Complementary Medicine, Padualaan 8, 3584 CH Utrecht, 1992.

7. D. J. Matzke, 'Prediction: Future Electronics Will Be Disrupted due to Consciousness', paper at Towards a Science of Consciousness conference, Tucson II, University of Arizona, 1996

8. Lawden DF, Separability of Psycho-physical Systems, Psycho-Energetics. The Journal of Psycho-physical Systems; vol 4, no 1, 1-10 (1981).

CHAPTER 17

1. E. Rasche, Elektronische Homeopathie (Friesenheim: Medtronik Trading GmbH, 1998)

2. H. Gaier (ed), Thorsons Encyclopedic Dictionary of Homeopathy (Thorsons, 1991): 57

3. Quoted in H. Brügemann (ed), Bioresonance and Multiresonance Therapy (vol 1; Haug: Brussels, 1990 [English edn, 1993])

4. Brügemann, op cit

5. Cahill K, Stead LF, Lancaster T (2011). Cahill, Kate, ed. "Nicotine receptor partial agonists for smoking cessation". Cochrane Database Syst Rev 2 (2): CD006103. doi:10.1002/14651858. CD006103.pub5. PMID 21328282

6. Rasche, op cit

7. Fawthrop, Tom (November 4, 2004). "Agent Orange Victims Sue Monsanto". CorpWatch

8. Personal communication, 14 Jan 2015

CHAPTER 18

1. E. Hamlyn, The Healing Art of Homeopathy (The Organon of Samuel Hahnemann, Beaconsfield Publishers, 1979).

2. H.-H. Reckeweg, Homotoxicology – illness and healing through anti- homotoxic therapy, (Albuquerque, NM: Menaco Publishing Co, 1980).] [A. Pischinger, Matrix and Matrix Regulation, Basis for a Holistic Theory in Medicine (Brussels: Haug International, 1986).

3. H. Gaier (ed), Thorsons Encyclopedic Dictionary of Homeopathy (Thorsons, 1991): 66.

4. Personal communication from George Burns, Manchester homeopath.

5. Gaier, op cit: 345

6. K Mumby, The Allergy Handbook (Thorsons, 1989)

7. Personal communication, 1998 and beyond

8. E Bach and F J Wheeler, The Bach Flower Remedies (New Canaan, CT: Keats, 1977)

9. E. Rasche, Elektronische Homeopathie (Friesenheim: Medtronik Trading GmbH, 1998)

10. M. Bastide, M. Doucet Jaboeuf, V. Daurat. Activity and Chrono pharmacology of very low doses of physiological immune inducers, Immunology Today (6:234-235) 1985] [B.J. Youbicier-Simo, F. Boudard, M. Mekaouche, M. Bastide, J.D. Baylé. Effects of embryonic bursectomy and in ovo administration of highly diluted bursin on an adrenocorticotropic and immune response to chickens. International Journal of Immunotherapy (IX: 169-180) 1993] [P.C. Endler, W. Pongratz, G. Kastberger, F.A.C. Wiegant, J. Schulte The effect of highly diluted agitated thyroxine of the climbing activity of frogs. Veterinary and Human Toxicology (36:56-59) 1994

11. http://onlinelibrary.wiley.com/journal/10.1002/(ISSN)1521-3773/homepage/press/201505press.html

CHAPTER 19

1. http://www.healthy.net/Health/Article/The_Past_Present_and_Future_of_the_Electrodermal_Screening_System_EDS/1086

2. Mumby K, The Complete Guide To Food Allergies and Environmental Illness, Thorson's, London 1993, p. 138

3. Ostrander S and Schroeder L, Super-Learning 2000, Souvenir Press, London, 1995, pp. 210- 211

4. Stortebecker P. Dental Caries as a Cause of Nervous Disorders, Bio- Probe Inc, Orlando, USA, 1986. p73

5. J. Diamond and L. W. Cowden, The Alternative Medicine Definitive Guide to Cancer (Tiburon, CA: Future Medicine Publishing Inc., 1997): 1027

CHAPTER 20

1. You may fnd useful clues in this very disjointed story from the ISTA website: http://www.scenartech.com

2. 1: Usp Fiziol Nauk. 2001 Jul-Sep; 32(3):79-86 (article in Russian)

3. http://www.scenarinstitute.org/file_storage/scenar_experience_dental.pdf

4. Travell J G and Simons D, Myofascial Pain and Dysfunction: The Trigger Point Manual, vols 1 and 2. See also Wikipedia - http://en.wikipedia.org/wiki/Trigger_point

5. Poltawski, L and Watson, T: Physical Therapy Reviews 2009 VOL 14 NO 2 (105-114)

6. Kirsch, Daniel L. PhD (2002) Pain Management: A Practical Guide for Clinicians (6th ed.) Boca Raton, Fla.: American Academy of Pain Management. Richard Weiner, Editor. CRC Press. 749-758

7. Odell, Robert H., MD, PhD, and Sorgnard, Richard E. PhD (2008) Pain Physician, 11:891-907 Las Vegas

8. Personal communication, Oct 2007

CHAPTER 21

1. R Weber, Dialogues with Scientists and sages: The Search for Unity, Routledge and Kegan Paul, London, 1986, pp 45 -48

2. Blavatsy H, The Secret Doctrine, Theosophical University Press, 1888, p. 579

3. Nature Photonics (2014) doi:10.1038/nphoton.2014.95

4. A.G. Gurwitsch: "Über Ursachen der Zellteilung". Arch. Entw. Mech. Org. 51 (1922), 383-415

5. F. A. Popp, 'New Avenues in Medicine' (two-part radio broadcast in the series Neues Aus Kultur und Wissenschaft; Deutschlandfunk Radio, Aug–Sept 1979. Published in H Brügemann (ed), Bioresonance and Multiresonance Therapy (vol 1; Haug: Brussels, 1990] [F. A. Popp et al., Experientia 44, 543 (1988)] [F. A. Popp et al., Recent Advances in Biophoton Research and its Applications, eds. F. A. Popp et al., World Scientific, Singapore, 1992

6. McTaggart L., The Field, Harper Perennial, London, 2001, pp. 50-54

7. M. Kobayashi, D. Kikuchi, and H. Okamura (2009), "Imaging of Ultra-weak Spontaneous Photon Emission from Human Body Displaying Diurnal Rhythm." PLoS ONE 4(7): e6256. doi:10.1371/journal.pone.0006256

8. Fröhlich H, 1988: Theoretical Physics and Biology. In: Fröhlich H (Ed.) Biological Coherence and Response to External Stimuli. Berlin: Springer-Verlag, 1- 24

9. Smith C W, Is a living system a macroscopic quantum system? Frontier Perspectives, 7(1), 9- 15 (1988)

10. Popp FA, et al. 'Biophoton emission' multi-author review. Experientia. 1988;44:543–600

11. Kobayashi M: Spontaneous ultra-weak photon emission of living organisms – biophotons - phenomena and detection techniques for extracting biological information. Trends in Photochem. Photobiol. 2003; 10:111–135

12. Merrow M, Roenneberg T. Circadian clocks: running on redox. Cell. 2001; 106:141–143

13. Photomed Laser Surg. Feb 2010; 28(1): 23–30. doi: 10.1089/pho.2008.2373

14. 1. Dou Z, Hu X, Zhu H (2003): The effects of two kinds of laser irradiation on patients with brain lesion. Chin J Phys Med Rehabil. 25(2): 86-88 (in Chinese).

15. J Cosmet Laser Ther. 2006 Apr; 8(1):39-42

16. Ann Allergy Asthma Immunol. 1997 Apr; 78(4):399-406

17. Biochem Pharmacol. 2013 Aug 15; 86(4):447-57. doi: 0.1016/j.bcp.2013.06.012. Epub 2013 Jun 24

18. http://www.alternative-doctor.com/bloodviscosity/

19. http://square.umin.ac.jp/mtnet/E/meridiantest.html as downloaded 25th August 2004, 15.00 Pacific Time.

CHAPTER 22

1. Szent-Gyorgyi, Introduction to a Sub-Molecular Biology, Academic Press, New York, 1960

2. Berezin Martinez, Artificial Light-Sensitive Enzyme Systems as Chemical Amplifiers of Weak Light Signals, Photochemistry Photobiology .29, March 1979, pp637-650

3. J Liberman Light: Medicine of the Future, Bear and Co, Santa Fe, 1991, p51

4. Beral V, et al: 'Malignant melanoma and exposure to fluorescent light' Lancet 2 (1982) pp 290-292

5. S. F. McDonald, "Effect of Visible Light Waves on Arthritis Pain: A Controlled Study," International Journal of Biosocial Research 3, no. 2 (1982): 49–54; Rodrigo Noseda et al., "A Neural Mechanism for Exacerbation of Headaches by Light," Nature Neuroscience 13 (2010): accessed December 2013, www.nature.com/neuro/journal/v13/n2/full/nn.2475.html.

6. www.whalemedical.com

7. B. Bhattacharya, Gem Therapy (Calcutta: Firma KLM Private Ltd, 1993)

8. Whale J, The Catalyst Of Power, Findhorn Press, Forres, UK, 2001, p. 114

9. T. Engineer, P. Richards, 'VRIC Imaging the Photon', paper presented at the International Forum of New Science, Denver, Colorado, 1997

10. T. Engineer, 'Biolumanetics – The Science of Life-Light', Positive Health March 1998: 23–7

CHAPTER 23

1. Anderson, C.H. et al. (2005) Directed visual attention and the dynamic control of information flow. In Neurobiology of Attention (Itti, L. et al., eds), pp. 11–17, Elsevier

2. http://www.aarda.org/autoimmune-information/autoimmune-statistics/

CHAPTER 24

1. J. D. Beck, S. Offenbacher, R. Williams, P. Gibbs and R. Garcia, 'Periodontitis: A Risk Factor for Coronary Heart Disease? Annals of Periodontology vol. 3, no. 1, July 1998: 127–41

2. Stortebecker P.: Dental Caries as a Cause of Nervous Disorders, Bio-Probe Inc, Orlando, USA, 1986. P74

3. Stortebecker P.: Dental Caries as a Cause of Nervous Disorders, Bio-Probe Inc, Orlando, USA, 1986. P34

4. Ibid: p.116

5. www.MRSAhotline.com

6. H. Raue, 'Resistance to Therapy; Think of Tooth Fillings', Medical Practice vol 32, no 72, 6th September 1980: 2303 - 9

7. J. E. Bouquot, In Review of Nico, G V Black's Forgotten Disease, The Maxillofacial Centre, 583 Tibbs Rd, Morgantown, West Virginia, Third Edition, 1995

8. G. Meinig, Root Canal Cover-up (Ojai, CA: Bion Publishing, 1995)

9. Radio interview of the Laura Lee Show, transcript published in the Townsend Letter for Doctor and Patient August/September 1996

CHAPTER 25

1. Mumby K, *The Allergy Handbook*, Thorson's, London, 1988, p. 119

2. Lamont, J. V. (1862). *Der Erdstrom und der Zusammen desselben mit dem Erdmagnetismus.* Leipzig und Muenchen: Leopold-Voss-Verlag.

3. K. Mumby, The Complete Guide to Allergy and Environmental

4. Illness, Thorsons, London, 1993, p. 90

5. *ibid.*

6. Freier von Pohl F, *Erdstrahlen als Krankheitserreger – Forschungen auf Neuland (Earth Currents–Causative Factors of Cancer and Other Diseases).* 1932, Republished in 1978 and still commercially available.

7. http://www.geopathologie.ch/pdf/Info_2010_A.pdf

8. http://www.geopathologie.de/studien/studie-2

9. https://geobilogiaparanovatos.wordpress.com/2014/06/24/earth-radiation-geopathic-stress-and-ley-lines/

10. http://swissharmony.com/us/earth-radiationgeopathic-stress-ley-lines-and-how-they-are-rendered-harmless

CHAPTER 26

1. New Scientist, Meet Your Unborn Child before It's Conceived, volume222 No. 2964, p.8

2. Meek G W, "After We Die, What Then?" Ariel Press, 1987, Columbus, Ohio, pp. 153- 165

3. Accessed 13th Apr 2008, 2.50 pm PDT

4. Quoted in October 30, 1920 issue of Science magazine but now hotly denied by the curators of the Thomas Edison National Historic Site, who insist that Edison later admitted that he had made the whole thing up - but surprisingly they provide no source for such a statement

5. Senkowski, Ernst (1995): "Analysis of Anomalous Audio and Video Recordings, presented before the "Society for Scientific Exploration" USA – June 1995". Retrieved 2014-05-30 5.15 pm PST

6. http://www.victorzammit.com/afterlifearticles/bacci.html

7. Talking to the Dead by George Noory and Rosemary Ellen Guiley, Forge Books, 2011, p. 275

8. Talking to the Dead by George Noory and Rosemary Ellen Guiley, Forge Books, 2011, p. 103

9. Raudive K, Breakthrough, Taplinger, New York, 1971, p. 15

10. Meek G W, "After We Die, What Then?" Ariel Press, 1987, Columbus, Ohio, pp. 153- 165

11. Spiricom booklet, study it on-line here: http://www.worlditc. org/h_07_meek_spiri_000_007.htm accessed May-1-2014, 9.32 PST

12. Rogo, D S, "Phone Calls From the Dead", Prentice-Hall, Englewood Cliffs, NJ, 1979

13. Watson L, "The Secret Life of Inanimate Objects", Destiny Books, Rochester VT, 1992, pp. 206-7

14. Peasboro J, The Devil in the Machine: Is your computer possessed by a demon? Unable to find the real publisher, though there is reference to it all over the Web: http://www.liberator.net/articles/ TremblayFrancois/digital.html

15. Regal, Brian; (2009): Pseudoscience: A Critical Encyclopedia. Greenwood. p.62 ISBN 978-0-313-35507-3

16. http://en.wikipedia.org/wiki/Electronic_voice_phenomenon

17. Skeptic's Dictionary. Retrieved 2006-12-01

18. Tommy Dunbar, personal communication (email) 6 Jun 2015

CHAPTER 27

1. Paul Davis and John Gribbin, The Matter Myth, Penguin Group (Viking), London, 1991, p. 303

2. Tiller AW, Science and Human Transformation, Pavior, Walnut Creek, 1997, p. 264

3. http://www.1911encyclopedia.org

4. Turing, A.M. (1950): Computing machinery and intelligence. Mind, 59, 433-460

5. Embody A Robot With Your Mind, New Scientist, 23rd July 2012, p. 19

6. http://consc.net/papers/matrix.html

7. From agencies: http://www.telegraph.co.uk/news/ health/10240400/Scientists-trigger-out-of-body-experience-using-heartbeats.html. Accessed 7 mar 2015

8. Jeans J, The Mysterious Universe, Rede Lectures delivered at the University of Cambridge. Nov 1930, p. 137

Index

G

H

Popp, Fritz 69, 195, 371, 372, 373, 514
Power of Movement in Plants, The 249
Poynard, Thierry 2
Pratchett, Terry 382
Prediction 43
Price, Weston 435
Prigogine, Ilya 159, 160, 418, 505
Prioré, Antoine viii, 117, 118, 503
Pyle, Walter 43, 45

Q

Quantum Jazz ix, 142
Quantum mechanics 1, 8, 11, 98, 203, 285, 483

R

Rackham, Karen 266
Radin, Dean 100, 502
Rainbow and The Worm, The 142
Rambeau, Dr. Viktor 446
Randi, James 70, 103, 459
Ransom, Dr. J.B. 43
Rasche, Erich 289, 290, 299, 300, 354, 511, 512
Raudive, Dr. Konstantīns 461, 462, 464, 465, 472, 473, 517
Raue, Dr. Helmut 430, 516
Ravitz, Dr. Leonard 114
Reagan, Harley "SwiftDeer" 208
Reckeweg, Hans-Heinrich 112, 313, 314, 315, 338, 382, 511
Regal, Brian 477, 518
Regis, Ed 487
Reichmanis, Maria 119
Reich, Wilhelm 414, 415
Relativity 1, 8, 12, 111
Report on the Discovery of Animal Magnetism 203
Revenko, A.N. 353, 354
Rey, Louis 149, 150
Rhine, Joseph B. 100, 502
Richardson, Stan 269
Richards, Patrick 400, 401, 402, 515
Rife, Royal Raymond ix, 175, 176, 177, 178, 179, 180, 181, 182, 183, 413, 477
RITM 353, 359, 361
Roberts, John 421
Robinson, Sir Kenneth 418
Rogo, D. Scott 464, 517

86299835R00300

Made in the USA
Columbia, SC
12 January 2018